Rebuilding Our Broken Faith

June 21/98

My very best wishes
In Christ,
L.G. Rigos

Rebuilding Our Broken Faith

by

CIRILO A. RIGOS, D.D.

Published by
Cosmopolitan Church
United Church of Christ in the Philippines
1368 Taft Avenue, Manila, Philippines

Rebuilding Our Broken Faith

A reprint of sermons originally published under the following titles:
  Rebuilding Our Broken Faith, © 1964 by C. A. Rigos
  Christians And Revolution, © 1972 by C. A. Rigos
  Love Is Involvement, © 1988 by C. A. Rigos

Printed in the Philippines

Contents

	Foreword	ix
1.	Christ Versus Prodigality	1
2.	The Staying Power of Prayer	9
3.	Hate and Forgiveness	15
4.	Singing Faith	21
5.	Is Death a Calamity?	27
6.	The Meaning of Worship	35
7.	A Man Called Simon	41
8.	The Rewards of Discipleship	49
9.	The Priesthood of Believers	55
10.	Lead Us Not Into Temptation	63
11.	Where Your Treasure Is	69
12.	The Rich and the Kingdom	75
13.	Learning from the Sons of the World	83
14.	The Sainthood of Believers	89
15.	The Pope and the Protestants	97
16.	The Church and Population Problem	103
17.	Labor and Christian Conscience	111
18.	Periscoping the Reformation	117
19.	Christmas and the Cross	123
20.	Christmas and Protestantism	129
21.	Christ's Royal Entry	137
22.	Christ and Pilatism	143
23.	The Paradox of Calvary	149
24.	The Road to Emmaus	157
25.	The Bible in Our Day	165
26.	What it Means to Believe in God	171
27.	Christians and Revolution	179
28.	"Shall We Strike with the Sword?"	185
29.	The Faces of Violence	191

30. "Righteousness Exalteth a Nation"	197
31. How to be Sober	203
32. The Golden Rule	207
33. Mission Possible	213
34. "Be Not Anxious"	217
35. From Suffering to Hope	223
36. Water and Wine	229
37. "It Is Finished"	235
38. The Regnant Christ	239
39. The Joy of Easter	245
40. Christmas and Crisis	251
41. Invitation to Live	257
42. Tension and Peace	263
43. "Only Believe"	269
44. The Living Water of Life	277
45. When You are in Love	283
46. Mary and Martha	289
47. Courage and Strength	295
48. Belief and Unbelief	299
49. Love is Involvement	305
50. The More Excellent Way	311
51. The Saving Love	317
52. The Other Prodigal	323
53. The Good Samaritan	327
54. The Nature of Hope	333
55. The Angry Prophet	339
56. Youth and Discipleship	345
57. The Stewardship of Health	351
58. Stephen: A Model Layman	357
59. O Man Greatly Beloved	363
60. Heroes or Villains?	369
61. God's Patience and Ours	375
62. Come, Everyone	381
63. In the Hour of Trial	387
64. Poor Man, Rich Man	393
65. Elisha's Faith and Ours	399

66. THE KING AND THE PROPHET	405
67. A POOR MAN'S VINEYARD	411
68. THE PHARISEE AND THE PUBLICAN	415
69. THE BEGINNING OF WISDOM	421
70. "A BIG MAN IN A LITTLE CHURCH"	427
71. THE WHEAT AND THE TARES	433
72. THE APPEARANCES OF THE RISEN LORD	439
73. ONE FOOT IN HEAVEN	445
74. THE FEEDING OF THE MULTITUDE	451
75. THE MAN WITH ONE TALENT	457
76. "DO YOU WANT TO GET WELL?"	463
77. THE PROMISE OF PARADISE	469

Foreword

I

Around early 1955, Cirilo A. Rigos, a senior student in the Union Theological Seminary, then located on Taft Avenue, Manila, was assigned as the Junior Church Pastor of Cosmopolitan Church.

I barely noticed the presence of this young man from Candelaria, Quezon, although I should have, as I was the chair of the Official Board of Cosmopolitan Church at the time. It was only after the Chairman of the Pulpit Supply Committee, Mr. Tito Dans — a kind, dedicated Christian who had gone through a lot of suffering during the Japanese occupation —invited him to preach during the English morning service at ten o'clock that his name came to my attention. The Committee was considering several names for the position of Associate Pastor for submission to the Official Board. After listening to several preachers, the Dans Committee recommended Cirilo A. Rigos (who had been requested to deliver not one but two sermons) to be the Associate Pastor of Cosmopolitan Church, although he had not yet finished his seminary studies. The Official Board approved the recommendation and issued the call, but not without the dissenting observation of an elderly lady, Ms. Paz Reyes, who made the remark— *"Batang-bata yata iyan at payat pa."*

In March 1955, shortly after he graduated *summa cum laude* with a Bachelor of Theology degree from the Seminary, this young man of great promise, then twenty-two years of age, accepted Cosmopolitan's call. After nine months of careful listening and evaluation, Ambassador Melquiades Gamboa, then a member of the Official Board of Cosmopolitan and one of its leading founders, moved that Associate Pastor Cirilo A. Rigos be appointed full pastor of Cosmopolitan Church. The motion was unanimously carried, including the vote of Ms. Reyes who became Pastor Rigos' ardent supporter. The new Cosmopolitan Church building was then under construction and it was under his leadership that it was finished and inaugurated. The congregation grew from Sunday to Sunday. We were all proud of our new pastor, a young man with a sense of mission and high purpose. Thus began a long and fruitful relationship which has no precedent, as far as I know, in the history of Cosmopolitan Church.

In September 1957, with the blessing of the Official Board of Cosmopolitan, he left for the United States to pursue graduate studies at the Union Theological Seminary in New York. Here, he studied under eminent theologians and philosophers, led by the eminent Reinhold Niebuhr. This must have been a broadening, uplifting experience for the young minister. Parenthetically, apart from picking up the degree of Master of Sacred Theology from the Seminary, he also obtained another degree when he married Ms. Lydia de Guia on January 1, 1959, a charming young lass, a native of Samal, Bataan, who had finished Nursing at Mary Johnston Hospital in Tondo, Manila and was taking postgraduate studies at the St. Luke's School of Nursing in New York as an exchange student. Lydia recalls that it was Dr. Albert Sanders, the former president of Union Theological Seminary in Manila, and the Rev. Donald Smith, a former pastor of Cosmopolitan (from 1948-1951), who officiated at their wedding. Ambassador and Mrs. Gamboa were among the guests. The Rigos couple came home on June 14, 1959 and together they became members of the Cosmopolitan family and served the congregation faithfully for around 25 years. Meanwhile, Pastor Rigos pursued higher studies at the University of Chicago, and a little later, at the San Francisco Theological Seminary in California, where he was awarded the Doctor of Ministry degree. In recognition of his preaching ministry, Coe College in Iowa, U.S.A. conferred on him a Doctor of Divinity degree (*honoris causa*) in 1970.

Pastor Rigos published three books of sermons and left another collection of sermons which were delivered in Cosmopolitan during the last years of his ministry. In honoring this man of God who passed away on June 21, 1996, and in helping rebuild and strengthen our faith, the Church Council of Cosmopolitan decided to republish them in one volume and make them available to a bigger number of people.

The first book of sermons of Pastor Rigos, *Rebuilding Our Broken Faith,* was published by the Men's Club of Cosmopolitan Church in 1964, shortly after his return from another year of in-depth studies and reflection at Union Theological Seminary in New York. This was the book that marked the style and approach of this young pastor. In the Introduction to that particular volume, I wrote:

> "God has endowed him with a sharp mind and an unusual depth of perception, and Rev. Rigos makes full use of his talents, as his flock will readily testify, to God's honor and glory. The light of His countenance

> shines upon this young man with brilliance, and His loving-kindness is reflected in Rev. Rigos' humility, warmth, compassion, and generosity of spirit... There is one note that runs through these sermons. I would like to call it by just one word: **relevance**."

For as was his wont, he would relate biblical facts and events of long ago to our everyday world. And because he did not cater to the weaknesses and prejudices of his audience, but spoke the truth no matter how uncomfortable, I then wrote that **integrity** was the essence of his preaching.

A good number of the sermons published in the second volume under the title *Christians and Revolution* were delivered in Cosmopolitan Church during the turbulent years preceding the proclamation of martial law in 1972. They are not necessarily discourses on revolution in the usual sense—in fact, they may be considered essentially moderate, given the spate of riots and demonstrations after the elections of 1969—but, as explained by Dr. Rigos, the whole book was dictated by the conviction "that the gospel is revolutionary and that Christians on fire for God can revolutionize the world."

It was in the Social Hall of Cosmopolitan Church where he, along with some lay leaders of Cosmopolitan and other Protestant churches, organized the *Wednesday Forum* in 1973, to enable an ecumenical group of socially-concerned ministers, priests, nuns, and lay leaders to openly and courageously discuss with high public officials and key opposition leaders the crucial issues of injustice, untruth and lack of freedom during martial law, always from the perspective of the Christian gospel. It was the only free forum in Metro Manila at the time where a group of Christians, at great risk, asserted their right to be free. In point of fact, several pastors attending the *Forum* were arrested and detained.

Dr. Rigos' involvement in the *Wednesday Forum* and his frequent criticism of martial law from the pulpit did not sit well with a few members of Cosmopolitan who were somehow linked with some people in power. Not wanting to divide the Church, Pastor Rigos came to see me and asked that he be allowed to resign, to which I reluctantly agreed. I was chair of the Official Board at the time. I then noted during the *despedida* party in his honor that his leaving us would be the loss of Cosmopolitan but would surely be Ellinwood's gain. Rev. Moley Familiaran from Bacolod and Iloilo replaced him and served Cosmopolitan with distinction, until he and his family had to leave for the United States. Bishop Pedro Raterta ably succeeded him.

Meanwhile, Dr. Rigos answered the call of Ellinwood-Malate Church, which he later served for eleven years. It was while he was pastor of Ellinwood that the EDSA "people power," non-violent revolution suddenly erupted in late February 1986 and overthrew the dictatorship in several days. Shortly after the installation of the new democratic government on February 25, 1986, President Cory Aquino requested Pastor Rigos to be a member of the Constitutional Commission which drafted the Constitution of 1987. Thus, he remained pastor of Ellinwood while in the Con-con until his work there as a Commissioner ended with the ratification of the new Constitution on February 2, 1987. In 1988, he resigned from Ellinwood due to his appointment as General Secretary of the London-based United Bible Societies.

His third volume of fine sermons, delivered during his stint in Ellinwood, appeared in Manila in 1989 under the title, *Love Is Involvement*. The Foreword to this third volume, written by former Justice Abraham F. Sarmiento, refers to the following characteristics of the Rigos style of sermon-making and delivery, none of which can be disputed: simplicity, commonness of themes, new perspectives, use of street jargon and a sense of humor, brevity, direct and forceful delivery.

Dr. and Mrs. Rigos returned to the Philippines in 1990. Dr. Rigos was conferred the title of Pastor *emeritus* by Cosmopolitan Church as a simple token of our love. In the meantime, he accepted the pastorate of the Community Church of Las Piñas (UCCP). With the resignation of Rev. Reynaldo Desenganio as pastor of Cosmopolitan Church in 1993, Dr. Rigos was called and installed for the second time as Minister of Cosmopolitan Church on July 1 of that year. In 1994, the dream of Pastor Rigos, the construction of a new church building for Cosmopolitan— a four-storey edifice fronting Taft Avenue and a renovated sanctuary—was approved by the Church Council (the new name of the Official Board). The ground breaking ceremony was held on February 7, 1995 and a month later, the construction was started under the close supervision of the pastor himself who watched the progress of the project from day to day. In the midst of this construction, Dr. Rigos eventually fell ill, a victim of colon cancer which, without his knowledge, had already spread by October 1995. The whole congregation was in gloom, but with rare valor, he lifted the morale of the leaders and members, performed his duties and preached with great eloquence and boldness from Sunday to Sunday. The Sunday attendance increased as friends and sympathizers joined the members in sheer admiration of this man of courage.

During the 63rd anniversary celebration of Cosmopolitan Church on March 23, 1996, the renovated, fully air-conditioned sanctuary was used for the first time with around 1000 people in attendance. Mrs. Mary Ruth Webb (the daughter of Mother Mary Boyd Stagg, pastor-martyr of Cosmopolitan Church during the Japanese Occupation) was the Special Guest. Three wartime heroes were honored, with President Fidel V. Ramos as Guest Speaker. More than one month after this event, on May 5, 1996, Dr. Rigos could no longer preside and preach during the Communion Service. After a short meeting with some officers of Cosmopolitan in his private room in the parsonage, Dr. Rigos, exhausted and feverish, had to be brought to the Makati Medical Center.

In a special meeting on May 15, 1996, the Cosmopolitan Church Council unanimously approved the motion to name the new four-storey building fronting Taft Avenue in honor of Dr. Cirilo A. Rigos, with the understanding that the appropriate marker of Rigos Hall would be placed in the new edifice in God's own time. Dr. Rigos was promptly informed, and although he had demurred when it was first broached to him, he eventually agreed and expressed his thanks.

On May 19, 1996, the new four-storey building and the renovated sanctuary were blessed and dedicated, again with the President as Guest of Honor. One person was missing — Pastor Rigos, who had served Cosmopolitan Church for around 25 years, but who was now bedridden. The action of the Church Council naming the new building fronting Taft Avenue in honor of Dr. Cirilo A. Rigos was ratified without any objection from the Cosmopolitan congregation during the morning service, and ratified again in the afternoon of the same day by the donors, friends, and other members of Cosmopolitan. Dr. Rigos, then seriously ill in the hospital, was promptly informed about this action of the various Church entities and about the tremendous outpouring of affection for him by those who had invested in his dream for Cosmopolitan Church. His reaction was something to this effect: *"Salamat ng marami, ngunit masyado naman yata ang ginawa ninyo."*

He passed away quietly on June 21, 1996. Three days later, during the last necrological service held in the Sanctuary of Cosmopolitan Church, the new building was named Rigos Hall and a marker was there unveiled by the officers and members of Cosmopolitan Church and by his friends and fellow workers including ministers and bishops from various churches.

A few weeks later, the Church Council unanimously approved the motion to publish in one volume all the sermons of Pastor Rigos, including the ones he delivered during his last years of ministry.

Thus, we have in this one new volume all the sermons in the three previously-published books of Dr. Cirilo A. Rigos. Only one more collection of sermons delivered in the 90's remains unpublished, due to a few missing pages which will undoubtedly be retrieved in due time.

Perhaps, what we said about the three essential qualities of Dr. Rigos during the last service before his remains were buried on June 24, 1996 is worth recalling since we cannot separate the sermons from the man behind them, however much we try.

II

Like a true disciple of Jesus Christ who lived and died in poverty, Pastor Rigos left no material wealth to his family nor the kind of earthly power some ministers and religious leaders obviously love and enjoy. But these three qualities of Dr. Rigos were probably his most treasured possessions.

The first is his humility of spirit. Although Pastor Rigos was appointed full pastor in 1956, he was still a *probinsiyano* since his pronunciation was sometimes faulty. The polished, well-educated Pearl Gamboa-Doromal thereupon appointed herself as the tutor of the young pastor in pronunciation. A *summa cum laude*, he did not consider it beneath his dignity to be tutored like a high school kid. He was willing to learn and in the fullness of time, Pastor Rigos became one of the finest, most eloquent Protestant ministers in this country. In my own experience, Pastor Rigos, despite his doctorate from a U.S. seminary, was prepared to accept his mistakes, not only in pronunciation but also in other areas of human knowledge. For to paraphrase one writer, all of us are ignorant without a single exception, the only difference being that we are ignorant on different subjects. Pastor Rigos knew it is not bad to be ignorant; what is pathetic is "to be ignorant of our own ignorance."

There was something about Dr. Rigos that was not mentioned in the marker we unveiled — his moral courage which was the very essence of his ministry. There are many pastors and priests in this country who possess— perhaps, even surpass— his intelligence, wit, and eloquence, but only a few may have the kind of moral courage Pastor Rigos possessed especially in times of crisis.

Long before martial law, Dr. Rigos did not confine himself to a safe, sanitized, harmless exposition of the Bible that would not offend the people in power. Like the prophets of old —from Isaiah to Jeremiah, from Micah to John the Baptist and Jesus Christ Himself, Dr. Rigos boldly denounced the wrongs, the evils and injustices of Philippine society, and gave a vision of what our society could be in light of the Christian Gospel. In short, he did not tailor his message to appease or flatter the men and women in power.

But the litmus test of his prophetic ministry came when martial law was imposed supposedly to build a "New Society" that would replace the sick "Old Society." Upon his return from the United States in 1973, he organized, with a group of ministers and lay leaders, the *Wednesday Forum* in light of Jesus' teaching: "...you will know the truth, and the truth will set you free" (John 8:32).

From Sunday to Sunday and during the free and open discussions in the *Wednesday Forum,* Dr. Rigos spoke with great moral courage. I stress the word courage, for in the language of Winston Churchill, "Courage is the one virtue that makes all the other virtues possible." *Ano 'ng saysay ng ating pag-ibig sa Kanya at sa ating kapwa tao, kung wala naman tayong tapang at lakas ng loob na ipaglaban ang ating pananampalataya't pag-ibig sa Kanya at ang ating paglingap at paglilingkod sa ating kapwa tao?*

At that time, I was one of the lawyers of Ninoy Aquino and, like Dr. Rigos, an outspoken opponent of martial law. In October 1980, I was arrested for alleged subversion, having been suspected of being one of the brains behind the series of bombings that hit Metro Manila. Immediately after my arrest and detention, Dr. Rigos received a telephone call saying he would be the next to be arrested. He dressed up and prepared his small bag of clothes, ready to be imprisoned. In a rare display of wisdom, the military held back and did not detain him. *Ngunit sa aking palagay, gustong-gusto sana ni Pastor Rigos na mapasok sa bilangguan para maging political detainee at makasama niya ang mga taong kanyang pinaglingkuran — ngunit hindi siya pinagbigyan.* For how can anyone knowing him believe that he would lend himself to any bombing activity? But this did not prevent him from working for the release of political detainees. With his assistance,

Operation Paglingap, of which he was a moving spirit, succeeded in causing the release of many political detainees.

If humility is the most attractive virtue of a person, moral courage is the one that is most highly-admired and respected. Like Peter and John during the first days of the Christian Church, Dr. Rigos spoke with great courage because he preferred to obey God rather than man.

This brings me to the third quality of Dr. Rigos—his sacrificial service. Pastor Rigos could not have been a minister of God in this church for 25 years if he did not lose himself in service to God, to the entire Cosmopolitan fellowship, and to the least of our brothers and sisters outside Cosmopolitan Church.

As I said when he resigned in 1977, he became part of our lives in more ways than one. He baptized our children, confirmed them in their faith, solemnized their marriages, interceded in their quarrels and differences, and buried our loved ones with dignity and grace. He shared our most intimate confidences, counseled us, and encouraged us in times of doubt and despair. His prayers accompanied us through many difficulties and his inspired, inspiring messages lifted us up from Sunday to Sunday.

Beyond the confines of Cosmopolitan Church, he interceded for pastors who were about to be arrested and detained. He worked for the release of many political detainees, mostly Roman Catholics. More than 90 detainees he had worked for were released during the height of the Marcos dictatorship.

Eventually, he came back to Cosmopolitan— his first "love" — to serve God and the church fellowship without counting the cost. In October 1995, after he was told his disease had spread all over his body, instead of going to the U.S. for medical treatment as he had been advised by some close friends, he stayed and continued to serve the church to the very last days when he could no longer bear the pain. In the words of the Gospel — *"No greater love hath any man than this, that he lay down his life for his friends."*

A young man once asked an old man: "What is the meaning of life?" The old man answered: "If we have learned to live without fear, to drop our hate and bitterness toward others, to go through pain and suffering without complaining, to see beauty in common things around us, to love and serve the poorest and the lowliest without counting the cost, to be glad to be alive and unafraid to die, then we are advancing toward the meaning of life." Pastor Rigos has done all these and more.

III

As stated earlier, in publishing in one volume the sermons he had put out under three titles, our desire is to honor Dr. Rigos and, at the same time, help in the rebuilding of our faith. In my case, there was an experience of spiritual satisfaction bordering on bliss when I finished a number of sermons in the entire series. I had heard some of them before particularly those that had been delivered in Cosmopolitan, but I felt an unspeakable lift when I read them anew. Apart from the lead sermons in each volume, "Hate and Forgiveness," "The Paradox of Calvary" and "The Road to Emmaus" in the *Rebuilding Our Broken Faith*, "Shall We Strike with the Sword?," "Righteousness Exalteth a Nation," and "From Suffering to Hope" in *Christians and Revolution*, and "The More Excellent Way," "The Good Samaritan," "O Man Greatly Beloved," and "The Appearances of the Risen Lord" in *Love is Involvement*, are some of the homilies that are both inspired and inspiring. I commend each of these sermons in this new volume to be read and reread by the earnest seeker in the spirit of love, humility, and understanding.

As I wrote years ago, in the same way that Pastor Rigos' preaching stirred his flock and multiplied it many-fold, my prayer is that each of these sermons may touch the reader, deepen his faith in God, give him hope in a world of despair and, above all, enlarge his love for the least of our fellow pilgrims.

JOVITO R. SALONGA

March 12, 1998
Pasig City

1

Christ Versus Prodigality

It was meet that we should make merry, and be glad: for this thy brother was dead, and is alive again; and was lost, and is found. — Luke 15:32

In the Parable of the Prodigal Son, the father was a man of means and, therefore, was enjoying a certain degree of popularity. He must have been a prominent figure in society. We can be sure that he was also a godly man. He was close to God, and must have been active in the work of the church. We wonder, however, whether he was a success in rearing up his two sons. Perhaps, in the end, we would say he was. But he went through some real difficulties dealing with his sons. He shared in the common problem of many parents today who find it hard to understand their children, especially the teen-agers. Even those who know something about adolescent psychology somehow find the actual dealing with their children a very trying experience. The father in our parable had to face a similar situation in the case of his younger son, who was perhaps still a teen-ager, or in his early twenties. To that young man, the world was beginning to unfold, dormant thoughts were stirring and he wanted to enjoy the liberty of youth. The father's handicap was that he had no wife to help him manage the house and the children. She might have died while the children were still young, and he, therefore, became the father and the mother to his two growing sons.

Could he have spoiled the younger son? He did not seem to be able to say "no" to the wishes of that boy. Maybe he knew it was useless to say "no" and that the wiser thing for him to do was to let his son do as he pleased, hoping that someday the lad would realize what was best.

The young man said, "Father, give me the portion of goods that falleth to me." It was an imperious demand. He knew that he was entitled to a portion of his father's property, and he wanted it for himself now. He did not say, "Father would you be kind enough to let me have my share in your property?" or "Would you please allow me to manage that portion of your wealth I am supposed to inherit from you?" No, he did not say "please." He did not say, "Would you be kind enough." He demanded, "Give me!" He was, in effect, saying, "Don't you ask me why. And don't you say 'no'. That belongs to me and I want to spend it in my own way. Come on, give it to me now." He was, shall we say, discourteous in his demand. He could not afford to be polite. He lacked the virtue of respect for one who was older than he was, even for his own father.

Modern Young People

The young people of today may well remember that whenever they behave unseemly and their conduct betrays their lack of courtesy and respect, they truly reincarnate the spirit of the prodigal son and become a thorn in the flesh and a disgrace to society. Many homes today are wrecked by prodigal sons and daughters who cannot control their passion and their temper, and who find it unpleasant to be disciplined by the guidance of filial love. When a young man or a young woman talks to his parents in a language that is bereft of any dignity, in a language that is filled with puerile liberty and juvenile arrogance, he or she has the stigma of the prodigal son and may someday end up in bitter disappointment. Very often the speech of a person is an index to his character, and his conversation with his parents or with his brothers and sisters reveals his spiritual maturity or immaturity.

The Death of Liberty

The story says that there in a far country the prodigal son lived in riotous living. That is a brief description of a wild life, of liberty turned into license. What he did exactly we are not told, but we are sure he spent his money right and left, he must have gone to expensive pleasure spots and before he knew it, his pocketbook was empty. He was a wastrel because he did not sweat to earn his money. He did not know how hard it was to earn a living. He never worried about money, neither did he help his father in their business. So he did not have an idea of the difficulties involved in saving and in earning their daily bread. All that he knew was to spend and to squander. Is this not the story of many young people until now? Their parents work hard to save, and sometimes forego with some of their own necessities in order that their children may not be wanting; but the heartless *señoritos* and *señoritas* who never cared about how their pocket money was secured carelessly spend their allowance and get broke even before the next supply comes in.

"No Vacancy"

The prodigal son, being penniless, now realized that he had to work in order to eat. He should have a job to support himself. So he went from one employment agency to another, from one company to another, asking if there was any vacancy for him. Perhaps one personnel manager who interviewed him was merciful enough to find out how he could take the young man in. He must have asked: "What can you do?" And the applicant, hoping that he had a chance, eagerly replied: "Anything, sir." "Can you type?" asked the manager. "No, sir," said the applicant. "Well," said the interviewer, "do you know stenography?" The young man paused for a moment and then innocently remarked, "I write faster in longhand than in shorthand." "Are you a college graduate?" asked the interviewer who was becoming a bit impatient. "No, sir." "But I thought you went to college and that your father paid for your matriculation fee for your senior year." "That's right, sir, but I did not quite make it because you see, sir, I was always absent and I got an F grade in most of my subjects." This time the personnel manager rose from his swivel chair, walked to his window, scratched his head and had a mixed feeling of pity and disappointment. He wanted to give that young man a good paying job but the applicant did not know anything. He went over the list of positions in the company only to discover that the applicant was not fit for any of them. Finally, he approached his young friend and said, "Brother, I am sorry but there is no place for you here. You cannot type, you don't know anything about bookkeeping and you cannot be even just an elevator boy. But if you like, you can work in my piggery in my farm. Your job will be to feed the pigs morning and afternoon, and I will pay you whatever your work is worth." The young man thought that since, anyway, he was good for nothing, he would at least try the job. After all, he need not be a college graduate to feed the pigs. It was one job that he could do.

It is, indeed, a pity that many young people do not take advantage of their educational opportunities. Some of them even take pride in being delinquent in their studies. They would rather go gallivanting than stay at home and study. And when circumstances force them to be on their own, they find themselves unfit for any job. It may be sad to note that there are those who cannot go to college because of lack of means, but it is tragic to see those who are in school but are not making the most out of it.

For the first time in his life, the prodigal learned what it meant to be hungry. Before, whenever he felt like eating, he would just run to the refrigerator and grab whatever he wanted. Now out there in the field he could feel the pain of hunger. There must be nights when he had to sleep with an empty stomach. "He would have been glad to fill his belly with the pods that the pigs were eating; and no one gave him anything" (v. 16). No one extended a helping hand. Now that he was in abject poverty, he had no friends to go to. Could they have been always with him when his pocketbook was fat? He must have taken them for a free ride in his Volkswagen in the Luneta; he must have brought them to first-class *panciterias* downtown; he must have given them tickets to the coliseum and the movies. Now that he was penniless and starving, where were they? Perhaps we would like to examine what kind of friends we are and what kind of friends we have. Are we the friends who can be depended upon in times of need? Will your friends avoid you when there is nothing more they can suck from you? Are they your friends because at the moment you can give them what they want and they can always come to you because you are ready to help? But whatever they may be to you, may you be their friends indeed.

A Repentant Sinner

And so the prodigal realized his serious blunder. "He came to himself" was Jesus' description of him. This phrase suggests that all folly is madness. It is not consistent with our real selves. Our true nature reflects the image of God; our perversity indicates our need of divine redemption. Repentance is the recovery of selfhood for it is the experience of coming back to God in whom we have our being. Of course when we go into the depth of folly we oftentimes do it consciously and deliberately, and yet to the eye of faith it is no less than cruel madness. The prodigal realized that, so he resolved to arise and go to his father and to confess: "Father, I have sinned against God and against you..." Incidentally, without being fully aware of it the prodigal caught a deep insight into the nature of sin when he said, "I have sinned against heaven and before thee." Sin is sin because it is a sin against God, and the sin committed against individual or society is at the same time a sin against heaven. The young man in the parable must have prayed hard for God's forgiveness and for reconciliation with his earthly father.

The Loving Father

And the merciful God heard the prayer of this repentant sinner, so that "while he was yet at a distance, his father saw him and had compassion, and ran and embraced him and kissed him." How could his father have recognized him at that distance when he looked like a beggar, pale and weak? The father must have been waiting for him to come home. He must have been at his veranda most of the time praying for his dear son and waiting for him all the day long. And this is the heart of the parable: that the waiting love of God can easily recognize the appearance of a repentant soul, and that there is great rejoicing among the angels in heaven for every lost sheep that has been found again. So the father ordered his servant to bring quickly the best robe, and to put it on his son, to put a ring in his hand and shoes on his feet. Chickens were killed and pigs were roasted and perhaps an orchestra was hired, and they had a big celebration in the house with music and dancing.

The Elder Brother

But remember that the elder brother was still in the field and he did not know all about the merrymaking. When he was nearing home he wondered what the fiesta was about. All lights were on and he could hear some singing. He called one of the servants and asked what it was and he was informed that his brother had returned. Did you expect him to run to the *sala* to shake hands with his brother and say, "Hello, Junior, how was your adventure?" We know he did not do that. His reaction was extremely unfavorable and bitter and sour. Jesus said he got mad and refused to go in.

The good father, seeing his elder son would not come in, went out to him and talked with him. He pleaded with his son to come in, but the son would not. Then angrily the son retorted, "Lo, these many years I have served you, and I never disobeyed your command." Did he say "All these years I have loved you?" No, he only served. And obviously his service was servile and was devoid of love. He had not disobeyed his father's command but could not love a repentant brother. He was indeed a prodigal himself, a prodigal in his heart. He did not leave his father's house, but his heart was in a far country. While working on his father's field, his heart was in the land of greed and envy and bitterness. Indeed, he did not like anymore to call the younger son his brother. He said to his father, "This son of yours ..." He did not say, "My brother." Is that not the language of an embittered person? When a wife complains to her husband about their child, she says, "That child of yours." When an employee speaks to a co-employee about their manager, he says, "That boss of yours." When a church member speaks to a fellow-member about their minister, he says, "That pastor of yours." The elder son would not say "My brother." He said, "That son of yours" and thereby exposed the ugliness of his soul.

The wise good father, who knew how to handle the situation, answered back and said, "Your brother." Not that he did not like to call his younger son his son, for the merrymaking alone and the giving of robe and ring and shoes was enough indication that the prodigal was received again as his son, but he wanted to impress upon the mind of the elder son that he who came home was his brother. "Your brother was dead, and now he is alive; he was lost, and now he is found."

A Happy Reunion

Was the older son after all persuaded to come in? We are not told about that. But I wish to believe that he was, that he finally mustered enough courage to greet the guests and embrace his brother and that by the grace of God they were reconciled to each other. I would like to believe that the elder son also realized the terrifying emptiness in his soul and his lack of love for the members of their household. And perhaps he talks to us today, and tells us that we need not leave our homes in order to become prodigal children. We need not go to a far country to indulge in riotous living, for right in our place, in our homes, in our church, in our community we can be the lost sheep. When we cannot love a brother or sister, father or mother, son or daughter, especially when that brother or father or son is truly repentant, we become prodigal in our hearts as we have chosen not to be found in the forgiving grace of God. When we do not care what happens with our neighbors, and our self-righteousness causes us to rejoice at the failure of a weak brother, we exemplify the spirit of the elder son that can be saved only by some kind of spiritual surgery. He who is lost in the jungle of sin and resentment cannot have God's peace even in a palace, but he who has found favor in the eyes of the Almighty will feel at ease even in the shanty surroundings of his poverty-stricken home.

If there are lost souls in this congregation this morning, they are hereby reminded that Christ came to seek and to save that which was lost. You therefore need not remain hiding in the pews, you need not go home the same old, ugly creatures. For here you can find God, and when you find Him it is because He has found you here. Then shall there be music in your heart and meaning in your life and a change in your outlook, and somehow you will feel within you the rejoicing of the angels above over one lost soul that has been found again.

2

The Staying Power of Prayer

Then Hezekiah turned his face toward the wall, and prayed unto the Lord. — Isaiah 38:2

Dr. George A. Buttrick, in a book on prayer, says that "prayer is the heart of religion." Stressing this same idea, Dr. P. T. Forsyth in his *The Soul of Prayer* says:

> "All religion is founded on prayer, and in prayer it has its test and measure. To be religious is to pray, to be irreligious is to be incapable of prayer. The theory of religion is really the philosophy of prayer; and the best theology is compressed in prayer."[1]

Prayer and the Great Religions

Alongside with Christianity, think of other religions such as Islam, Buddhism, Hinduism, Shintoism. Is not prayer a common element in them? Prayer surely is an essential property of religion and no religious system can survive without it.

Students of comparative religions note among other things the universality of prayer. Prayer is so common that we look upon it as a human instinct. The atheists are no exception for, as someone has observed, an atheist is one who thanks God that there is no God.

In the Christian religion prayer is so essential that prayerlessness is inescapably the worst sin. Not to pray is the sin behind sin. It is spiritual suicide of the highest degree. "Overt sins or crimes or the glaring inconsistencies which often surprise us in Christian people"[2] are the effects of prayerlessness, or its punishment. When we neglect prayer, we deprive our souls of the greatest blessing that can come from the window of heaven.

---

[1] Dr. P.T. Forsyth, *The Soul of Prayer*, p. 44.
[2] *Ibid.*

A Serious Business

The importance of prayer in our Christian life makes it necessary for us to deal with it with seriousness. Indeed to pray is a serious business, for while it can be a means of grace it can also be a curse. For instance, do we not sometimes find ourselves, in moments of carelessness if not of total ignorance, asking God to run errands for us? Do we not sometimes ask Him to put His stamp of approval on something we have already decided? This is not to say that petitions have no place in prayer. Petitions we should make, and make often. But the Christian way is first of all to seek God's will and then in obedience to that will we live and move and have our being. Prayer in this sense is not telling God what we want Him to do for us. Rather it is asking Him to reveal to us the highest purposes of our life.

A Freudian Reminder

There is a prevailing notion today that prayer is only an illusion of the mind, or a projection of desires. This is a grave and dangerous idea, for while prayer may have some psychological values, it is primarily a spiritual exercise. We should thank Freud for reminding us that religion can be an escape ("a hiding in time from the demands of eternity"), but prayer need not be an empty autosuggestion. It need not be less than what it is. We do harm to the cause of religion if we make it into a hiding place to evade the issues which put character to a test. That is not prayer. It is poverty of soul, the result of acquisitiveness and foolish rebellion against the disciplining of life.

What Prayer Is

From the standpoint of the Christian faith, prayer is communion with God. We pray because first of all we believe in a personal God who is concerned with the welfare of His children. He is the God who listens to the cries and praises of men, of every man. The burden of Jesus' teaching about God is that God is our heavenly Father, One who can discern our deepest thoughts and feel our purest longings. To pray is to bring our hearts to the glorious presence of God where life becomes full and meaningful and rich. It is spiritual fellowship with the Lord of all creation, an encounter with the living God.

Necessarily, therefore, prayer is a cry of guilt. Before God we see our depravity and sinfulness. Before the throne of the perfect God our brokenness lies uncovered. The nakedness of human frailty cannot be hidden. We see ourselves as we really are. Prayer is the most honest endeavor we can engage ourselves in for if it is not honest then it is not prayer at all.[1] In prayer we do not and cannot hide our inward ugliness, because God can see what is in the heart of man. A soul that is brought face to face with God – unless it is fatally benumbed by persistent sinning – makes a clean breast with God, and admits its paralyzing guilt. The prophet Isaiah, seeing the Lord upon a throne, high and lifted up, cried in repentance: "Woe is me for I am a man of unclean lips." It was a confession of sin, a recognition of his unworthiness.

As a cry of guilt, prayer is a cry of the finite to and for the Infinite. St. Augustine said, "Our souls are restless until they rest in God." This is not acquisitiveness because the motive is not for self-satisfaction. It is an upward lift, a Godward move made possible not by human power but by the grace of God. Prayer is a response to divine influences working within. It is looking up to the Author and Finisher of our Faith.

Prayer, in the words of Dr. Frank Laubach, is conversation with God. It is reverently talking with God and God revealing His will to us. But it is more listening than talking. When we keep still, we wait for the still small voice. Then we know that God is. Prayer is approaching the throne of God so that we may hear Him more clearly. We speak only to affirm our attentiveness and willingness to listen. Like Samuel, we say: "Speak Lord, for thy servant heareth."

And, of course, it is also talking . Indeed prayer is "the highest use to which language can be put." It breaks through language as a matter of fact. Words fail us in prayer. The Spirit comes to our aid, delivers us from the limits of our words and brings us to the realm of the living Word. Prayer takes us from mere human speech into action and achievement; it is "word become work" because it is the victory of the Spirit. Communion with God transcends speech; it is a living contact, energizing, empowering, enriching.

Reasons for Praying

Let us now mention some of the specific reasons for praying. For one thing, we pray to thank the Lord for the mysterious ways He works

---
[1] Forsyth, *op. cit.*

with us, for the untold blessings we enjoy, for all things that make life pleasant and meaningful. A prayer of thanksgiving is a song of faith; it is the core of worship. The eagerness of God to hear thanksgiving prayers was dramatized by Jesus looking for the nine who were cleansed of their leprosy. Gratefulness is a great virtue. It can cause rejoicing in heaven. It ennobles human relationships.

Let us thank God for the gift of life, for the means of livelihood, for health and strength, food, shelter, clothes; for air, rain and sunshine; for our family and friends; schools and hospitals and markets; for the many conveniences around; above all for Jesus Christ. Thank God for the salvation of our souls, for the promise of eternal life, for peace which passes understanding; for pain that serves to purge our souls; for disappointments that make us realize our inadequacy and need of forgiveness; for sorrows that deepen our life of prayer. We have many things to be thankful for, and we should not withhold our prayer of thanks.

Again, we pray to intercede for others. We are a part of the great human race. We are a family of men. Jesus teaches us to pray: "Our Father ..." We cannot say that unless we recognize our brotherhood. The Apostle Paul in his letter to Timothy says: "I exhort therefore that first of all, supplications, prayers intercessions and giving of thanks be made for all men ..... For this is good and acceptable in the sight of God our Saviour" (I Tim. 2:1). In Galatians 6:2, we read: "Bear ye one another's burdens, and so fulfill the law of Christ." Surely intercession is a Christian privilege. It is remembering to God a brother in need or in trouble. It is invoking God's mercy upon the rulers and the subjects, upon men and nations the world over. It is praying for others. Jesus prayed for Simon Peter that his faith might fail not. Jesus teaches us to pray for those who persecute us and say all manners of evil against us. James, the Lord's brother, admonishes us to intercede for one another: "Is any sick among you? Let him call for the elders of the church; and let them pray over him, anointing him with oil in the name of the Lord; and the prayer of faith shall save the sick, and the Lord shall raise him up; and if he has committed sins, they shall be forgiven him . Confess your faults one to another, and pray one for another, that ye may be healed. The effectual fervent prayer of a righteous man availeth much." (5:14ff).

Intercession brings healing not only to others but also to us. When we pray for someone who has done us wrong, we keep ourselves from bitterness and hate. It enables us to control ourselves and even to be forgiving. Think of the persons who constantly irritate you, who cause you embarrassments and disappointments, whose irresponsibility scandalizes you, who have failed you, who have turned unfaithful and brought you disgrace, and then pray for them that they may change for the better, that God may guide them to moral rectitude and truth, and the urge to hate shall find no lodgment in your heart. Do not do it with a sense of spiritual superiority, for that will be fatal. Do it in the spirit of real intercession, and Satan will give up kindling the fire of your anger.

We pray also because we need to ask God's help. Very often knowingly or unknowingly we trespass against the law of God. The world is so full of temptations that even the greatest of saints can commit hideous sins when he is not on guard. Who can imagine that such a man as the author of the 23rd Psalm could commit the crime which David committed against Uriah, the Hittite? The 51st Psalm is a prayer for the remission of his sins, a passionate plea for forgiveness and sanctification. Surely we daily need to purge our souls from all pollutions of evil and guard against the cancerous effects of callousness and moral laxity. This kind of petition is suggested in the Lord's Prayer. It is legitimate to pray for deliverance from evil, just as we pray for God's forgiveness.

Again, we pray because we know that God is Creator and Sustainer of life, so that when pain and sickness assail us God may embolden us to walk through the valley of the shadow of death. While food and medicine are means of God's healing grace – and indeed the ministry of healing has a place in the order of creation - nevertheless the best medical care cannot take the place of a simple, sincere prayer for the mercy of God. We certainly need the services of doctors and hospitals, but more than that we need to be near our God.

The Case of Hezekiah

Our Scripture lesson describes King Hezekiah as a very sick man. He surely had the privilege of being attended to by the best physicians in his kingdom. For all we know he summoned also the leading specialists in the neighboring kingdoms, and yet in spite of that the prophet Isaiah pronounced him a hopeless case. "Thus saith the Lord," declared the prophet to the king, "Set thine house in order, for thou shalt die, and not live." Who can imagine the agony and grief and pain of Hezekiah at that dark hour of total hopelessness? He must have spent sleepless nights wrestling with the fact of his coming death. But, ah, the king knew how to handle his disparagement. The Scripture says he turned his face unto the wall and prayed unto the Lord. And the good Lord, whose thoughts are higher than our thoughts, granted the prayer of the king and gave him fifteen more years to live.

Prayer Guides

Let us now review some guides to be followed in the cultivation of our prayer life. First, before we pray we need to enter into the atmosphere of humility. That spirit is in itself an answer to our prayer. Arrogance and boastfulness are injurious to the soul. Meekness and lowliness of heart open wide the gate of heaven.

Second, if growth in our Christian life is to be achieved, our prayer should also be regular. The Apostle Paul advises us to pray without ceasing (I Thess. 5:17). Sometimes we don't feel like praying. That's just the time we need to pray more. If we are to learn to pray in freedom, we should force ourselves to pray more. Someone said, "The great liberty begins in necessity." But again we might say, "That is lip-service." That is not the lip-service which God dislikes. What God dislikes is the lip-service which is undisturbed at not being more. "As appetite comes with eating, so prayer with praying." Is it not that when we need rest most, we are too restless to lie down? But when we force ourselves to lie down and be still, in ten minutes or so, we fall asleep and we feel refreshed. Let our lips mention the detailed needs of our souls, and our heart will soon listen to the language of our lips.[1] Then shall we be instant in season and out of season.

Third, let us pray with a sense of expectancy. Tennyson said, "More things are wrought in prayer than the world dreams of." Great things can happen within us. Believe that God will not cast away all who come to Him in faith. Earnestly seek His holy will, let our spirits bear witness with His Spirit. Pray hard, pray fervently and wait patiently for Him to hear our supplications.

Daring and adventurous Christians will find great thrill in the adventure of prayer. For there we experience the true romance of religion. In prayer we enter the sanctuary of God's being and behold the perfect beauty of His love. It surely makes us feel inadequate and focuses before us our unworthiness and shame, but then a mysterious power fills our souls, cleanses away our guilt, and we feel strengthened and brave to enter the strait gate and tread on the narrow way. That is the power of prayer which we should harness to the limit for the living of these days.

---
[1] Forsyth, *op. cit.*

3

Hate and Forgiveness

But he that hateth his brother is in darkness, and walketh in darkness, and knoweth not whither he goeth, because that darkness hath blinded his eyes. — I John 2:11

One of the Old Testament characters who knows the destructiveness of hate was Esau, the brother of Jacob. He was cheated by his brother who took from him not only his birthright but also his father's blessing. And Esau was so embittered that he pursued his fleeing brother to take his life. For many, many years he harbored that resentment, and those long years must have been a rosary of restlessness.

Then there was Cain. Why did he kill his brother? Was he jealous or envious because his offering was not honored by God while that of his brother's was accepted? One may conjecture that such petty jealousy or envy grew into burning hatred and at the impulse of such evil spirit the crime of murder was committed.

In the book of Esther, the story of prime minister Haman is an illustration of what hate can do upon the man who nurses it. As Haman went out of the king's palace one day, he met a Jew, Mordecai, who refused to salute him because he was an enemy of the Jews. Haman was so enraged that he planned a ferocious vengeance not only against Mordecai but against the whole of the Jewish race. He built a gallows 50 cubits high where Mordecai and his people were to be hanged. One morning as the people passed by the city gates on their way to their places of work, they saw a dead man dangling to and fro on the gallows built by Haman, but the body was not that of Mordecai; it was the body of Haman himself, executed there at the king's command.

Was not Peter expressing his personal experience of getting tired with the failures of a brother when he asked Jesus, "Lord, how often shall my brother sin against me and I forgive him? till seven times?" He must have been greatly troubled by some wrong done him by a dear friend, brother or relative.

Causes of Hatred

From these examples we get the suggestion that sometimes hatred is caused by the folly of another. To be cheated, for instance, is a painful experience and that is fertile soil for the seed of hatred to grow. To be maltreated, to be deceived, to be a victim of ingratitude and disloyalty and insincerity – that is a supreme test on one's patience and faith, and the soul with a weak spiritual foundation easily falls into the grip of bitterness and hate.

From the case of Abel and Cain, we have the intimation that hate can evolve from envy or jealousy. It can grow out of an inward spiritual malady, and its destructiveness is equally monstrous. Again, hate can just be acquired. It can evolve from something outside, and has no rational basis at all. Sigmund Livingston, in his *Must Men Hate?* gives a penetrating analysis of anti-Semitism. He submits that it is a result of emotionalism and a fruit of superstition, ignorance and frustration. A person from childhood can acquire a mental picture of a Jew which creates prejudice and which can stir into action on unpredictable events. The point is that whether hatred is justified or not, whether it has rational basis or not, whether it springs from maltreatment or it issues in envy, its destructiveness is unspeakably horrible. Hatred poisons the mind and the body and the spirit. It produces man's inward deterioration. It reduces man into the purely biological creature and usurps his power of self-transcendence.

The Holy Bible has much to say about this spiritual dilemma. For the Bible is essentially the story of God's love overcoming the hatred of men. The devil knows that hate is a powerful weapon and his mission is to transform man's wounded love into hate. But God saves and His mission is to transform hate into love.

Men's Hate and the Cross

Review, if you please, the life of our Lord Jesus Christ. Was it not man's hate that led Him to the cross? Did not the scribes and the Pharisees hate Him for liberating the people from the bondage of the law? Did not the businessmen hate Him for turning their tables upside down in the tabernacle? And yet it was the voice of God's love that echoed across the hills of Calvary and down thru the centuries when Jesus prayed for the shouting mad crowd: "Father, forgive them for they know not what they do."

And so from the very heart of the gospel story we have the message that to overcome the sting of hate we should by necessity have the forgiving love of God. That love of God is first of all forgiveness, and forgiveness is the only power that can drive away the evil of hate.

The Nature of Man

At this point it should be said that man by nature is unwilling to forgive. When man has wronged someone he wants to be forgiven, but when someone has wronged him he is not willing to forgive. Jesus Christ related a parable to stress this fact. He said a man owed a king 10,000 talents. When the date of payment came, he begged the king saying: "Have patience with me, and I will pay thee all." For he was not able to pay his debt on the promised date. And the good king, touched by the pleadings of the servant, forgave him his debts. But on his way home, the servant met his fellow servant who owed him 100 pence and he demanded for the payment of the debt. But the fellow servant begged him and used the very same words he said to the king: "Have patience with me, and I will pay thee all." But he did not forgive. He took his fellow servant by the throat and shook his head vehemently, and finally he cast him into prison. Translated into the language of today, the "man was forgiven $10,000,000, but was unwilling to forgive $17.00." Jesus concluded the parable by saying that God will not forgive us if we from our hearts do not forgive those who trespass against us.

The Nature of Forgiveness

Attention should be called to the phrase, "forgiving from our hearts," because the legalistic concept of forgiveness has no place in Christian life. We cannot, for example, lightly condone the ungratefulness of a friend to us only to secure God's divine clemency on our sin of greed or pride or idolatry. We cannot manipulate the method of forgiving those who do us wrong in order to earn God's pardon on our trespasses against Him. The forgiveness that has healing power is one which comes from the heart and it is there only because it is planted by God. Therefore we can truly say that to forgive is the working of God in and thru the human heart and while to err is human, nevertheless to forgive is divine.

This being the case we cannot forgive others from the resources that are ours. There is only human weakness in us which tends to be unforgiving.

We can forgive only on the basis of God's goodness which, if penitently appropriated, empowers the heart to forgive and to forget, and to restore the fellowship both with God and with one another.

If there is a two-way traffic in the Christian religion, it is in the area of forgiveness. For God is ready to forgive only those that are truly repentant. The two thieves on the cross dramatized the truth that God forgives those who are truly sorry for their sins but does not impose His pardon upon those who determine to be stubbornly unrepentant.

A Hard Lesson

One of the hardest lessons in the subject of forgiveness, and one that is hard to face, is the fact that the duty of forgiveness is unlimited. This is what Peter learned when Jesus told him to forgive 70 times 7, not that on the 491st time he may be free to be unforgiving but that always he should recognize that God's heart is an everlasting well of love and that His forgiveness flows to everlasting shores. At the same time such forgiveness does not encourage the repetition of sin, for it is granted when man repents, and repentance is turning away from sin and living anew with God. Hence, forgiveness is redemptive; it has healing grace and it solidifies character.

And so, if hatred can poison the moral and spiritual life of man, forgiveness can revive the image of God in man. If hatred can destroy the citadel of the soul, forgiveness can rebuild the broken faith and the broken spirit. Before Pilate, thousands of voices trembling with hate clamoured "Let Him be crucified," but the voice that showered the mercies of heaven was the voice of Him who cried: "Father, forgive them."

The Church Needs Forgiveness

The Church today stands in need of that divine forgiveness. If it is to carry out faithfully the mission of love, it must bear the mark of a forgiven community. The preaching of the Word is the preaching of God's forgiveness and we have not truly heard the Word unless we receive God's pardoning grace.

Our Highest Duty

Our need of divine forgiveness is an imperative need because the practice of Christian forgiveness is our highest duty. The life of many has been a life of misery and fear, of tormenting restlessness and artificial happiness because within their hearts is the poison of hate. As St. John says, "He who hates his brother is in darkness, and he walks in darkness and knows not where he goes, because darkness has blinded his eyes" (I John 2:11). We say: But men revile us, cheat us, fail us; they are irresponsible, annoying, impatient, intolerant. And yet Jesus says: "Forgive 70 times 7... Love your enemies; bless them that curse you, do good to them that hate you, pray for them that despitefully use you... if thine enemy hunger, feed him... if he thirst, give him drink... overcome evil with good... be of good cheer...."

Are we not sometimes wearied by the overpowering impulse to hate? Do we not sometimes succumb to the consuming passion for the downfall, and even destruction, of another? If this is our weakness, I suggest that we keep ourselves close to God. Why? Because hate is a spiritual disease which only God can cure; because hate if not overcome by forgiving love paves the way to self-destruction; because hate if not controlled will control us.

Keeping Close to God

Let us keep close to God in the reading of the Scriptures. The stories of men who have overcome their hatred are inspiring and challenging. Esau's forgiveness to his brother is a mighty testimony on the redemptiveness of love. Philemon's welcome to repentant Onesimus demonstrates the practicability of Christian forgiveness. Jesus' compassion for the erring sons of God and the way He fought the hated power of the Roman Empire established the landmark of spiritual superiority of forgiveness over hate.

Let us keep close to God in the discipline of prayer. Our greatest sin is prayerlessness. It is the sin behind sin. It is independence from the Guardian of our souls. The poet was right when he said:

> O what peace we often forfeit,
>
> O what needless pain we bear,
>
> All because we do not carry
>
> Everything to God in prayer.

Jesus calls us to unearth the wisdom of His words when He says: "Pray for them that persecute you."

4

Singing Faith

Speaking to yourselves in psalms and hymns and spiritual songs, singing and making melody in your heart to the Lord.
— Ephesians 5:19

Appreciation of music varies according to one's cultural orientation. A song may be beautiful to some, it may be boring to others. Nevertheless, it is a fact that music is the universal language of the soul.

Today music serves not only as a medium of cultural expression but also as a therapeutic device. Modern hospitals all over the world make use of selected music in restoring the mental balance of the patients. There are parts of the human personality which can be touched only by music.

Therapeutic Values of Music

This method of healing, by the way, is not an entirely new system. It was used before and during the days of Socrates. Plato tells us that "the Corybantic priest treated hysterical women with pipe and music, which excited them to dance and dance till they fell to the ground exhausted and went to sleep; when they woke, they were cured."[1] Mr. Beneridge testifies: "Music calls in my spirits, composes my thoughts, delights my ears, recreates my mind, and so not only fits me for after business, but fills my heart, at the present, with pure and useful thoughts, so that when the music sounds the sweetliest in my ears truth commonly flows the clearest into my mind."

Plato saw the importance of music not only in restoring mental health but also in achieving an ideal utopia. He proposed that the first years of a person's schooling should be spent in physical education. Every pupil should be a good and healthy athlete. "The Utopia must begin in the body of man." Then with physical education should go music because the prize-fighters and weight lifters must also have a disposition to justice. Through music the soul learns harmony and rhythm. He who is harmoniously

---
[1] Durant, *Story of Philosophy,* p.23.

constituted "cannot be unjust, because rhythm and harmony find their way into the sacred places of the soul bearing grace in their movements and making the soul graceful. Since music molds character... it shares in determining social and political issues."[1] That theory invited serious criticisms, but Plato held fast to his belief that a person disciplined in the harmony of music would at least feel uncomfortable at the sight of disorderliness and injustice. Martin Luther said, "Music is a discipline and a mistress of order and good manners, she makes the people milder and gentler, more moral and more reasonable."

Music and Worship

We need not wander far to realize how greatly music can enrich our life. Without music, this worship service can be dry and boring. Without the choir and the organ, without congregational singing and choral responses, many of us will fall asleep. If our radio programs were all speeches and talks, how many would care to listen? Addison said, "Music wakes the soul, and lifts it high, and wings it with sublime desires and fits it to bespeak the Deity."

It is not a mere coincidence, therefore, that the Christian faith is a singing faith. Evangelical Christianity especially is a great patron of music. There are churches which have no musical instruments at all, but they sing. There are those who sing with simple accompaniment of the organ or piano. And there are those who sing with guitar, banjo, violin, trumpets, saxophone and all kinds of musical instruments. They may differ in the quality and quantity of music and in instruments, but all employ music during the worship ceremony.

Even the Old Testament people, let us remember, loved music and used to sing on special occasions. Moses and his sister Miriam, as well as the congregation of Israel, sang antiphonally beside the bank of a river. That was done reverently and in the spirit of worship. For, as Chalmer said, "music is the language of praise."

There was David, the king whose ability as a musician can be traced thru the pages of the book of Psalms. "No other poetry has been so constantly used by the church through all the centuries as the Psalms of David," someone noted. In many instances, whenever he would breathe a prayer unto God, he would do it with his harp and thru his songs.

---

[1] Durant, *op. cit.*, p. 22.

Music and Christ's Birth

In the fulness of time, when in the village of Bethlehem Jesus Christ was born, the angels of heaven sang the hallelujah song and filled the air with heavenly music and the believing hearts with joy. In fact, even while He was yet in the Virgin's womb, Mary sang the great *Magnificat* confirming the truth that the coming Saviour would make the hearts of men sing. And so, that Man of Galilee whose life was hard and whose death was a shame is now the resurrected Christ whose message is Good News.

Reasons for Singing

In Jesus Christ, we discover why Christians sing. We sing because Christianity is a religion of a happy life. To be a Christian is not to put on long and sour faces. It is to discover the joy which the world can never give. What greater joy can there be than the joy of a life with God? To worship God is to put life on the highest level. It is to make a joyful noise unto the Lord. (It may be noise, but it is joyful.) That is why life in the hands of God is a happy life. It may be a life of difficulty, of banishment, of unpopularity, of persecution — but it is strong and secure. It is a blessed life. Jesus underscored the blessedness of life with God in His Sermon on the Mount. When He said, "Blessed are the poor in spirit," He meant "Happy are the poor in spirit." In some translations of the New Testament, the word **happy** is used instead of **blessed**.

> "Happy are those who mourn, for they shall be comforted.
>
> "Happy are the meek, for they shall inherit the earth.
>
> "Happy are the merciful, for they shall receive mercy.
>
> "Happy are you when men revile you and persecute you and utter all kinds of evil against you falsely on my account.
>
> "Rejoice and be glad, for your reward is great in heaven, for so men persecuted the prophets who were before you."

Those pictures of Jesus depicting Him as a stern, sad-looking Man miss the blazing heroism of the Master's soul. He who perfectly obeyed His Father's will could not have attracted the little children if He looked so stern and sour. There must be a radiant, happy expression on His face which children saw and felt. All those who come and follow Him, both young and old, confirm the happy life they have in Him. Therefore they sing.

In the second place, Christians sing because Christianity is a religion of love. When a person is in love, he will surely sing. When a young man or woman sings or hums or whistles while he or she is walking or doing anything, is that not often a sign of being in love? When a person is in love he can be a poet. He can also be a singer.

Love is the keyword of the Christian faith. St. John defines God as love. Human relationship can be terrible without love. Family life without love can be unbearable. Religion without love cannot be Christian. Christians sing because their faith is a loving faith.

In the third place, Christians sing because Christianity is a religion of the Holy Spirit. There are two spirits which can make a man sing: One is the spirit of liquor, and the other is the Holy Spirit. It is not unusual to see a man singing when he is drunk. He who is most shy and reserved when drunk makes a lot of speeches even without making any sense – and sings as well. You will be surprised that when a person is drunk, he composes his own music or revises the works of the masters. And he sings with feeling.

In our text, however, the Apostle Paul reminds us not to get drunk with wine, "for that is debauchery; but be filled with the Spirit, addressing one another in psalms and hymns and spiritual songs." Do you remember that on the day of Pentecost when the Holy Spirit filled those that were with one accord in the tabernacle, the outsiders thought that they were drunk? It was Peter who stood up and said, "Men of Judea and all who dwell in Jerusalem, these people are not drunk with wine as you suppose. They are filled with the Holy Spirit." Then Peter continued to preach on the saving power of Jesus Christ. We sing because God's Spirit fills our hearts.

Congregational Singing a Serious Business

Our church people should take congregational singing seriously because singing is an act of worship, an expression of our faith. You say you are monotones; never mind, just sing. You can produce a joyful noise unto the Lord. You say you are not a singer; never mind, just sing. After all, it is the harmony of our inward life that God wants. You say how can we sing when we are low-spirited and brokenhearted and heavy-laden and burdened with cares and problems? That is precisely the point. A man or woman who can sing in spite of life's bitter experiences is a great child of God. God knows the distress of our souls. Some of us may be victims of some malignant disease and our days are numbered. Others may be suffering from mortal pain inflicted by the ungratefulness of a trusted friend. Some of you may be treading along the narrow path of uncertainty, not knowing clearly what may come out of your plan or business. And it grieves you to be walking in the dark. Still some may be burdened with the cares of your own homes, finding it harder and harder to live with your wife or husband, finding it more difficult to understand your son. Others may be beset by financial worries, or by many obligations that need to be fulfilled soon, or by anything which disturbs their nerves. Whatever be the pain in our hearts, singing hymns and spiritual songs is one remedy prescribed by the Holy Scriptures. That is what Jesus did at one of the most crucial moments in His life. During the Last Supper which He instituted in the Upper Room, one of His disciples went out to betray Him and He knew the hour of His death was drawing nigh. And yet after the Communion, He and the rest of the disciples sang a hymn and went to the Mount of Olives.

But while vocal singing has great values, it is not the final goal of the Christian life. The goal, rather, is the making of melody in our hearts unto the Lord. We may be still and quiet, but our hearts are singing unto God. That is the art of singing which every Christian should learn. A person who makes a melody in his heart unto the Lord may be a poor singer, but His music is most acceptable unto the Great Musician. And if our hearts will sing to God even while we work and labour, if our lives are attuned to God's Holy will, the shadow of death may fall upon us but we will never want. That is the secret of a fully surrendered life. It knows no end, no fear, no death. It only knows that God is almighty and that in Him all is well.

And so, whoever you are and whatever your sorrow, make melody in your hearts unto the Lord, and the world cannot undo you. Remember that you are not alone, that there is Someone who cares for you. Someone who assures you, "In the world ye shall have tribulations, but be of good cheer, I have overcome the world."

5

Is Death a Calamity?

O death, where is thy sting?
O grave, where is thy victory? — **1 Corinthians 15:55**

The sermon-topic is borrowed from Leslie D. Weatherhead's last chapter in *Why do Men Suffer?* It fairly puts in the form of a question one of the deepest problems that haunt every human mind. The fact of death is a tremendous fact, and all of us sooner or later will have to face it as a burning issue. To talk about death may not always be pleasant, and yet it is always unavoidable. Indeed, we cannot fully understand life, even only its most pleasant aspects, apart from death. If our Christian faith is a faith in the resurrected Christ, it is because we also believe in His crucifixion. And so our religion is concerned not only with our life but also with our death.

The Unpredictability of Death

This concern is a very needful one because we do not know when our "time" will be and sometimes it comes to us when we are least ready for it. It may come to some in the innocency of their childhood, as well as in the golden age of their life. It may come in the fullness of health and strength as well as in the midst of suffering and pain. It may suddenly come at the height of laughter and merrymaking, as well as in the desert land of a gripping loneliness. And even if its coming is announced, like the sun setting in the west announces the coming of the night, the thought of death can be horrifying and its coming a very shocking experience. It makes the last few moments of life the summit of despair, if not a part of death itself. A portion of our earthly life can be seriously damaged by our fear of death, whether it be our own death or the death of a loved one.

Death and Sin

The biblical view of death is always associated with the fact of sin.

The Apostle Paul tells us (Rom. 6:25) that the wages of sin is death. Therefore, contrary to the thought of the Greek philosophers, death is not something natural or something willed by God. It is unnatural and opposed to God. The book of Genesis tells us that death came into the world by the sin of man. It is a curse in which the whole creation has become involved. It can be conquered only by conquering sin. It is the dark presupposition of the whole drama of Christian redemption.

Death is the enemy of God. For God is Life and the Creator of Life. It is not His will that there be withering and decaying, sickness and pain and suffering. These things happen not because of God, but because of sin. James in his Epistle (1:15) confirms the fact that sin bringeth forth death. It should not be a surprise to us that in the book of Job death is spoken of as the king of terrors (18:14). It is loneliness beyond description. It is being away from the presence of the Holy One.

A Review of Jesus' Death

A brief review of Jesus' death will clearly illustrate the point. St. Mark in his Gospel tells us that Jesus in Gethsemane, knowing that His death was at hand, "was greatly distressed and troubled." Speaking to Peter and James, Jesus said, "My soul is very sorrowful, even to death" (Mk. 14:32 ff). We have here a picture of a human being who shares in the natural fear of death. Jesus knew that death was not something divine, but dreadful. He was afraid of death. He prayed to God and said, "Abba, Father, all things are possible unto thee; take away this cup from me" (Mk. 14:36). He knew that to die was to be alone, and He did not want to be alone. He did not want to be forsaken. He cried to God and petitioned that if it was possible, He be spared from drinking from that bitter cup. He wanted the companionship not only of God but also of His intimate disciples. He would interrupt His prayer every now and then to go to His disciples who were fighting off sleep. He woke them up again and again because He did not want to be alone. As the Epistle to the Hebrews says, Jesus "offered up prayers and supplications with strong crying and tears unto [God] that was able to save him from death" (5:7). He was, please note the word, strongly crying to God for deliverance from death. Those of us who have a picture of a purely divine Christ may find it hard to imagine Him crying and weeping, but the Evangelists did not gloss over their records of Jesus' tears at His death.

And what did we hear from the Cross? It was a cry of dereliction:

"My God, my God, why hast thou forsaken me?" (Mk 15:34). Only a gravely desolated spirit could have cried that way. It was, for Jesus, the darkest night of His soul when God, who had been close to Him all His life, forsook Him. Jesus saw the most frightful face of death and He felt the greatest loneliness in His life. As far as the Gospel records are concerned, there is no glossing over the terribleness of Jesus' death.[1]

But of course we know that the life of Christ did not end at the grave. We know that the cry of dereliction was not the last word. We know that even before He gave up the ghost there was something in the manner of His death that foretold the victory of life. Someone in the crowd, sensing such signal victory, muttered, "Surely, this is the Son of God." And when on the third day the cover of His tomb was rolled away, there spread in Jerusalem and all over Palestine the glorious news that He who was crucified rose again from the dead. The event of the resurrection shattered all the power of death and assured all men that death is not the end. The gloom of the Holy Friday had passed away and the Crucifixion was no longer a tragedy, for on the Cross the king of terrors and the King of kings met and Jesus the Christ won the victory. The resurrection event was the event of life's triumph over the horror of death, when the mighty Son of God robbed death of its power. So now the Christians can rejoice with Paul: "O death, where is thy sting? O grave, where is thy victory?"

It is in the light of the resurrection that we see the wondrous power of God which can make use of death. Death is no longer the end of life but the beginning of another life. It is, in the words of Herman Hooke, "the foreshadowing of life. We die that we may die no more." That which was feared as dark wall is now seen as the door to life eternal; that which was thought to be the end of the road now looks like the gate to eternity. Death is no longer a curse but a crown to them that walk with Christ. It has acquired a certain beauty which can be seen thru the eye of faith.

Cyprian's Views of Death

The early Church Fathers[2] tried to bring out that beauty in their sketches of the face of death. Though sometimes the sketches are unsatisfactory, they nevertheless give us some insight into the meaning of death. Cyprian, for instance, distributed literature on the notion that death is "rest from the labour and sorrow of life." Admittedly, this concept is not

---

[1] Cullman, *Immortality of the Soul or Resurrection of the Dead*, pp. 19-27.
[2] See Pelikan, *The Shape of Death*, pp. 60-63.

uniquely Christian since Stoic writers like Cicero and Seneca shared the same thought. But Cyprian stressed that the rest which death gives is only for believers. This is in consonance with the promise in Rev. 14:13, where the voice from heaven says, "Blessed are the dead who die in the Lord henceforth. Blessed indeed, says the Spirit, that they may rest from their labors."

Cyprian also spoke of death as the soul's return to its native land. To die is to go home. This is the picture we get from his peroration: "What man, after having been abroad, would not hasten to return to his native land? Who, when hurrying to sail to his family, would not more eagerly long for a favorable wind that he might more quickly embrace his dear ones?" Surely this statement is a commendation of death, a tribute to the blessedness of going home.

We remember Cyprian for his metaphor of death not only as rest and return to native land, but also as victory. This figure of speech is also used in the New Testament which speaks of the crown of life or the crown of victory. The resurrection event enables us to see that Christ on the Cross was not the victim but the Victor. His death was a victory over sin. He rose again from the grave. So, St. John in Revelation can say to the churches that everyone who remains faithful will, at the time of his death, receive the crown of life.

Cyprian also suggested that we may think of death as a summons. He said, "Let us show that this is what we believe, so that we may not mourn the death even of our dear ones and, when the day of our own summons comes, without hesitation but with gladness we may come to the Lord at His call." The early Christians took it as a euphemism, even as a "summons to higher service." It was Cyprian's aim to emphasize the supreme authority of God as Judge who can summon anyone for an accounting of his life. A response to God's call is, at the same time, "going to Christ." To die is to be called to Christ, and, to use Cyprian's words, "to be changed and reformed to the image of Christ and to the dignity of heavenly grace." There is no place for regret in the death of a Christian for to go to Christ and be with Him is a joyous privilege.

Death As Sleep

Another metaphor of death closely related to the ones suggested by Cyprian and which was perhaps quite common to the early Christians is the metaphor of death as sleep. Jesus Himself used this metaphor in describing the death of His friend Lazarus. He told His disciples that Lazarus, who had been in the grave for four days, was only sleeping. And when they could not understand Him, He had to tell them plainly that Lazarus was dead. The writer of the Book of Acts describes the death of Stephen, the first Christian martyr, as falling asleep. The Old Testament does not seem to be unfamiliar with this concept. The Psalmist, for instance, speaks of the sleep of death (Ps. 13:3). When Paul in Ephesians (5:14) quotes the prophet Isaiah, he says, "Awake thou that sleepest, and arise from the dead." He pictures the dead as sleeping, or are at least in a deep, luxuriant slumber.

All these metaphors of death are characterized by the conspicuous absence of anything disconsolate. Nowhere in the New Testament can we find death as a terror, although, as the Apostle Paul says, it is still our last enemy. Victory over it has already been achieved. Because Christ has drawn the sting of death — which is sin — we need not be afraid. Therefore, in a very real sense, we can thank God for death and for the glorious life that can be ours beyond the end of our earthly pilgrimage.

Death As Last Enemy

All these beautiful affirmations of the defeat of death are not an attempt at obscuring its empirical reality. We have noted that the Apostle Paul does not allow us to forget that it is the last enemy we have to face. Although its sting is already broken to pieces, it still lies across the path of every life and all of us, without exception, will someday cross that bridge. And because we do not know when that someday will be, the big question we have to answer is whether we are prepared for it anytime. Some preachers take this question seriously and their preaching is not complete without asking the people if they are ready to meet their death. Those who elect to ignore the question for reasons of good health or great fortune may remark with an air of sarcasm, "What do we care? We have goods laid down for many years. Let's eat, drink, and be merry!" Let the Gospel remind us, if we happen to be like-minded, of the folly of such complacency for it is not within our power to fortify ourselves against the forays of our last enemy.

The answer to the question, we see, depends on the degree of our intimacy with Jesus Christ. If the early Christians and the church fathers saw nothing horrible in the face of death, it was because, in the first place, there was beauty in their inward life. Their sweet friendship with the Creator of the universe enabled them to transcend the bitterest of tragedies. They knew they were not alone though they walked thru the valley of the shadow of death.

Serenity Before Death

In these our days when the death of mankind can easily be caused by miscalculation or fear, we need a staying power to keep us calm and alert. And that sense of security even in the face of an impending gloom cannot be generated by the invention of more satellites, but by deepening our trust in Him who is Life and the Creator of life. As Fuller says, "There is no better armor against the shafts of death than to be busied in God's service." A godly character that has been pruned of its greediness and pride, the life that has been disciplined in righteousness and love—that is our strong shield against the onslaughts of death. They who are at peace with God can never be troubled by the specter of the grave. They are lives built upon the Rock which the storms cannot destroy.

So in the providence of God, a saintly life knows no fear of death. But this also means that the ungodly are not so. Men who have courage to defy the law of God are, by the nature of things, cowards in the face of death. They are afraid to die because they have not lived well. And their fear of death is a sign of a bad conscience.

The ungodly life which creates fear of death is, in the strong language of the New Testament, death itself. St. Paul, in his letter to Timothy, reminds us that "she who indulges in pleasure is dead even while she lives" (1 Tim. 5:6). If the New Testament speaks of the dead as living souls because of their faith in Christ, it also speaks in equally plain language of the living as dead because of their indulgence in sin. And if sin separates us from God who is life, then the sin-stricken souls are in the hands of death. Then we can be dead even in the midst of life.

If we are afraid more of death than of sin, we have the symptom of spiritual bankruptcy which only God can cure. We have not yet understood that in the divine scheme of things, it is spiritual death which is our tragedy. We should strive to concern ourselves not only with meeting the legitimate claims of our bodies, but also and especially with attending consistently and conscientiously to the admonition of the Lord all the days of our life. For only by humbly yielding to the holy claim of God and by firmly clinging to His pardoning grace can we hope to stand face to face with death with quietness and confidence. Only by completely committing ourselves to the serious intention of Christian discipleship and by being daily nurtured in the truth of faith can we be persuaded that neither death nor principalities nor powers shall be able to separate us from the love of God in Jesus Christ.

> So live that when thy summons comes
>
> To join the innumerable caravan
>
> Which moves to that mysterious realm
>
> Where each shall take his chambers
>
> In the silent halls of death;
>
> Thou go not like a quarry slave at night,
>
> Scourged to his dungeon,
>
> But sustained and soothed by an unfaltering trust,
>
> Approach thy grave like one who wraps
>
> The drapery of his couch about him,
>
> And lies down to pleasant dreams.[1]

---

[1] William C. Bryant, From *Thanatopsis*.

6

The Meaning of Worship

I was glad when they said unto me, Let us go into the house of the Lord. — Psalm 122:1

One thing common among our churches is that in every congregation, there are professional latecomers to worship services, or to any church-sponsored activity. We do not need to be keen observers to note this fact. I am afraid this is true in all other churches all over the world. There are times, of course, when people cannot help but be late because of some urgent matters that should be attended to, or because something unforeseen and beyond control unexpectedly comes up. We should grant that there are reasonable excuses for being late, and that be they reasonable or not, we should not look derogatorily upon anyone entering the sanctuary ten or fifteen minutes late.

A More Regrettable Fact

Even more deplorable is that in many congregations, there are professional absentees. And again we should understand that sometimes people cannot go to church because of sickness, because they have to travel, or because something very important has to be done. But again there are those who do not go to church because of sheer laziness. Or could it be because they simply have not developed the habit of churchgoing? Could it be that they have not fully understood the meaning of Christian worship?

Then look at the respectable churchgoers, those who are not always late and not always absent. Look at those who are punctual and meticulous in the observance of their religious duties. Do we not find some with an overly critical attitude toward worship? They are the people who withhold their good comments about the service, if they have any, but quite vocal about the things they cannot fully appreciate. Could they have possibly forgotten the essential intent of spiritual gathering?

And how about those who do not actively participate in the act of worship? Those who are in the service more as spectators than as participants? The hymn may be familiar to them and yet they do not sing. They may be able to read the notes and yet would rather be silent. When the morning prayer is being offered, they do not close their eyes. They only look around to see what others are doing. When the choir is singing or when the preacher is preaching, they make drawings on the pages of the hymnals or on the order of worship. Could they be uninformed about what it means to worship God?

Undeniably, there are also ministers and lay leaders who do not seem to know the real value of public worship. Until now, we have churches where the worship leader or minister, after announcing that the congregation will sing a hymn, scans the pages of the hymnal to select the hymn they are to sing. Some preachers prepare their message on Sunday morning just before the service begins. Sometime ago, *Time* magazine carried a news item about a certain Rev. Jackson Burns of St. Paul's Methodist Church in Cedar Rapids, Iowa who tape-recorded one of his Sunday sermons. While listening to its playback, he fell asleep.

Stages in Worship

Dr. Edgar S. Brightman, in his *Religious Values* suggests that a fully developed worship has four distinct stages or elements, since they are vitally interrelated. The first stage, he says, is contemplation. Man meditates on the mysteries and majesty of almighty God. His consciousness is directed to the reality of the Supreme Being. He is made aware of God's omnipotence. He realizes that the Lord is great, worthy of all his praise and thanksgiving, admiration and adoration.

The second stage in the experience of worship is revelation. Here the worshipper is confronted by a divine Presence. God is giving Himself. The resources of His grace are made available. Contact with the Divine is firmly established. Our spirits bear witness with His Spirit. The dark shadows of the heart are illuminated. In contemplation, man is seeking; in revelation, God is giving. The prophet Isaiah in the temple first saw the Lord — that was meditation; and then, he said: "One of the seraphims flew unto me" — that was revelation. God always takes the initiative in the God-man relationship.

The third stage is communion. It is a living fellowship with God. It is more than a mere contact. It is a vital encounter between God and man.

Communion is a created community where God is Lord and Sovereign Power. It is the experience of harmony which is beyond all earthly cares. It is the redemption of existence, the triumph of holiness over sin, the subordination of the flesh to the spirit. Communion therefore is a blending of the divine and the human, the harmony of material and spiritual interests.

Communion is between God and man, but also among the worshippers. In worship, they discover unity of spirit. They may come from diverse backgrounds and different cultures and races, but worship makes them one. They serve one God and Father. They see that they are brothers. Communion among the worshippers is the birth of brotherhood, the crystallization of man's true nature and destiny.

The fourth stage of worship is fruition. The fruit of the Spirit — love, peace, joy, meekness, gentleness, patience, temperance, faith — that is the true goal of worship. Strictly speaking, fruition is a natural result of the Christian worship. A man who places himself under the transforming influence of God cannot remain an old creature. Everything shall be new again. Worship is the event of the second birth, the refuelling of love, the rekindling of hope.

Communion and Commemoration

I shall now further elaborate on some of these elements of worship. The communion with God is unavoidably a commemoration of His mighty acts. In the Old Testament, the psalms and the hymns are mostly about God's great deliverance of the Israelites from the bondage of slavery in Egypt. Among the major and the minor prophets, the statement of authority is "Thus saith the Lord, who hast brought you out of the land of Egypt." God Himself, so the prophets testified, reminds the people of what He had done for them before conveying His message. In Isaiah 51:15, God says, "I am the Lord thy God, that divided the sea."

Preaching in the New Testament

In the New Testament, preaching is the proclamation of what God had done in Jesus Christ. Peter's inspired sermon recorded in the Book of Acts is a stirring testimony on what God had done in Christ. St. Paul's sermon before King Agrippa is a touching confession of God's redeeming power in Jesus Christ and how such grace so touched his heart that he could not be disobedient to the heavenly vision.

The Lord's Supper

This element of commemoration is so essential in worship that Jesus Christ, in instituting the sacrament of the Holy Supper, commanded us to observe it in remembrance of Him. Whenever two or three are gathered in His name, the presence of the Unseen One in their midst beckons them to look back to the Cross and remember the glory of His resurrection. Worship, then, is a commemoration of the past, a communion with Christ and with all those who laboured in the Vineyard of the Lord. It is beholding God as Lord of time, One who has entered into the history of His own creation.

Thus rooted in the past, worship generates power for the present and equips the worshippers for the living of these days. Men do not enter the house of worship to flee from the burdens of the world. Worship is not an escape mechanism whereby all cares and problems, all tears and griefs miraculously disappear. Rather, to worship God is to realize the sufficiency of His grace in all our needs — good cheer in tribulations, peace in the restless sea of sins, courage in the face of seemingly insurmountable difficulties.

This is the foundation of our hope for eternal life. The future is secure in the hands of God. We can look forward with jubilant spirit. Christ is the same yesterday and today and forever. And because He lives we shall live also. In worship we have a foretaste of the life in the Kingdom of God.

The Ministry of Worship

What else can the human heart crave for? What yearning can be deeper, nobler, purer? Worship is the highest activity of the soul, the most sublime duty of a Christian congregation. In worship we look through the windows of eternity and then the purest longings of our finite and mortal spirits are met and richly satisfied. In worship we commune with One whose demands are exacting, who wishes to be the sole Master of life and who requires absolute obedience.

But while in worship God purifies man's experience, the attitude of the worshipper should not be what he can get, but what he can give. Too often we miss the blessing of worship because the idea of getting something from worship has set the mind in the wrong perspective. While there should be expectancy in receiving the grace of God thru worship, worship is nevertheless the giving of praise, the surrender of the will, the submission of self. Only in worship can we discover that giving is receiving, and being captured by Christ is the crown of liberty. A man may not get anything from the service (the anthem may be poor, the sermon empty, the prayer too long) but if in worship he gives his time, his thoughts, his loyalty and his love to God, he has the joy of having felt the sustaining presence of the living God.

Worship and Our Churches

It is incumbent upon our churches to make the service solemn and impressive. The people are entitled to a replenishing spiritual experience during the service. The worship of God should always be an offering of gratitude, a presentation of ourselves as a living sacrifice. In worship we recover the image of God in us, and the enjoyment of His gifts comes only as we give ourselves. To be sure, we make petitions and offer supplications, but they are a part of a full surrender to the Lordship of the Heavenly Father.

Only in this light can we speak of the creative values of worship. It is necessary that we manifest the fruits of the Spirit if we do worship God in spirit and in truth. We go to church not to observe a decent ceremony or an approved custom, but to praise the Lord in the beauty of His holiness. We go to church not primarily to meet our friends and relatives. The house of God is a house of prayer. We go to church to pray. The greatest value of worship is the enthronement of God in our life, the flowering of His love in our hearts. After the service we should go out with a sense of mission, and as men and women who are not afraid to do justly, to love mercy, and to walk humbly with our God. Jesus Christ defined worship when He said, "Come unto me..." and "Go ye into the world."

7

A Man Called Simon

But there was a certain man, called Simon, which beforetime in the same city used sorcery, and bewitched the people of Samaria, giving out that himself was some great one.
— Acts 8:9

Biblical literature is replete with characters by the name of Simon or Simeon. Jacob's second son by Leah bears that name. It comes from the Hebrew word *shama*, which means to hear. Leah called her son Simeon because, according to Genesis 29:33, God heard her. In Luke, chapter 2 (v. 25-32), a man by this name is called "just and devout," waiting for the consolation of Israel. He had upon him the Holy Spirit who revealed that "he should not see death before he had seen the Messiah." In Matthew 13:55, one of Jesus' brothers is named Simon. We also read of Simon the leper in Matthew 26:6. The rich Pharisee, in whose house a sinful woman washed Jesus' feet, was also a certain Simon (Lk.7:44). The Cyrenian, who was forced by the Roman soldiers to help Jesus carry the cross, was called Simon (Mk. 15:21). The Simon with whom Peter lodged in Joppa was a tanner (Acts 9:43).

In Acts chapter 8, we have a man called Simon who bewitched the people of Samaria with his sorcery, and proclaimed himself as "somebody great." Obviously he got a good following because the people gave heed to him, "from the least to the greatest, saying, This man is that power of God which is called great" (v. 10).

Philip's Ministry

For the meantime, however, there came Philip preaching the Kingdom of God and the name of Jesus Christ. Indeed, he performed wonders and miracles by healing the sick of their organic and psychological disorders. These miracles, we can be sure, were the result of his preaching, or rather manifestations of a life that had been released from the burden of guilt by the forgiving love of God. The book of Acts says, "The people with one accord gave heed unto those things which Philip spake, hearing and seeing the miracles which he did." Their attention, in other words, was turned from Simon to the witness of Philip, and indeed, submitted themselves to baptism. The record says Simon himself believed, and was baptized. God surely blessed Philip's ministry in Samaria, for the people responded faithfully to the message of the Gospel, and there was great joy in the city.

Peter and John

Our Scripture lesson says that when the apostles in Jerusalem heard that Samaria had received the Word of God, they sent Peter and John to see for themselves the new developments in their missionary work. And there in Samaria they prayed for the people and, while laying their hands on them, an act that became customary among the apostles, the Holy Spirit descended upon them. And when Simon saw that through the laying on the apostles' hands the Holy Spirit was given, he offered them money saying, "Give me this power, that on whomsoever I lay hands, he may receive the Holy Ghost." But Peter rebuked him and said, "Thy money perish with thee." The New English Bible translates it this way: "You and your money, may you come to a bad end." J. Phillips' translation perhaps conveys the idea most clearly. It says, "To hell with you and your money!" This, I guess, is the translation we would prefer because, I am afraid, we are quite familiar with that kind of a language. When we recall that Peter was a very impulsive person, and in fact became outspoken among the Twelve because of his impulsiveness, then we know that such rebuke on Simon was typical of Peter and could come only from him.

Simon's Half-Baked Conversion

This brief account of Simon Magus, as he is traditionally called, gives us some insights into the nature of man which may help us understand the futility of half-baked Christianity. For one thing, in the case of Simon, we have a man who believed but was not really converted. Simon became a baptized member of the Christian fellowship, but was obsessed with the thought of becoming great and popular and somebody. When he saw the apostles bestowing upon the people the gift of the Spirit thru the laying of their hands, he desired not to be filled with the Spirit himself, but to possess the power so that he, too, could be like the apostles. He wanted always to be on top, and he would offer anything he had just to get to the top. He did not have the humility of spirit that should characterize a Christian believer. It is not surprising, then, that though he was a baptized member of the church, his burning passion was to have his own way and to get what he wanted.

It is obvious that I am describing here not only a forgotten person in history but also the living men and women of today whose Christianity is only superficial and whose membership in the Body of Christ is no more than a fashion or a formality. I am describing here a host of Christians whose faith is only intellectual, who believe that Jesus is the Christ and yet have never known the cleansing power of His love. They are those whose baptism was only a ceremony and not a replenishing experience of being born again. They sometimes come to church and may be in the forefront of the church's affairs, mixing freely with bishops and ministers, not so much for the enjoyment of the fellowship, but for the advertisement of their schemes and business. People of this kind cannot be depended upon. For they will shirk from the slightest demand of discipleship and will be afraid to share in the burden of the church's witness. Like Simon the charlatan, they need to be converted.

Magic vs. Miracle

Again, in the case of Simon, we have the image of a Christian who is more after magic than miracle. And magic, as Theodore P. Ferris notes, is "man's attempt to change the natural course of events for his own benefits. It is the imposition of man's will upon a higher will."[1] In Simon's case it was self-centeredness. A miracle, on the other hand, is "the surrender of the lesser to the greater will in order that the will of God may work thru the will of his servant."[2] And yet our weakness is precisely our tendency to look for magic rather than miracle. Our prayers sometimes betray this. We tell God what we want Him to do for us, rather than ask Him what He would have us do. How many, for instance, are motivated during worship by the thought of success, rather than by the spirit of surrender? This attempt of making religion into a magic is always a perversion of the Gospel.

Dr. Ferris further observes: "There is always the temptation to use the sacraments of the church as magic rather than miracle, as techniques by which we control the forces that are greater than ourselves, rather than the means by which we become channels for those forces."[3] One mark of maturity in our Christian faith is to see that the greater virtue we have to

---

[1] *Interpreter's Bible*, vol. on Acts, p. 111.
[2] *Ibid.*
[3] *Ibid.*

strive for is to seek the avenues of Christian service which demand great things from us, and not to recluse to the narrow interests of self.

Simon's Serious Blunder

Perhaps the most shocking blunder of Simon the Magician was his daring proposal to buy God's power with his money. Such an offer was so vicious that **simony** has become the word for the ugly and unscrupulous practice of getting ecclesiastical position and honor thru bribery. Simon's serious blunder was the thought that he could buy God's gift and that the Holy Spirit could be enticed with the glitter of his gold. Only moribund greed could poison the mind to think that way. It was filthy ambition and just the thought of it can be horrifying.

Simony in Our Society Today

Now, while this was the sad plight of that man called Simon, the fact is that simony has been an endemic spiritual disease until these days. It was the evil which tainted the purity of the Church during the medieval period and it is the same evil which is at work in many places until now. If the Church today is enjoying relative peace and moral cleanliness, it does not mean that simony has become an obsolete disease. On the contrary, simony has been victimizing every institution where human beings are to be found. We may not call simony the act of bribing a judge for a desired decision, but it is no different from simony itself. If it has another name, at least it is still the spirit of Simon Magus. Simon Magus is at work whenever money is employed to buy the influence of politicians, to secure the favor of those in the high places, and to corrupt the officials who are supposed to serve for public welfare. And they who betray the public trust by allowing their offices to become tools of vested interests actually sell their souls to Simon Magus, the Father of graft and corruption. The pandemonium over the fabulous Stonehill case, I would like to submit, is essentially a sample of simony which can only be partly remedied by juridical means and a more strict implementation of the law. But the root cause of that anomaly is the iniquitous disposition of the human heart which seeks nothing but the self even in God. This is why the task of a Christian citizen in a case like that is not only to take active part in the formation of a sound public opinion on such an important matter which affects the welfare of the state, but also and especially to implore in earnest prayers the guidance of the

Holy Spirit that we may act and speak with calmness and conviction and that those who are involved in the case may finally embrace the pardoning grace of God. Simony in the church or in the state, in religion or in politics, in business or anywhere is the enemy of Christianity, and if we are to uphold the banner of the Christian faith, we should fight against it with all the forces of our conviction. We should resist its seductive approaches which come to us everyday. This calls for a constant spiritual exercise to cultivate the strength of character which all those who call upon the name of the Lord should possess.

Unrepentant Simon

Now, when Simon was reprimanded by Peter for his offer to buy the power of bestowing the Holy Spirit, he said, "Pray ye to the Lord for me, that none of these things which ye have spoken come upon me." Note that his words reveal fear of punishment rather than hate for sin. And that is not the language of a repentant soul. All that he was saying was that he did not like to perish. He never asked for the forgiveness of his sin. The extra-biblical record of his life does not suggest any serious attempt on his part to live soberly and honestly. On the contrary, he must have gone deeper into the pit of folly and shame and infamy. From the writings of Justin Martyr and Irenaeus, for instance, there seems to be "little doubt that Simon claimed to be Messiah, and instituted in Samaria a movement that was intended to rival Christianity."[1] Dr. G.H.C. MacGregor, in his exegesis of the book of Acts, contends that Simon's messianic pretentions seemed to combine " Gnostic speculations, including the common conception of a hierarchy of divine emanations or powers, serving as mediators between God and man, of which he claimed himself to be chief."[2] Again, Justin Martyr tells us, Simon Magus in Rome was honored by the Senate by putting up the statue erected between two bridges, with the Latin inscription Simoni Deo Sancto, or To Simon the Holy God."[3] The so-called *Recognitiones* and *Clementina* documents quote Simon to have said, "I am the Word of God, the paraclete, omnipotent." In fact, he claimed to be the incarnation of the word (or the Logos)."[4] Josephus, the Jewish historian, tells us that Simon was "Felix' tool to seduce Drusilla away from her husband Azizus, king of Emes."[5] In the Christian tradition, Simon came to be regarded as the Father of all heresy. During the first century of the

---
[1] *Interpreter's Bible, loc.cit.*
[2] *Ibid.*
[3] *Ibid.*
[4] Fausset, *Biblical Encyclopedia,* p. 644.
[5] *Ibid.*

Christian era, the heretics were called Simonians. In the Pseudo-Clementine literature, he appears to be the foremost opponent of St. Peter in public debates. In Rome, when outwitted by Peter, Simon tried to redeem himself by "a superlative feat of magic" and offered to fly. But the experiment was a tragic failure.

We have here a picture of how far a man can go in defying the power of God in the name of religion. He was not content to be just one of the holy angels; he wanted to be god himself! This is why I suspect that when the Roman senate conferred upon him the title of "the Holy God," and to that end erected a monument in his honor, there was behind that congressional act an immoral transaction which we can read only in Simon's own "blue book." I would not be surprised if he bribed those senators to confer upon him the title of a deity, for if he had the courage to tempt the ministers of God with his money, he would not have hesitated to do the same to those worldly politicians whose weakness was the love of money.

In these days of ours when many events seem to be but sad appearances of Simonism in modern forms, it will comfort us to remember that God is still the Lord of history; that the ultimate triumph of righteousness over sin is sure; and that we really need not be weary or faint. For in these days, as in every dark period of life, we can experience the personal presence of God in our hearts. This is what we mean by being filled with the Holy Spirit. The elements of sordidness in our world today should serve to underscore the necessity of living in the power of the Holy Spirit to fortify ourselves against the onslaughts of life.

Paul's Admonitions

The apostle Paul, in his letter to the Galatians (5:22), concretizes this Spirit-filled life by enumerating the fruit of the Spirit. He says among other things that it is a life characterized by love. And by that the Apostle means the love that is kind and patient, that suffereth long and rejoiceth not in iniquity. It is the love which alone can overcome the bitterness and hatred rampant in our midst.

Again, the Apostle says, it is a life of joy. The author of the book of Acts tells us that when Samaria responded to Philip's preaching and received the word of God, there was great joy in the city. The Christian life is not the sad experience of being deprived of the things we want or being restrained from doing certain things. It is rather the experience of that abiding happiness which the world can never give.

Now, the fruit of the Spirit, which is love and joy, is also peace — perfect peace, peace that emanates from fellowship with God and cannot be disturbed by the shifting sands of time. The fruit of the Spirit is also long-suffering, which will help us endure the heavy burden of discipleship; gentleness, which is so much needed in a world dominated by unfriendliness and cruelty; goodness, for the relief of the afflicted and the sorrowing; faith, for the strengthening of the hopeless and the weak; meekness, for the salvation of the vain and the proud; temperance, for the deliverance of the self-indulgent, the greedy, and the materialistic.

This is the Spirit-filled life; to know and be known by the all-knowing God; to possess and be possessed by the power of the Holy Spirit. It is this life which we wish to experience in these days of great confusion and fratricidal partisanship, when nations rise up against nations and friends betray friends. It is the life which can withstand the brutal attacks of Simonism, because it is securely anchored on the solid foundation of Jesus Christ our Lord.

Pray, then, that even now the Spirit of God may descend upon us, so that in the face of all impending gloom, in the bivouac of life, we may stand courageous, heroic, invincible.

8

The Rewards of Discipleship

For if ye love them which love you, what thank have ye? for sinners also love those that love them. And if ye do good to them which do good to you, what thank have ye? for sinners also do even the same. — Luke 6:32-33

There is within us some natural inquisitiveness about the purpose of the Christian life and we wonder if the end of all our strivings is really what we most ardently crave for. In many cases our decision on whether or not it pays to be a Christian depends on our concept of the rewards. St. Peter expressed our natural craving for rewards when he asked Jesus: "Behold, we have forsaken all and followed thee; what shall we have therefore?" (Mat. 19:27). It was indeed a mercenary question, but it is the question of every man. In other words, Peter was saying: What's the use risking our lives for Jesus if we are not to be satisfactorily rewarded? From the purely legal standpoint, there is sense in Peter's question.

The Sermon on the Mount

At the outset, we should note that Jesus Christ has some definite things to say about reward. In His Sermon on the Mount, for instance, He is quite vocal about the rewards of the Kingdom of God. The Beatitudes, we may say, are not only descriptions of the pristine happiness of Christian living but also affirmations of the fact that God does reward us for our faithfulness. "Blessed are the pure in heart, for they shall see God. Blessed are the meek, for they shall inherit the earth. Blessed are the merciful, for they shall obtain mercy." His teachings are replete with assurances of reward. "Love your enemies, and do them good; lend, never despairing; and your reward shall be great, and ye shall be sons of the Most High" (Lk. 6:35). Even our acts of charity done in secret are to be rewarded. He said, "Thy Father which seeth in secret shall reward thee openly" (Mat. 6:4). Again, He said, "Whosoever shall give to drink unto one of these little ones a cup of cold water only in the name of a disciple, verily I say unto you, he shall in no wise lose his reward" (Mat. 10:42).

The question, therefore, that we would naturally raise is, What is that reward? What exactly do we get for following Jesus Christ? Is it material wealth? Is it material blessings? In Mark 10:29, Jesus promises a hundredfold of all the houses and lands given up for the cause of the Kingdom of God. This verse is usually cited in support of the contention that our reward will take the form of material blessings. Then there is the favorite verse, "Seek ye first the Kingdom of God and His righteousness, and all these things shall be added unto you" (Mat. 6:33), where the words "these things" mean food and clothing and shelter. But a thorough exegetical study of this verse will disclose that Jesus never makes the promise of reward as primary motivation in seeking the Kingdom of God. To be in God's Kingdom is something infinitely more than having thousands of houses and acres of land. And the promise of food, clothing and shelter is not a decoy for seeking God's kingdom first. When Jesus said those things would be added unto us, He was only underscoring the point that our primary concern is spiritual. Although we need to meet the basic needs of our bodies, and indeed to that end He taught us to pray for our daily bread, nevertheless, the full measure of our devotion should be to Him who is the Giver rather than to His gifts. It is this faith in the loving God which enables us to see that He cares, and that He is concerned about our daily needs and about our difficulties. And it is in the light of this faith that we see His providence upon us everyday. This is the testimony of the Psalmist who said, "I have been young, and now am old; yet I have not seen the righteous forsaken or his children begging bread" (Ps. 37:25). We can hold fast to the words of Him who said, "Ask, and it shall be given you; seek and ye shall find; knock and it shall be opened unto you" (Mat. 7:7). God is so good that He causes His sun to shine upon both the just and the unjust.

What the Reward Is Not

Surely, in the Gospel, we have the incentive to work hard for material progress and improvement. The abundant life which Jesus speaks of should find expression in terms of economic well-being. To work honestly and faithfully is a Christian imperative, and we trust that God will bless our efforts. At the same time, however, material wealth is not necessarily a blessing from heaven. We can have food and clothing and shelter without seeking first the Kingdom of God. Even the atheists and those who have no regard for moral values can enjoy material prosperity. We should not easily mistake material progress for the rewards of discipleship because it can be the reward from the evil one. When Jesus was tempted in the wilderness, Satan was telling Jesus that if Jesus would worship him, he would give Jesus all the kingdoms of the world. Wealth can come from the enemy of God. This is why Jesus admonishes us to beware of covetousness, for a man's life consisteth not in the abundance of the things which he possesses. Jesus Himself died a poor man, materially speaking. He had no place to lay His head on. He was buried in a borrowed graveyard.

Again, the reward of discipleship is not "immunity from physical ills." Some sincere Christians are of the belief that if we trust in Christ, we need not fear dangerous animals or bodily ills. They quote Luke 10:19 where Jesus says, "Behold, I have given you authority to tread upon serpents and scorpions, and over all the power of the enemy; and nothing shall in any wise hurt you." The fact, however, is that even the members of our Visiting Committee, when they go out in the name of the Lord to visit members of the church who are sick or are in trouble and they see at the gate of the house the sign "Have dog, will bite," they are afraid to get in right away until they are sure the dog is not around to bite. Did not Jesus Himself drink of the bitter cup of death? And were not the sons of Zebedee to drink of the same cup? History tells us that Christian martyrs are not free from physical ills. They who follow Christ in one way or another meet trials and persecutions and even death.

What the Reward Is

Now, therefore, if the reward for obedience to the will of God is neither wealth nor immunity from physical ill, then what is it? What reward would be adequate for taking up our cross and following Christ? In his book, *The Teachings of Jesus*, Harvie Branscomb submits that "no reward could be equal to the sacrifice demanded (in Christian discipleship) except one, the obtaining of a fuller and richer life,"[1]

Eternal Life as Reward

It is in the Fourth Gospel where we find a consistent reference to life as reward for discipleship. Here we find the words of Christ: "I came that they may have life, and have it abundantly" (John 10:10). "He that hath the Son hath life, and he that hath not the Son hath not life" (5:12). In the Synoptic Gospels the word "life" is sometimes used as a substitute for the

---

[1] Harvie Branscomb, *The Teachings of Jesus,* p.253 ff.

Kingdom of God, so that "the kingdom of God is the reward of the righteous." But in any case, it is the life that is full and rich which is promised to those who love the Lord.

This life, in the language of the New Testament, is eternal. It does not perish with the mortal flesh. It transcends the limitations of time and the barriers of space. In the Great Judgment, so Jesus tells us, the righteous shall enter into life eternal (Mat. 25:46).

A Life of Fellowship

That life is also a life of fellowship with the great figures of the past. Describing the life in the Kingdom, Jesus says, "Many shall come from the east and the west, and sit with Abraham, Isaac, and Jacob in the kingdom of heaven." They are the patriarchs and the prophets and the heroes of faith. The promised life, then, is in association and fellowship with all those who, in every age and circumstance, have endeavored to do the will of God. It is a life which releases us from the bondage of the present, and yet wrestles with the present with the faith that if God feeds the sparrows and clothes the lilies in the field, how much more shall He take care of us who trust in His providence. It is a life of peace and confidence in the midst of uncertainties and sickness and difficulties.

Having said this, we see that the reward of discipleship is only from God and never from men. Indeed, Jesus warns us not to act merely for social recognition. He indicted the scribes and the Pharisees who loved to pray at street corners that they might be seen of men. Their goal was the praise of men rather than the approbation of God. They already had their reward. Jesus said they were hypocrites who would not give alms without first sounding their trumpet. They wanted the glory of men, and they got it. And that was all that they got. Giving, therefore, even to the cause of the church is not always a Christian virtue. It is not Christian when it is motivated by the desire for publicity. It is just another form of paid advertisement. I am not saying here we have no use for publicity. Indeed, it is sometimes good for the church to publicize our giving. But once publicity becomes the decoy for giving, it becomes a pharisaic way of exposing our self-righteousness.

Reward Is From God

Another thing that should be said is that in the ultimate analysis of the Christian faith, we cannot really earn any reward from God. No amount of goodness and good works will ever enable us to merit the blessing of God. We do not deserve it. We cannot have it by merit. We can only have it by grace. It is therefore a gift. It can only be given to us. We are like the workers in the vineyard who were hired at the eleventh hour. They did not earn their pay. But they got it because of the goodness of the master. Jesus says, "It is your Father's good pleasure to give you the kingdom" (Lk. 12:32). "Verily I say unto you, Whosoever shall not receive the kingdom of God as a little child, shall in no wise enter therein" (Mk. 10:15). "Even so ye also, when ye shall have done all the things that are commanded you, say, We are unprofitable servants" (Lk. 17:10). We have in these verses the truth that God's reward is really a divine gift. We cannot earn it because "we all like sheep have gone astray." Our attitude, therefore, when God blesses us for our faithfulness should not be that of boasting pride but that of humble gratitude, knowing that even our faith is also a gift from Him.

Therefore, if we seek the kingdom of God because the other things shall be added unto us, we tragically miss the whole point of Christian discipleship. If we follow Christ because He would give us what we want, we have not truly understood what it means to follow Him. Paul Ramsey, in his *Basic Christian Ethics*, emphasizes that if anyone "acts for the sake of the reward, he has not yet done what God requires of him in readiness for the kingdom, he has not yet become entirely trusting and obedient, not yet single-minded in obedient love."[1] Jesus' promise of reward, he says, may be the "condition of action, the ground or premise of strength, but reward is never action's goal. Reward is always added to the nature of the act, not a direct result of it such as might become a part of the agent's own prudential calculation."[2] Martin Luther, echoing the spirit of the Protestant Reformation, condemned anticipation of rewards when he said:

> "If they should work good in order to obtain the Kingdom, they would never obtain it, but would be numbered rather with the wicked, who, with an evil and mercenary eye, seek the things of self even in God. Whereas the sons of God do good with a free-will, seeking no reward, but the glory and will of God only; ready to do good; even if (which is impossible) there were neither a Kingdom nor a hell ... Even though they knew that there were no heaven, nor hell, nor

---

[1] Paul Ramsey, *Basic Christian Ethics*, p. 133.
[2] Quoted by Ramsey, *Ibid.*

any reward, they would nevertheless serve God for His own sake."[1]

Luther argued that action which seeks reward is just the opposite of the action for which reward is promised. He said:

> "Be not thou concerned about the reward, ...For although it is impossible that the reward should not come to them who worship God... without consideration of gain or wages; yet, certain it is that God hates those mercenary characters, who seek themselves and not God and will never give them any reward at all."[2]

This is why the Christian life, in the words of St. Francis of Assisi, is not so much to seek to be consoled, as to console; to be understood, as to understand; to be loved as to love; and yet we know that if we try to understand we will also be understood; if we try to love we will also be loved. For, as Jesus tells us, if we are merciful we shall obtain mercy, and if we mourn we shall be comforted.

It is unfortunate that until now we have church people who seek nothing but themselves even in God. They are the people whose giving is inspired by the thought that the Lord will open the windows of heaven for them and pour out great blessings for which there shall not be enough room. Their service is motivated by the promise that they who serve shall be the master of all. They call Jesus Lord and King and offer unto Him the adoration of their lips, but actually they try to reduce Him into a family physician to take care of them when they are sick; into a bodyguard to protect them when they are in danger; and even into a talisman to insure success in their enterprises. But that is a sacrilege in the guise of piety; it is a desecration of the Christian faith, an insult against Almighty God! They need the forgiving love of God which alone can deliver them from the bondage of their selfish eudaemonism.

So let us pray that we may continue growing in the knowledge of our faith, until we reach that maturity which though certain of reward nevertheless does not seek for it, but makes it easier for us to offer ourselves as a living sacrifice. Perhaps we will discover that only by forgetting the reward of discipleship can we be more assured of it, and that consequently our Christian conduct may be ordered by a self-giving love. We would do well to continue trusting in the wisdom of God's will, until we realize that obedience to the will of God is itself a reward of discipleship.

---
[1] Ramsey, *op. cit.*
[2] *Ibid.*, p. 134.

9

The Priesthood of Believers

But ye are a chosen generation, a royal priesthood, an holy nation, a peculiar people; that ye should shew forth the praises of him who hath called you out of darkness into his marvellous light. — 1 Peter 2:9

In countries like ours where the religious atmosphere is predominantly Roman Catholic, the priesthood is generally associated with that group of men who have given themselves to chastity, poverty and service. Although some non-Catholic communions continue calling their pastors priests, in our country the priesthood is very much identified with the religious vocation supposed to be much higher than the secular professions. The Reformers, however, who found it hard to distinguish between the sacred and the secular, suggested that the priesthood, thus interpreted, could be a barrier to the spiritual growth of men. They uncovered an important message of the New Testament by proclaiming the priesthood of all believers which became one of the cardinal teachings of Protestantism.

Paradoxically, however, in spite of our firm belief in the tenet, (the privilege of every Christian to take part in the priesthood of Christ), the word **priest** or **priesthood** is slowly disappearing in our religious vocabulary. Therefore, we need to rethink the meaning of our common priesthood, and see how we can more effectively manifest it in our individual and corporate life.

Priesthood and the Roman Church

First of all, this priesthood of believers is not to be understood as a negative reaction to the institutionalized priesthood of the Roman Church. Although it cannot be denied that the Reformer's assertion of the priesthood of believers is tantamount to a repudiation of the institutionalized Roman priesthood, we misunderstand the doctrine unless we see that it is essentially and first of all a declaration of Christian liberty. The negative aspect of the doctrine becomes inevitable only because every assertion of Christian truth is at the same time a repudiation of anything against that truth.

On the other hand, an understanding of the Roman concept of the priesthood will at least give us an idea of what a priest should not be, in the light of the Holy Scriptures. It is for this reason that we take a glimpse at a priest as understood in a culture like ours. From there we can proceed to seek guidance on the nature of our calling, so we may resolve to relate our daily conduct more closely to our Christian beliefs.

A booklet entitled "The Priest" written for the edification of the so-called faithful, and which carried the imprimatur of the Archbishop of Ottawa, Canada, quotes the venerable J.B.M. Vianney in his speech delivered to a throng of pilgrims. Some of the sentences are the following:

> "Where there is no priest there is no sacrifice, and where there is no sacrifice there is no religion."
>
> "Without the priest, the death and passion of our Lord would be of no avail to us."
>
> "See the power of the priest ! By one word from his lips, he changes a piece of bread into a God! A greater feat than the creation of the world."
>
> "If I were to meet a priest and an angel, I would salute the priest before saluting the angel. The angel is a friend of God, but the priest holds the place of God."
>
> "Next to God Himself, the priest is everything."
>
> "Did we understand him and appreciate him in this life, we should die, not of fear, but of love..."[1]

We have in these statements the indispensability of the priest, without whom there will be no religion. The priest is the needed intermediary for the people to avail of the death and passion of Christ. The priest is also a dispenser of grace, and by the power of his words the elements at the Eucharist are transformed into the actual body and blood of Christ. If man according to the Psalmist, is created a little lower than the angels, the priest, according to Father Vianney, is to be regarded a little higher than the angels.

---

[1] Quoted by J. C. Macaulay, *Truth Vs. Dogma,* Moody Press, 153 Institute Place, Chicago, Ill, p.57.

The Priest's Prerogatives

Cardinal H.E. Manning, in his book *Eternal Priesthood*, speaks of the priest's two prerogatives which give him a dominating place in the lives of the people. First, he has jurisdiction over the natural body of Christ; and second he has jurisdiction over the mystical body of Christ. "Jurisdiction over the natural body of Christ means the consecration of the sacrament of the altar in which the bread becomes, at the word of the priest, the very flesh of our Lord. . .The jurisdiction over the mystical Body of Christ, namely, the church, signifies the priest's power to give absolution, to forgive sin." We will not discuss the merits or the demerits of this claim. but we need to emphasize that the priesthood of believers knows nothing of these prerogatives.

The Priest in the Bible

What then, in the light of the Holy Scriptures, is a priest? In most cultures it is recognized that sometimes things go wrong in the relationship between the people and their god. Always there is a need for someone to help straighten things out. And such an intermediary is called a priest.

The practices of the priesthood vary according to culture, but in the Old Testament the priestly office is said to be transmitted by heredity.

We read, for instance, of the Levites as a tribe of priests. In the book of Leviticus, we have the rites which the priest should observe to safeguard his holiness. For instance, he is forbidden to shave his head or beard (21:5); he should not touch a dead body (21:1); he should be free from physical defects (21:16). But the important things to note are: (1) the priest is God's representative to man, the one authorized to interpret God's will to the people; and (2) he is also man's representative to God, one who offers sacrifices to the deity in behalf of the people.

In the New Testament, these two important functions of a priest were fulfilled in a very unique way by Jesus Christ. The author of the Epistle to the Hebrews speaks of Christ as our High Priest. Jesus, as God's representative to man, mediates the Word of God to us. Indeed, He is Himself the Word of God. He is the Word made flesh. And as man's representative to God, He offered a sacrifice for us — not a goat or a lamb — He offered Himself. He is the "lamb of God who takes away the sins of the world" (John 1:29). In the words of Robert McAfee Brown, "He is both sacrificer and sacrificed. He is the high-priest who comes as the suffering servant and offers himself, sacrifices himself, on behalf of those to whom he has come."[1]

The Perfect High Priest

So in Christ, man's alienation from God is overcome. In Him, the fellowship between Creator and creatures, broken by sin, is restored. Things that have gone wrong in the relationship are straightened out. In Him, the salvation of mankind is assured. Jesus is the perfect High Priest because in Him the priesthood and the sacrifice are one, the office and the offering are one, and therefore it is in Him that we find our oneness with God and with one another.

Christ's Supreme Sacrifice

Now, the sacrifice offered by Christ the High Priest was done "once and for all." It is unrepeatable. We cannot and need not supplement His sacrifice. Christ's offering of Himself is the supreme sacrifice that embraces all eternity. Therefore, His death and resurrection is not only the death of the old priesthood, but also the birth of a new one which has a greater dimension and a more stringent demand. In the eyes of faith, the church itself, the church as a whole, is a royal priesthood — not just those set aside to serve at the altar but all who belong to the body of Christ. To be in Christ is to participate in the life of Christ, and our baptism into the Christian faith is our ordination into the priesthood of the church. That is what we mean by the priesthood of all believers.

The emphasis, therefore, is not that "every Christian is his own priest." This might lead to individualism that is detrimental to the harmony of communal living. The emphasis, rather, is that "every man is priest to every other man." The stress is on the necessity of a community. "Christians are to offer themselves to one another, to pray for one another, to sacrifice themselves on behalf of one another, so that through them all the high priesthood of Jesus Christ may be more effectually communicated to them all."[2]

The Christian Ministry

Actually, in this doctrine we have the clue to understanding the Christian ministry. The ministry, we see, belongs to the whole church.

---
[1] Robert McAfee Brown, *The Spirit of Protestantism*, p. 96.
[2] *Ibid.*, p. 97.

Every Christian is a minister in the sense that he is called to a life of Christian service. The burden of Christian duty rests upon the shoulder of every church member.

It is clear, then, that this concept of the ministry does not invalidate the place of the ordained clergy in the life of the church. The ordination to the ministry is not a promotion to a higher standard of Christian life, because the Christian faith does not know of inequality between laity and clergy. It is only an assignment to a specific function within the body of Christ, so that the priesthood of the entire body may be exercised more efficiently. In other words, the function of the professional minister is within the ministry of the church, but specifically to edify and train and equip the members of Christ's body for the exercise of their priesthood in the world. The minister, therefore, should among other things constantly remind us of our calling to the royal priesthood, and that such holy office cannot be delegated to the professional minister, or to anyone.

So our common priesthood is really a tribute to the spiritual possibilities of men, a solemn symbol of God's claim upon every life. It is the image of a life that has found transforming grace in Christ. For if to believe in Christ is to be ordained to his royal priesthood, then to be a Christian requires some cost and sacrifice. It requires a certain heroism and chivalry which emanate from a pure love of God. It demands a stubborn courage to launch out into the deep, to fight the good fight, to cling tenaciously to that which is good and pure and honorable and of good report.

Manifestations of our Priesthood

A more aggressive expression of our priesthood will certainly take the form of concern which goes beyond the boundaries of self and home and country. For sure it will liberate us from self, from the narrow demands of vested interests, from self-centeredness. For to be a priest is to be obsessed with the welfare of others, and even intercede to God on their behalf, to the end that what is good for all may be done on earth. In other words, to fulfill our priesthood is to be possessed with a sense of mission, to be moved by compassion for the touching needs of men. It is to realize selfhood by forgetting self, by self-denial and by the giving of self.

Again, an awareness of our priesthood will cultivate our sense of responsibility. It will redeem us from carelessness and complacency, from the sordid tendency to take things for granted. For we are persuaded that we will give account of our life before the judgment throne and that every minute of existence in this world is to be utilized in preparation for that momentous event. It is the eternal repose of our soul that is at stake and only fools will squander their time in riotous living. But the Christian who is aware of his priesthood will daily submit himself to the searching of God in the hope that in all things he may do that which is well-pleasing in the sight of the Lord. He, therefore, will regard the discipline of prayer and meditation as absolutely necessary for the health of his soul, and indeed will strive to make his own way of life as a prayer in itself.

The Recovery of Priesthood Today

It is almost needless to say that there is urgent need for us today to manifest this priesthood of ours especially in our church life. For our priesthood is the priesthood of the church, and the church is you and me, and all those who profess to believe in Christ. To be a priest means we cannot elect churchgoing as an optional subject. On the contrary, it is to be taken as a duty because we know it first of all as a Christian privilege. You do not see a priest who goes to church only when he feels like going. He has to go. He has a sense of responsibility which converts his duty into a joyful freedom. A true and faithful priest finds great delight in the house of God. For him, worship is the most sublime expression of his priesthood, the noblest experience of free access to God. It is the experience of Christian worship which drives away the clouds of moodiness and emptiness and meaninglessness. A loyal priest aspires for power that will transcend all temptations to take churchgoing for granted.

And yet when I look at the way some of us spend our Sunday mornings, I wonder whether we really know what worship is . When I see that even our ushers come to church late, I doubt whether we really believe in the priesthood of believers. No priest worthy of the office comes to church late. I can excuse the *sacristan* for being late, but not the priest. And all of us are priests. Of course you can tell me, "You have to be in church on time because you are the preacher." But I tell you that unless you feel that my being the preacher is your assignment to me and that even the act of preaching is done on your behalf and on behalf of the whole church, you have not really understood what it means to be a part of the body of Jesus Christ.

And so I plead that you reconsider this matter of your priesthood, and see whether you can muster enough courage to translate it into life. The assurance is ours that if we would but trust in Him who has called us to the royal priesthood, we will not drag ourselves into doing what we ought to do, for the grace of God will work in us to do that which we ought. We can be equally sure that a deepened sense of our priesthood is really a key to the enjoyment of life, the core of discipleship, and the sum of all piety. It is the secret of victorious living, of rediscovering the sacredness of human toil and labour.

It will be a glorious day when our church people begin to realize the high calling of the Christian life and resolve to act as holy priests of God. For that would mean the revival of faith which the early disciples sedulously possessed and which enabled them to conquer pride and hate and sin. It would mean the resurgence of the Militant Church which will surmount every obstacle to the preaching of the Gospel until everyone is confronted with a call to repentance. Then shall the rays of the sun of new hope penetrate through the dark clouds of life to illumine every corner of the earth, and great shall be the rejoicing of the angels in the kingdom of heaven.

We are "a chosen race, a royal priesthood, a holy nation, God's own people" and therefore nothing should stop us from declaring "the wonderful deeds of him who called us out of darkness into his marvelous light."

10

Lead Us Not Into Temptation

*And lead us not into temptation, but deliver us from evil:
For thine is the kingdom, and the power, and the glory, for
ever. Amen.*— Matthew 6:13

The sixth petition in the Lord's Prayer, "Lead us not into temptation," is a phrase vaguely understood if not misunderstood by church people. It seems to suggest that God leads us into temptation, and we beg Him not to. One has to be Jewish to understand the meaning of the phrase, or at least be acquainted with the idioms of the Aramaic dialect. We are not competent enough to dig into this subject very thoroughly, but it is not difficult to see why the sixth petition is far from implying that God leads us into temptation.

For one thing, there is no passage in the Holy Scripture that will support the alleged implication. Indeed, the suspicion that God leads us into temptation is contrary to the testimony of the Bible writers. St. James, for instance, advises us: "Let no one say when he is tempted, I am tempted by God, for God can not be tempted with evil and he himself tempts no one." In the second place, Jesus Christ reveals to us the nature of our God. We see in Him the God of love and purity, and not One who takes pleasure in tempting His children.

In Genesis 22:1, we read that God tempted Abraham. You will note, however, that in the Revised Standard Version, the word used is **tested**, and not tempted.

The Meaning of "To Tempt"

At this point it will be profitable if we review the meaning of the term. In the *Interpreter's Bible*, the meaning rendered to the word temptation is "trial" or "testing". In John 6:5, we read that Jesus asked Philip where to buy bread to feed the 5,000 only to prove the disciple. The word **prove** here is often rendered **tempt**. In II Corinthians 13:5, Paul admonishes us to examine ourselves whether we are in the faith. **Examine** here is also rendered **tempt.**

Dr. John F. Scott, in his little book on the " Lord's Prayer" observes that the word temptation means not only trial but also suffering, or allurement to sin. Further, he notes that the word **lead** is a mistranslation of the Aramaic idiom which means to **fail** or **succumb** or **yield**. That is why he believes that a truer conception of what Jesus means by the petition "Lead us not into temptation" is "Let us not yield to temptation," or "Grant that we fail not in time of testing." Seen in this light, the petition is a prayer for strength to overcome trials, and not a plea for God to stop plaguing us.

Now, if temptation in the Lord's Prayer conveys the idea of testing, suffering, trial or examining, it is natural and legitimate to pray that we be spared from it. Washington Gladden in his *The Lord's Prayer*, points out that suffering can be a means of good, and yet in itself it is an evil. We are willing to endure it if we must, but it is natural and right to shrink from it. Those who pray, "Lead us not into trial" are offering the same prayer Jesus Himself offered in Gethsemane: "If it be possible let this cup pass from me." The thing to remember, however, is to subject this natural desire unto the judgment and will of God. Hence, Jesus prayed, "Nevertheless, not as I will but as thou wilt." And so we pray to be delivered from sickness, or poverty, or humiliation, but if in the providence of God we have to go through it, then we pray God to let us not fail in time of such testing.

The Ministry of Suffering

Let us stress that we do not deny or in any way diminish the usefulness of suffering. It can be God's instrument to rectify a person's life. Some of the most moving stories in the Bible are the suffering of men whose faithfulness was tested in the fire. The offering of Isaac by Abraham, the many crises in the life of Moses, the suffering of Job, the humiliation of Hosea — these are eloquent testimonies on the ministry of tribulations. It is not surprising, then, that when Jesus resolved to fulfill the role of the Messiah, He chose to walk through the path of suffering love.

Two Affirmations

"Lead us not into temptation," I repeat, is a humble cry of the soul for strength. And two things are affirmed by that prayer: (a) The universality of temptation. The experience common to all men in all places and in all ages is the experience of being tempted. Even the Son of God was not spared from the experience. He was tempted in all points as we are, according to the Epistle to the Hebrews. Temptation comes to everyone regardless of his status or dignity of his office. (b) The second fact affirmed by the petition is the frailty of human nature and our tendency to lose a moral battle. On our own strength we cannot stand; only by the grace of God can we.

The Peril of Courting Evil

We should observe that if Jesus teaches us to pray for deliverance from temptation, it is because there is great danger in being exposed to it. One is spiritually irresponsible if he courts temptation. Evil is an ugly thing, and one should shudder at the sight of it. It is childish to think we are strong enough to withstand the allurement of sin. We should not overestimate our spiritual stamina. Many have failed because of too much confidence. The downfall of men and nations is usually preceded with pride and false belief in their impregnability. In Paul's first letter to the Corinthians, he says, "Let him who thinks he stands take heed lest he falls" (10:12). To entertain some little vices or commit some little sins in the thought that we would not lose control anyhow is to embrace a morbid and heathenish notion that can be the beginning of moral deterioration and the breaking down of character.

Ezekiel's Experience

There is a passage in the Book of Ezekiel which perfectly illustrates the work of evil. The prophet was asked to take a look at the abominations of Israel. He was brought to a wall where he found a hole through which he saw some people behaving like men not seen by God. Then the prophet was encouraged to dig in the wall and to his surprise, he saw a door. Then he was led through the door into a big chamber inhabited by all kinds of creeping things and abominable beasts. Then he walked into the inner court where he saw men and women worshipping the sun. That was the plight of Ezekiel. He began by peeping through the hole and ended up standing in the inner court where everything laid bare before his naked eyes.

That has been the strategy of Satan. Evil is dressed up nicely as if it is a very harmless thing. It entices a man to peep through a small hole and yet before he knows it, he is led inside the inner court. Take the alcoholics as a case in point. They begin by just tasting liquor, by drinking just a few drops of it. And they like its smell, and the more they drink the sweeter it tastes. But as the days go by, they are being drawn into the inner court where big jars of wine are a source of great delight. The first Psalm is saying exactly the same thought when paraphrased negatively : A man at the beginning simply passes by the group of ungodly people; later, he stands in the way of those sinners; and then finally, he is seated with them in the seat of the scornful. It is dangerous to take little temptations for granted because they can grow up to monstrous size and make us slaves.

The slightest suffering or pain, I repeat, can be a big temptation to some people who know not the virtue of patience or the sufficiency of God's grace. Little affliction easily assails them and makes them poor.

A More Deadly Evil

And yet that is not the worse temptation, though a lot fall under its prey. The more virulent evil and the more destructive sin is the feeling of being virtuous. Martin Luther said: "Temptation is of two kinds: one on the left which makes us suffer, and one on the right which makes us feel virtuous, and this is the deadly one." Here is where many Christians fall. Not a few feel spiritually superior. Because they are respectable members of a church, because they worship regularly, it is easy for them to look down upon those who are not as active as they are. Like the Pharisees of old, we take pride in bringing a woman before Jesus and say: This lady is caught in the act of adultery. Now, Master, what shall we do with her? It is not until Jesus bids those of us who have no sins to cast a stone upon her that we realize our own moral poverty and begin to walk away. How often has our sanctuary been desecrated by those who come to pray: God, we thank thee that we are not like others who are sinners! Jesus' denunciation of spiritual superiority should teach us that the temptation which makes us feel virtuous is a very deadly evil.

Avoid Temptation

Now, to guard ourselves against the enticement of sin, two things should be done. First, let us avoid temptation. Paul suggested to the Thessalonians: "Abstain from all appearances of evil." This is more than not courting temptation. It is a deliberate effort to shun evil, to flee from places that may occasion sinning. It is avoiding the company of hoodlums, of grafters, of people engaged in filthy business. Solomon, in the Book of Proverbs, told his son to stay away from bad women and never to set his feet at the door of their house. We would do well to keep ourselves away from evil and from all of its ugly appearances.

Overcome Evil with Good

The other thing to do to guard ourselves against the allurements of sin is to overcome evil with good. There are occasions when we cannot extract ourselves from the inner court. Jesus Himself was often with the company of publicans and sinners, but He did not become one of them. He tried to lead them to God. When one cannot escape from evil and has to deal with it face to face, the only weapon one can use to overcome it is goodness. That is what Jesus meant when He said: "In the world ye shall have tribulations, but be of good cheer.. ." He said also that there shall come into our midst many anti-Christs who will deceive many; there shall be wars and rumors of wars; there shall be famines and pestilences, earthquakes in divers places. Many will be afflicted and killed. Friends will betray friends and iniquity shall abound. But they who shall endure until the end, the same shall be saved. That strength to endure comes only from the Good Teacher who Himself was despised and rejected of men, yet He opened not His mouth. Christ is the assurance that love is stronger than hate and that goodness can conquer evil.

Some Practical Steps

I have been suggesting ways of dealing with temptation. Now I wish to advance some more practical measures to ascertain victory over sin. One of them is keeping our health in the best condition. John Scott observes:

> "People who are tired and below par, physically and nervously, yield to temptation more readily than others; people living under tension, people whose strength is depleted through illness, seem to lose something of their power to resist evil:"[1]

Of course, this does not mean that we should overlook the fact that character can be made more radiant in the experience of physical pain or

---
[1] Scott, *The Lord's Prayer*, p. 93.

sickness, as history can prove. Dr. Scott only wishes us to see that good health is not only God's will for us but also can be an aid in resisting evil, as well as in causing it to others and ourselves. For surely a person suffering from a slight headache or toothache can easily become careless in his speech while talking to his driver or employees or students. We should learn to use our health as a weapon against temptation.

Another way of making more certain our resistance to temptation is the preventive discipline in righteousness and religion. We all value preventive medicine in physical health. We try to have regular exercise, balanced diet, plenty of sleep, vaccination against common infections, good sanitation, etc. Those will keep our bodies resistant to disease. The same principle is true in the moral and spiritual realm. A regular exercise of righteousness and a constant application of religious discipline will aid much in preserving the strength of our faith.[1] That is why the church urges us to pray and meditate and worship regularly. The greatest battle we are waging is in the realm of the spirit, and we need to be always revitalized if we are to win the fight.

Another great help in overcoming temptation is an absorbing loyalty to Christ. St. Paul discovered this when he said, "For me to live is Christ." In Christ, said Paul, he found both peace and strength.

Most of us, I am sure, have experienced the tremendous power of an absorbing central loyalty. A young man, for instance, will cut his classes just to see his sweetheart somewhere. To others, it is their family that is dearer than life itself. Still to others, it is their country, or the institutions that are dear and sacred to their hearts. And still to others, it is their business. They will prefer to miss their lunch or supper or family just to work overtime.

How is it with you and me? How controlling is our loyalty to God and His church? This is an embarrassing question especially to those who often feel they would rather be with their friends or family or stay in their shops or offices than be with God in the house of prayer. But let me tell you this: that when the world seems cruel and friends betray and even the dearest in the family cares no more, God alone can sustain and deliver us from any evil thought or deed. To all of us come the onslaughts of temptation and only God can give us the power to overcome. Paul declares, "God is faithful, who will not suffer you to be tempted above that ye are able." This is the promise that will keep us strong, triumphant, and steady.

---

[1] Scott, *op. cit.*

11

Where Your Treasure Is

For where your treasure is, there will your heart be also.
— Matthew 6:21

The stewardship of money should be understood in the context of total Christian discipleship, or in the light of the stewardship of the whole of life. Stewardship need not be identified with money alone, because there is such a thing as stewardship of time, stewardship of talents, of influence, of character. Stewardship is the management of life with the keen consciousness of God's ownership of everything entrusted upon our care, including ourselves. The giving of time, talents and means is not a separate aspect of the Christian experience; it is only one expression of a vital religious faith. Unavoidably, therefore, giving becomes an index to the depth, or to the emptiness, of our faith because faith expresses itself in self-giving.

We believe that when a person has given himself to God, the giving out of his abundance or out of his poverty, naturally follows. Dr. Nels F.S. Ferre, in his book *Making Religion Real,* says : "If we give ourselves completely to God, there is little question about the giving of our money. The reason that money looms large for many is that they have never given their whole selves to God."[1] And so in this business of following Christ, the first step is to touch man's spirit, and then he will joyfully surrender whatever he possesses.

The hard fact of life, however, is that most of us would like to think that we do give ourselves to God, and yet find it quite unpleasant to dedicate our pocketbooks. Martin Luther understood this most perfectly when he said that man needs two conversions, namely; the conversion of his heart and the conversion of his pocketbook. It is not enough that we give our hearts to Christ; we should also give our means. It is this double conversion of our hearts and our pockets that we need to experience today.

---

[1] Nels F.S. Ferre, *Making Religion Real*, p. 160.

Many people think that if our hearts are dedicated, the money will follow. But have you ever realized that Jesus puts it the other way around? Jesus says, "Where your treasure is, there will your heart be also." If your treasure is dedicated, then your heart will also be dedicated. If it is not, the likelihood is that your heart will not be dedicated either. If we put our treasure in heaven, our hearts will be in heaven. Why? Because, as a piece of secular wisdom goes, "a man's real interests are where his investments are . . .If you want to get a man interested in something, get him to put his money into it." By nature, we learn to love what we work for and give to. So that "where your treasure is, there shall your heart be also."

The Rich Young Ruler

Let us go back to the story of that rich young ruler because his experience may be similar to ours. In all appearances, he was a devout believer. He believed in God. He obeyed the commandments. He did not commit murder. He did not commit adultery. He did not steal, did not bear false witness. He honored his father and mother, and loved his neighbor as he loved himself. Certainly, no one would doubt that he was a lover of God. But the acid test on his discipleship was given when Jesus told him, "Go and sell that which you have, and give it to the poor, and thou shalt have treasure in heaven." The young man did not pass the test. He went away sorrowing, for he had great possessions.

How is it with us? Do we not also believe in God? Assuredly, like that young man, we do not kill. We do not commit adultery. We do not steal. We love our neighbor as we love ourselves. We do not bear false witness. We practice the golden rule most of the time, if not always. We go to church. We pray. We perhaps read the Bible. In all appearances, we have given our hearts to God. What else do we lack?

Lesson from Statistics

Dr. Charles N. Crowe, in his book *Stewardship Sermons*, compiled the findings of an agricultural college which made a study of the things which went into the production of one hundred bushels of corn on one acre of land. He said that man contributed the labor, but God also contributed a few things:

> "4,000,000 pounds of water, 6,800 pounds of oxygen, 5,200 pounds of carbon or 19,000 pounds of carbon dioxide, 160 pounds of nitrogen, 125 pounds of potassium, 40 pounds of phosphorous, 75 pounds of yellow sulphur, 50 pounds of magnesium, 50 pounds of calcium, 2 pounds of iron, and smaller amounts of iodine, zinc, copper, and other things, including the annual migratory habits of billions of birds."[1]

How often do we assure ourselves, saying: "Soul, you have many goods stored up for many years. Eat, drink and be merry?" When our barns are full and our pockets are bulging, do we not say **our** good? **Our** money? When such thought visits us again, it is good to remember that only God can make a tree. God is the real owner of our wealth.

Our Modern Dilemma

One trouble we have these days is that we hardly believe in investments in the Kingdom of God, or at least we do not find it challenging to put our treasure there. Dr. Earl H. Cressy, some years ago, after making a study of 10 typical urban churches in the Philippines, discovered that the people's giving represented only 1-1/2% of their income. When we remember that 10% is the minimum expression of our stewardship, we realize how far we fall short in our Christian concern. Certainly, we should be embarrassed with the amount of our giving. In many cases, our giving is at a pittance. And yet we know the church of God deserves more than that. It deserves to be the depository of all our treasures. Jesus says, "Lay up for yourselves treasures in heaven..." And by treasure, He means that which is most precious to us, that which is diamond and gold and silver to us — not the useless stones and unwanted leftovers.

Starting from the Wrong End

One defective practice we have which betrays the blind spot in our understanding of Christian stewardship is that in giving, we begin at the wrong end. After receiving the pay envelope, we first deduct the amounts for movies, cigarettes, food, educational expenses, water bills, electric bills, gasoline, clothing and everything, and then if there is anything left we give 10% of it to the church. Our giving is from the residue, rather than

---

[1] Charles N. Crowe, *Stewardship Sermons,* p.113.

from the top. But the biblical injunction is that it should be from the top — the first fruit, the first born, the first tenth. But no, we don't give from the top, we give from the bottom. No wonder our gift is meager. Is this our answer to the threat of communism and secularism, to the resurgence of the non-Christian religions, to the problem of a decaying moral order?

The Church Deserves Our Best

If we believe in the church of God, why do we treat it the way we do? There is no doubt in our minds that the church stands for the purity and the love of God, for the brotherhood of men, for truth and service, for character and integrity. The church of the living God, the evangelical church for sure, is a strong defender of freedom and the sanctity and dignity of man. The church of God is the spiritual crusader and the conscience of society. It is the Guardian of Faith in God which is our sure defense against the threats of atheism and materialism of the ages. As Dr. Crowe says, there is nothing more pressing than our support of the church of God. If we are in Christ, as we believe we are, there is nothing optional in our support of the church. It is the most pressing obligation that we have. If the church is to march forward and win victories for God, if it is to continue planting the seeds of the gospel and making men whole, we need the maximum expression of Christian stewardship. Miserly giving cannot bring it far. We do not honor God, nor ourselves, when we give only at a pittance.

Dr. Crowe's observation

Charles M. Crowe, in his book I cited above, makes an interesting observation of people whose giving is pathetically small. He says that the stingy, the niggardly in giving are not only unhappy, but are hard to get along with. He says: "Most stingy Christians are sideline sitters, always ready to criticize and discount the Christian program. It hardly ever fails that the people who give the least are the fussiest and most critical of the church. Far too many Christians are unhappy in their Christian lives because they have never learned to give."[1] How true this is in many of our churches. Whether that is an indication of a more basic spiritual disease we do not know, but people of that kind suffer from the double tragedy of being unhappy in their Christian life and of missing the opportunity of helping enhance the cause of the kingdom.

---

[1] Crowe, *op. cit.*, p. 127f.

An Adventure of Faith

So now let us be reassured that putting our treasure in the Kingdom of God is the most thrilling adventure of faith we can ever experience. For one thing, it is the will of God. We are called to fix our eyes on the eternal values of life. It is not His will that we perish with mammon, or be a slave to its evil power. The will of God is that we trust in Him alone. We dare not trust in gold. A baptized pocketbook is one which delivers us from the slavish influence of mammon and leads us to the worship of the one true God.

We see, as sinful human beings, as members of the fallen human race, that the natural tendency of our heart is to indulge in frivolity, in transient pleasure, in false security, in worldliness. And money, being able to buy all these, is usually the most powerful controlling factor in directing our heart's desire. Put that money in the Kingdom of God, and we will discover to our own surprise that our highest and lasting joy is one which money cannot buy. There, both hearts and treasures find their true place in the service of God. It is the birth of man's redemption, the discovery of life abundant, the realization of the will of God and the enjoyment of human freedom. Such a life of blessedness with God is a treasure beyond measure which neither moth nor rust can take away, nor death destroy.

Let us try, therefore, to overcome that unholy feeling of uneasiness when we are asked to sign a pledge card or when we are challenged to write a check for the church. This tendency to shy away from our share in carrying on the church's ministry makes it terribly hard for us to even just consider the challenge of the Master to put all our treasure in the Kingdom of God. And yet, we cannot hope to please our God unless we face this stringent demand of the Christian gospel. It is my prayer that none of us will go away sorrowing, after hearing the Voice of Him who bids us to lay up for ourselves treasures in heaven, in the sure hope that where our treasure is, there will our hearts be also.

12

The Rich and the Kingdom

For it is easier for a camel to go through a needle's eye, than for a rich man to enter into the kingdom of God.
—Luke 18:25

Scripture Reading: Luke 18:18-30

In the Scripture Reading cited above, Jesus is recorded to have said these words: "How hard it is for those who have riches to enter the kingdom of God! For it is easier for a camel to go through the eye of a needle than for a rich man to enter the kingdom of God." This figure of speech, a camel going through the eye of a needle, is used in all the three synoptic gospels to emphasize the difficulty, nay the impossibility, for rich people to enter the kingdom of God. The three evangelists must have been impressed by the vividness of such language that all of them recorded it in their gospel accounts.

The Rich in the Light of Biblical Faith

We wonder why the rich are singled out. Is the New Testament apathetic to the wealthy? Why does Mary, for instance, in her *Magnificat*, praise God for "he has filled the hungry with good things, and the rich he has sent empty away?" (Lk. 1:53). Is she rejoicing over the disappointment of the rich? Then there is the Epistle of James which contains uncomplimentary remarks on the wealthy. James says: "Listen, my beloved brethren. Has not God chosen those who are poor in the world to be rich in faith and heirs of the kingdom which he has promised to those who love him? But you have dishonored the poor man. Is it not the rich who oppress you, is it not they [the rich] who drag you into court? But you have dishonored the poor man. Is it not they [the rich] who blaspheme that honorable name by which you are called?" (2:5-7). Surely, these words are a tirade against the rich. The rich are singled out as oppressors who not only cause the poor to suffer but also desecrate the holy name of God. In chapter 5 of the same Epistle, James has this to say: "Come now, you rich, weep and howl for the miseries that are coming upon you. Your gold and silver have rusted, and their rust will be evidence against you and will eat your flesh like fire" (vs.1-3a). These are strong words that should make the rich tremble.

Now, while these passages do not sound pleasing to the rich, let us note that there are also passages in the Bible which regard riches as a reward for man's piety. The first Psalm, for instance, likens the blessed man who walks not in the counsel of the ungodly to a tree planted by streams of waters which bears fruits in due season and prospers in all that he does. Again, in Psalm 112, we read: "Blessed is the man who fears the Lord, who greatly delights in his commandments... Wealth and riches are in his house, and his righteousness endures forverer." This thought, that material prosperity is a sign of God's favor, was quite popular among the Jews in the Old Testament and in the early part of the Christian era. It is possible the disciples held this doctrine because when Jesus said it was easier for a camel to pass thru the eye of a needle than for a rich man to enter the kingdom of God, they (the disciples) were, in the words of Matthew, so "exceedingly amazed" ("greatly astonished," RSV) that they asked, "Who then can be saved?" (Mat. 19:25). Obviously, the disciples were of the belief that if the rich, whose wealth is, or should be, the manifestation of their closeness to God, couldn't be saved, then who would be saved?

Jesus and the Wealthy

How, then, are we to understand Jesus' hyperbole of the camel and the rich man? I suggest, first of all, that we take note of the fact that Jesus did not sweepingly condemn the rich because they are rich. There is no record in the New Testament of Jesus' indifference toward the rich because of their wealth. On the contrary, there is the moving story of Zacchaeus who became rich by cheating the people in taxes, but it was in his house where Jesus lodged one day. We can be sure that was the beginning of a lasting friendship between Jesus and the tax collector. There is the story of Nicodemus, a doctor of laws who must have done well in his legal practice. There is the story of Joseph of Arimathea, certainly a man of means. The owner of the Upper Room where Jesus instituted the Lord's Supper with His disciples was probably a rich man. And all of them were Jesus' friends. And so we can be sure that whenever Jesus speaks of rich people, however strong His words may be, it is not because He dislikes rich men. The Gospel tells us that the rich can be Jesus' friends.

Again, we should understand the hyperbole of the camel and the rich man in the light of its context. In the Synoptic Gospels, Matthew, Mark and Luke record that Jesus said it after a certain rich man had come to Him to solicit His advice on how to inherit eternal life. The man began with courtesy and politeness in addressing Jesus "Good Teacher." Of course, from Jesus' remarks we can gather that the rich man, while doing good, actually did not know what being good meant. He was content with doing good, as attested by the fact that he did not steal, he did not bear false witness, he did not commit adultery, he honored his father and mother. He had been doing all those things since he was a youth, he said. It never occurred to him that doing good was not enough. That was the crux of his problem. So that when he was put on a test, he did not pass it. "One thing thou lackest," said Jesus. And that thing was that he did not have the compassion for the poor, for the needy, for those who had not been touched by the hand of human sympathy. He did not have concern for the poverty-stricken sons of men because he lacked inward goodness which alone could generate concern. No wonder he went away sorrowing because he had great possessions. He was so attached to his material wealth that he could not leave it for the sake of Christ, and therefore it became a hindrance to his discipleship. Hence, Jesus said, "How hard it is for those who trust in riches to enter the kingdom of God!" And in that context Jesus proceeded to say, "It is easier for a camel to go through the eye of a needle than for a rich man to enter the kingdom of God."

Barclay's Comments

Dr. William Barclay, in his commentary on this passage, says that the possession of riches means at least two things: namely, (a) "It is an acid test of a man. For a hundred men who can stand adversity, only one can stand prosperity. Prosperity can so very easily make a man arrogant, proud, self-satisfied, worldly. It takes a really big and good man to be worthy of prosperity." (b) Secondly, it is a responsibility. Man is to give account for the way he secures his possession and the way he uses his possessions.[1] In other words, Jesus would have us understand that the possession of wealth, to serve the highest purpose of life, requires a tremendous sense of Christian responsibility. Wealth is a form of power

---

[1] William Barclay, *On Mark*, p. 257.

which can be harnessed for the good of the kingdom of God, but once it becomes the controlling power, the master rather than the servant, it will surely lead men to egocentricity and spiritual ruin.

In his exposition of the parallel passage in the Gospel of Matthew, Dr. Barclay speaks of the peril of riches in the following terms:

(1) Riches encourage a false independence. He notes that "if a man is well-supplied with this world's goods, he is very apt to think that he can well deal with any situation which may arise." And truly there are those who believe they can buy their way into happiness as well as their way out of sorrow. Indeed, the logical result of such cynical attitude is the illusion that we can get along without God. But Dr. Barclay observes, "there comes a time when man discovers. . .that there are things which money cannot buy, and things from which money cannot save us." It is not until we come to our senses that we realize that in this moral universe we cannot get along without the help of God.

(2) Riches shackle a man to this earth. Did not Jesus say, "Where your treasure is there will your heart be also?" Barclay comments, "If a man has too big a stake on earth, he is very apt to forget that there is a heaven. After a tour of a certain wealthy and luxurious castle and estate, Dr. Johnson grimly remarked: 'These are things which make it difficult to die.' " In our Scripture Reading, it is the wealth of the rich young ruler which made it difficult for him to follow Christ.

(3) Riches tend to make a man selfish. Someone has remarked, "Enough is always a little more than a man has." In the words of Barclay,

> "... once a man has possessed comfort and luxury, he always has to fear the day when he may lose them. Life becomes a strenuous and worried struggle to retain the things he has. The result is that when a man becomes wealthy, instead of having the impulse to cling to them, his instinct is to amass more and more for the sake of safety and the security which he thinks they will bring. The danger of riches is that they tend to make a man forget that he loses what he keeps, and he gains what he gives away."[1]

You will note that this emphasis on the danger of wealth does not in any way imply the undesirability of material possessions. The implication, rather, is the supreme importance of responsible management of wealth.

---
[1] All quotations from pages 240-241, Barclay, *On Luke*.

For Jesus Christ is not against possessions. He is against possessiveness. Christ felt sorry for the rich young ruler not because he was rich, but because he was selfish.

The fact of the matter is that there is danger not only in wealth but also in poverty. For the poor may be morbidly obsessed with the thought of wealth in their frantic effort to achieve economic security and social prestige. Poverty can be a fertile ground for the seeds of criminality and delinquency and even communism to grow. It can make man look up to material security as the ultimate goal of life.

Salvation and Human Power

And so the passage teaches us that the salvation of mankind is not within the power of man. We can only improve the economic condition of men. We can only hope to minimize, if not totally eliminate, the danger of poverty. We can only do good to our fellow men. But we cannot be good apart from God for, as Jesus says, only God is good. So in the end we repeat the same question of the disciples, "Who, then, can be saved?" And we get the same answer, "With men it is impossible, but with God it is possible."

We have been saying here that salvation and getting rich are not necessarily incompatible, although there are dangers in wealth that are hard to overcome. And poverty is not necessarily an asset for the soul, although it can be turned into the soul's account. Discipleship demands that we be God's faithful stewards in all circumstances of life, favorable or unfavorable. It demands that we keep a sense of value which places spiritual interests over and above the purely personal and material pursuits and, at the same time, keeps body and soul in the unity of human personality.

Some Guiding Principles

In this connection, let us briefly state some principles that may guide us in our search both for the fulfillment of our bodily needs and for the kingdom of heaven. George F. Thomas, in his book *Christian Ethics and Moral Philosophy*, observes that "virtually all moral philosophers as well as religious thinkers have agreed that material possessions have only instrumental rather than intrinsic value and that they belong at the bottom of the scale (of values)."[1] Bodily or biological values, such as the pleasure

---

[1] G.F. Thomas, *Christian Ethics and Moral Philosophy*, p. 471.

of eating and drinking, are inferior to mental values, in spite of the modern cult of health and long life. And even higher than both economic and bodily values are worship, love, goodness, truth and beauty. The point to note is that while certainly material possessions have only instrumental value and lower than the values of worship, love, truth and beauty, the two values cannot be really absolutely separated. They are so interwoven in human life that, while they can be distinguished from each other, they cannot be completely separated. Therefore, as Christians, we should regard the lower values of material possessions as fundamental to the achievement of spiritual values. Dr. Thomas observes that "a scientist in quest of truth needs a laboratory equipped with suitable apparatus; an artist must have paint and canvas and a musician, an instrument; members of a religious community must have a church (building), books (hymnal), and other material objects for their corporate worship."[1] Of course we can worship God even without church building and without hymnbooks, but worship can be more meaningful and deeply enriching with the aid of these material things. The presence or absence of material things can profoundly affect our spiritual values. A Christian without a Bible cannot grow spiritually as fast as when he has one. A painter without paint and without canvas would have difficulty expressing his sense of beauty. A musician without an instrument may only waste his talent. Therefore, we are not to dispose material possessions. Neither should we make them the end of all our living. Their true place in life is to enhance the cause of our spiritual values — the cause of the kingdom of God.

"Spiritual values bestow upon lower values a higher significance that they would otherwise possess."[2] Eating and drinking, for instance, become an occasion not only for the fulfillment of the need of hunger and thirst, but also for gathering friends and loved ones. The fellowship of kindred minds bestows upon material things a significance that is more lasting than food and drink. This place of worship becomes a hallowed place because here we commune with God and have fellowship one with another. Thus, the blending of spiritual and material values ennobles life itself and meets the needs of the entire person.

Finally, George Thomas would like us to remember that our pursuit of "spiritual values as well as of other values is (often) corrupted by sin." It is possible to seek high values from low motives. A man may pray to God only to secure divine favors. A man may speak the truth only to glorify himself.

---

[1] Thomas, *op. cit.*, p. 472.
[2] *Ibid.*

On the other hand, the pursuit of what we regard as of lower value may be ennobled by a spiritual motive. You may be engaged in the production of soap and toothpaste and lumber and milk and money, but if you are motivated by a deep love of God and neighbor and family, your work becomes a holy office for the exercise of the Christian ministry.

> "It is easier for a camel to go through the eye of a needle than for a rich man to enter the Kingdom of God."

Jesus, in this statement, does not define who a rich man is. A man may be considered rich in one community, but poor in another place. But that is immaterial. For the fact is that it is truly easier for a camel to go through the eye of a needle than for any man, rich or poor, to enter the Kingdom of God. It is impossible for any man to enter God's Kingdom. But we can rejoice that in God's great mercy we can enter His Kingdom, and once we are there, we are truly rich. Not all of us can possess wealth on this earth, but in God's Kingdom we all become rich.

13

Learning from the Sons of the World

No servant can serve two masters: for either he will hate the one, and love the other; or else he will hold to the one, and despise the other. Ye cannot serve God and mammon.

— Luke 16:13

In the parable of the Dishonest Steward (Lk.16:1-13), we read these words: "And the lord commended the unjust steward, because he had done wisely." Does this verse mean that Jesus Christ approves of the dishonesty of that man who cheated his master? Here is a man whose rascality reminds us of the graft and corruption in our society, and yet he was commended by his employer. Is this not an encouragement to our people to indulge in roguery?

You will note that the parable ends at the middle of verse 8; from the latter part of that verse to verse 13, we have the comments of Jesus Christ on the parable. The words in the second half of verse 8, "for the children of this world are in their generations wiser than the children of light," cannot be attributed to the rich man in the parable, because that phrase was used only by those who were thoroughly familiar with the language of the Hebrew faith. The rich man seemed to be a son of the world himself, and most probably an alien to the heritage of the Jewish tradition.

The Jewish Background

This consideration of the parable in the light of Jewish background is supremely important because it is the key to getting the meaning which is usually obscured in many translations. This method, for instance, is most helpful in understanding verse 9. Take the phrase, "Make for yourselves friends of the mammon of unrighteousness," or, as other translations have it, "with the mammon of wickedness," or "by means of unrighteous mammon." The word mammon, though not identical with Plutus, the Greek god of wealth is, to the Hebrew mind, the symbol of wealth and represents money. But the mammon of unrighteousness does not mean, as Goodspeed translates it, ill-gotten wealth. Mammon in this regard is called unrighteous "by metonymy because the abuse of riches is more common than their right use." As Prof. Albert Barnett of Scarritt College suggests, the Evangelist Luke "seems to feel that the possession of wealth has a morally corrosive effect on the human spirit. It is the possession of wealth, not merely love for it, that is dangerous. Perhaps, he (Luke) thinks that a man cannot possess it without loving it." Of course, in the Gospel of Luke, it is certain that wealth can be used in ways which God commends, but the point which is strongly emphasized is that "God alone has the wisdom and the goodness to own it in an absolute sense because He alone sees its proper relationship to spiritual ends. The conclusion is that man's relationship to wealth must be kept strictly to that of trusteeship."[1] And so, contrary to the common belief that the mammon of unrighteousness means ill-gotten gain, we are inclined to regard it as simply money "with its inevitable taint," and which easily leads to moral deterioration. In the words of Dr. George A. Buttrick, "wealth does provide a ready occasion for pride and greed. . . The biography of any worn coin would turn the average drama into dullness, and the story would not lack elements of sordidness."[2]

" Make for yourselves friends of the mammon of unrighteousness, that, when ye fail. . ." In the Revised Standard Version, the translation is "when it fails." The phrase simply means "when you die," and so the King James Version, though regarded as inferior reading, gives the meaning more clearly than any other translation.

"When ye fail, they may receive you into everlasting habitations." In this phrase, the word **they** seems to refer to the friends who are won by means of wealth. This, we would suspect, would mean that eventually we can buy our tickets to heaven, that salvation can be bought, that we can bribe the keepers of the gates of glory. How are we to reconcile this with the fact that true friends cannot be bought and that salvation is not for sale? And what right have those friends to receive us into eternal habitations? On this point, Bible scholars are agreed that the "whole clause is a circumlocution to avoid the use of the divine name," that it should really read, "That God may receive you into His eternal habitations."

---

[1] Albert Barnett, *Understanding the Parables of our Lord,* p. 154f.
[2] Buttrick, *Luke*, p.282.

The Stewardship of Wealth

So this verse, seen in the light of this explanation, is actually a teaching on the proper use of wealth. "He who is faithful in that which is least is faithful also in much: and he that is unjust in the least is unjust also in much. If, therefore, ye have not been faithful in the unrighteous mammon, who will commit to your trust the true riches? And if ye have not been faithful in that which is another man's, who shall give you that which is your own? No servant can serve two masters... Ye cannot serve God and mammon" (vs.10-13).

It is clear, therefore, that making friends with the unrighteous mammon is being faithful in that which is least. In other words, as Dr. W. O. E. Oesterley submits "it is an earnest of what he will be in greater things, and therefore his reward of being received in eternal tabernacles is regarded as assured."[1] The verse, then, may be paraphrased this way: "Be ye faithful with the mammon of unrighteousness, i.e. in your dealings with money matters, which is one of the lesser duties, so that when all is over here on earth, ye may be received into abiding dwelling-places."[2] Dr. J. R. Dummelow, in his *Commentary on the Holy Bible*, held this same interpretation of the verse when he wrote: "We turn mammon into a friend and make ourselves friends by its means when we use riches not as our own to squander, but as God's to employ for deeds of usefulness and mercy."[3] This interpretation, I believe, is consistent with the teachings of Jesus, especially with His Sermon on the Mount where he says, "Lay up for yourselves treasures in heaven where neither moth nor rust consumes, and where thieves do not break in and steal" (Matt. 6:20).

The Unjust Steward

Now, let us turn our attention to verse 8, which reads: "And the lord commended the unjust steward, because he had done wisely." The RSV has it this way: "The master commended the dishonest steward for his prudence." Lina Flor of *Daily Mirror* observes that her Missal, commenting on this verse, says: "Only his foresight is praised — not his injustice." Interestingly, this is the same interpretation given by most Protestant scholars. Dr. Alexander Maclaren, for instance, in his *Exposition of the Holy Scriptures*, says "What is praised is not the dishonesty but the foresight, realization of the facts of the case, promptitude, wisdom of various kinds exhibited by the steward." He contends there is "eulogism

---

[1] W.O.E. Oesterley, *The Gospel Parable*, p. 200.

[2] *Ibid.*, p. 201.

[3] *Ibid.*, p. 265.

here, recognition of splendid qualities prostituted to low purposes; a recognition of wisdom in the adaptation of means to an end."[1]

Charles R. Eardman, in *Exposition of St. Luke's Gospel*, writes: "A more careful reading shows that the praise was bestowed, not for dishonesty but for prudence and foresight, that our Lord would have his followers imitate these good qualities in a bad man."[2]

Donald G. Miller, *The Layman's Bible Commentary*, Vol. 18: "Jesus obviously did not approve the dishonesty of the steward, but commended solely his prudence; that is, his wise use of present opportunities in a way which resulted in his future welfare."[3]

R. R. Dummelow, *A Commentary on the Holy Bible*: "The prudence [foresight] of the steward is commended in this parable, not his dishonesty."[4]

A brief review of the story will emphasize the point. Here was a rich man whose farm manager was reported to be wasting his goods. We are not told who brought the charges, but we can be sure the boss was rich enough to hire the services of some detectives. And he said to his steward: "What is this that I hear about you? Turn in the account of your stewardship, for you can no longer be steward." We wonder why the dismissal was done that hurriedly. Even before the steward could answer the question and defend himself, he was fired without the benefit of a formal investigation. And perhaps he thought it was useless to defend himself since after all he no longer enjoyed the confidence of his master. His problem was what to do next, now that he was to lose his job. He said, "What shall I do, since my master is taking the stewardship away from me?" So he faced the facts of life, but was a bit worried because it seemed he had not saved enough for the hard times like that. And he noted his limitations. He said "I am not strong enough to dig," he could not be a manual laborer; "and I am ashamed to beg." But then, after much thinking, he said, "Ah, I have decided what to do, so that people may receive me into their houses when I am put out of stewardship." And we know what he did: he called his master's debtors one by one (obviously giving them the impression that he was still his master's official collector) and asked them: "You, how much do you owe my master?" The reply came swiftly, "A hundred measures of oil, sir." "Come on, take your bill, and write fifty. . . Now you there, how much do you owe my master?" "A hundred sacks

---

[1] Alexander Maclaren, *Exposition of the Holy Scriptures*, Vol. on Luke, p. 75.
[2] Charles R. Eardman, *Exposition of St. Luke's Gospel*, p. 147.
[3] Donald G. Miller, *The Layman's Bible Commentary*, vol. 18, p.122.
[4] R. R. Dummelow, *A Commentary on the Holy Bible*.

of palay, sir." "Come on, take your bill, and write eighty." So he made those people feel indebted to him, so that if someday they learned that he was fired from his job because of his "unethical" dealings with his master's debtors, they would welcome him into their homes and return the hospitality to him. Clever? Yes — and wise, and prudent in his own way. He typifies the children of this world who are determined to have their own way, and would not waste any time to realize their selfish schemes. He used his mind, though devilishly, but he used his mind anyway. Can we imagine the tremendous gain we can have if such prudence were applied on spiritual matters?

Lesson from the World

In this parable, Jesus is telling us that the Christian can learn something from the children of this world. For is it not true that in many cases, "the sons of this world are wiser in their own generation than the sons of light?" Our trouble is that, as Dr. Buttrick observes:

> "[While] the worldling thoroughly cares for his senses, the follower of Christ becomes casual about his soul. The golfer takes lessons and reads books, while the religious man forgets his prayers. The salesman becomes an evangelist for some gadget, while the disciple of Jesus rarely mentions the Savior of the World. . . Most men believe in savings accounts, pensions plans, annuities, insurance — various forms of preparedness for this world. But what about a home in the hidden land? 'I go to prepare a place for you;' said Jesus; but those who most profess to love him are sometimes careless about that welcome."[1]

Surely, the Christian may learn something from the children of the world. If church meetings, for example, can be conducted the way the Rotarians conduct their meetings, what an orderly and inspiring program we will have! And yet, it is sad to note, most of our churches do not even have an order of worship. When the worship leader mounts the pulpit to announce the singing of a hymn, he at the same time scans over the hymnal to choose the hymn to be sung. While some businessmen have "blue books" and records of money they have given to their political patrons, many of our churches do not issue receipts for the payments of pledges.

---

[1] Buttrick, *Luke*, p. 281.

Then, there are those who cannot get by without reading even the headlines of the newspapers everyday; but the Christians feel they can get by without touching the Bible for weeks and months and years. While a concert singer would not dare present a musical program without a thorough practice, the members of the choir who are supposed to sing for the glory of God feel they can get by even without attending choir rehearsals.

Can we imagine, I repeat, the great benefit we would get if only this virtue we find among the children of the world is applied on the welfare of the spirit? It would be a revolution — a benignant revolution — if we read the Bible as much as we read the newspapers, and treat our church the way we treat our business. There would be a tremendous spiritual revival once we invest as much in the Kingdom of God as we invest in our recreation and leisure.

Certainly, we have every right to expect the church to be a model institution in the operation of its program and in its ministry to the world. This is possible only if we are smart enough to care for the welfare of our souls. If the influence of the church cannot be felt in the community, if it does not contribute to the moral and spiritual regeneration of the people, it may be because our Christianity is only superficial and that we have not really experienced what it means to be converted. This is why I believe we should plead for a living faith and sincerely demonstrate our love for God's church in the face of this world which demands absolute loyalty from men. It would help us to remember that like the unjust steward in the parable, we too would be required to give an accounting of our life, and if we lose time to prepare for that day of reckoning, our sweetest victories in our earthly enterprises will only turn out to be the bitterest failures that can grip us to the bones. But how wonderful it would be, how glorious, how majestic if, upon reaching our journey's end, we would hear the voice of Him who would say: "Come, thou good and faithful servants, enter thou into the joy of the Lord."

14

The Sainthood of Believers

Paul, called to be an apostle of Jesus Christ through the will of God, and Sosthenes our brother, unto the church of God which is at Corinth, to them that are sanctified in Christ Jesus, called to be saints, with all that in every place call upon the name of Jesus Christ our Lord, both theirs and ours: Grace be unto you, and peace from God our Father, and from the Lord Jesus Christ. — 1 Corinthians 1:1-3

Sometime ago, there was published in a certain magazine an article on the cost of canonization. Accordingly, in Roman Catholic tradition, canonization is the process whereby the Pope, or the hierarchy, proclaims a person to be a saint. Usually, it takes fifty or more years after a person's death before he can be pronounced a saint. There were very, very few cases in which a Christian was given the title of a saint just a few years after his death. Dr. Pitirim A. Sorokin, in his book *Altruistic Love*, tells us that "the death of a saint is actually his birthday — the day of the saint's entrance into the Kingdom of God." Christians are therefore usually canonized on the anniversary of their death.

The *Catholic Dictionary* edited by Attwater defines a saint as "one whose holiness of life and heroic virtue have been confirmed and recognized by the church's official process of beatification and canonization."[1] These "holy people," says the *Catholic Dictionary*, may be given public veneration and liturgical honour. This is why the images or statues of those pious men and women may be found in family altars and in Catholic churches.

Dr. William Adams Brown, in his *God at Work*, observes that the "Catholic saint is most often a mystic." He, of course, engages himself in creative activities, but his is essentially a contemplative life. This image of a saint is so popular in Christendom that even Protestants coming from a culture infused with the "medieval view which divides the Christians

---
[1] *Catholic Dictionary*, ed. by Attwater, p. 444.

into secular and the religious" think of a saint as one who is always serious, pious, aloof, and with an exceptional depth of spirituality. Listen to this fragment of conversation common to many:

"You are a Christian, aren't you?"

"Yes. At least, I try to be."

"Then you are a saint."

"What? "

"I said, you're a saint. To be Christian means to be a saint."

"Who, me? Goodness knows, I never claimed to be a saint. I hope I'm a Christian, as far as that goes, but I don't expect I'll ever make enough headway at it to be enrolled with the saints."[1]

This sounds like us. We admit and sometimes claim that we are Christians, but we blush at being called saints or saintly. And yet the serious intention of a true and vigorous Christianity is to make us saints. As a matter of fact, the biblical view is that to be a Christian is to be a saint. The New Testament does not know of a Christianity that is apart from saintliness. To be a saint is not the exclusive privilege of a few. It is the description of all true believers in Christ.

The Pauline Concept of a Saint

The Apostle Paul, in his letters, calls the Christians **saints**. Read his greetings in II Corinthians: "Paul, an apostle of Jesus Christ by the will of God, and Timothy our brother, unto the church of God which is at Corinth, with all the saints which are in all Achaia" (1:1). Also, greeting the Christians in Philippi, he says: "To all the saints in Christ Jesus which are at Philippi" (1:1). He also calls the Colossian Christians saints. In I Corinthians 1, Paul does not withhold the title **saint** even from the quarrelling divided members of the church. Before upbraiding those Christians for their sexual sin, drunkenness and factionalism, Paul greets them and says: "Unto the church of God which is at Corinth, to them that are sanctified in Christ Jesus, called to be saints, with all that in every place call upon the name of Jesus Christ the Lord"(1:2). Thus to Paul, if a man is a Christian, he is a saint. The early Christians were called believers, brethren, disciples, those of the Way—they were also called saints.

---

[1] Stevenson, *Faith Takes a Name*, p. 63.

The Meaning of Saint

Dr. Dwight E. Stevenson, in his *Faith Takes a Name*, notes that the term saint is an English translation of three biblical words, two of them Hebrew and one Greek. The Hebrew *hasidh* means "one who is filled with love and loyalty to God;" *qadhash* means "the loyal ones." The Greek *hoi hagioi* may be translated "those who belong exclusively to God." Stevenson suggests that a Christian, "being a saint, is to be counted among the loyal ones, who love God, and who belong exclusively to Him."[1]

The Saint is the First

This definition intimates that sainthood, or belonging exclusively to God, can be realized not by isolating ourselves from the world but by living up faithfully to God in the place He has called us to be. The Christian's demand for a better world is a prayer for renewal beginning with himself. This is a reversal of the method usually advocated in bringing about social reform. We sometimes say "Why don't **they** stop this evil or that injustice" and by **they** we mean the President and those who are in power, the congressmen, the governors and mayors, or even the bishops and cardinals and moderators. Unless **they** pay their taxes, unless **they** do this and that, I will not do my part. There is no sense for me being honest if they are not. The world will not become any better with my small, meager goodness.

In 1812, the Quaker Joseph Hoag was preaching to a London audience, and as he was pressing home the urgent claim for converts, someone in the crowd cried out and said: "Well, stranger, if all the world were of your mind, I would turn and follow after." But Mr. Hoag quickly answered, "So you have a mind to be the last man in the world to be good. I have a mind to be first." Surely a saint has a mind to be first. His prayer is: "O God, create a new world, beginning with me." It is not for us to say that we are only a drop in a bucket; it is ours to inquire what is right. It is not for us to judge the consequences, it is ours to do our duty and leave the outcome to God.

Again, a saint is aware that he is a member of a minority. He associates with the others who are also loyal to God. The Apostle Paul never speaks of an isolated individual Christian. He always speaks of Christians as groups in churches, and members of a fellowship. They belong to the party of the concerned which, though a minority, is nevertheless

---
[1] Stevenson, *op. cit.*, p. 64f.

God's minority. Did not the Christian church start as a minority movement? Jesus had only twelve disciples. But the strength of their faith as well as of those who joined them later turned the world upside down.

Prof. Dwight Stevenson made a penetrating analysis of man and society when he said the following:

> "The redemption of a decaying order can never be the work of a majority. Majorities can muster political power, financial power, or even the power of armies and these powers can multiply and extend the existing order; but they cannot redeem that way of life. What is wanting for that task is moral power, and this is to be found internally in the few who value the call of God above every other vocation."[1]

Did not Jesus have this in mind when He said, "Ye are the salt of the earth?" Salt savors and preserves, and only a little of it is required. "A pinch of salt will season a whole kettle of food." The saving power of a consecrated minority can save our decaying civilization from planetary death. If Gomorrah long ago needed only ten righteous men to stop the rain of fire, we can be sure that God will bless the labors of His minority to effect our social redemption.

A Saint's Staying Power

So a saint is a Christian who begins with himself in seeing to it that the task of social redemption is carried out, and associates with those who also give themselves to the work of God's redemption. More than that, he has staying power. Being anchored on the sure foundation of God's love, he is not swept off his feet by opposition. He has that holy courage exemplified by Peter and John who, standing before the state tribunals that wanted monopoly of their loyalty, said: "We must obey God rather than men." A saint has staying power which keeps him from being swayed by lesser values and from being wrecked by the tides of earthly pleasures and low ambition. He stands firmly on what is right, facing opposition with dignity and poise.

Such staying power is manifested not only in standing firmly against popular opposition, but also in keeping oneself loyal to God in the familiar

---

[1] Stevenson, *op. cit.*, p. 69.

ground where there is no opposition. One big test of Christian character is whether it can remain saintly in the ordinary events of life, when there is no crisis to meet. Human beings have the admirable capacity of rising to the heights of heroism when faced by a massive danger. Many people in the recent war were surprised by the amazing deeds of valor performed by those whom they never thought could be valiant. They tell themselves: "Who would have guessed that Mr. Juan de la Cruz after all is capable of such heroic act?" Perhaps, de la Cruz himself did not know he could do it, but the uncommon challenges of the battle line drew from his prosaic breast that courage and that self-forgetfulness which had been lying dormant within his being. Thus, he became a heralded hero for mustering courage during those few days of dangerous fighting. But now that he is back in his home and work, does he have enough courage to live an unchallenging life of nagging selfishness and petty irritation and common annoyances? Does he have enough courage for the commonplace?

Such saintly courage for the commonplace cannot be generated by a major outward crisis: it is generated only by a living faith. It springs from the believing heart and remains faithful in all circumstances. During occasions of ecstasy and months of dull and hard duty, through times of glory and of misery, the saint lives by his faith. He has the capacity to endure in the unusual and in the commonplace, of "being prepared in season and out of season."

Secular Substitutes

The terrifying scarcity of Christians with staying power of faith is one big dilemma our church is facing today. The world, however, does not seem to feel this great spiritual poverty because whether we like it or not, there are secular substitutes for the saint. One of those substitutes, and most characteristically modern, is the scientist. The scientist is in a sense a priest of the modern world not only because he gives us new insights into truths, but also because he brings new things to pass. He says: "Let there be light," and there is light. He works miracles. He makes the winds his messengers, he travels faster than the sound, he flies higher than the clouds. Hence he becomes the object of public veneration.[1]

Dr. Brown, in his book I already cited, remarks that it is not the scientist's capacity of being a practical helper that most commands our admiration. It is the type of character which he illustrates. "There is about

---
[1] Brown, *God at Work*, pp. 249-252.

him something simple unselfish, outward-looking. He is not thinking about himself, but only about truth; and for truth's sake, he will sacrifice everything."[1] There is, therefore, a certain religious quality in the scientist's attitude. He knows what it means to stand before a mystery and to risk all that he has for the sake of new insight. And that is the very thing which brings him close to a saint. The competing world powers, knowing the tremendous advantage science can give them, may be tempted to canonize their scientist even while they are still alive.

Another secular substitute for the saint is the philanthropist, or the man who deliberately chooses the life of helpfulness and "devotes all that he has of time, or money, or privilege, to alleviating human misery and fostering human welfare."[2] Such a man may be one who has accumulated great fortune and has made his wealth his servant rather than his master. Or he may have just enough, but with a loving spirit and a cheerful face is trying hard to share every bit he can with his less fortunate fellow men. And it is that spirit of helping, more than the material help given, which makes the philanthropist a saint in the modern world.

Another secular substitute, for lack of a better term, should be described as the statesman or one who has a genius for social organization and has the ability to have an insight into the complex problems of men and society. Such a man may be a politician or a businessman, a labor leader, a social worker. They have that insight into the problem and have the spirit to do their best to remedy the situation in the right way.

Those stouthearted men whose selfless devotion to truth or duty helps us see what ought to be are, on closer inspection, saints in the making. They only need to be directed to the highest good of God to convert their humanism into the highest expression of a vital Christian faith. The world may gain materially to increase and multiply these substitute saints, but we may just as well see that unless we become saints, our material gain may only aggravate our spiritual loss.

We Can Be Saints

To the eye of faith, our highest purpose in God's holy scheme is not to become substitute saints, but to become saints. This is God's will for the scientists, philanthropists, statesmen, as well as for the humble workers, the peasants and the ordinary citizens.

---

[1] Brown, *op. cit.*, p. 247.
[2] *Ibid.*

It is true that some people are capable for deep spiritual insight and pious service. St. Francis of Assisi, for instance, was of that category. But it is wrong to think that because we cannot attain that high level of spirituality which St. Francis of Assisi attained, we cannot be saints. If the image of St. Francis of Assisi makes it hard for us to believe that we too are called to be saints, then I suggest that we think of the disciples and the early Christians who were not so different from us and yet, by the grace of God, were called to be saints. Peter, for instance, was a man of strange moral mixture. He was the fearless spokesman of the group. He had a terrible temper, capable of cutting somebody's ear at the impulse of a moment. We like that impulsive disciple because he is one of us, and we are like him. And we call him a saint.

And was not Paul hard to get along with? His friend, Barnabas, could not get along with him in their second missionary journey. The two had to part ways. Paul himself tell us, in his letter to Timothy, that he is the chief of all sinners. Yet, the Christians of his age and of our generation have no hesitation to call him a saint.

It will help us to remember that a saint, as far as the New Testament is concerned, is not a sinless person. For who is sinless aside from Jesus Christ? A saint is a forgiven sinner — a sinner but a forgiven one. A saint is a sinner who has been justified by the love of God. He is one who is totally dependent upon God for guidance and power. Saints are they who live up to God in the difficult atmosphere of home, office, shop, factory, in the market places and in the school, and to whom the law of Christ matters more than the law of their social set. Saints, to quote again from the Apostle Paul, are Christians who strive to follow the mind of Christ and whose loyalty to God determines the course of their conduct. Surely, the recovery of primitive Christianity is the revival of the sainthood of all believers. As long as we Christians remain timid to become saints, our Christianity is more of a label rather than life. As long as our loyalty to God is regulated by our own convenience, the profession of our faith is more of a ceremony rather than experience.

My prayer, therefore, is that we may reconsider very seriously God's claim on our obedience and loyalty to Him, knowing that He is a jealous God who wants us to be His alone. To be a Christian is to yield to God's holy claim and to give ourselves exclusively to Him. The call for us to follow Christ is a call to sainthood. It is a call to be like the Master.

15

*The Pope and the Protestants**

Last Tuesday morning, when the world woke up to learn that Pope John XXIII had died, a terrible sense of loss gripped the heart of mankind and the whole world felt the pang of sadness. Not only the Roman Catholic Church but the whole Christendom felt the loss of a leader whose brief stay in the Pontificate left pleasant memories that will be long remembered. And not only non-Catholic ecclesiastical leaders but also leaders of civil governments, including Nikita Khrushchev, sent letters of condolences to the Vatican.

Significance of Pope's Death

One significance of the Pope's death is that it reveals quite clearly the fact that the Papacy has at last victoriously emerged from the prison cell of its own history. There is no denying that, especially during the Medieval Period, some occupants of Peter's throne brought shame and embarrassment to the church. There was a time when the Pope was the symbol of intolerance and greed. The enemies of the Roman See must have prayed for the death and destruction of the Catholic Faith. Some of them must have been tempted to wage an armed rebellion against the Pope and his church. The Protestant Reformation came about partly as a revolt against the immorality of the Catholic clergy.

After the Reformation, however, the Popes who ruled the church have been among the finest of saints on the surface of the earth. They have been known not only for their intellectual greatness but also for the shining example of their Christian life. And last week, while Pope John was at the brink of death, Christians all over the world — Catholics and non-Catholics — were imploring God's blessings on his soul. Even the churches that are theologically antagonistic or indifferent to the Holy See encouraged their flocks to intercede to God for the health of the Supreme Pontiff. He was loved so much that the world felt it was too early to lose him even at the ripe age of 81.

---

* A sermon delivered on June 9, 1963, five days after the death of Pope John XXIII.

The Pope's Humanity

There are some reasons why the late Pope endeared himself to the Christian world, especially the Protestants. One reason is that he was a very human pope. He had the touch of a common man. He himself loved to recall his boyhood experiences on the farm in Sotto Il Monte, "a mountain village in northern Italy," where he was born. His parents were peasants and he himself was a tiller of soil. Belonging to a family of 13 children, of whom he was third, he had to work hard to help his parents earn their living.

Mr. Emmet John Hughes, writing about the late Pope in the *Newsweek* magazine (June 10, 1963), contrasted John to his predecessor, Pope Pius XII. "In daily routine, Pius was methodically precise; John was bewilderingly unpredictable. In theology, Pius was scrupulously cerebral and thorough; John was candidly casual and unscholarly." Of course it was incidental that while Pius was the son of Roman aristocracy, John was from the rank of farmers.

The humanity of John XXIII was further underscored by the fact that aside from rice and cheese and coffee, his favorites included wine — certainly, as an appetizer. He smoked 3 to 4 cigarettes a day, and perhaps the first Pope who smoked. He made no less than 140 visits to schools, hospital and orphanages, most of which were unannounced visits. He delighted the people with his unexpected appearances in the Vatican gardens and sometimes in the market places. He broke some of the old practices of the Papacy. For instance, as a rule, the Pope should eat alone. He observed this rule only for a few days, then he invited guests to the papal dining room because he said he could not eat much without some companions. And to top it all, he disobeyed some of the advice of his physicians. Dr. Antonio Gasbarrini said of him, "He is a man who does not pay attention to his doctors."

Furthermore, the late John XXIII had a remarkable sense of humor. When he was to appear on television, he looked at himself and, seeing through the mirror his own full frame and bulging ears, he said, "Oh Lord, this man is going to be a disaster on television." He was reported to have said this statement: "In Italy, there are three ways of losing one's money: women, gambling, and farming. My father chose the most boring of the three."

Aside from his admirable personal characteristics, the late Pope became dear to the non-Catholic world because of the liberality of his thoughts and his skillful diplomatic relations with the communist states. In his encyclical, *Pacem in Terris,* he was firm but gentle in his appraisal of communism as a movement sparked by "false philosophical teachings," and predicted that such movements would be subject to changes, "even of a profound nature." His words revealed his brilliant understanding of history, not a rejoicing over the heresies of communism. No wonder Khrushchev's daughter and her husband, when they visited Rome, thought it worthwhile to seek the Pope's audience. He received them warmly and gave her a gift of a rosary. When the observers from the Russian Orthodox Church were having difficulty getting Soviet permission to attend the Vatican meeting last October, it was Pope John who interceded for them with a promise to the Soviet government that no anti-Communist oratory "would spice the solemn deliberations" at the Vatican. We should not forget that John was, for 25 years, the Vatican envoy to Bulgaria, Turkey, and Greece. He was a seasoned statesman and diplomat.

The Pope's Encyclicals

Protestants are happy to note that in his *Pacem in Terris,* the late Pope had shown no small amount of religious tolerance which only a few pontiffs would publicly advocate. In said encyclical, the Pope spoke of the right to worship God according to one's conscience. He wrote, "Every human being has the right to honor God according to the dictates of an upright conscience and, therefore, the right to worship God privately and publicly." He was, in effect, saying that religion cannot be legislated and that the practices of other religious faiths should be respected. A bold answer to such a challenge would mean the death of religious bigotry and fanaticism, and the birth of human brotherhood which transcends cultural and religious barriers. Once again we are reassured that whatever contradictions there may be in the actual practice of Catholicism, the true spirit of the Catholic faith is one which gives way for religious tolerance.

In his other encyclical, *Mater et Magistra* (May, 1961), the Pope showed social concern which is as embracing as Protestantism's social gospel. Among the problems considered were the plight of the farmers, the disparity between the rich and the poor, the obligations of the more advanced nations to the underdeveloped countries. He was concerned with the universal common good, with making the peoples of the world realize that we are living as members of the human race, that in our pursuit of life and the means of livelihood we cannot afford to ignore the welfare of our neighbors.

The Second Vatican Council

A third reason for John XXIII's enthronement in the hearts of the non-Catholic Christians is to be found in the profound significance of the Second Vatican Ecumenical Council. As we know, this council meeting started last October, recessed in December, and is scheduled to resume this coming September. Of course, the new Pontiff may or may not call for the resumption of the meeting, but whatever he decides, he can no longer stop the theologically revolutionary air which the first session had generated.

Some of the items on the agenda are of great interest to the Protestants. Take, for instance, the suppression of the celibacy of the clergy. In other words, it is being proposed that the priests be allowed to get married. Such proposal is just a sample of the revolution going on in Catholic theology today. We can only pray that if and when the Council meeting is resumed, the Spirit of God may guide them in their deliberations on this important proposal.

Another item on the agenda that will certainly arouse lively discussion is a restudy of the doctrine of the church. The official Catholic doctrine of the church as of now is that the church is the extension of the Incarnation. This is perhaps the major theological basis for the claim that the church is sinless. Of course, this ecclesiology has always been rejected by some Catholic theologians, but the 1943 encyclical *Mystici Corporis* defended the traditional position of the church, and the doctrine continued to be popularly supported. The II Vatican Council, however, proposed to look at the church as the *People of God* which is the phraseology used in Catholic liturgy. As people of God, therefore, the church cannot be sinless, just as the people of God in the Old Testament were never sinless. The church needs to pray for forgiveness, for the redemptive grace of the Divine Saviour. The church stands under the judgement of God.

I am led to say that this trend in Catholic theology, especially the proposed doctrine of the church, is quite biblical. Should the Council continue to move towards this direction, we can never imagine the tremendous changes that will subsequently come about. Corollary to this problem of the doctrine of the church is the proposal of the II Vatican Council to reconcile the Holy Scriptures and tradition as sources of authority. The method of Bible study called "higher criticism", a method recognized by the encyclical of 1943, is to be employed. This means that a serious and thorough study of the Scriptures will be undertaken. Those of you who love the Bible so dearly will shed tears of joy to know that the highest council of the Catholic church does not neglect Bible studies in its ecumenical gatherings. Again we should be in prayers for God's blessings on the Council's inquiries into the Scriptures, and hope that they may submit to the authority of the Bible even at the cost of giving up some of their hallowed traditions.

Another proposal scheduled for discussion at the II Vatican Council is the saying of mass in the vernacular. The present practice as we know is that mass is said in Latin, a language which none of the worshippers can understand. The proposal, if approved, will mean that time is coming when mass in our country will be said in Tagalog, Ilocano, Cebuano, Bicol — in the respective dialects of the people where the church is located. Should we not feel happy even only for the plan of such a change? Is it not our desire, as Protestants, that the language of worship in any church, Protestant or non-Protestant, should be in the language that has meaning to the people in the pews? Certainly, we can say that this proposal is a step in the right direction because if the Christian faith is to be a dynamic power in the life of men, its resources should be available in the language of the common *tao*.

Another major item on the docket of the II Vatican Council meeting is the study of ways and means to achieve unity among the divided members of the Christian Church. And to emphasize the importance of this work, Pope John created the Secretariat for Christian Unity with Augustin Cardinal Bea, the only Jesuit cardinal, as the head of the Secretariat. It is to be admitted that such a move is a very bold one. Indeed, it seems to many that a union between the Roman and the non-Roman churches is a historical impossibility. But we should not underestimate the power of the Spirit. We can at least begin working for such unity. This is why, for the first time in the history of the Catholic Church, leaders of non-Roman churches were invited to the Council as official observers.

These proposals, which affect the entire system of the Catholic Church, can be described only as revolutionary. The Roman Church, which used to be the symbol of *status quo*, has acquired a new image in the eyes of the world. The late Pope declared in his opening address at the II Vatican Council that the Church should be brought up to date. The *Pax Romana Secretariat Bulletin* (July-August issue,1962), confirms that the aims of the II Vatican Council "are meant to cope with the various needs and surging emergencies of the times."

Let us pray that the conclave which will meet on June 19 to elect a new Pope may be guided by God so that the noble dreams of John XXIII may be pursued further. For the meanwhile, let us hope that the spirit of tolerance, which the late Pope magnificently displayed, may continue to spread until it becomes the very foundation of our hope for the achievement of Christian unity. So if someday such a dream becomes a reality, we know it is partly because there was a man who worked against the odds of time and in spite of the pessimisms of men; perhaps with the knowledge that such unity is not possible within the realm of history, and yet with faith that what is impossible with men is possible with God.

This is also the faith which I covet for ourselves, the faith which is in the heart of the gospel message and delivered unto us by Jesus Christ Himself. With this faith we can face the vicissitudes of the present, and look forward to the coming of the day when men will fight no more but live together in harmony and peace. We can be grateful that in the providence of God, our life in the here and now can be a foretaste of the gloriousness of such wondrous hope.

16

The Church and Population Problem

For a number of years now, there has been much talk about population explosion as a grave problem of our time. Biologist Julian Huxley believes it is "more serious in the long perspective than war or peace." Karl Sax reminds us it "could be a greater threat to world peace and prosperity than the atomic bomb." And this is something that should concern both the church and the civil governments.

Facts and Figures

A brief review of the population growth will underscore the gravity of the situation. In 1650, the world population was estimated at 625 million. Barely two hundred years later (1830), it reached the billionth mark (1.25 billion). And it took only 100 years more to double that number. In 1950, it was 2.5 billion. Today, the estimate is three billion, and some scientists predict that by the end of this century the number would soar up to 7 billion, if the present rate of growth continues.

This means that every second, three babies are born. Before we are able to mention the name of one, another is born. Every year, 44 million people are added and they need food, clothing and shelter. Of course, everyday thousands of people die, but the surplus of births over deaths is 120,000 each day.

Karl Sax, professor of botany at Harvard University, traces the problem to be most acute in Asia where we have more than half of the world's population. Communist China, for instance, has an estimated growth of 15 million people every year, more than the people living in all of Canada.

The Philippines is one of the fastest-growing nations in the world. While the world population is growing at the rate of 1.6 percent, the Philippines is increasing at the rate of about 3 percent. At the turn of the century, there were only about 7.5 million Filipinos. In 55 years, the number trebled to reach 24 million. Today, there are about 28 million Filipinos. In 1956, the Philippine Statistical Survey of Households interviewed married women over 45 years old, and asked them how many children they had in their lifetime. The answer was that the average woman had 7.1 children, indicating a birth rate of 50 per 1000.

Some Conflicting Views

Before saying anything more, let us observe that the term "overpopulation" as noted by James J. Norris, President, International Catholic Migration Commission, is a relative term which brings into play not only the density of people, but also the resources and the economic situation of a country. And there has been some theorizing about the number of the people which the world can support. Colin Clark, for instance, a well-known British scholar, contends that the world can support a population of between 10 to 15 billion, "if all the cultivable land in the world were farmed at Dutch standards of skill and hard work and if the consumption of farm products per capita were at the present-day Dutch standard." Dr. James Bonner of Caltech, on the other hand, estimates that the world can support 50 billion people. Only history can pass judgment on the theories of these men. For the meantime, we are openly alarmed by the staggering growth of the world's population. For the fact is that two-thirds of mankind are hungry, and if this is the situation, even those who have three square meals a day cannot have peace of mind. Our own leaders tell us that our country can support 80 to 100 million people, but the trouble is that even at our present number, poverty walks like rags in almost every corner of the land.

Cause of Population Growth

When we look for what has brought this problem about, we see, for one thing, not so much the increased birth rate, but the decreased death rate. Modern science is able to eradicate much of the disease which used to be a horror to society. In India, for instance, 60 years ago, for every 1000 babies 330 died at birth. Today, the mortality has dropped to 95 per 1000. Just a generation ago, the life expectancy of an Indian was 23 years. Today, it is 48 years. In our country, the death rate has gone down from 31.7 per 1000 after the war to less than 20 per 1000 at present.

Migration as a Remedy

Now, what are some of the remedies which the experts suggest? One is free migration. The July 23, 1962 issue of the *Newsweek* magazine observes that "much of the world today is not overpopulated but underpopulated. Giant Canada has fewer people than Burma, and the whole continent of Australia has fewer people than the city of Tokyo. Fertile Argentina has only 18 people per square mile, against 340 in the Netherlands... Russia, too, is underpopulated, and Khrushchev has said 100 million more people would not be enough."[1] Evgeny K. Federov, secretary-general of the Soviet Academy of Sciences, surmises that within a generation some people may settle on new planets. This reminds us of Earl Wilson who said, "Ten years ago, the moon was an inspiration to lovers and poets. Ten years from now it will be just another airport."

Increased opportunity for emigration is being solidly advocated by the Catholic Church. In a letter to the American Bishops in 1948, the late Pope Pius XII said that "a man had a natural right to emigrate, since God had provided material goods for the use of all." He said that if in some locality "the land offers the possibility of supporting a large number of people, the sovereignty of the state, although it must be respected, cannot be exaggerated to the point that access to this land is, for inadequate or unjustified reasons, denied to needy and decent people from other nations, whenever this does not hinder the public welfare as measured on honest-weight scales."[2] It is quite obvious that this step is not an easy one. Aside from the tremendous cost of migrating people from one place to another, there is in emigration the great obstacle of racial feeling. Someone has noted that "half-empty nations like Australia and Canada bar most colored immigrants, and Britain (just a few months ago) ended free immigration from its multiracial Commonwealth."[3] Furthermore, as Norman St. John-Stevas submits, the capacity of individuals to cross from one culture to another is clearly limited, "and a wholesale immigration would be destructive to the migrants and the social structure of the receiving countries."[4]

Foreign Aid Policy

Another measure being done to help alleviate the misery in the underdeveloped countries is the sharing of material resources thru financial

---

[1] *Newsweek*, July 23, 1962, p. 21.
[2] Quoted by Norman St John-Stevas, *Birth Control and Public Policy*, p. 71.
[3] *Newsweek, op. cit.*
[4] *Ibid.*

and technical assistance by the richer nations. The foreign aid program of the U.S. government, for instance, based on the philosophy of enlightened self-interest, certainly helps much. President Kennedy expressed a genuine Christian concern when he said, "The economic collapse of those nations (underdeveloped and rapidly increasing) would be disastrous to our national security, harmful to our comparative prosperity, and offensive to our conscience."

Increased Food Production

Again, to meet the problem caused by rapid population growth, efforts are being exerted to increase food production. United Nations experts believe that the production of many crops can be doubled in two decades or less. They believe that deserts can be converted into irrigation powered by atomic pumping stations. "Algae may be converted to human food. Yeast may make carbohydrate wastes fit for human consumption." It seems that with sufficient capital all these can be done.

Birth Control as a Solution

Another solution to the population problem on which Christians are not unanimous is birth control. The United Nations, realizing the seriousness of population problem, considered the policy of encouraging family planning, but the adoption of such policy was blocked by the delegates from Roman Catholic and Communist countries. The Communists opposed birth control on the Marxist theory that human labor is the measure of wealth. The World Health Organization in 1952 had to drop the Norwegian proposal to study contraception as part of its official program because of the Catholic opposition. Accordingly, the United Nations adopted the policy of neutrality on this subject to respect the different ethical and religious values of the member nations, but the advice of experts to individual states is available on request.

A Theological Tension

Protestants and Roman Catholics differ very sharply on this matter of birth control. To us, the issue is basically doctrinal and theological, so that while we handle it in the light of our Christian convictions, we should at all times be open to the leading of the Holy Spirit. The Catholic Church, let us note, is not against family planning. On the contrary, she encourages it. But only the "rhythm method" is the accepted method — either this, or complete abstinence. To the Catholic faith, contraception or the use of any means to prevent the meeting of the sperm and the egg is a mortal sin. In the words of Fr. E. P. Miller, "it is always a mortal sin. Always. Always. No doctor, no pope can ever give anybody permission to practice birth control." Contraception (which, according to Fr. Miller is synonymous to birth control) is a mortal sin because it is against Natural Law. The encyclical on Christian Marriage issued by Pope Pius XI says that "the conjugal act is primarily by nature for the begetting of children," and therefore, those who deliberately frustrate this natural course of the conjugal act contradict the intention of the Author of nature. "Man is free to act only within the pattern of nature." (Stevas)

The question is, if we are free only within the pattern of nature, why does not the Catholic Church condemn those who cut their fingernails and their hair, those who dam the rivers and those who try to produce seedless papayas? The answer is that there is no reason for allowing hair and fingernails to grow, whereas the chief purpose of sexuality is, undeniably, reproduction. In other words, Catholic natural law teaches that the primary end of marriage is the procreation of children, based on the biblical injunction: "Be fruitful, and multiply."

The Evangelical faith, on the other hand, holds that the primary aim of marriage is not the procreation of children although this is not overlooked, but the companionship of husband and wife. In Gen. 2:18, God said, "It is not good that the man should be alone; I will make him a helper fit for him." If procreation is the chief end of marriage, then those couples who have no children failed to achieve the chief end of matrimony; then nature has not been kind to them.

Of course, in the Evangelical faith, children are to be desired. And the Bible speaks of the kind of relationship that should exist between parents and children. But if the couple are childless, they need not be in despair. They need not feel that their marriage has gone into the rocks.

Again, Catholic theologians oppose the practice of birth control because they believe it is against the teaching of the Scriptures. St Thomas Aquinas, in his book *Summa Theologia*, cites the case of Onan, the son of Judah, as recorded in Gen. 38:8-10. "And Judah said unto Onan, Go in unto thy brother's wife, and marry her, and raise up seed to thy brother. And Onan knew that the seed should not be his; and it came to pass when he went in unto his brother's wife, that he spilled the semen on the ground, lest he should give offspring to his brother. And what he did was displeasing in the sight of the Lord, and he slew him." Aquinas contends that Onan was punished by God because he indulged in *coitus interruptus*. This interpretation is not universally accepted by Bible scholars. Onan was punished not because he practiced *coitus interruptus*, but because he broke the levirate law requiring a man to raise children to his brother's widow. Had he not married his brother's wife, just the same he would be punished, because that, too, would be breaking the levirate marriage law.

Responsible Family Planning

Certainly, the Evangelical churches would render valuable service not only to our country but to the rest of mankind by advocating the idea of an intelligent family planning as a major Christian responsibility. We should teach the people that large families, especially at this stage of our economic development, are not necessarily the Christian ideal. We should feel terribly uneasy to have children who cannot be given fair opportunities in life because of carelessness on the part of the parents. Planned parenthood will help avoid illegal abortion which is being madly resorted to by those people who are not ready to shoulder responsibilities; it will greatly lessen the birth of unwanted children.

And so, in the light of this fact, I am inclined to suggest that our Evangelical churches and other sympathetic Christians should work hard for the amendment of our Tariff and Customs Code, so that Sec. 102, par. d. may be eliminated or at least modified. This provision states that we cannot import into the Philippines "Articles, instruments, drugs and substances designed, intended or adapted for preventing human conception or producing unlawful abortion, or any printed matter which advertises or describes or gives directly or indirectly information where, how or by whom human conception is prevented or unlawful abortion produced." By all means we should stand against unlawful abortion and do our best to stop such crime, but importation of contraceptives and printed matters containing information on birth control should be allowed, not for reckless and immoral use, but for the implementation of sound family planning programs. In the states of Connecticut and Massachusetts, where prohibition on birth control information is also prevailing, Evangelical Christians are relentlessly working for the modification of the law. There was a time when, in Massachusetts, 7,000 laymen, 1,300 doctors and 400 ministers signed a petition to amend the law. And though their efforts were unsuccessful, they have high hopes that someday the legislature would change its mind. It is that kind of determination, undaunted by unsuccessful attempts, which we need to have in this country today. We should at least begin rallying together and lobby for the amendment of our Tariff law. The Philippine Federation of Christian Churches[1] should provide the leadership and initiate studies on strategy.

The Family Relations Centers

For the meantime, we should support the program of our Family Relation Centers and make use of their services. While India has 4,300 family clinics, there are only two Family Relations centers in our country, both operating in Manila. One is the Center for Planned Parenthood launched in November, 1960, and is a project of the Manila Health Department. The other is the Family Relations Center begun in July, 1961 and is sponsored by the Philippine Federation of Christian Churches. We should urge our civic and government leaders to put up more Family Relations Centers all over the Philippines to help those millions who cannot afford to come to the city. This is one of the practical things which we can do.

Lastly, let us not forget that the problem of rapid population growth is ultimately the problem of stewardship of family living. This is why to the Christian conscience, the problem is not simply how to limit the size of the family according to the material resources of the family or as agreed upon by the husband and wife, but also how to make every member of the family conscious of the priority of the spiritual over the material interests of life. Our task, as Christians, is not only to work for the relief of mankind from all sorts of ills and miseries caused by population explosion, but to bring to every living creature the message of hope and comfort and the love of Jesus Christ which alone can enable them to transcend not only the misfortunes of life but even the threat of death itself. And if we are to do that effectively, a living faith in the God and Father of Jesus Christ should first be real in our homes. This is the supreme task of the Christian family whether it is large or small.

---

[1] This is now the National Council of Churches in the Philippines.

17

Labor and Christian Conscience

(A Labor Sunday Sermon)

Let us note at the outset that in a religious observance of Labor Day, nothing could be more fitting than the consecration or reconsecration of our talents to the purposes of God, the dedication of our work to the fulfillment of life as we know it in Jesus Christ. This means that whether we are manual laborers or personnel managers, whether we are farmers or landlords, our duty is to acknowledge our occupation as a vital area of Christian witness, a sacred trust for the exercise of our ministry.

In sociological parlance, the word **labor** is used not only to designate those in the rank and file of laborers as distinguished from the managers or employers; it is also used as a general term for any kind of labor or work. Someone has observed that the word labor suggests the negative image of a labor union on strike against an employer. We will have something to say about this today, but only for the purpose of clarifying our social concerns as responsible members of the body of Christ.

Generally, there are three things needed in the production of wealth: land, labor, and capital. Many of us have neither land nor capital, but all of us have some ability to work, some talent to earn a living. Labor, therefore, is one thing we have in common, and to talk about it is to talk about our common stewardship.

Attitude Toward Labor

There are some labor conditions in our country which are quite obnoxious to a Christian conscience and, therefore, pose a tremendous challenge to the Christian community. One is the general attitude to labor itself, especially manual labor. We tend to classify people into those who work on the land and those who own the land, an attitude inherited from Spain. Bruno Lasker puts it this way:

" . . . In the Philippines, anyone whom industry, thrift,

or luck had placed in possession of money almost invariably invested it in land and thus changed his social status. To engage in any kind of physical labor would have held down his social position. The process of industrialization, thus, was greatly handicapped not only by the export of potential capital, but also by the absence of a class of manual workers who, when successful, would invest their savings in technical training for themselves or their children and thus build from the ground up enterprises of growing complexity. Instead, the successful man became an *ilustrado* whose son, if of a progressive frame of mind, might prepare himself for a career of industrial management or teaching, but always with a view to functioning in the office or the classroom, never in the shop."[1]

Richard Poethig, in his newly-edited book *Philippine Social Issues from a Christian Perspective*, submits that the American occupation in the Philippines tried to eradicate this false exaltation of the white-collar job to the desecration of manual labor by introducing industrial training and vocational education. The result of such an attempt had been quite impressive, but it made "little change in the overall attitudes of the people toward labor."

It appears, therefore, that if our country is to become more and more industrialized, Christians in their churches, in the schools and in their civic and business groups should continue upholding the dignity of honest labor so that the next generation may find their true places in the development of a sound economic order where there are no occupational prejudices.

The Unemployed and Underemployed

Another deplorable social condition prevailing in our midst is the unusually high number of the unemployed and the underemployed. Under this category are 2 ½ million of our 10 million labor force. This situation is being made more serious by the fact that 360,000 persons join the labor force every year. This means that even only for the purpose of arresting the growth of unemployment and underemployment, there should be at least half a million new jobs every year. Norberto Romualdes, Jr., in his article in the *1962 Fookien Times Yearbook*, observes that "for a single employment opening you can expect about a hundred applicants to vie."

---
[1] Quoted by Hunt in *Sociology in the Philippine Setting,* p. 330ff.

The Labor Movement

Another area of modern life which needs the guidance of a Christian conscience is the labor movement. The labor movement started as a social reformation movement led by the late Isabelo de los Reyes and Dominador Gomez. It is also the result of industrialization. In an industrial community, the workers are forced by circumstances to unite together to protect themselves from any possible exploitation by the capitalists, to safeguard their rights and privileges, and to effect collective bargaining for what they consider to be legitimate demands.

Some labor leaders feel that the labor union becomes some kind of a substitute for the rural community life from which most laborers are uprooted and where fellowship is intimate and personal. In the factory, men can become depersonalized because their attachment is to the machine, but in the labor union, they find their identity, and the need for fellowship is met.

A young Filipino economist observed that the labor movement in our country started as a secular movement. In other words, it presents a challenge to the church to offer some Christian guidance on the movement. Leadership, for instance, should be guided by a Christian conscience. Incidentally, this is what our friend Cipriano Malonzo wrote a few years ago. "Organized labor in the Philippines is sadly lacking in Christian leadership. Most of the labor leaders I have met are wanting in moral idealism and vision of Christian service. The sad consequence of this is that many unions are run for the personal benefit of labor leaders. The workers are exploited by their leaders."[1] We may say that not only the labor movement but any social, religious or political movement will not go far unless its leadership has a sense of mission and is thoroughly dedicated to the cause it seeks to champion.

The Role of the Church

At this point, let us note that the greatest contribution the Christian church can make towards the noble cause of the labor movement is not to be partisan to labor, not to be identified with the unionists, but to be the conscience of society. The labor-management issues are sometimes technical in nature, and members of the church are apt to differ in their opinions on technical questions. It is wrong for the church as an institution to be partisan because the members of the church come from the ranks of

---

[1] Malonzo, *Philippine Christian Advance,* August, 1951, p. 7.

labor and also from management. But the church as an institution should expose its members to the searchlights of God's Spirit so that, as individuals, they may think and speak and act in accordance with the dictates of their Christian conscience. The church should remind its members of the righteousness of God and of the love of Christ which they should manifest in their daily life. The church should help the people to get rid of their selfish motives which usually control their acts and which are often hidden beneath the cloak of piety. The church should make the people realize that if the love of God is real in us, then somehow we will hate evil and the appearance of evil in our relationships, and therefore we will strive to solve the problems that may come up in the farms or shops or factories in the spirit of a forgiving love.

And so, if the church is to be the conscience of society, it is within the scope of its duty to conduct seminars and conferences on labor problems. Indeed, it would be good for the church-related schools to offer formal courses on trade unionism, labor laws, business management and other related subjects. For we need to have an intelligent understanding of the situation and a firm grasp of the subject, so that our course of action may be guided by prudence and sobriety.

A Wider Distribution of Wealth

An enlightened conscience would also be concerned with a more equitable distribution of the nation's wealth. Mr. Candido Ordinario of the Bureau of Census and Statistics has suggested that the annual family income of P1,500 is the poverty line, below which the families may be considered poor. The 1957 Statistical Survey of Households reveals that 71.4% of the Filipino families earn less than P1,500 a year, and only 3.9% have an annual income of P5,000 and above. We cannot spell out here how an equitable distribution of the nation's wealth should be carried out, but let us emphasize that a Christian conscience would not let us rest unless we share the fruits of our lands and the fruits of our labors with those who have not been touched by the hand of human sympathy. The heart that has known the love of Christ would not send a brother away empty-handed, if he comes to knock at our doors in the middle of the night for a loaf of bread and a cup of water.

One practical way by which we can express this Christian concern for the less fortunate is to treat our household helps with fairness and understanding. Our conscience should disturb us if we know we pay them less than what we should, and yet enjoy their services because we know they have no choice. If it is at all possible, we should encourage them to have some vocational training if they have talents for it, so that they need not remain household helps throughout the rest of their life. Hiring household helps should be dictated not only by our need of their services, but also by our desire to help people as much as we can.

The Judgment of God

Again, an enlightened Christian conscience would submit the labors of our hands unto the judgment of God, so that whether we be laborers or managers, whether we toil in the classroom or in the shops, we become aware that we work not only to earn a living but also to exercise our ministry in this world. Our work becomes more meaningful when we remember that it is the phase of our life which reflects the riches or the poverty of our worship. For it is in work where worship finds its true expression. Incidentally, the Greek word for worship can also be translated service, or work. Liturgy, in Greek, literally means "the work of the people." Therefore, we are to be aware of God's presence not only in the sanctuary but also in the farm, in the shops and factories. He is at our places of work.

Viewed from this Christian perspective, work is to be done responsibly. In the final reckoning, the question is not what kind of work we do, but how well or how faithfully we do our work. This is to say that we have to work even if sometimes we are not inspired to work. This is true especially among the employees. They have to work if it is working day. Those who are clever enough to fabricate some other reasons for not working when the truth is that they simply feel lazy may not have fully understood that work is a sacred trust they have to give account of. Our Christian conscience should not allow us to yield to laziness and to any form of complacency.

And so for us Christians, the conviction that God is the Master Workman of the race is the solid foundation of any act toward the building of a responsible and prosperous economic order. For we see that to lift the country from the debris of poverty and want is not only a human necessity but also a divine imperative. We are persuaded that worship is not an isolated religious ceremony, but a rich spiritual experience intended to be a source of strength we need in our daily struggle for survival. We realize that our work should reflect the content of worship and that it is a trust given for our responsible stewardship. This is why we cannot help but be concerned about the meaning of labor and the plight of the laborers, trusting always that whatever social status we find ourselves, we, as followers of Christ, may be used by God in the preservation and propagation of His love, so that in all our relationships there may be equity and justice, dignity and honor, gallantry and peace.

18

Periscoping the Reformation

(Reformation Sermon)

It is good that the Reformation Sunday is observed at least once a year, for it gives us an opportunity to trace and to remember the rich heritage of our faith. Especially now that many of our people do not seem to be acquainted with the history of our church, such opportunity is the more welcome.

Understandably, our view of the Reformation can easily be coloured by our denominational background. And yet, if we are to be objective, we should be willing to consider the different views and thresh out the grains of errors which our finite mind may be able to detect. I am referring particularly to how the Catholic Church views the Reformation because it was the Catholic Church that was most seriously affected by it. As you may expect, the Catholic Church does not have anything good to say about it.

The Frankness of Some Catholics

First of all, we should appreciate the frankness of some Catholic historians, like Fr. Reginald F. Walker and Fr. John O'Brien, who admit that some of the causes which gave way to the Reformation movement were: (1) the weak theological orientation of the church to meet the threats of pagan humanism which was quite reckless in its criticism; (2) the "decay of Scholastic philosophy" or the decay of the church's intellectual life; (3) the age-long struggle between the Holy Roman Emperors and the Pope; (4) the widespread social unrest caused on the one hand by the grasping after wealth and power on the part of the greater nobility and higher clergy and, on the other hand, by the discontent of the lesser nobility, the lower clergy and the peasantry; and (5) the appalling immorality even of the outstanding religious leaders, including some popes.[1]

---

[1] Fr. John O' Brien, "The Reformation," *Outline History of the Catholic Church,* pp. 37-44.

Various Descriptions of Luther

Jacques Maritain, in his biography of Luther, says that the Reformation was an anti-Christian revolution and that it was nothing but a historical dramatization of Luther's personal egocentricism. The Protestant Reformation, says Maritain, was an immense disaster for humanity, "the effect of an interior trial which turned out badly in a religious who lacked humility."[1] This brave spokesman of the Catholic Church pictures Luther's person at the very center of the Reformation so that Lutheranism, especially, is but "the overflow of Luther's individuality."[2]

While Fr. Walker thinks of Luther as the greatest of all heretics, even greater than Arius, Maritain on the other hand describes Luther as a fallen monk, a victim of sensuality and a man tormented by pride. Luther was the Augustinian priest who perverted the Gospel and caused untold harm to the church of God. Luther was "an inverted Pharisee, a runaway victim of scruples,"[3] relying on his own works and not on the grace of God. "What was lacking in him," says Maritain, "was force of intellect... Luther was not intelligent, but limited — stubborn, especially."[4] However, this man who lacked the force of intellect became a professor at the University of Wittenberg at the age of 25 and won his doctorate in theology at 29.

Other writers call him the fallen angel, but Father Walker describes him simply as one of the fallen sons of Adam, "the young friar who seldom prayed... and one who, little by little, forsook the interior life of personal union with our Divine Lord."[5]

Luther: A Man of Prayer

Perhaps there is not much need to argue with the Catholic biographers of Luther and say that the Reformer was not really as they think he was; that, indeed, Luther was a man of prayer, with a good amount of intelligence, if not a genius, and a sincere monk whose desire was to have peace with God. If we go into the basic issue, we might get a better picture of the Reformer. And the issue was the nailing of his 95 theses to the door of the Castle Church in Wittenberg, which were solely directed against Father John Tetzel and Albert of Brandenburg in their "unbridled pretensions as to the efficacy of indulgences." As you know, Father Tetzel was a Dominican monk, commissioned by Pope Leo X to issue letters of

---

[1] Jacques Maritain, *The Three Reformers*, p. 13ff.
[2] *Ibid.*, p. 15.
[3] *Ibid.*, p. 11.
[4] *Ibid.*, p. 5.
[5] *Ibid.*, p. 40.

indulgences to raise funds for the building of the new St. Peter's Cathedral. According to Fr. John A. O'Brien in his *The Reformation*, "The preaching of Tetzel, a monk of blameless life and impressive eloquence, conveyed the essential teaching of the Church, and barring a few rhetorical exaggerations, did not merit reproach."[1] But Luther thought that it was so grave an issue affecting the salvation of men's souls that he could not bear being silent about it.

Dr. Roland Bainton, an authority on the Reformation at Yale University, in his book *Here I Stand*, quotes a paragraph from the sermon of Father Tetzel which was delivered by the monk wherever he went before selling the indulgences:

> "Listen now, God and St. Peter call you. Consider the salvation of your souls and those of your loved ones departed. You priest, you noble, you merchant, you virgin, you matron, you youth, you old man, enter now into your church which is the church of St. Peter. Visit the most holy cross erected for you and ever imploring you. (NOTE: Fr. Tetzel's men always erected a big cross beside the improvised pulpit in the market places where they sold the indulgences.) Have you considered that you are lashed in a furious tempest amid the temptations and dangers of the world, and that you do not know whether you can reach the haven, not of your mortal body, but of your immortal soul? Consider that all who are contrite and have confessed and made contribution will receive complete remission of all their sins. Listen to the voices of your dear dead relatives and friends, beseeching you and saying, 'Pity us, pity us. We are in dire torment from which you can redeem us for a pittance.' Do you not wish to? Open your ears. Hear the father saying to his son, the mother to her daughter, 'We bore you, nourished you, brought you up, left you our fortunes, and you are so cruel and hard that now you are not willing for so little to set us free. Will you let us lie here in flames? Will you delay our promised glory?'
>
> Remember that you are able to release them, for
>
> As soon as the coin in the coffer rings

---
[1] John A. O'Brien, *The Reformation*, p. 22.

> The soul from purgatory springs.
>
> Will you not then for a quarter of a florin (or 12 cents, American currency) receive these letters of indulgence through which you are able to lead a divine and immortal soul into the fatherland of paradise?"[1]

Such was the kind of appeal made to the common people for contributions to the building of St. Peter's Cathedral. Dr. Roland Bainton says that so much money was going into the coffer of the vendor that new coins had to be minted on the spot. Perhaps you would like to ask Fr. O'Brien, Is that the essential teaching of the Church? And if that was the preaching of Fr. Tetzel, should it not be readily reproached?

Luther's Attacks

But while Fr. Tetzel preached that men, to gain salvation, should not only give contributions but also have contrite hearts and confess their sins, Albert of Brandenburg, in his printed instructions of indulgences, made it clear that those "securing indulgences on behalf of the dead already in purgatory need not themselves be contrite and confess their sins." Such pronouncements and doctrines were offensive to Luther's conscience and he revolted against them. Some selected passages from his 95 theses reveal how seriously Luther was concerned with the issue. He said:

> "Papal indulgences do not remove guilt... I claim the Pope has no jurisdiction over purgatory... If the Pope has power to release anyone from purgatory, why, in the name of love, does he not abolish purgatory by letting everyone out? If, for the sake of miserable money, he released uncounted souls, why should he not for the sake of the most holy love empty the place? To say that the souls are released as soon as the coin in the coffer rings is to incite avarice. The Pope would do better to give away everything without charge."[2]

In another section, Luther said something more devastating:

> "Indulgences are positively harmful to the recipient because they impede salvation by diverting charity and inducing a false sense of security... He who spends his money for indulgences instead of relieving want

---

[1] Quoted by Dr. Roland Bainton, *Here I Stand*, p. 78.
[2] *Ibid.* pp. 81f.

receives not the indulgence of the pope but the indignation of God...Indulgences are most pernicious because they induce complacency and thereby imperil salvation. Those persons are damned who think that letters of indulgence make them certain of salvation."[1]

Luther and the Roman Church

With these strong words which rang like roaring guns across Germany and all over Europe, we begin to understand Luther's unpopularity with the Holy See. It did not take long and he was exiled to Wartburg. And so today the Catholic Church speaks of him as a fallen angel and the son of iniquity. He was attacked by his mother Church on many points: on his alleged inconsistencies, on his insubordination, on his break with the Roman Church, and especially on his doctrine that salvation is a free gift from God and that we are saved by the grace of our faith in Jesus Christ. Faith in Jesus Christ is the only requisite for salvation and that, in Luther's own words, we are justified by faith. This doctrine is heretical to the mother Church because, according to Fr. Reginald Walker, the Church position is that faith and good works are necessary for salvation.[2] To the Catholic Church, faith should be supplemented by good works. To the Reformers, good work is only the product or the expression of faith. In fact, in this sense, faith without work is really dead. This is the position also of Calvin, Zwingly, John Knox, Melanchton, Wesley and a host of others.

Salvation in Biblical Thought

The point, however, is that this doctrine is not the mere invention of the Reformers. Rather, it is the very message of the New Testament. St. John, for instance, makes this abundantly clear in the Gospel that bears his name:

> "For God so loved the world that He gave His only begotten Son, that whosoever believeth in Him should not perish but have everlasting life." (3:16)

> "These things are written that ye might believe that Jesus is the Christ, and that believing ye might have life through his name." (20:31)

And this is also the testimony of the Apostle Paul:

---

[1] Quoted by Bainton, *Here I Stand*, pp. 81f.
[2] Walker, *op. cit.*, pp 75.

> "There is none other name under heaven given among men whereby we must be saved (except that of Jesus Christ)." (Acts 4:12)
>
> "Whosoever shall call upon the name of the Lord shall be saved." (Acts 2:21)
>
> "Therefore being justified by faith we have peace with God through our Lord Jesus Christ." (Rom. 5:1)

A Philippian jailer asked Paul and Silas: "What must I do to be saved?" And they answered: "Believe on the Lord Jesus Christ, and thou shalt be saved, and thy house" (Acts 16:25-31). And did not Jesus Himself say,

> "I am the resurrection and the life: he that believeth in me, though he were dead yet shall he live: and whosoever liveth and believeth in me shall never die."(John 11:25,26)
>
> "I am the way, the truth and the life." (John 14:6)

The Reformation and the New Testament

We see then that the message of the Reformers is the message of the New Testament — the sufficiency of Jesus Christ to save us from our sins. The aim of the Reformation is to proclaim the Lordship of Jesus Christ as the greatest Reformer of all history and the only Head of the Christian Church. Jesus Christ is the Reformer who denounces the self-righteousness of the scribes and the Pharisees, who fights against making the house of God a den of robbers. Christ is the Reformer who makes the sinful Samaritan woman into a happy, radiant person; the fascinating and good Teacher who makes the Sabbath for man and not man for the Sabbath; the tender Healer who makes the lame walk and gives sight to the blind; the powerful Preacher who proclaims the love of God even to the dying thief; the faithful and constant Friend who gives peace to a troubled breast; the only Saviour of the world before whom all knees shall bow.

And so if we are to recapture the spirit of the Reformation, we should allow God to mold our character, our habits and our life in the way He wants us to be. After all, this is what it means to be a Christian and to be justified by faith. May the peace of God find lodgment in our hearts and take away the stain of prejudice within us, so that we may always speak the truth in love, and love the truth which makes us free.

19

Christmas and the Cross

He came unto his own, and his own received him not.
— John 1:11

It is very seldom that Christmas is associated with the name of St. Francis of Assisi. But it was that stouthearted saint who introduced Christmas into the calendar of the church's festivals. During the first 13 centuries of the Christian era, the Church did not put much emphasis on the event of Jesus' birth. There were, of course, occasional celebrations of Christmas but its significance was lightly taken. But when Francis of Assisi visited the Holy Land, he caught a holy vision and somehow the sweet music of the Christmas story, long unsung though not forgotten, came to him like the voice of the angel that sang in heaven when Jesus was born. Tears of joy rolled down his cheeks while he recalled Jesus' birth in Bethlehem of Judea. Years later, the whole of Christendom was with the saintly man of Assisi in celebrating the birth of the Messiah, recalling the Saviour's humble birthplace, the lowly manger, the shepherds watching their flocks by night, the song of the heavenly hosts, the wise men's journey, and all the happenings attendant to the Incarnation. Never before did the Church discover such a gloriously rich meaning of Christmas. And so if we today rejoice at the coming of the Son of God, and solemnly thank God for the unfolding of His divine salvation, it is because seven centuries ago, a man of God saw the beauty of the Christmas spirit and shared it with the rest of mankind.

The problem, however, which we have to face is that while Christmas has become an institution in our Christian life, we are not quite sure whether it has any redemptive influence upon us. Indeed, if we may say it bluntly, Christmas in our country has become so secularized that during the Christmas season, we think more of mundane things than of the bigger needs of our spirit. Such materialistic tendencies often obscure the message of the Incarnation and reduce Christmas into an occasion for selfish revelries.

Christmas Wishes

You perhaps would recall that sometime ago, the *Daily Mirror* carried an article on three wishes for Christmas. Most of the people mentioned were Filipino actors and actresses, some politicians and newspapermen. Eddie Garcia, for instance, would ask first that he become a successful bullfighter so that he could win Ava Gardner; second, he wished to have an island paradise where he could spend his honeymoon with Ava Gardner; third, that he be endowed with a good singing voice so he could lull Ava Gardner to sleep. Tony Marzan's three wishes were: for the night to be longer and darker, for the women to be prettier, and for the wine to be more plentiful. Daisy Romualdez' three wishes: Rock Hudson, Rock Hudson, Rock Hudson. Priscilla Valdez would like to have a salary raise, more pictures and that her boyfriend would not stray away from her. Dominador Castillo, a lawyer, had just one ambition: to be a successful politician. He said, "I don't care if my two other wishes would not materialize. I only hope to capture the mayoralty of a Laguna town."

It is not for us to pass judgment on the statements of these people, yet we cannot help but feel disappointed that they somehow represent a great number of our countrymen who, during the Christmas season, think more of salary raise and Ava Gardner and Rock Hudson than of our Lord and Saviour Jesus Christ. It is imperative that we remind ourselves that Christmas is not a glorified time for personal aggrandizement or an occasion for magical fulfillment of our childish dream. If we are to capture the real spirit of this season, we should not eliminate Christ from Christmas. To do so would only expose the depravity of our human nature.

Christmas and the Cross

A review of the record of Jesus' birth would help us see that if Christmas is the birth of the world's Redeemer, then it should be understood in the light of the Cross. Let us note first of all that the world into which Jesus came was plagued by a dismaying medley of social evils and interracial tensions. Fear, for instance, was a haunting terror in the minds of the Israelites who knew not what the future had for them. For years and years, they had not known the joy of national independence. They had been the sorry victims of foreign domination and their destiny was in the hands of the enemies. The opening words of the angel that appeared to the shepherds in the field were meant not only for them but also for their fear-stricken fellow men who were at the mercy of the Roman conquerors.

"Fear not," the angel said, "for unto you is born this day a Saviour, which is Christ the Lord."

Hate was also a fomenting storm raging in the human hearts. Herod typified those whose suspicions and jealousies were eating up their life. It was consuming selfishness and burning hate which led him to issue a decree to kill all children two years old down to be sure that the newborn king would not rival with him for the throne.

James S. Stewart, in his *The Life and Teaching of Jesus Christ*,[1] takes note of the fact that the world into which Jesus came was also morally sinking. "The depravity of the human spirit was literally shocking. Youth was so wasted that only grief could represent it. Womanhood was so defamed and desecrated that the Apostle Paul, in his letter to the Corinthians, admonished the Christian women to keep silence in the church."

Furthermore, the religious life was not deep enough. The Jews kept their religion as a matter of convention. The Pharisees and the Sadducees, the scribes and Zealots and the rest of the religious hierarchy were dry ecclesiastics, and not saints on fire with God. In spite of the Jewish faith in the one and holy God, the Graeco-Roman world was a pagan world. Idolatry was rampant and polytheism was popular.

Politically, the ancient world was rotten. Not that graft and corruption was the issue of the day – though certainly the tax collectors were unpopular for their filthy business. Graft and corruption, to be sure, was a real problem, and yet in the government of the Roman conquerors, it was a minor evil. Indeed, those who disobeyed the law were severely punished. Nevertheless, the Roman governors scattered throughout the empire were drunk with power. The Roman emperors were deified. Dictatorship consecrated tyranny. The pursuit of life, liberty and happiness was a mirage, and the promise of independence was a political comedy.

Economically, the world into which Jesus came was in a mess. While luxury and sinful extravagance flourished in the royal palaces, poverty walked in rags and restlessness filled the air. Misery was in every nook and corner of the land. Of the 400,000 citizens in Athens a few years before Christ came, 250,000 were slaves, mere commodities at the disposal of their masters. Starvation was hovering in the sky, and anxiety was written deeply on the face of everyone.

That was the world into which Jesus came. It was a world in the

---

[1] James Stewart, *The Life and Teachings of Jesus Christ*, pp. 18-25.

brink of death and in need of God's redeeming grace. And it cost the life of the Son of God to impart such redeeming grace. The price for the world's salvation was the long procession from Bethlehem of Judea to the Hill of Calvary.

This is why the Christian faith holds that Christmas should be understood in the light of the Cross. The birth of Christ is an event that is not separate from the events of His death and resurrection. The message of Christmas, Holy Friday and Easter is essentially evangelistic, and anything less than that is a perversion of the Gospel. The Old Testament messianic prophecy was fulfilled not only in the Cradle but also on the Cross. The Holy Child of Bethlehem is also the Crucified and Risen Lord.

The World Has Not Changed Much

The thing that we would like to note is that the world into which Jesus came has not really changed so much. Fear is still mankind's great enemy. Fear of old age, fear of war, fear of sickness, fear of death, fear of failure, fear of the reign of terror – all kinds of fear are invariably known to us.

Hate has now acquired greater dimensions of destructibility. It can inspire the dirtiest political vendetta and pave the way for global annihilation. It can commit physical murders and moral murders as well. Satan has doubled his efforts to plant the seed of hate in human hearts.

Morally, our world is no better than the world into which Jesus came. For sure, we have these days more motels for immoral business and more telephones through which some people sell sex.

Our religious life cannot be said to be any better. For while the Jews at the age of seven knew by heart the basic teachings of the Old Testament and the Temple rules, the average Christian today does not know his Bible and the fundamental teachings of the Christian faith.

Politically, our world needs to be redeemed. In our country, political redemption is not necessarily the defection from the NP to the LP. As long as our leaders are drunk with power and are determined to do anything to get what they want, even the best political system will fail.

Economically, our world is in a sorry mess. Two-thirds of all mankind are daily beset by the pangs of hunger and disease. There is a need to translate into economic terms the abundant life which the Gospel is speaking of.

Now we may say that this is not a time for sentimentalism, nor is this an occasion even for a passing survey of our national and individual shortcomings. Why think of the gloomy side of life when the hour calls for rejoicing and singing and merrymaking? The fact, however, is that Christmas does not allow us to forget the malignancy of the human situation. We cannot help but be reminded of our moral blindness, of graft and corruption in the high places, of juvenile delinquency.

Indeed, it is only when we realize our helplessness and apostasy that Christmas becomes a redemptive experience. And, by the very nature of things, Christmas reminds us of the sinfulness of man. It is because of our sins that the Father sent the Son. The dark presupposition of the Incarnation is the sinfulness of man.

The Transcendent Power of God's Love

Our consolation, however, is that while Christmas necessarily reminds us of our care-ridden life, its dominant note is the love of God which takes away the sins of the world. There is in the spirit of Christmas something which enables us to transcend selfishness and bitterness and failure. It is something akin to the magnanimity of the Galilean who prayed, "Father, forgive them for they know not what they do," even while He was being subjected to the most brutal form of human punishment.

And so, if we today speak of moral degeneration among leaders and followers, of social evils and personal sins, it is with the conviction that Christ has the power to overcome them and to cleanse us from all unrighteousness. The Incarnation is a divine assurance that no one is beyond redemption if he looks to God with faith.

The redemptiveness of the Christmas spirit was dramatized in the hallowed experience of the shepherds as they went back to the field. They were still shepherds after visiting the Holy Child, but there was something in their hearts that made them different. The Scriptures say they returned to the field "glorifying and praising God for all the things that they had heard and seen." That was the difference. They went back to their work with a sense of God's nearness. Tending the sheep was no longer a mere means of making a living, but a dignified occupation where God's presence could be real.

A Sense of God's Nearness

It is very likely that after the Christmas season is over, we will still be in the same occupations as we are now — teachers, businessmen, employees, students, lawyers, etc. But there should be a difference: the sense of God's presence in our work. The angel said that the newborn Child shall be called Emmanuel which is *God with us*. That means that the influence of Jesus' birth is intended to be permanent and, therefore, the keeping of Christmas is the experience of God being with us and we being with Him. It is unfortunate if God is real to us only on Sundays or only when we are in church. For the reality of God is too great to be confined only within the narrow walls of the sanctuary. Like the shepherds of old, we need to experience the abiding presence of God in our places of work, in the fields and in the factory, in our homes and in our offices, in all walks of life. Unless we feel God's nearness in our work, then we may well suspect that our Christmas celebration is but a dry ceremonialism.

Let us then resolve to make this season a period for solemn self-retrospection. God has intended it to be that way. It is a time for an honest reappraisal of life and how we have been getting along. It may be that there is some corner in our soul, some aspect in our business, some place in our heart where Jesus Christ should be born. We would do well to remember that unless Jesus is born in us, we cannot be born again. What a pity if we do not avail ourselves of such glorious experience. It would be to repeat the tragedy of Herod who did not know the joy of the Christmas spirit. But if in humble faith we commit ourselves to the love of the Holy Child, we can be sure that though the going is rough and hard, we will hear music in the air and see some star to follow in the night. Certainly, there can be nothing more wonderful in this time and age, when the world is sinking fast in sin, than to see men and women who would rise up in the name of Christ, to take the armour of righteousness and the sword of love and the shield of faith, and march unto the highway of life with unfaltering steps to conquer in His name and to snatch the world from the clutches of death and put it under the dominion of God. For that would mean the resurgence of a revolution for the cause of Christian brotherhood. And to have a part in that great cause is to rediscover the joy which the shepherds had when Jesus Christ was born. It is the joy which can carry us through every steep and rocky hill; it is the joy of Christian discipleship. May we know something of that joy this Christmas, because it is a foretaste of the life in the Kingdom of God. Once that is the case, this season may soon be buried in the past, but Christmas it shall always be for us.

20

Christmas and Protestantism[*]

And suddenly there was with the angel a multitude of the heavenly host praising God, and saying, Glory to God in the highest, and on earth peace, good will toward men.
— Luke 2:13-14

I would like us to consider this morning the great parallelisms between Christmas and Protestantism. This, I believe, would give us a good review of the basic tenets of the Evangelical Faith and how they are related to the spirit of the Christmas season. This is an attempt to show that the real spirit of Protestantism is what we know to be the spirit of Christmas, and that, therefore, for people who embrace the Evangelical Faith, everyday is Christmas day.

Rejoicing of the Heavenly Host

The first thing we would be interested to note is that when Jesus Christ was born, there was great rejoicing among the angels in heaven. The Evangelist Luke tells us that while the shepherds were keeping watch over their flock by night, "the angel of the Lord came upon them, and the glory of the Lord shone round about them: Fear not: for, behold, I bring you good tidings of great joy, which shall be to all people. For unto you is born this day in the city of David a Saviour, which is Christ the Lord. And this shall be a sign unto you: Ye shall find the babe wrapped in swaddling clothes, lying in a manger. And suddenly there was with the angel a multitude of the heavenly host praising God, and saying, Glory to God in the highest, and on earth peace, good will toward men." (Luke 2:8-14).

We should underscore the last verse in this passage: "And suddenly there was with the angel a multitude of the heavenly host praising God, and saying, Glory to God in the highest, and on earth peace, good will toward men." To praise God is not necessarily to sing, and yet the great

---
[*] Delivered on December 23, 1962.

interpreters of this verse always think of these angels as a big heavenly choir singing, "Gloria in Excelsis." In the book *Raphael, the Herald Angel*, for instance, the authors depict the heavenly host as a group of singers and musicians always rehearsing before Jesus was born and did an excellent performance at the birth of the Messiah. The book, of course, is a fiction, but it is an evidence of the fact that our deepest joy for God's goodness is best expressed in songs and music. Therefore, it is not whimsical to imagine that the rejoicing among the heavenly host at Jesus' birth was coupled with melodious singing which only the angels of God can do. Indeed, we are constrained to say that Christmas can be a very drab affair without any Christmas music. For it is the Christmas songs and anthems and hymns which fill the atmosphere with joy and help create the spirit of Christmas that should characterize this season of the year. A truly merry Christmas is not without a song.

A Singing Faith

The Protestant Faith, on the other hand, is a singing faith. It is a faith that is known, among other things, for its hymns and gospel songs and anthems. A Protestant service is a dry service without any music. Music has become an indispensable means of worship. It is generally observed that a Protestant is one who possesses not only a Bible but also a hymnal. His worship consists of meditating on the Word of God and singing the wonderful words of Life.

Admittedly, Protestant denominations differ on tastes for church music to be used during worship and on the use of musical instruments. There are some who would not allow the use of any musical instrument, not even a Hammond organ. Others would use almost all kinds of instruments, including the bass drum, the *tumpiang* and the guitar. Again, some prefer the jazzy gospel songs for worship, while others use only hymn tunes which are conventionally formal and distinctively religious. But all do make use of music and hymns and anthems.

Indeed, we may say with pardonable pride that one of the greatest contributions of Protestantism to making Christmas a season of music is the tremendous number of Christmas hymns which Christians and non-Christians have loved to sing during this season. Except for "Silent Night" and "O Come, All Ye Faithful" and a few other hymns which were written by Roman Catholics, almost all the rest of the Christmas hymns we sing these days are a contribution from the musical talent of Protestantism.

"Silent Night" was written by Fr. Joseph Mohr, assistant Pastor of St. Nicholas' Church in Oberndorf. "O Come, All Ye Faithful" was written in 1744 by John Francis Wade, a man whose business was to copy music for Catholic institutions and families.

But the other popular Christmas hymns were authored by Protestants. Charles Wesley, for instance, one of the pioneers of Methodism, wrote that immortal hymn, "Hark the Herald Angels Sing." Martin Luther, the sparkplug of the Reformation in Germany, wrote: "Away in a Manger," "Ah, Dearest Jesus, Holy Child," and "All Praise to Thee Eternal Lord." The Rev. Isaac Watts, one of the most brilliant ministers Congregationalism has ever produced, wrote "Joy to the World, the Lord is Come," which is based on Psalm 98. The Rev. Edmund Hamilton Sears, a Unitarian, contributed "It Came Upon the Midnight Clear." John Browning, another Unitarian, authored "Watchman, Tell Us of the Night."

Among the Anglican divines, we can mention the Rev. John M. Neale, the prince of all hymn translators, who popularized "Good Christian Men, Rejoice" and "O Come, O Come, Emmanuel." Bishop Phillips Brooks, an American Episcopalian born in Boston, wrote the famous hymn "O Little Town of Bethlehem." These are the hymns brought into our living rooms during the Christmas season not only by the carolers, but also thru radio and television. They are hymns that come mostly from the musical treasury of the Protestant faith. They are hymns that make Christmas alive and joyous and happy.

Now, after having said this, let me remark that it is good we sing these hymns without thinking much about who the authors were. For if music is to fulfill its mission, it need not be the exclusive property of the writer's denomination. Perhaps it is in the singing of Christmas hymns where our churches can be more ecumenical in spirit. I would like to believe that when Protestant churches use "O Come, All Ye Faithful" as a processional hymn, we are not prejudiced by the thought that it was written by a Catholic priest. In like manner, we may be sure that when our friends sing "Hark! The Herald Angels Sing," they do not care whether it was a Protestant Reformer who wrote it. This is a type of ecumenicity which we should encourage. It truly transcends the barriers of denominationalism. It liberates us from the shackles of sectarianism and gives us the joy of seeing ourselves as one in the worship of the Holy Child.

Emphasis on Christ

Another major parallelism between Christmas and the Protestant faith is their common emphasis on Jesus Christ as Lord and Saviour. Indeed, this is the reason why most Christmas hymns have gained ecumenical acceptance. While Christians cannot be together in singing "Ave Maria," we can be together in singing songs that enthrone Jesus Christ as God's Messiah and the World's Redeemer. And they are the songs of Christmas.

The message of Protestantism is, like Christmas, Christocentric. The Protestant faith is not primarily a rebellion against Rome; it is a positive witness to the love of God in Jesus Christ. When Martin Luther defended the biblical doctrine of justification by faith, he meant faith in God thru Jesus Christ. "For there is none other name under heaven given among men, whereby we must be saved." (Acts. 4:12). Jesus Christ is the center of the Protestant faith. As a matter of fact, the Evangelical faith cannot be understood apart from its Christology. Schleiermacher is to be commended for his courage in defining Christianity as "a monotheistic religion of a teleological kind in which everything is related to Christ, the Redeemer." It is significant to note that the theme of the World Council of Churches in the past year was "Jesus Christ: the Light of the World," and for the present, "The Finality of Jesus Christ in an Age of Universal History."

The Immanence of God

Another Christmas message which is corollary to the one we just mentioned is the indwelling presence of God with us. **Emmanuel**, the Gospel tells us, means God with us. The Incarnation, we see, is the great drama of God becoming flesh in Jesus Christ. While God remains transcendent, He, at the Incarnation, also becomes immanent. Christmas is the divine assurance that God is not too far away, that He is not beyond the reach of a longing heart, that He is not unconcerned about what's going on on earth. When the Word became flesh and dwelt among us, it was God who came into our midst in all His glory. Christmas is the story of God's search for man rather than of man's search for God. We find Him only because He first found us.

And is this not also the message of Protestantism? Are not our evangelistic enterprises propelled by the conviction that God seeks to meet us in our sinful conditions so that we may experience the power of His forgiving love? Protestantism is a faith in the One and Holy God whose presence can be felt in all walks of life. If it is a rebellion at all, it is a rebellion against confining God within the walls of the sanctuary, against compartmentalizing life into the religious and secular, against making religion into a Sunday affair. Protestantism is for the experience of God's presence with us in the shops and factories, in the homes and offices, in all places of work. It is, indeed, for the sanctification of all of life with a sense of God's abiding nearness.

It is this faith in the indwelling presence of God which makes the secular vocations a vital area of Christian witness. It is this faith which tears down the wall separating the clergy from the laity. Thru the eye of this faith, we see ourselves as a company of God's people called to serve Him in the different capacities we have and in the different strategic places we find ourselves to be .

The Paradox of Jesus' Birth

A review of the gospel records will enable us to see that the event of the Incarnation is shrouded by paradoxes which humble our expectations. St. Luke, for instance, tells us that the child was born to be the Saviour of the world, that He was wrapped in swaddling clothes and lying in a manger. Pick out those key words: child... Saviour ... wrapped in swaddling clothes ... lying in a manger — and we get a picture that arrests one's curiosity. How can a child be the Saviour? Is the manger the place where one can find the Saviour? Is the Son of the Most High to be found in a stable? He was a king, but born in an animals' cave. He was not born in a royal palace. And His first visitors were humble shepherds. He was prophesied to become great and would liberate the people from the bondage of sin, and yet the religious dignitaries of Israel were fast asleep when He was born. He grew up in Nazareth, a small town from which people thought nothing good could come out. He called Himself the Son of God, but people derogatively called Him the son of a carpenter. We believe Him to be a Good Teacher, yet His band of followers were uneducated fishermen.

And what about Mary, the mother of Jesus? She was warned that her child was conceived by the Holy Spirit, that He would be Lord of lords and King of kings. Did she not, therefore, expect God to give her a decent place to deliver her child? How come now in Bethlehem there was no room for them?

Certainly, the story of Christmas is a sublime paradox. But is not our Christian faith also paradoxical? Did not the Apostle Paul say "the foolishness of God" is "wiser than men?" (I Cor. 1:20f.). Is it not paradoxical that we believe Jesus Christ to be God and also man? Surely Jesus Christ Himself is the supreme paradox. Soren Kierkegaard, emphasizing this paradoxical nature of the Christian faith, said, "It is the duty of the human understanding to understand that there are things which it cannot understand, and what those things are. Human understanding has vulgarly occupied itself with nothing but understanding, but if it would only take the trouble to understand itself at the same time, it would simply have to posit the paradox."[1] The best of human reason is limited not only by the formal character of its logic but also by sin, and the answer to such dilemma is the assurance that God loves us even while we are sinners.

The Blending of the Spiritual and the Material

Finally, let us be reminded that Christmas is the great drama of that perfect blending of the spiritual and the material. The Bible holds that God is a spirit, and yet this God became fully known to us in the person of Jesus Christ. And to believe that Jesus is both human and divine is to confirm that in the eternal wisdom of God, the spiritual and the material are intended to be blended. We do not live by bread alone, neither can we live by prayers alone. We need both bread and the Bread of Life, even Jesus Christ our Lord. Christmas is a reminder that in our longings for better living and better homes and bigger salaries, we should not forget that our deepest needs are spiritual.

The Evangelical faith stands for the conviction that our bodies are the temple of God, that the body and spirit are a unity and not a duality, that true piety can be experienced in the fields and in the factories as well as in the church and in the monasteries. Protestantism holds that poverty is not necessarily a virtue, though it can be turned into the soul's account; and that wealth is not necessarily evil. The materialistic tendencies of our generation often obscure the message of the Incarnation and reduce the Christmas season into a period for selfish revelries. But if we are to capture the spirit of this day, we should put Christ back to our Christmas celebration. We insult our God and we insult ourselves by being totally forgetful of our spiritual needs even as we celebrate the birth of Him who came that we may have life. If it is tragic to see men and women pining away day by

---

[1] Journals, Dru, 623, quoted by Hopper, *Handbook of Christian Theology*, p. 262.

day and morbidly obsessed with the thought of economic survival, it is more tragic to see those who can afford to enjoy sumptuous Christmas dinners without pausing to acknowledge that God is the Giver of all good and perfect gifts.

And so if we, Evangelical Christians, are to salvage Christmas from being further secularized and desecrated, the fire of pure faith should be rekindled in our hearts. We have to see for ourselves that the message of Christmas and that of our Faith are completely identical because they center around the same Lord and Saviour and emanate from the witness of the same Gospel. The world has the right to expect of us to keep Christmas everyday because the profession of our Faith is not a seasonal affair nor is it only a Sunday morning exercise. We may rest assured that once we revive our sense of militant discipleship, ours will be not only a deepened appreciation of our Evangelical faith but also the key to a fruitful and rich experience of the Christmas season.

PRAYER: Almighty God, who at sundry times and in diverse manners spake in time past unto the fathers by the prophets but now speakest to us thru Thy Son, we thank Thee for the knowledge that Thou art in Christ reconciling the world unto Thyself. May we, at this time of the year, behold the wonders of Thy love, and in Thy love live and move and have our being. In Jesus' name. Amen.

21

Christ's Royal Entry

And the multitudes that went before, and that followed, cried, saying, Hosanna to the Son of David: Blessed is he that cometh in the name of the Lord; Hosanna in the highest.

— Matthew 21:9

On Palm Sunday, the whole Christendom looks back to that event in the life of Jesus Christ when He, together with His 12 disciples, entered the city of Jerusalem, riding upon a lowly ass, the symbol of meekness. He was greeted by the people with great enthusiasm. They laid their garments on the road and gathered palm branches and accorded Him a royal welcome given only to kings and conquerors. Today, we rightly call that dramatic entrance the triumphal entry for, indeed, it was the entry of the royal King whose kingship is to last forever. And although that entry sparked the fire of mad hostility against the Son of God, and indeed led Him to Calvary, yet it was truly triumphant as it disclosed the sovereignty of God over history and human freedom.

And is it not a miracle that the divided churches on all parts of the globe are today one in commemorating the triumphal entry? Ours should be a sense of oneness with the Christians the world over as we look back to that day when Jesus rode on to give His life a ransom for many. And we can hope that if we keep our eyes on Christ, we will ultimately be drawn together and thus fulfill the wish of Him who prayed "that they may be one."

Jesus and Politics

Dr. Harold Cooke Phillips, one of the greatest Baptist preachers in the United States, in his book, *The Timeless Gospel,* has a sermon entitled "When Jesus Entered Politics." Interestingly, it is a sermon on Jesus' triumphal entry. The author suggests that though the phrase "to enter politics" has a connotation which does not apply to Jesus in the generally accepted meaning of the words, nevertheless the charges against Jesus before the Roman tribunal were certainly political in nature. He was charged with being a political revolutionary: "He stirs up the people" say the accusers in Luke 23.5. He was charged with being disloyal to the Emperor: "We found this man perverting our nation, and forbidding us to give tribute to Caesar, and saying that he himself is Christ a king" (Lk. 23:2). And then the threat to Pilate was politically inspired: "If you release this man, you are not Caesar's friend... We have no king but Caesar" (Jn. 19:12,15). In other words, Jesus was crucified because He was allegedly an enemy of the state. The accusation, of course, was false, but the point is that it had some political implications.

Jesus' Friend in Jerusalem

And really, if we recall how our politicians conduct their campaign these days, we realize that Jesus' entry into Jerusalem could be a very good opportunity for politicking. He was popular. The trip was well-planned. Halford E. Luccock, in his exposition of St. Mark's Gospel in the *Interpreter's Bible*, observes that Jesus had an "underground" working in Jerusalem. He believes that the ass used by Jesus in entering Jerusalem was given by friends and adherents who knew about His coming to the city. He was hailed by men and women and children as a great political figure. The people whose religious faith was identical with their political aspirations looked up to Him as one who could deliver them from the bondage of Roman imperialism. In our country, if anyone is popular and is looked up to by the people as capable enough to save the nation from poverty and unemployment, he is sure to go to the House of Representative or to the Senate.

The Crowds in Jerusalem

Now, in the case of Jesus, what did He find in Jerusalem? Dr. Phillips submits that there were at least three distinct groups: first, "there were the people, or the Passover pilgrims who were looking for someone to take a sword and lead a revolt against Rome."[1] For sure they were tired of being slaves in their own country and their supreme desire was the independence of Israel. On the other hand, there were the Roman officials, Pilate and Herod and the rest who could not allow any Jewish nationalism to come to the surface. It was enough that they give the Jews considerable liberty in

---
[1] Phillips, *The Timeless Gospel*, p. 145.

their religious practice, but it was anathema to the Romans for any Jew to challenge Caesar's authority. In short, a political Messiah was a hero to the people, but a bitter enemy to the Romans. But in between these two groups, says Dr. Phillips, were people like the Sadducees who, while professing to be loyal Jews, yet were collaborating with Rome because of the constant favors they received from her.

The Big Question

The question therefore is: With whom should Jesus side? With the people? Well, they had the votes. If there would be a democratic election, surely He would have the majority. But no, Jesus did not side with them. Should He, then, cast his lot with the Romans? Well, they had power and prestige. They were the ruling class. But, as we know, Jesus did not side with them. Then with the party in between? It would seem safe to stand on both sides of the fence. He could be one of the Sadducees playing cards left and right. No, not that group, we know. Jesus took no sides. Phillips said Jesus entered politics on God's side, "in the name of the Lord." That was the theme of the song of the Palm Sunday pilgrims: "Blessed be he who comes in the name of the Lord." Jesus was guided not by the claims of men but by the claims of truth. Jesus would not take the people's party and at the same time give them what they wanted. He would not be a puppet ruler. Of course, the Roman power was finally broken by Christ, but not in the way the people wanted. And Jesus would not take the side of Rome. He was quite vocal in his opposition to the selfish use of power. He taught the people that the greatest of them shall be the servant of all. And surely, Jesus would not take a stand with the Sadducees, the dishonest men who converted His Father's house into a den of robbers. Therefore, Jesus would not come in the name of anyone of them. He came in the name of the Lord and therefore His coming was to bear witness to the truth.

The application of this principle, revealed by Jesus on the first Palm Sunday, is a much needed virtue in our present-day political life. This would mean that the individual politician should put the best interests of his community above his own selfish interests. This would mean that the interests of the country should transcend those of the party. And this would mean, ultimately, the redemption of politics itself.

Let us hope that most politicians are in their churches today. And let us pray that the Holy Spirit may guide them to see that He who rode upon a lowly ass and whose entry into Jerusalem we now celebrate is, to all eternity, a model Politician whose loyalty to the cause of truth transcends earthly ambitions for popularity and power and privilege. May they realize that politics, when entered into with a sense of mission, can be a vital area of Christian witness and need not be reduced into a sorry mess that it is now in. We can be sure that if Jesus were to enter this city of ours today, as indeed He is in our city to judge or to bless, He would take a look at the Congress of the Philippines and the City Hall and Malacañang Palace and see if the occupants of those places, upon whose hands is committed the government of the people, are faithful in their sacred tasks of guarding the best interests of the country.

And this is why we believe Jesus entered Jerusalem. He could have gone to Capernaum or to Nazareth. But while what happened in those places were important, nevertheless what happened in Jerusalem was decisive. Jerusalem was the center not only of religious activities but also of political life. It was the political center of the nation's hope. And His entrance into that city symbolized the fact that God's domain should not be limited to the periphery but should also extend to the citadel. Of course, the first Palm Sunday was not the only occasion on which Jesus made clear the social implications of His teachings. But the royal entry dramatized, in concrete fashion, that which is always implicit in His preaching: God's claim is on the whole man. It is also on the whole nation and the whole world. The rule of God demands not only the sanctification of the church but also the redemption of the state. "The redemptive work of God is for all of life, including Jerusalem."[1] Christianity should face not only the religious problems of man, but also the social, the economic and the political.

The Cleansing of the Temple

Now, after saying that Jesus' triumphal entry has a direct message on the stewardship of politics and the conduct of public servants, let us emphasize that the event on that first Palm Sunday cannot be understood apart from the cleansing of the temple. Students of the Bible believe that this was what Jesus did first the following day. While His entry into Jerusalem was a proclamation of the kind of politician He was, He did not go to the city hall the following day, or to the Bureau of Customs or Internal Revenue. Rather, He went to the Temple. And seeing the people more intent in making money the Saducean way than in worshipping God, He

---
[1] Phillips, *op. cit.*, p. 148.

turned the tables upside down and drove them out of the Temple premises. So Jesus entered the Temple for it was there where spiritual cleansing should begin if His spiritual conquest was to affect the whole community. Jesus knew that if the people's business and political affairs were far from being manifestations of their faith in God, then there must be something wrong at the center of their religious activities. There must be something defective in their religious education. He who knew that religion is a way of life and not simply the observance of decent customs and ceremonies, had the right to plead with men to make the house of God what it ought to be and, therefore, live by what they believe in, everyday of their life.

Applying this in our situation, we see that the church is, in the Providence of God, meant to be the chief moral and spiritual guardian of the community. It should strive not to make its laws the laws of the state as that would mean a church-controlled state and will not work in a religiously pluralistic society; but should rather aim at cultivating the moral character of the citizens, nurturing them in the love of God and teaching them to do justly and to love mercy and to walk humbly with their God. The church fulfills its mission by being the conscience of the state, by faithfully reminding the people of God's holy expectations in their various secular engagements. The church is charged with the task of instructing its members on the bearing of the Christian faith on questions of practical conduct, of making the life of the people a living witness to the power of the Gospel.

This being the case, therefore, the quality of life of the citizens reflects the kind of church they belong to. For the moral and spiritual level of the church cannot rise higher than that of its members. This is so because the church is the people and not the few erring ecclesiastical leaders set aside by ordination. The degree of the church's faithfulness to its calling is to be gauged in the way its members conduct themselves outside the four walls of the sanctuary.

The Royal Christ

Therefore, the regnant Christ, who comes to see how we go about with our business and looks at our every movement in the *sari-sari store*, in the classroom, in courts, in offices, in shops, in the farms and in the factories, will most certainly subject the church to serious questioning to find out how far we have been faithful in the exercise of our discipleship. This is why in this fellowship, and in all other Christian fellowships that seek to please the Lord, we are careful not to isolate the profession of the

Christian faith to the congregational worship service on Sunday morning alone. Here we are reminded that the true heroes of faith are not those who piously join in the service of worship but those whose loyalty to God directs their ways with men and whose presence in the sanctuary is solely a response to the leading of the Spirit. Here we are reminded that our beautiful affirmation of faith in the sufficiency of Christ are not of any value unless they are demonstrated in the daily course of life. Here we are reminded that the vital witness of the church is not so much in the elaborate programs of activities as it is in what we say and do in the many places we happen to live and work.

Let us today rededicate ourselves to the Lordship of Christ the King by giving Him a royal welcome to our hearts and homes. And if we welcome Him to stay with us forever, He will someday welcome us into His own.

22

Christ and Pilatism

Pilate saith unto them, What shall I do then with Jesus which is called Christ? They all say unto him, Let him be crucified. — Matthew 27:22

The Scripture passage indicated above is only a part of the tragic story which culminated "on a hill far away." In this passage, we have the trial of Jesus before Pontius Pilate, the name which throughout the centuries has been sadly associated with everything vain and weak and cowardly. It was a mock trial, we know, because the Prisoner was already prejudged and because the Roman tribunal was only made an instrument of judicial murder.

The Inescapable Jesus

So we have this picture, in our mind, of Jesus being tried by the Roman Procurator. Here, I believe, we have the symbol of the fact that paganism, as typified by Pilate, will also have to face the inescapable Christ. Pilate, we can be sure, was least interested in the religious issues of the Jewish people. He did not care about their messianic expectation. He was in Judea primarily to keep order especially during the celebration of the Jewish paschal festival when many people from all over Palestine would gather in Jerusalem for the affair. It was not a mere accident in history that Pilate was there and, as the Roman tribunal reserved the right of final judgment on cases involving death penalty, he had to try the case of Jesus. The gospel account of this mock trial suggests quite clearly that Pilate wanted to evade the responsibility of being involved in the issue. His wife, we remember, sent him a message asking him not to have anything to do with the righteous Man, the Prisoner. But the governor could not be neutral on the matter. He had to face the inescapable Christ.

So is every living creature on the surface of the earth. Jesus Himself said that "the gospel of the kingdom shall be preached throughout the whole world as a testimony to the nations." The Apostle Paul, in his letter to the Romans, reminds us that "everyone of us shall give account of himself to God" (14:12). We leave it to the wisdom of God as to how those who have not heard of the good news should ultimately be confronted with the demands of the Gospel. But we can rest assured that in God's own time His will shall be brought to pass. Jesus Christ is simply inescapable.

Pilate and Christ

When Pilate said, "What shall I do with Jesus?" he asked the question of every man. It is the "crux of life and death." Business and businessmen will have to ask the same question. The tragedy on Calvary was partly the answer of the business tycoons in Jerusalem. They perhaps detested Jesus' interference with the business management in the city temple where He turned tables upside down and reprimanded the people for making the house of God a den of robbers. They must have heard about Jesus' demand on a tax collector to return to the people whatever was taken from them feloniously. They must have heard about His teaching on honesty as a virtue to be sedulously cultivated. And now this religious Leader who claimed to be a Teacher of righteousness was going about the market places and the business sections of the Temple pleading with them, in the name of God, to make their religion real in daily life.

Businessmen and Christ

Business and businessmen must ask, "What shall I do with Jesus?" Politics and politicians, too, will have to ask the question. We cannot help but note that in the past few years there has been a revival of interest in what Christianity has to say about politics. Indeed the problem is that some churches overdo this by constituting themselves into a political power and interfering too much in the internal affairs of the government. Rightly or wrongly they are led to do this in the conviction or under the pretext that the Christian faith, which is oftentimes interpreted in a narrow sectarian spirit, should be expressed in the management of their temporal affairs.

The church and the Christians will have to ask the question. And it is to us that the question is most acute. For if our Christianity means anything at all, it should constantly pose before us the question of Christ's presence and what to do in His sight. To anyone, therefore, who has had a taste of Christian discipleship, Christ is most certainly inescapable.

Pilate Before Christ

Now let us see how Pilate conducted himself in the presence of the unavoidable Christ. His first question, dictated perhaps by the Roman instinct of respect for justice, was "What accusation do you bring against this man?" (John 18:29). And when they could not give any definite answer, Pilate talked with Jesus privately. We do not know what happened exactly during that closed door meeting. But the record tells us that Pilate found no fault in Christ. According to Luke, Pilate said so twice. According to John, Pilate declared it three times. Indeed, his declaration has become a confession of the Christian church about the sinlessness of Christ. St. Paul, in his letter to the Corinthians, describes Jesus as One who knew no sin (II Cor. 5:21). The author of Hebrews speaks of Christ as One like us, tempted in all points, "yet without sin." The Roman governor was convinced that his Prisoner was innocent. Furthermore, he knew that the case was far from being a legal one. We read from Matthew that Pilate knew that for envy the people delivered Christ to him.

Should we not, therefore, expect the governor, as an agent of the law, to do what he knew was right? Was it not his duty to dispense justice? As a representative of Tiberius, the emperor, he should neither condone treason nor punish the innocent. We can be sure that he had wanted to acquit the Prisoner, but was not Jesus after all just a simple Carpenter from Nazareth, a religious Teacher whose followers were only humble fishermen? The crowd, on the other hand, was led by the chief priests and rulers of people. They were perhaps the cream of Jerusalem. Annas was there and Caiaphas was there. Businessmen and intellectual leaders and socialites were there – all clamouring for the blood of the innocent Man whose only hope was in the justice of Rome. How, then, could the governor protect the Prisoner and at the same time please the crowd?

Three Expedients

So in his efforts to evade responsibility, he tried three expedients. First, he sent the Prisoner to Herod, who was then taking a vacation in Jerusalem. Anyway, Jesus was a Galilean, and it was but proper that the case be referred to the governor of Galilee. Such courtesy did no more than heal the enmity between the two Roman officials who were not in speaking terms. But it did not work. After Herod's share in the mocking of the Christ, the Prisoner was sent back to Pilate. The second expedient which Pilate tried, so Luke tells us (23:16), was to scourge Jesus and then release Him. Maybe Pilate was hoping that savage punishment, given only to die-hard criminals and disobedient slaves, would cause the people to take pity on Jesus and finally let Him go. But it did not work. Pilate then proposed that since it was the custom that the governor should release one prisoner every year the Passover festival was celebrated, he would set Jesus against Barabbas, hoping against hope that of the two, the people would prefer Jesus to go free. But the people's choice came like thunder, acclaiming Barabbas. The echo of that mad cry had barely disappeared when another voice suddenly called out and said, "If you let this man go, you are not Caesar's friend" (John 19:12). That settled it. Pilate knew what the threat meant. It was a choice between his career and Jesus. But to him he would give up anything to save his career. A bad report about him to his master in Rome would mean the loss of his position, as his conduct would not bear examination. And so borrowing the Jewish ceremony of washing hands, he asked for a basin of water and a towel, publicly washed his hands as a sign of innocence and at the same time officially authorized the crowd to proceed with the crucifixion. "Take him and crucify him."[1]

Jesus' Mock Trial

In that mock trial, we see not only the blazing heroism of Christ but also the contemptible cowardice of Pilate. His perversity is so obnoxious that even the Apostle's Creed would not allow us to forget it. Such reminder is important because although Pontius Pilate is no longer a terror to mankind and is nothing but a hated name in history, Pilatism is still very much alive. It looms in every dark corner of social and political life. It lives in the sinful heart of every generation. It grows in the swamps of vested interests and selfishness. It commands the loyalty of those who have not known the abiding peace of God. Pilatism comes to life when people evade responsibility which they alone have to shoulder. Pilatism is resurrected when one accepts a ritual but avoids discipline. Pilatism is reincarnated when men say one thing and do another thing. Pilatism is the vain attempt of pleasing everyone by standing on both sides of the fence. It is the surrender of reason to the rule of evil passion; the giving up of justice for the sake of popularity and position and power.

Look at every aspect of our modern life and see if Pilatism is not a malignant cancer. Study the many problems which beset us as a nation and see if it is not a source of confusion and disharmony.

---

[1] Stewart, *Life and Teaching of Jesus Christ,* Lesson XVIII.

Modern Pilatism

There is a form of Pilatism being practiced by many people today which should alarm us if we are really concerned about the welfare of the church. And that is "the adoration of Jesus as a substitute for facing the challenge of the gospel."[1] It is the practice of calling Jesus, "Lord, Lord," but not doing what He wants us to do. It is the practice of paying Him lip-service, but doing something else which is even against His will. Did not Pilate admire Jesus? Did he not say repeatedly that the Galilean was innocent and that he found no fault in Him? But what he did was not what he said. He sent Jesus to the Cross and allowed the people to get rid of Him. Are we different from Pilate when we all say nice things about the Saviour of mankind, but do something that contradicts our testimony? Yet we say we believe in Jesus, He is the Son of God, He is a good man, He is a true friend, but do we not sometimes behave as if Jesus is not alive, as if His lordship over us does not matter at all? Pilatism, we see, can take the deceiving form of discipleship where faith is no more than a mere intellectual belief.

There are, however, some other mild forms of Pilatism which may not be a complete negation of Christ but which, nevertheless, betray the lack of faith in Him. Dr. Harold Cooke Phillips, in his book, *The Timeless Gospel*, suggests that we get rid of Jesus by saying He is outdated. People who advance this argument may not be spiritually bankrupt, but they cannot see the relevance of Jesus Christ to the contemporary world. Because Jesus lived twenty centuries ago in a place without any political or economic significance, because He had no technical and scientific knowledge which our century considers essential, because He knew nothing about horsepower and never traveled more than a hundred miles from the place of His birth, He is, therefore, a misfit in our generation. The logic is that if Jesus is outdated, we need not pay attention to His Sermon on the Mount, to His ethics of love, and to His other teachings on the cultivation of the spiritual life. This view, we see, betrays a grave misunderstanding of Christ and fails to see the timelessness and the perennial timeliness of the Gospel. It fails to note that Christ has gone into the deep areas of life and has revealed life's unchanging realities. Or we get rid of Jesus by saying that He is impractical. That He set a lot of ideals that will not work in the brutal facts of life. That the power of the hydrogen bomb and not of love is what we need these days. That Jesus was too sentimental about the worth of an

---
[1] Phillips, *The Timeless Gospel*, p. 35.

individual. That His teaching on stewardship is not applicable during these days when human needs are vastly multiplied.

We should admit that under the conditions of existence, and knowing how sinful men are, we are sometimes driven to meet force with force and threats with threats. But it is wrong to throw our faith in the power of love into the winds. That would be the greatest blunder we can commit. That would be tantamount to spiritual suicide. In the words of Willard L. Sperry, our "skepticism [about] the ultimate power of the Christian ideal to work its own final victories in our world is a sin against the Holy Spirit." Our problem actually is that we have never really given Christianity a serious try. We have not really tried to follow Christ on His own terms.

There is another form of Pilatism which is perhaps the most popular one. It is, in the words of Dr. Phillips, just ignoring Jesus. We go about our business from day to day unmindful of Christ, not thinking that "more things perish from neglect than from aggressive assault." We don't care about Him and His church. We don't mind Him so much except perhaps on Good Friday and on Christmas.

But this kind of Pilatism is doomed to be frustrating. For whether we ignore Christ or brand Him to be outdated and impractical, the fact is that we cannot get rid of Him. Why? Because we cannot get rid of God. We can only get rid of ourselves. God is in Christ reconciling us unto Himself. God is our Father who would not let us go, although He would not coerce us into loving Him if we don't like to. He follows us into the valley of our moral blindness and sinful ways; He lingers behind us in the corridor of our ugly thoughts and devilism; He stands before us when we are at the brink of giving up the true and the good and the beautiful, pleading with us that for His sake and for our sake we go back to Him and thus find the fulfillment of our fondest dreams.

Let us pray that our observance of the lenten season may not be just another empty ceremonialism, but that it may be a replenishing spiritual experience for us to keep until the end of time. We can do this by first giving up our own versions of Pilatism in our church, and then the good Lord who brought Jesus up from the dead will, in the fullness of time, give us the crown of everlasting life.

23

The Paradox of Calvary

(A Good Friday Sermon)

The event of Jesus' death, like the Incarnation and the Resurrection, is shrouded by transrational realities which we can describe only as paradoxical. In the Incarnation, the Saviour of the world came as a helpless child. The King of kings was born in a lowly manger. The first visitors were not the bigwigs in government or in business. They were humble shepherds. And yet the Holy Child, born in an obscure village of Bethlehem, was the Son of God. In the Resurrection, the grave lost its power to bind the dead. The Victim became the Victor. The cross of shame and infamy became the symbol of God's love.

Calvary is equally paradoxical in that it symbolizes both the suffering love of God and the waywardness of sinful men. It represents both the agonies and magnanimity of Christ and the barbarity and inhumanity of men. Indeed, we can truly say that the crucifixion was on the one hand the greatest tragedy in human history and, on the other hand, the miraculous fulfillment of the divine plan.

The Illegality of Jesus' Trial

Let us then, first of all, recount why the crucifixion, as well as all the other sordid events connected with it which we associate with Calvary, was a tragic misdoing that may shock our imagination. For one thing, the trial of Jesus was brutally illegal. It besmeared the legalism, the stringent devotion to law of both the Jews and Roman leaders. It was a double trial and it was a mistrial. He was tried before the Sanhedrin, an ecclesiastical court, and before the Roman tribunal.

Jesus' appearance before the Sanhedrin informally began when he was presented to Annas. This old man was the high priest for 20 years, and therefore had tremendous influence in the Jewish community. This part of the proceedings was informal and arbitrary because Annas held no official position. He was no longer the high priest at that time. But, as Prof. James S. Stewart observes, "Annas was the evil genius behind the plot that had led to Jesus' capture... It was probable that it was Annas who established the bazaar within the Temple courts which Jesus had so sternly denounced."[1]

The news of Jesus' arrest easily spread and that brought the members of the Sanhedrin to the High Priest's house. And the high priest, Caiaphas, was Annas' son-in-law. He was, in the words of Dr. Stewart, the accredited guardian of the nation's soul. He was supposed to be the supreme representative of the Most High. To him was given the glorious privilege to enter the holy of holies once a year to offer to God the prayers of his people. Yet it was this man of great spiritual responsibility who condemned the Son of God. Is this not a case where the best religious opportunities and the most promising environment do not guarantee a man's salvation? John Bunyan might be thinking of Caiaphas' superciliousness when he wrote in one of his books, "Then I saw that there is a way to hell, even from the gates of heaven."

Trial Before the Sanhedrin

So when Jesus was delivered to Caiaphas, the trial before the Sanhedrin formally began. We can imagine the boisterous commotion of the crowds around the court as they watched the scribes and elders conduct themselves during the proceedings. We can be sure, however, that the Accused was a picture of peace and calmness, standing valiantly before the Court, and perhaps silently praying for them whose murderous plans were eating up their hearts. But it was a mock trial and illegal for the following reasons:[2]

(1) The trial was illegal because according to the Jewish constitution, the Sanhedrin could not be legally convened before the hour of sunrise. Yet the trial started a few minutes after midnight. Perhaps the whole council was in haste and they thought it would save time to continue with the proceedings at that early hour and then have the formal ratifications of their decisions at the rising of the sun.

(2) The trial was illegal because according to its constitution, the Sanhedrin could not be legally convened on the day before the Sabbath day. Sabbath was then interpreted as Saturday, and therefore there should be no session on a Friday, according to the constitution. And yet the trial

---

[1] Stewart, *Life and Teaching of Jesus Christ*, p. 172.
[2] *Ibid.*, pp. 174-175.

and the crucifixion were done on the day before Sabbath.

(3) The trial was illegal because the members of the Sanhedrin were inextricably implicated in the secret plots that culminated in Judas' deed of treachery. "The court that was to decide Jesus' case was also an accomplice in His betrayal."[1] It was the chief priests and the scribes and the elders that bribed Judas to betray his Master. And those same people were now to decide the case.

(4) Moreover, Caiaphas, who was the head of the Sanhedrin as the high priest, was also the leader for the prosecution. He was the man who advanced the idea that "it was expedient that one man should die for the people" (John 11:50).

(5) The trial was illegal because it did not begin with a definite charge against the Accused, as the Jewish law demanded. Indeed, in the beginning, this was the difficulty of Caiaphas and his friends. In Mark 14:56, we read, "Many bare false witness against him, but their witnesses agreed not together." When witnesses disagreed and there was no definite charge, it was the duty of the court to abandon the case. But Jesus' case was continued to drag on.

(6) The trial was illegal because no witnesses for the defense were summoned. In cases involving death penalty, the defense should be heard. But Jesus was not heard. He was against the world. And the world was against Him. Only the voices of the prosecutors were heard.

(7) The trial was illegal because according to the constitution of the Sanhedrin, the death sentence should be pronounced 24 hours after the trial. But in Jesus' case, he was tried and sentenced to death almost at the same time. The court could not wait for 24 hours to elapse before pronouncing the death sentence on the Accused.

We can see, therefore, that the entire proceeding was a deliberate perversion of the constitution of the Jewish Sanhedrin, an insult to their delicate sense of justice; but they closed their eyes to those important technicalities because from the very beginning, they had been after the blood of the sinless Son of God. And now that they had sentenced Him to death, the next step to do was to deliver Him to the civil court because the Roman tribunal reserved the right to have a final say on cases involving death penalty.

---

[1] Stewart, *op. cit.,* p. 174.

Trial Before the Roman Tribunal

The light of dawn was beginning to dispel darkness when Jesus was brought before Pilate. According to St. John, Pilate demanded a charge, saying: "What accusation bring ye against this man?" (John 18:29). And the Jews, knowing that their accusation of blasphemy which they formed just before the civil trial convened was outside the concern of the Roman court because their charge was a purely religious matter, answered evasively, "If he were not a malefactor, we would not deliver him up unto thee" (John 18:30). But according to St. Luke, (23:2), they accused Jesus of (1) perverting the nation; (2) forbidding the people to give tribute to Caesar; and (3) that Jesus was a king in the military sense of the word.

Nevertheless, after the cross-examination, Pilate told the people, and his words were resonant and clear, "I find no fault in this man" (Lk.23:4). But the crowd, for reasons we cannot fully understand, grew mad and shouted, "Let him be crucified!" The Roman procurator was in a dilemma. He tried to evade responsibility by sending Jesus to Herod who, at that time, was taking a vacation in Jerusalem. After all, Jesus was a Galilean and therefore subject to the rule of the governor of Galilee, Herod. The governor, according to Luke, was delighted to see Jesus because he had heard a lot about this Jesus, but he politely sent back the Prisoner to Pilate. Pilate suggested that Jesus be scourged and then be released, but even that did not do the trick. The people clamoured that Christ be killed. Finally, Pilate tried setting Jesus over against Barabbas, hoping that of the two, the people would prefer Jesus to live. But the more the shouting of the crowd became tumultuous. They said, "If thou let this man go, thou art not Caesar's friend" (John 19:12). Those words came to Pilate as a threat. It was now a choice between his political career and Jesus. But Pilate was a politician who would give up anything to save his career. He could not afford to displease the Emperor. For if loyalty to truth would mean disloyalty to Rome, then he would rather be loyal to Rome, though it meant turning his back to the claims of justice. And so in an effort to please the crowd and at the same time wash his hands off the case, he said, "Take ye him, and crucify him, for I find no fault in him" (John 19:6).

Jesus was Condemned

Thus, the sorriest tragedy in all history occurred, and Calvary was the scene of it. The Son of God, in whom people found no fault, was crucified and given a crown of thorns. He who came to save the world was rejected by men at the instigation of those who were supposed to lead the people in moral uprightness and in religious devotion. A grave injustice was committed before the face of God. Annas and Caiaphas and Herod and Pilate, deep within their hearts, knew that the Accused was innocent, that they found no fault in Him. Their sin was the blackest of all because the victim of their barbaric maneuvering was the Messiah, the Son of God. The crucifixion was no less than a judicial murder.

A Fulfillment of God's Plan

The paradox, however, is that while the crucifixion was the most tragic event in all history and the most cruel perversion of human freedom, it was at the same time the mysterious fulfillment of the divine plan. From the perspective of eternity, Jesus' death accomplished a plan that was prophesied long before the coming of Christ. The New Testament tells us that when Jesus entered the city of Jerusalem, it was to fulfill the prophecy of Zechariah (9:9) who said, "Rejoice greatly, O daughter of Zion; shout, O daughter of Jerusalem; behold, thy King cometh unto thee; he is just, and having salvation; lowly and riding upon an ass, even upon a colt the foal of an ass." When His disciples were dispersed during the crucifixion, we recall the words of prophecy: "Smite the shepherd, and the sheep shall be scattered" (Zech. 13:7). The remembrance of His sacrificial death is often associated with the 53rd chapter of Isaiah: "... He is despised and rejected of men; a man of sorrows and acquainted with grief; he was despised and we esteemed him not... Surely he hath borne our griefs and carried our sorrows...he was wounded for our transgressions, he was bruised for our iniquities: the chastisement of our peace was upon him, and with his stripes we are healed..."

The Emmaus Journey

We would recall that on the first Easter morn, when two disciples were on their way to Emmaus, they were discussing the news of Jesus' rising from the grave. It was obvious that those men could not fully believe the news. And Jesus, who appeared to them as a Stranger, told them in loving tone: "O fools, and slow of heart to believe all that the prophets have spoken: Ought not Christ to have suffered these things, and to enter into his glory? And beginning at Moses and all the prophets, he expounded unto them in all the scriptures the things concerning himself" (Lk. 24:25-

27). Note the phrase, "Ought not Christ to have suffered these things," and there we get the suggestion that His suffering was foreordained. In the same Lucan passage, when Jesus appeared to the eleven gathered in Jerusalem, He said, "These are the words which I spake unto you, while I was yet with you, that all things must be fulfilled, which were written in the law of Moses, and in the prophets, and in the psalms, concerning me. Then opened he their understanding, that they might understand the scriptures. And said unto them, Thus it is written, and thus it behoved Christ to suffer, and to rise from the dead the third day" (Lk. 24:44-46).

The Apostle Paul, according to the book of Acts, when confronted by the Jews in Thessalonica, argued with them "out of the Scriptures that Christ must needs have suffered," always emphasizing the point that His death and passion were to fulfill what was written in the Scriptures (Acts 17:2, 3). Therefore, it is no wonder that Jesus Himself could say that His death on the cross was an act of offering, of loving and sacrificial and voluntary giving of Himself. In John chapter 10 verse 17, Jesus said, "...I lay down my life, that I might take it again. No man taketh it from me (v. 18), but I lay it down of myself. I have power to lay it down, and I have power to take it again." In other words, Jesus was saying that no man, no spear, no sword, no cross could ever take His life from Him. He died not because He was crucified, not because the Roman soldiers pierced His body with their bladed weapons; He died because He laid down His life. "No man taketh it from me." He said, "I lay it down of myself. I have power to lay it down, and I have power to take it again."

Bible scholars tell us that generally it takes 20 hours or more before a person, hanging on the cross, dies of exhaustion. Sometimes it takes several days before the victim passes away. Crucifixion is a very slow process of killing a person. But in the case of Jesus, He gave up the ghost after only six hours of suffering. And His last words could have been uttered only by a perfectly tranquil mind. "Father, into thy hands I commend my spirit" (Lk. 23:46). It was a fulfillment of His promise to lay down His life.

The question that we may raise is, How can human tragedy be a fulfillment of God's plan? Was it God's will that Jesus be humiliated and subjected to the most brutal form of punishment known to man at that time? Should we not congratulate Pilate and Herod and Caiaphas and Judas and all those who had a part in the crucifixion for their role in the fulfillment of God's plan? This precisely is what the paradox of Calvary emphatically rejects. The tragedy of the cross was first of all committed in the context of human freedom. Pilate and Judas and Caiaphas and all of them did not have the least consciousness that their treachery and perfidiousness would somehow redound to the accomplishment of some divine purpose. They acted in the freedom of their personal decision.

Human Freedom

God's foreknowledge, we see, does not eliminate human freedom. When Peter denied Christ three times before a helpless maid, he was not consciously fulfilling Christ's prediction that such would be the case. There is absolutely no evidence that Peter tried to justify his cowardice with the pretext that he made denials of his Master to fulfill Christ's prophecy. God's foreknowledge, before the eye of Faith, is a mark of God's greatness, a divine assurance that no amount of human folly can ever defeat the purposes of God. The events of history, though very often contradicting the will of God, are somehow moving towards the final consummation of God's plan. We may choose to wallow in the quagmire of sins because of the hardness of our hearts; we may destroy the temples of God and desecrate His holy name and consecrate tyranny, but let us remember we cannot outwit God, we cannot outdo Him, we cannot overpower Him. God is so great that He can turn even human failure into the account of the soul. He can make the tragedy of Calvary a fulfillment of His plan. Our God is omnipotent.

Implication of the Tragedy

Now, if this paradox of Jesus' death is to be of help to us these days, it should first of all remind us that whatever tragedy befalls us, we can still be grateful to God in the sure knowledge that God can make use of our misfortune. This does not mean that we should intentionally court disaster and invite tragedy. That would be equally tragic. Rather, it means that when the going is rough and hard, when the world looks dark and cruel, when misfortune and calamity and death knock at the door of our homes, we can look up to God for strength and peace. When enemies persecute us and friends betray us, when loved ones turn their backs on us and leave us languishing in solitariness, there is One who watches over us and in whose care we will find rest. To have faith in that great God, whose love shone most brightly on Calvary, is to know that though we be troubled on every side, we will not be distressed; though perplexed, we will not be in despair; though persecuted, we will not be forsaken; though cast down, we will not be destroyed (II Cor. 4:8,9). The observance of Good Friday and the remembrance of Calvary become gloriously meaningful once we are reassured that the travails of this life may lead us to the gates of eternity. The Apostle Paul understood this most perfectly when he said, "All things work together for good to them that love God" (Rom. 8:28).

24

The Road to Emmaus

And they said one to another, Did not our heart burn within us, while he talked with us by the way, and while he opened to us the scriptures? — Luke 24:32

One of the most dramatic stories connected with the event of the Resurrection is the story of the two disciples recorded for us and for posterity by the author of the Book of Acts. Those two men, according to Evangelist Luke, were on their way to Emmaus, a village about 7 miles from Jerusalem. The passage does not tell us who Cleopas' companion was, but tradition has it that the third century Christians began calling him Simon. They were engaged in a solemn conversation about all the things which happened in Jerusalem during that stormy week. The gloomy memory of Holy Friday, with all its harrowing experiences, must be haunting them to their very souls as they walked through the barren road to Emmaus that melancholy afternoon. The day was dying in the west. It was possible they were dazzled by the setting sun which would account for their failure to recognize Jesus who joined them in their journey. Their hearts were heavy and laden with grief. The world looked so empty to them at the death of their Master. Gripping sadness was deeply written on their faces.

Luke tells us that "while they were talking and discussing together, Jesus himself drew near and went with them" (v. 15). And in a tender tone that was characteristic of Him, He asked: "What is this conversation which you are holding with each other as you walk?" Cleopas answered marvellingly, "Are you the only visitor to Jerusalem who does not know the things that have happened there in these days?" "What things?" asked Jesus innocently. And they answered, "Concerning Jesus of Nazareth, a prophet mighty in deed and word before God and all the people. The chief priests and the rulers condemned him to death, and he was crucified on the cross. But we had hoped he was the one to redeem Israel." That was an expression of despair. Their hope was shattered and their dream did not come true. I would guess their voices were strained by hopelessness and by a sense of tragic failure. Then after a pause, they continued: "Some women of our company amazed us. They were at the tomb early in the morning and did not find his body; and they came back saying that they had even seen a vision of angels, who said that he was alive. Some of those who were with us went to the tomb, and found it just as the women had said; but him they did not see." From these statements, it was evident that they did not believe Jesus rose again from the grave. The women were told by the angel that Jesus was alive, but they saw Him not. Others verified the report of the women; they also went to the tomb, but did not see Jesus. If they only knew that Jesus was risen, had they believed the angel's good news, they would not have tasted the pang of despair and loneliness and grief. But because it never occurred to them that the prophecy was fulfilled, that Jesus on the third day would rise again from the dead, the tragedy on Calvary looked like a disaster, and their hearts were sorely desolated.

Jesus' Remarks

Now, after hearing their sorry tale, it was Jesus' turn to speak. He said to them, "O foolish men... and slow of heart to believe all that the prophets have spoken!" Let me say, parenthetically, that the word **foolish** as used by Jesus here does not mean wicked or evil. The New English Bible uses the word **dull**, which is closer to the meaning of the Greek word *anohtoi*, to talk without sense. For truly, were the disciples quick to believe the prophets, they would have talked with sense. So Jesus "expounded unto them in all the scriptures, beginning with Moses and the prophets, all the things concerning himself" (v. 27). He tried to teach them that according to the Scriptures, God had ordained the sufferings of Christ. It was therefore necessary, He said, that Christ should suffer and enter into His glory.

For the meanwhile, their journey was coming to the end. They were now at the village of Emmaus. Just a few more steps and the two disciples would be at the door of their humble cottage. But when they reached the place, Jesus appeared "to be going further." We can be sure He really meant to go on further since after all He was just a Stranger to them and He feared it might be an unholy intrusion to lodge with those men in their modest nipa hut. But, the Evangelist Luke tells us, the disciples invited Him to come in and lodge with them, for the day was far spent and the night was drawing nigh. And Jesus, as we know, graciously accepted the invitation, led in prayer at supper time, and while He was breaking bread the disciples recognized who He was. They perhaps were taken aback to see that the Man whom they thought was only a Stranger and with whom they had animated conversation about the resurrection was after all the Christ Himself, the Risen Saviour of mankind. But miraculously Jesus vanished out of their sight, and they said to themselves, "Did not our hearts burn within us while he talked to us on the road, while he opened to us the scriptures?" And because they could not contain within themselves the swelling joy of that wonderful experience, they rushed back to Jerusalem, perhaps almost running all along the way, and finding the eleven gathered in the city, they told them that Christ indeed had risen.

Talks on the Resurrection

I suggest that we pick out some points in this dramatic story which may be relevant to our life today. For instance, let us note that the subject of their conversation was the Resurrection. On the part of Jesus, who was no more than a mere Stranger to the two disciples, there was earnestness in showing to them that the events of that week, hectic as it was, were a fulfillment of what was written in the books of Moses and the prophets and in the Psalms. Luke says that Jesus "expounded" the Scripture unto them. Where He got a copy of the Bible we do not know. It is probable, however, that the two disciples had a copy with them, and that Jesus borrowed it for the purpose of citing the biblical references on the subject under consideration. What a wasted opportunity if they had no Bible with them. They would have missed the penetrating exposition of the best Sunday School Teacher.

What They Lacked

The two disciples were absorbed in the study of the Resurrection. But what was conspicuously lacking in their life was the consciousness of the presence of the Risen Christ. With Jesus as their Bible Study leader, we can be sure that they were finally convinced that as far as the Holy Scripture was concerned, Christ had to suffer and then enter into glory; and that He who was crucified three days ago must have risen from the dead. And yet we know that those two men did not feel the fullness of the Biblical message. There is no glossing over the record of St. Luke. Those men simply did not have the certainty of the Resurrection.

How is it with you and me? Here we are joining the rest of the

Christian world in celebrating the triumph of the Risen Lord over the grave. Do we really know the reality of Easter joy? Are we really convinced that Christ is the living Lord? We see, it is possible to talk and study about the Resurrection; it is possible to celebrate Easter by getting up early enough to be at the Luneta for the Sunrise service – and yet deep within our hearts there is no Easter joy, and Christ is only an ordinary Stranger. This is what we mean by empty ceremonialism or shallow piety, an observance of the day without spiritual content, without meaning, without sincerity. It is traditionalism and formalism, rather than life and experience. We have to emphasize again and again that Easter services and Easter ceremonies are nothing but forms of spiritual deception unless they represent the gloriousness of faith which knows the deepest joy of the Resurrection.

The Invitation

Again, let us recall that when the disciples reached their home, Jesus appeared to be going further. But they invited Jesus to stay with them overnight. They perhaps thought that wherever Jesus was going, He might proceed with His journey the following day after resting with them that night. In the King James Version, the word used is **constrained**. "They constrained him, saying, Abide with us; for it is toward evening, and the day is far spent" (v. 29). The translation in the New English Bible is, "They pressed him." In either case, the verb used is strong. They were violently friendly, firmly gentle in their invitation. They really meant it.

We Filipinos, and most Orientals for that matter, have the so-called *pabalat-sibuyas* way of inviting people. That is a part of our culture. When people come to our house at meal time, we invite them to join us. But the truth is that we do not mean it, especially when we are not ready. Our invitation is *pabalat-sibuyas*. And the person being invited is not expected to accept the invitation. He is expected to say, "Oh no, thank you." Of course, we know when the invitation is genuine. If the host insists that we join them for lunch or supper, we really feel at home and eat to our heart's content. And in the case of the two disciples, Jesus knew their invitation was not *pabalat-sibuyas*. And so He graciously accepted it.

The Guest Became the Host

But a most surprising thing happened in their home. He who was invited to be a Guest actually became the Host. In Palestine, it was the host who should break bread at meal time and lead in prayer. But in that home of the two disciples, their Guest broke the bread and gave thanks. And it was only then that they recognized their Guest to be the Risen Christ Himself.

And so I am constrained to say that if we invite Jesus to be our Guest in our homes, we will discover somehow that He is the Host. He becomes the Head of the family and the Master of the house. He will be there to remind us that we are His guests. Then we begin to see that even our home is not really ours; it is God's and that we are there only as His guests. We are reminded that life itself upon this earth is only temporary, and that our destiny is the eternal dwelling place in the Kingdom of God. But we have to insist persistently for Christ to abide in our home before He comes in to be our Guest and therefore to be our Host.

To Give is to Receive

The other point which is corollary to this one I have just mentioned is that to give of what we have to Christ is really to receive from Him. The two disciples thought that by inviting Jesus to be their Guest, they would give Him what they had and share with Him what they possessed. Perhaps all that they had in their house was bread for supper, but anyhow they were ready to share it with the Stranger who, they knew, was tired after the day's journey. And yet, acting as the Host, Jesus appeared to be the Giver of the bread, and that the men who had intended to do the giving became the recipients of the Host's hospitality. They extended hospitably to Jesus, but it was they who received from Him – an acted parable of the truth that those who give to God with a cheerful spirit are actually receiving. This is perhaps what the Lord meant when He said, "It is more blessed to give than to receive." But it takes intimacy with God and some maturity of faith to know that in the divine scheme of things, giving is receiving and prayer is its own answer. The experience of those stouthearted Christians tells us that when they give to God, they discover it is God who is the real Giver.

And so I suggest that the Easter message is not detached from stewardship. After all the death of Christ was an act of giving – the giving of His life for the redemption of mankind. And, therefore, when He rose again from the dead, the substance of His great commission is that those who believe in His resurrection should become great givers, for to believe in the Risen Lord is to give our all to Him. But Jesus would like us to remember that, like the two disciples, once we open our treasures for Him and ask Him to lodge in our house, He will come in, not as our Guest to receive the best which we can offer, but as Host to give us the best that we can receive. That is what we may call "The Paradox of Easter" or "The Paradox of Christian Giving."

Easter's Evangelistic Note

Now, let us mention briefly the evangelistic note of the Resurrection. When the two disciples recognized Jesus as He broke the bread, soon after Jesus vanished out of their sight, they went back to Jerusalem and, finding the eleven gathered together, they told them of their unique experience. Perhaps they missed their supper that night, like the Samaritan woman who left her waterpot at Jacob's well when she discovered that the Man she was conversing with was the Son of God. Such enthusiasm, generated by the joy of Christ's presence and by the urgency of the Gospel message, has always characterized the brave advances of all missionary movements. Jesus' great Commission, the basis of Christian evangelism, could have been given before the tragedy of Calvary in one of Jesus' sermons. But He waited until after the crisis of Holy Friday. He gave it when He was about to go up to heaven. It is therefore the commission from the Risen Christ.

I need not now emphasize the fact that Easter should make us heralds of the Risen Lord, for this truth, I repeat, is not new to us. But let me say that sometimes in our earnestness to witness for Christ, we unconsciously distort the message of Easter by overemphasizing its evangelistic note. I refer to the slogan, which has now become quite popular, that "Christ is not Lord at all, unless He is Lord of all." That is a Christian heresy. For Christ is not a despot who would not be willing to be Lord unless we give a unanimous vote on His Lordship. The fact is that even if men reject the Lordship of Christ, He is still Lord. God has made Him Lord over us, whether we like it or not. I cannot believe that because the communists, for instance, publicly ridicule Christ and denounce the power of God, that because there are people in our homes and in our land who do not acknowledge the Lordship of Christ, Christ is not Lord. The event of the Resurrection is enough guarantee that Christ is our living Lord even if many do not yet recognize His Lordship. Here we need to resolve to be more aggressive in our Christian witness, but for the meantime let us not be uselessly saddened by the false claim that Jesus is not Lord at all, because He is not the Lord of all.

A Concluding Appeal

Cleopas and his friend speak to us today thru the pages of the New Testament. The story of their trip to the village of Emmaus is not even one chapter in the Gospel of St. Luke, but the magnificence of their experience on that first Easter is something that should be coveted by Christians of all ages. They tell us that if we desire to discover the joy of Easter, which alone can dissipate the heavy fog of grief and loneliness, we need not go to far places and look for it in running brooks, in majestic sunrises, in verdant fields, in giant trees, in singing birds, in blooming flowers – we only need to open our homes for Christ to enter and to stay. And it is not enough that we meet Jesus on the road, that we look up to Him as the Great Teacher when we are earnest to know the truth of our faith; it is not enough that we see Him in the garden of His empty tomb, that we feel His nearness in the quietness of the night, and His presence in the house of worship—we also need to invite Him most sincerely to abide with us in our homes. The joy of Easter, the meaning of the Resurrection, does not come to its fullest blessedness unless it is a real, vital, energizing experience in the homes of men.

Today, we are here to celebrate Easter – the glorious event of the Resurrection, the victory of life over the power of death. This is the Queen of the Christian festivals. It reminds us that Christ is alive, as symbolized by the empty cross. But let us not forget that this celebration is never complete unless it is supplemented by the hospitality of our homes to Him who rose again from the dead. "Behold, I stand at the door and knock," says Jesus, "if any man hears my voice and opens the door, I will come in to him and will sup with him, and he with me."

25

The Bible in Our Day

(Message for Universal Bible Sunday)
Scripture Reading: Psalm 119:1-16

The 1963 report of the Advisory Council of the Philippine Bible House presents both the triumph and the ever increasing possibilities of Bible distribution in the Philippines. Accordingly, more than half a million volumes of Scriptures (whole Bibles, New Testaments, and Bible portions) were distributed. At the request of Mayor Antonio J. Villegas, some 18,000 Bibles were given to senior students in the Manila city high schools.

The report also includes an estimate of people in the Philippines who most probably do not own a copy of the Scriptures. Some 23 million Filipinos, says the report, are "bibleless." This, admittedly, is a conservative estimate. But if this figure means anything, it means that the Christians and the churches have a long way to go before we can reach the goal of "one Scripture to each person."

We should be glad to note that the Catholic Church has also launched a program of Bible distribution. According to the *Sentinel*, a Catholic weekly,

> "The daughters of St. Paul have so far made home-to-home campaigns to 37,612 Catholic and non-Catholic families in 14 parishes in the archdiocese of Manila. They have distributed 19,192 Bibles and Gospels in English, Tagalog, Cebuano and Bicol." (Quoted from the 1962 report of the Bible House, p.8).

Let us pray that other Christian groups may be led to do the same until the Word of God becomes a treasured book in the home of every Filipino family.

Mr. Béguin's Observation

But while we rejoice at the increasing number of people having a copy of the Scriptures, we have no guarantee that the Book is being read as faithfully as it should be. Two years ago, Mr. Olivier Béguin of London, General Secretary of the United Bible Societies, made the observation that though millions of additional people are acquiring Bibles, the book is not being read much except by non-Christians. He said that "distribution has climbed steeply, but the actual reading is much less than it had been presumed to be." He noted that the new interest in the Scripture is from an "intellectual rather than religious motive." The non-Christians, he said, read the Bible only to know more about the faith that has made Western culture and civilization. He cited studies in Germany, Britain and the United States showing that only a small proportion of the people read the Bible regularly. "They've lost contact with the message," he sighed. "They don't see its relevance in many cases today."[1]

The Popularity of the Bible

In our country, there are some pleasant facts which attest to the popularity, if not usefulness, of the Holy Bible. For instance, a good number of our politicians seem to be quite familiar with the beautiful passages in the Holy Scriptures. In the last elections, a lot of campaign speeches were coated with biblical references. Indeed, some of our candidates felt, rightly or wrongly, that they were the political messiahs our country needed. Today, it is no longer unusual to hear politicians quoting from the Bible in their speeches in congress and in other public gatherings. Of course, we do not know whether this means that our politicians read the Bible or that their ghost writers are smart enough to capitalize on our people's abiding reverence for the Word of God. But, at any rate, we should be glad that the Bible is somehow being popularized and that the Book, which used to be a censored book in this country, is now being recognized as a source of divine guidance and authority.

Resurgence of Biblical Preaching

Even more significant than this is the fact that the pulpits of both Catholic and Protestant churches are today becoming more and more resonant with biblically-oriented sermons. In other words, there is an apparent resurgence of biblical preaching. There was a time when preaching was no more than catechetical discourses. Today, even social issues are discussed in the light of the Biblical faith, and though sometimes narrow

---

[1] *Sunday Chronicle,* June 18, 1961.

sectarianism only compounds the problems, there is, nevertheless, a serious attempt to seek guidance from the resources of the Scriptures. Admittedly, interpretations of biblical passages are sometimes conflicting, but the point is that more attention is now being given to the supreme value of the Bible. Unhappily, however, this revival of interest in biblical studies seems to be isolated at the present among theologians and Christian educators and preachers. It has not come down yet to the laity who really need it more. There is still in our country a certain amount of illiteracy in the Christian faith and in the Holy Scriptures. This is due to the fact that, on the one hand, in spite of the sustained efforts of Christian churches to distribute the Bible, still many, many more souls have not yet seen what the Bible looks like. On the other hand, there are those who are familiar with sight of the Book, and may even have a copy in their library, but somehow find no time to read it. No wonder, an average church member does not know what he believes in.

Causes of Biblical Illiteracy

This apathy or disinterestedness in Bible reading is partly reflected in the Sunday School. If the Sunday School is to be our gauge for the amount of concern we have for our Christian nurture, then our concern is pitifully meager. One common problem of the Manila churches (and also, I believe, of many other churches in the rural areas) is the poor attendance in the Sunday School. Compared to the total membership of the church, those who come to Sunday School are pathetically few.

At a meeting of the expositors for the Bible Study week last year, the chairman of the district, for the purpose of determining the approximate number of people who would attend the Bible study sessions, asked the representatives of local churches in his district how many from their congregations were coming. The spokesman of a church with a membership of 1,500 was not sure whether there could be 15 people from his church who might want to come. Representatives from other churches with 300 to 500 members could not guarantee more than 10 from each group to come. It was, of course, a very enriching Bible study week, but the attendance was less than the already conservative estimates. Is this not the irony of human nature? When it was a criminal offense to believe in Jesus Christ and sacrilegious to read the Bible, Christian martyrs gave their life and, thereby, defied the mightiest persecutions waged against the church. But now that the Christians are free to preach the Gospel even at public places, many Christians do not seem to have time to read it.

Last September, the *Newsweek* magazine[1] carried an article on the World's Fair held in New York in 1964-65. Accordingly, every religious group is allowed to put up a booth in the Fair. The Roman Catholics have decided to import the painting "Pieta," Michelangelo's life-size statue of Mary holding the dead Christ, to be exhibited at the Fair. The Jews, on the other hand, have agreed to display the Dead Sea scrolls to symbolize the Jewish faith. But the Protestants had a hard time deciding on what to exhibit. First, they considered the picture of "Praying Hands" by Albrecht Durer, but later on dismissed the idea on the ground that Protestants do not have a monopoly on personal prayer. Tentatively, they agreed on an open Bible as their symbol because they felt an open Bible symbolizes the prophetic ministry of the Protestant Church. Members of the Protestant committee, however, said: "If we are really honest, would not a closed Bible, covered with dust and crammed with yellowing obituaries, be a better symbol of the actual state of Protestantism?"

That is the embarrassing question we have to answer. For if the Holy Bible is a closed book in our homes, untouched for weeks and months and years, should we not feel ashamed to have it in our lecterns and altars? Should we not feel guilty when the symbol of an open Bible does not reflect the actual state of our Christian life?

Faith and Atheism

And yet we know that if we are to withstand the onslaughts of life, we should be deeply anchored on the solid ground of biblical faith. We are alarmed, for instance, by the threat of atheism and the mockery it openly makes of the Christian religion. Lately such mockery expressed itself in a brutally refined way in the joke of a Russian astronaut who, after visiting the recesses of space, said he did not find God there. We squirm at such ugly joke and wonder how God could forgive him for his nasty unbelief. We should realize, however, that we, too, are at the brink of atheism when we do not find God in the daily walks of life. Our spiritual complacency, our lack of consciousness of His presence, is the religious version of an irreligious philosophy which does not believe in God. And if we are to overcome such danger, then I repeat, we should by all means be securely founded upon the Word of God.

---

[1] *Newsweek*, Sept. 17, 1963, p. 56.

The Power of the Christian Message

This reaffirmation of the relevance of the Bible in our day is based on the conviction that the deepest longing of the human spirit and the gravest problems of our age can be met by the power of the Christian message. For the Bible witnesses not only to the reality of God, but also to His absolute sovereignty over His creation. And to believe in the divine omnipotence is to be liberated from the chain of despair and hopelessness; it is to be assured that in spite of the selfishness and inhumanity of man to man, God is the Ruler yet. Therefore, the Christian need not despair of the future for he knows it is in the hands of God; he knows that God is Lord not only of history but also over history. This is the faith which gives meaning to all our striving for peace, for progress, for brotherhood; it is the faith which comes from the heart of the biblical message.

The Bible and Its Unifying Influence

We should not overlook the unifying power of the Holy Bible. It is mystifying to note that while the Episcopalians, for instance, and those of the Reformed and evangelical tradition cannot come together at the Lord's Table for communion, they can come together for Bible study. Last summer, when the Philippine Theological Society met at St. Andrew's Episcopal Seminary, we could not be together at the Lord's Supper. But we had a nice time together studying the Bible. A few years ago, I attended a certain church in Guadalupe. The pastor, aware of my presence in the congregation, announced that those who were not immersed at baptism could not be allowed to take part in the holy communion. But we were welcome to the Sunday School. Which makes me think that the Bible has indeed some unifying influence. We can be sure that once we are led face to face with God through the pages of the Bible, we will see ourselves all in dire need of His pardoning grace to deliver us from the prison cell of denominationalism.

26

What it Means to Believe in God *

It is most fitting that before you receive your diplomas this afternoon, we gather here for the solemn purpose of reminding ourselves that the talents and skills acquired through education are a gift from Him who is the Source of all wisdom. This baccalaureate service, I would like to believe, is not just another date on the school calendar, not just to observe a decent tradition that has become popular among institutions of learning, but a day especially set aside for a grateful thanksgiving. Here we publicly admit that God is the Giver of all good gifts and that, therefore, our highest duty is to acknowledge His goodness with deepest gratitude.

What it means to believe in this God whom we now praise and worship is what I propose to discuss briefly this morning. This means that for our purpose, I am not interested in the problem of whether or not we believe in God. I know we do, or else this act of worship is nothing but an empty ceremonialism. But I feel we need to clarify what we mean by believing in God, especially in relation to the hard task of living in a world heavily burdened with miseries and sin. And I suggest that we approach this question in the context of a Christian experience.

First of all, when we say we believe in God, we mean the God who has revealed Himself through Jesus Christ. We mean the God and Father of our Lord, the One whose very nature has been disclosed in the life and teaching of Christ. Therefore, we do not mean the Unknown God of the Greeks in Athens in the days of the apostle Paul. We do not mean the God of philosophical speculations, whose existence or non-existence is at the mercy of fallible reasoning of finite minds. We do not mean the Mysterious Being who is detached from our world, or the Divine Power that is alien to human experience. To be sure, God remains hidden even as He reveals Himself to us. He is the *Mysterium Tremendum*, the unfathomable Reality,

---

* Sermon delivered at the Baccalaureate Service of the University of the Philippines held on April 7, 1963

the wholly Other. The Christians' God is One who is both hidden and revealed. In the words of Martin Luther, God is both *obscunditus* and *revelatus*. It is safe to say that God's revelation makes us aware, among other things, of His mysteriousness; that the more we know Him, the more we are sure that we cannot really know Him; His self-disclosure is at the same time an evidence of His hiddenness. But He is the God who comes to us through Jesus Christ and dwells with us through the Holy Spirit. He is the God of the Christian trinity.

Now, this God in whom we believe is the one true God. There is no other God beside Him. This is the faith of the prophets, the Apostles and the Christian Church. But this belief has some definite moral implications. It means we acknowledge Him to be the sole Object of our loyalty and devotion, of our allegiance and admiration. Christian monotheism is a response to the divine claim for monopoly of man's fidelity. To use a figure of speech, our God is a jealous God and does not want us to have other gods before Him. Idolatry, or the worship of other gods, is a grave offense to the Almighty. It belies our profession of monotheism and betrays our sordid fickle-mindedness.

The Apostle Paul, in his letter to the Colossians (3:5), says, "Mortify therefore your members which are upon the earth; fornication, uncleanness, inordinate affection, evil concupiscence and covetousness, which is idolatry." In other words, any form of bestiality, any act of self-gratification which makes man a prisoner of his carnal desires is a negation of monotheism. The certainty of monotheism is not established simply by giving an intellectual assent to the oneness of God. It should be validated by character and conduct. A contradiction between life and creed is a scandalous contradiction.

The scandal of Christianity is precisely its claim for monotheism while a great number of its followers are flagrantly immoral. We have been led into the false thinking that the soundness of a doctrine is its invulnerability to the searchlights of logic. We have forgotten that unless it is authenticated by the realities of life, it is just like a sounding brass or a tinkling cymbal.

Take the case of the scribes and Pharisees. They were men known for their much learning and their familiarity with the laws of Moses. People looked up to them as leading citizens of the land, as able interpreters of theology and religion. Yet to Jesus' searching eyes, they were but abominable hypocrites who could not escape the damnation of hell. Jesus' words about them, as recorded by St. Matthew, were obviously unpalatable. Listen to some of them:

> "Woe unto you, scribes and Pharisees, hypocrites! For ye devour widow's houses, and for a pretense make long prayer.....
>
> "Woe unto you, scribes and Pharisees, hypocrites! For ye compass sea and land to make one proselyte, and when he is made, ye make him twofold more the child of hell than yourselves.....
>
> "Woe unto you, scribes and Pharisees, hypocrites! For ye make clean the outside of the cup and of the platter, but within they are full of extortion and excess...
>
> "Woe unto you, scribes and Pharisees, hypocrites! For ye are like unto whited sepulchres, which indeed appear beautiful outward, but are within full of dead men's bones and of all uncleanness."

This rosary of lamentations from the lips of the Son of God certainly carries with it a deep note of pity and sadness over the plight of those people who had kept themselves in the sarcophagus of a lost religion! It must have broken the loving heart of God to see those keepers of the Temple gates helplessly imprisoned within the narrow walls of their home-made hell.

Now this one true God is also a holy God. He is a God of perfect purity and goodness and honor. His glory is transcending and evokes our deepest reverence. But to believe in the holiness of God is also to realize our utter sinfulness. To stand before His consuming Presence is to see our unworthiness. To proclaim His holiness is to own our unrighteousness. We would recall that this was the experience of the prophet Isaiah. When he saw the Lord sitting upon the throne, when he heard the seraphim and cherubim singing "Holy, holy, holy is the Lord of hosts," the prophet could not help but say, "Woe is me, for I am undone; for I am a man of unclean lips, and I dwell in the midst of a people of unclean lips; for mine eyes have seen the King, the Lord of hosts" (6:5). Surely, we cannot behold the glory of the Lord without being convicted of our inward ugliness. We cannot say God is holy without humbly admitting our awful sinfulness. One of the paradoxes of the Christian life is that the more we come close to God, the more we realize how far we are from Him.

But the disheartening fact about us is that we either ignore the reality of sin or we feel we are so close to God that those who are not with us are therefore far from the gates of heaven. Mr. Albert J. Portune, writing in the *Plain Truth* magazine observes that the key to present social decay is that "we are losing our sense of awareness of sin as a factor in human conduct." Sin, he says, is increasingly being ignored and made light of in modern society. There are those who do not believe in sin anymore. They believe in errors, in mistakes, in guilts, but not in sin. And how can the redemptive grace of Christ have meaning if the paralyzing power of sin is not even recognized? How are we to repent if we are not aware of sin?

Certainly, we should strive to attain the highest degree of spiritual growth. But let us not forget that religious emotionalism is a poor substitute for the real joy of salvation. It may even lead us to the graver sin of spiritual hypocrisy. The feeling that we are holier than those who are not with us may be a sign that we ourselves are in serious need of God's pardoning grace.

The holiness of God should be seen in the background of His love. Indeed, He is a loving God and His nature is love. It is His love that will not let us go. Our highest calling, therefore, is to respond to the love of God because in so doing, we take part in the being of God. As St. John says, "Love is of God, and everyone that loveth is born of God and knoweth God." In this we see that love is the fulfillment not only of the law but also of ourselves because to love is to be born of God.

Therefore, to believe in a loving God is to become loving ourselves, to forsake our unloveliness and to love even the unlovely. And in a world where there is so much hatred and jealousy and resentment, so much bigotry and bitterness, love is the only power that can give us peace.

Again, to believe in God is to see through our problems. In fact, it is to look beyond the problems and behold the farthest horizons with quietness and confidence. It is to be equipped with the knowledge that God is our Refuge in times of stress and strain. In other words, to believe in God is not to be free from the troubles of life. It is not to be exempted from the tumults of this world, from the terrible onslaughts of sin and death. If we believe in God only to escape from the grim facts of life, only to shun the path of the cross, then we reduce religion into a kind of magic which can be manipulated for our own pleasure.

History tells us that those who are faithful to God are not necessarily free from life's crushing burdens. On the contrary, their misfortunes are usually monstrous. Job in the Old Testament had a harrowing experience when his wife and children died. And yet, he was a righteous man. The disciples left their fishing nets to become fishers of men. They followed the Master wherever He went. But they ended up in dungeons and dens of lions. And there was Jesus Himself. He who taught men to feed the hungry and clothe the naked was given vinegar when He was thirsty. He who taught men to love each other, to turn the other cheek, to walk the second mile, to forgive without limits, was given a crown of thorns and crucified upon a cross. But all these men became heroes of faith because God was real in their life and because their life was entrusted in the hands of God.

There is wisdom in the advice of that Episcopal divine, Dr. Phillips Brooks: "Do not pray for easy lives. Do not pray for tasks equal to your strength. Pray for strength equal to your task." St. Francis of Assisi, that godly man who exemplified what it means to believe in God, asked for strength equal to his task when he prayed. "O Lord our Christ, may we have Thy mind and Thy spirit; make us instruments of Thy peace; where there is hatred, let us sow love; where there is injury, pardon; where there is discord, union; where there is doubt, faith; where there is despair, hope; where there is darkness, light; where there is sadness, joy."

Annie Johnson Flint, in her poem entitled *God's Promise*, understood this truth of the biblical faith when she wrote:

> God hath not promised
> > Skies always blue
> Flower-strewn pathways,
> All our lives through;
> God hath not promised
> > Sun without rain,
> Joy without sorrow,
> > Peace without pain.
> But God hath promised
> > Strength for the day,
> Rest for the labor,
> > Light for the way;
> Grace for the trials,
> > Help from above,
> Unfailing sympathy,
> > Undying love.

It is a happy coincidence that this affair falls on Palm Sunday because there are striking similarities between the Triumphal Entry and our experience here. For one thing, in the event of the Triumphal Entry we remember Jesus marching from Galilee to the City of God. "Destination Jerusalem" can be an apt description of His journey. From the start of His ministry, He had aimed at entering that city as King of kings. And today we commemorate the fulfillment of His aim. But is this not also a fulfillment of your aim? You have long dreamed to be an engineer, a teacher, a doctor, a lawyer — and now you have reached your Jerusalem. This is the culmination of your long journey.

But note that Jesus' Jerusalem lies on the road of the cross. And I am quite certain that your Jerusalem cannot be without Calvary. For if you live by the precepts of Christ, if you practice Christianity in your respective professions, you, too, have to tread the path of the cross.

It belongs to the wisdom of God that when we follow Christ, we should take up our cross. For we cannot be Christians without some cost or sacrifice. Christianity without a cross cannot be of Christ; it is pseudo-Christianity, and it is bound to fail. Jesus Himself said, "In the world ye shall have tribulations." He predicted that nations shall rise up against nations and friends will betray friends. But He also said, "Be of good cheer, I have overcome the world. . . Lo, I shall be with you always, even unto the end of the world."

All that I have been saying is that to believe in God is to live in the power of faith which can overcome the world. It is to have courage for the living of these days. As a brave disciple said, "If God is for us, who can be against us?" Neither tribulation nor distress, nor famine, nor sword shall be able to separate us from the love of God in Jesus Christ.

This blazing heroism, let us further observe, is generated by the conviction that the God we believe in is the Lord of history; that the events of time, though very often contradicting the will of God, are moving towards the final consummation of His purposes; and that human freedom which is often turned into a license will not in any way defeat the omnipotence of God.

This is the faith which can make us strong in this age of fear and anxiety. Almost anytime the world may perish with human folly; it may blow up to pieces at the outbreak of nuclear war. But faith in God, in whose hands is the destiny of mankind, does not allow us to be frantic about the precariousness of the world's situation. For we know that beyond the border of time, beyond the sphere of temporal existence, is the sunshine of God's love and the reign of righteousness and peace. As Christians, we believe in the ultimate victory of goodness and the final overthrow of evil. As Martin Luther said, "And though this world, with devils filled, should threaten to undo us, we will not fear for God hath willed His truth to triumph through us." This is the faith which will make us more than conquerors.

Certainly, to believe in God is to walk without fear through the valley of the shadow of death, and to be assured of His sustaining presence in our lonely struggle for honor and integrity. It is to surmount every obstacle that may come along our way with courage and patience. To believe in God is to know that when the storms of life are raging, when our homes are made desolate by the death of a loved one, when we are bitten by the serpent's tooth of disloyalty or ingratitude, when we are tired and heavy-laden, there is One in whose presence we can find peace, understanding, forgiveness and rest. To believe in God is to know that when things go wrong, it is not God's doing but only men's misdoing, that all things will work together for good to them that love Him, that the hardships of the present cannot be compared with the joy that awaits us in His kingdom. To believe in God is to know that Jesus Christ is our way when we are lost in the jungle of moral compromises; that He is our life when we are dying; that He is our truth which will make us free. To believe in God is to experience that His grace is sufficient for our needs and that our greatest need is His redeeming grace.

But when all this is said, we come back to the same question: What does it mean to believe in God? And we discover that the question demands an answer from our personal decision. For whatever may be said about belief in God, it is we who have to answer individually; and when we are honest with ourselves, we know that in many cases, our belief in God is but an empty piety, a religious sophistry to cover up our irreligiousness. So in the innermost chamber of the heart, where the issues of life are being fought, we can only repeat the prayer of that man in the Gospel story: "Lord, I believe; help thou my unbelief."

Today, while we wrestle with ourselves into believing in God, while our profession of faith in Him is polluted by unholy pretensions and uncertainties, one thing stands beyond the shadow of doubt: namely, God believes in us. God believes that we who have been blessed with a university degree can be a help in saving our country and the world from economic and moral decay. God believes that we who fail Him very often can, by

His grace, reach a certain maturity in faith and thus become pioneers of a movement that will draw men to Him. He believes, we can be sure, that in spite of our natural handicaps and limitations, we will commit ourselves to be the vanguards of His love, holding on to the light of His truth in the dark night of life, until the dawning of the day when all peoples shall bow in adoration and admiration before Him. God believes that you who are soon to leave the portals of this institution can become assets in the building of a nation where freedom truly reigns. God believes that even those who do not believe in Him can be channels of His love, that they can serve the cause of truth and justice for the benefit of the human race.

    Let us, therefore, examine ourselves and see what it means for us to believe in God. Let there be no doubt in our belief, lest we begin to believe our doubts. And as we march along the highway of life, where our faith in God and in our fellow men is on test, let us not forget that there is One who believes in us because He has created us in His own image.

PRAYER: Almighty God, our heavenly Father, in Thee we live and move and have our being. Teach us to number our days that we may apply our hearts to wisdom. Create in us a new spirit, and lead us in the way everlasting. In Jesus' name. Amen.

27

Christians and Revolution

Scripture Reading: Luke 19:41-48

There are at least two schools of thought in the current discussion of the likelihood of a revolution in the Philippines today. One believes that the revolution is imminent. Fr. Pacifico Ortiz, in his invocation at the opening of the Seventh Congress in 1970, used the phrase "trembling on the brink of revolution." A newspaper columnist, commenting on that invocation, wrote: "We are no longer on the brink. The revolution everyone copiously talks about is upon us." Our own President, sometime ago, described this country as sitting on a social volcano which could erupt violently anytime. Father Horacio de la Costa goes further by saying that we do not have much time to shape the coming revolution and therefore, we may just as well concentrate now on the reconstruction we have to do after the revolution.

The other school of thought does not easily subscribe to the pronouncements quoted above. There is, for instance, another Jesuit priest, Fr. John F. Doherty of Ateneo de Manila, who admonishes us to be cautious in predicting a Philippine revolution. "Prophecy," he says, "is tenuous and should, in any rational discussion, yield to the evidence of facts." He admits that there are "elements of a revolutionary situation present in the Philippine society today," but he believes that these elements "do not seem to be sufficient at this time to predict an imminent revolution."

The *Manila Times* editorial (February 3, 1970) took the same position. It said, "There is no room for smugness and complacency at a time like the present. But neither is there reason for believing that the country is facing imminent revolution and ruin ... Those who tell our people that there is no alternative to revolution are just as irresponsible as those who close their eyes to the need for change."

Whichever side we take in this on-going debate is, in a sense, immaterial. What is of immediate importance, especially to those who profess the Christian faith, is to find Christian guidance that will help us understand the meaning of our situation and determine the appropriate action we have to make.

For an answer, we must necessarily consider the pronouncements of the Church. For instance, there is the statement of Pope Pius XII to a group of Italian workers in 1943:

> "Salvation and justice are not to be found in revolution but in evolution through concord. Violence has always achieved only destruction, not construction; the kindling of passion, not their pacification; the accumulation of hate and ruin, not the reconciliation of the contending parties."

Speaking in the same vein, John XXIII, in his *Pacem in terris*, says, "It must be borne in mind that to proceed gradually is the law of life in all its expressions; therefore in human institutions, too, it is not possible to renovate for the better except by working from within them, gradually."

Then more recently, Pope Paul VI, in this *Popularum progressio*, declares:

> "A revolutionary uprising — save where there is a manifest, long-standing tyranny which would do great damage to fundamental personal rights and dangerous harm to the common good of the country — produces new injustices, throws more elements out of balance and brings on new disasters. A real evil should not be fought against at the cost of greater misery."

This is to say that on the whole, the Catholic Church is unwilling to recognize revolution as a legitimate means of solving social and political injustice. However, some official pronouncements of Pope Paul VI provide some leeway, however small, for revolution as a last resort. In the case of John XXIII, he admits that those who champion revolution are often "particularly endowed with generosity for bringing about justice." In the case of Paul VI, he qualifies his statement by saying: " save where there is a manifest, long-standing tyranny which would do great damage to fundamental personal rights and dangerous harm to the common good of the country."

This exceptive provision may be in the mind of some Catholic thinkers when they give a go-signal to an armed revolution, in the sincere belief that it is the only way left for men to do. George Celestin, a professor of theology at St. Edward's University in Austin, Texas, observes that "Christians are becoming determined to change unjust structures as quickly as possible. This will mean in some cases that the churches may have to preach violence." He regards the pacifist's total renunciation of power as irresponsible.

But perhaps, the most classic example of a Christian who feels he has no alternative but to be violent is Father Camilo Torres, a priest turned guerilla. Thoroughly convinced that an armed revolution was the only way through which his people could change things in Colombia, he wrote: "The people do not believe in elections. The people know that legal means are at an end... The people know that only armed rebellion is left. The people are desperate and ready to stake their lives so that the next generation of Colombians may not be slaves." He incited the people to follow him, declaring in no uncertain terms, "Every Catholic who is not a revolutionary and is not on the side of the revolutionaries, lives in mortal sin."

Now, what does the Protestant evangelical church say about revolution? Well, like the Roman Catholic we have many pronouncements against violent revolutions. In fact, the Quakers and the Mennonites strongly maintain until now that a Christian must be an absolute pacifist. Prof. Heinz Deitrich Wendland, in his paper at the Geneva Conference on Church and Society, maintains that "the rule of God indirectly has social and political repercussions, not by stirring up rebellion, not by the use of political and military force, but solely through the 'quiet' unarmed, loving action and service of Christian groups scattered all over the world, and yet united in Christ."

All official statements on nonviolence will not, for a long time, equal the emphasis given to it by the late Martin Luther King, Jr. Like Mahatma Gandhi, Martin Luther King was convinced that "to meet hate with retaliatory hate would do nothing but intensify the existence of evil in the universe." He believed that reconciliation and nonviolence is the only practical way of dealing with evil and effecting social change.

Of course, in the Protestant church, we also have people like Fr. Camilo Torres and George Celestin who find themselves in situations where the stark realism of evil compels them to use force. Among the most vocal ones is Prof. Richard Shaull of Princeton Seminary. Having lived in Latin America for many years as a missionary, he is convinced that "in certain situations, it might be incumbent upon Christians to take part in revolutionary action which involves the use of force." But it was Dr. Castillo-Cardenas of Colombia who verbalized this idea most emphatically. After pointing out that many forms of force were being employed to protect an unjust order against the underprivileged and oppressed, he said, "Revolution is not only permitted, but is obligatory for those Christians who see it as the only effective way of fulfilling love to one's neighbor."

Coming now to our own situation, what Christian guidance do we have in determining our reaction to the spread of evil in our society? To answer a question like this, our first impulse is to hear what the Bible says. Should we not at least presume that the Popes, Fr. Camilo Torres, Richard Shaull, de la Costa and Manglapus have read the Bible and that their statements, though seemingly conflicting at times, are nevertheless an honest expression of what they believe to be the mind of Christ? We must admit that the tenor of the New Testament is that of love and patience and nonviolence. Nevertheless, it gives us some clear hints that in this world of ours where sin and greed prevail, even love can take the form of anger. The Bible does not allow us to forget that Christ, who is ready to forgive and to understand, turned upside down the tables of the money changers. This means that if and when circumstances become such that we have to overturn the tables in Congress and in Malacañang, then we must prove ourselves capable of doing so even if in the process, we risk our lives and those of our loved ones.

Happily for us, a bloody revolution is not the only alternative we have at present. If we do not like someone in the government, we do not have to shoot him; we can demand for his resignation. It is our Christian duty to use all available legal and peaceful means before we resort to the use of force.

If we are to avoid a bloody revolution or if we are to make peaceful political and social changes that will minimize, if not totally eradicate, the inequalities and injustices we have at present, several things must be done with a sense of Christian stewardship. First, we must actively participate in insuring the election of the best qualified delegates to the Constitutional Convention.* This is a big order and may not be easy at all; but a serious attempt must be made to see to it that the men and women who will constitute the Constitutional Convention are among the best that we have in this fair land of ours — and not those who simply have more money to buy the citizen's votes.

---

* This was written before the election of delegates to the Constitutional Convention.

Second (and this is corollary to what has been said above), every Christian, and every Filipino for that matter, must read our present constitution. If we are to participate intelligently in the discussion of constitutional amendments, the least we should do is to read and reread the fundamental law.

In the third place, the rich and the well-to-do and those who can afford must learn to share voluntarily all that they can with those who have less in life. The widening gap between the rich and the poor in any country is not conducive to the maintenance of peace. If sharing cannot be done as an act of Christian stewardship, it must be done as a practical strategy for avoiding a bloody conflict that is likely to be initiated by those who have nothing to lose. Today, more and more people are beginning to believe that sharing with the poor is no longer a question of charity but of justice. Men are entitled to their basic needs, and those who have more than what they need must be persuaded to share. The tragedy of our age is not that there is not enough for all, but that those who can afford to give are too greedy to think of others. Such consuming selfishness is detrimental to the health of our world.

Finally, if we are to reform our society, we must begin with ourselves. It is easy to denounce the inefficiency of those in public offices, but it takes courage to overcome our own complacency and sluggishness. It is easy to join the crowd and carry placards that express our gripes against those in power, but it takes real guts to put our own house in order and to acknowledge the beam in our own eyes.

In the final analysis, what we ardently need is the sanctifying grace of God. We may write a flawless constitution, we may prescribe a perfect system of government, but if the human heart is manacled by bitterness and hate, there will be no peace, and we may yet end up in planetary death. Our social revolution is not worth our efforts if it leads to more injustices. This is what Jesus meant when He said, "What does it profit a man to gain the whole world if he loses his own soul?"

Today, the greatest challenge is not to die for our country, however glorious that may be. Our real challenge is to live for God. That includes not only true patriotism in times of crisis, but also Christian heroism in times of peace. May the good Lord give us the courage to face this challenge of our time.

28

"Shall We Strike with the Sword?"

Scripture Reading: Luke 22:47-53

Our Lord Jesus and His disciples just had their meal in the Upper Room where Jesus instituted the sacrament of the Lord's Supper. Judas had gone out to contact the authorities and to tell them where Jesus could be found. At that time, Jesus and the rest of the disciples were already on the Mount of Olives. At a certain place, the disciples rested while Jesus walked a few meters farther. And there, a stone's throw from His companions, in the deep silence of the night, Jesus prayed, saying, "Abba Father, if it be possible, let this cup pass over me; yet not my will but thine be done." The Evangelist tells us that while Jesus prayed more earnestly, His sweat fell like great drops of blood. Every now and then He interrupted His prayer to see how His disciples were. He found them sleeping. The second time He went to see them, they were still asleep. He did not bother them for He knew that they were tired. But on His third inspection, He woke them up and enjoined them to pray.

While He was yet speaking, a multitude of soldiers came to arrest Him. They were led by Judas who identified Jesus by kissing Him. It was customary among people in those days to kiss their teacher, especially their respected and favorite teacher, as an act of greeting. But Judas' kiss was a kiss of betrayal. Apparently, the disciples knew what that kiss meant, for when they sensed something wrong was coming, they asked Jesus, "Lord, shall we strike with the sword?" But before Jesus could answer, one of the disciples (identified as Peter in the book of John) drew his sword and cut off the ear of the slave of the high priest. (Also, in the Gospel of John that slave is identified as Malchus. Not Marcos. Malchus.)

Jesus would not allow such violence to go on unchecked. Speaking with firm authority, He said," Enough of this!" Then He restored the ear of the slave.

There are some interesting details in this passage. First, let us note that a big number of soldiers came to arrest Jesus. In the book of John, the word used is **band**. "Judas, then, having received a band of men and officers from the chief priests and Pharisees, cometh thither with lanterns and torches and weapons" (King James Version, John 18:3). In Luke, the word is **crowd** (Revised Standard Version). In the King James Version, the word is **multitude**. At any rate, it was a big group of men that came under the command of some well-trained officers from a nearby military camp. They were armed with swords and clubs — their swords were the equivalent of our modern armalites and their clubs must be similar to the truncheons of our policemen. We are not told whether they had white helmets on their heads.

Was that not an unnecessary, irresponsible, arrogant display of power which we even today find grossly obnoxious? They were to arrest one itinerant preacher who was not even a Jesuit. They must have known that Jesus had only eleven men with Him, and those men were but His students. They were only a very small segment of the student population in the city of Jerusalem and yet a multitude of soldiers came to get Him — as if they were to invade Vietnam! We would think that ten or eleven soldiers would suffice. The big number of soldiers sent is simply offensive to our sense of proportion.

This is one mistake that we in this country must always try to avoid. We expect our authorities to be prepared for any crisis that may be generated by riotous demonstration, but they should not exhibit the same folly of the Jerusalem Metrocom who seemed to gloat over their superior arms and strength. An arrogant display of power does not, in any way, contribute to the maintenance of peace and order. It may even provoke some rascals to resist arms with arms.

Today, we must reiterate our belief in the value and importance of police and military power. In societies like ours where law and order must be preserved, the use of police power is a legitimate necessity. But when such power is needlessly displayed when a hundred unarmed students gather at Mendiola bridge, the people get the impression that our agents of the law are getting excessively panicky. What we want to see are police authorities with confidence in themselves, with infectious sobriety and with admirable poise even in turbulent situations. We don't want them to behave as if they are being threatened by a host of *insurrectos*.

Now, let us ask: Why did the authorities send a multitude of men to arrest Jesus who was not armed? The answer put forward by some Bible scholars is that the authorities strongly suspected that Jesus' disciples were armed. This, of course, is only implied in their question: "Lord shall we strike with the sword?" You will recall that in the early part of chapter 22 in Luke, Jesus was giving instructions to his disciples on their evangelistic mission and on his coming death. At one point, Jesus said, "But now, let him who has a purse take it, and likewise a bag. And let him who has no sword sell his mantle and buy one." Then the disciples answered, "Look, Lord, here are two swords."

Where did they get those swords? They could not have rushed to town at that time of the night to borrow swords from their friends. They must be carrying swords with them. But there is no hint in the entire Bible that carrying arms was customary in those days. Swords were for the use of the police and the army, and when people carried swords with them it was a sign that they were ready for a bloody encounter. The passage seems to imply that the disciples had only two swords.

Even if we grant that all the eleven disciples were armed, still a multitude of soldiers was too big a contingent to arrest them. The authorities must have known that those disciples were mostly fishermen and did not have any training in military matters. In fact, they all slept while Jesus was praying. It did not occur to them that one should be on guard while the others slept. They were amateurs not good enough for a riot, much less for a revolution.

It was apparent that the disciples were not skillful in the use of the swords. If Peter was their model, they certainly were lousy swordsmen. For if Peter was right-handed, then he almost missed Malchus—unless of course he really did not intend to kill him but only wanted to scare him away. At any rate, the vast number of men and officers sent to deal with Jesus and His followers was a perfect example of overacting.

Paradoxically, in spite of all this, the Jerusalem policemen had one sterling virtue which our own authorities should try to emulate. One of their companions was wounded, but they did not gang up on Peter. They had all the reasons to retaliate; after all, Peter started it. But they did not beat him up. Their officers, whoever they might be, did not allow them to fight back violently.

Perhaps, we should require our anti-riot squads to read this portion of the Gospel. We cannot guarantee that their ears will be restored in case cut off by some knife-wielding fellows, but if this passage gives them some insight into how to remain poised in the face of a dangerous provocation, they may yet prevent the loss of many lives and the breaking of many limbs.

Peter started the provocation. It was he who drew his sword and cut off the ear of the slave. For what reasons, we do not know. Perhaps, he was so alarmed by the huge number of soldiers coming that he decided to start the work early to make up for the smallness of his own group. Perhaps, he just lost his temper. And if we know Peter, we will be inclined to believe that he was just carried by his emotion.

Many of our demonstrators today are like Peter. They are at the mercy of their emotion. Having been angered by the angry speeches of their angry leaders, they march down the Luneta to destroy the beautiful garden of Doroy Valencia. They go to the Chinese and American embassies to throw Molotov bombs. They burn cars parked along the way. And the rest of the citizens, instead of joining them in their demonstration, are kept busy covering their building with plywood boards. That is why the price of plywood is going up.

But breaking glass windows will not help our cause and throwing Molotov bombs cannot right the wrong. It will only increase the price of gasoline.

Going back to the story, the disciple's question has become our own question today. "Lord, shall we strike with the sword?" Shall we resort to the use of arms in effecting the changes we want? Shall we resort to violent revolution in order to achieve the social and economic changes we badly need?

In the case of the disciples, they did not wait for Jesus to answer. Perhaps, Jesus, at that very moment, was not prepared to give an answer. Or could it be that before Jesus could answer their question, Peter was quick enough to draw his sword? But Jesus was in their midst. He would not allow such violence to go on unchecked. Sternly, He said, "Enough of this!" "Stop it!" "That's enough!"

Today, I believe the church must echo those same words of Jesus. Some people are itching for the sword and are even publicly inviting us to join them in revolt. Already, we have seen some ugly samples of violence, and such bloody foretaste of an armed revolution must spur the church to say: Enough of this!

These words are not a confession of our cowardice. The teaching of the church is clear: Christians are not afraid to die, especially for the cause of Christ and for the virtues He represents. Our duty is to plant the seed of understanding wherever there is bitterness, of love wherever there is hatred, of justice wherever there is oppression. Christians are the first ones that should be seriously alarmed whenever basic human rights are being recklessly trampled upon by those who have no regard for justice.

The fact is that when Jesus was presented with two swords, He did not ask His men to throw them away. On the contrary, He advised His disciples to sell their mantle in order to buy a sword if they had none, thus, giving them the clear impression that in resisting oppression, the use of force might be necessary.

The Jesuits are right: revolution is justified if, and only if, it is the last recourse open for men to take. This means that we should first exhaust all peaceful and legal means before we consider striking with the sword. Once all peaceful and legal means are exhausted, then it becomes our Christian duty to resort to violence.

And so we ask again: Shall we strike with the sword? I believe the church must answer **no**. At least, not yet! The lines of communication are still open. The leaders of the Establishment are still willing to talk and negotiate with those who are anti-Establishment. We still have confidence in the integrity of the Supreme Court. Even our politicians are now trying their best to behave better. Peaceful demonstrations are still effective. There is no need to strike with the sword.

The other question is: How can we remain calm in the midst of a revolutionary situation? How can we be sober when evil is a stark reality in our country? The answer is: Do what Jesus did. In the face of an impending gloom, under the deepening shadow of the cross, Jesus prayed and thus built up His spiritual resources. That is why when the hour of testing came, when a multitude of soldiers surrounded Him and Peter began swinging his sword, Jesus alone had complete control of the situation, and His heroic handling of that crisis prevented the soldiers from slaughtering the provocateur and His helpless companions.

And that is what we also need to do these days. The time demands that we be on our bended knees. If we are to transcend the tumult of our age, we must stay close to God through prayer and worship. No tranquilizer, no sleeping pills, no hot drinks can calm our nerves. Only prayer can. Only God can. Only in fellowship with the Creator of mankind can we find peace of mind and peace of soul. And so, as we live during these troubled days, let Jesus be our true leader. For when we follow Him, we will never go wrong.

29

The Faces of Violence

Scripture Reading: Luke 20:9-18

The discussion of violence going on in our society today clearly suggests that violence has more than one form and, therefore, has more than one meaning. It appears that a rigid, dogmatic definition of the term is a barrier to an intelligent assessment of our revolutionary situation. It could be that those who are opposed to violence are themselves perpetuating violence, but are not fully aware of it. If they were, they would prefer to use another word to describe their role.

Let us, therefore, speak of at least four faces, forms, or shapes of violence. The first is that which we ordinarily have in mind: i.e., as sometimes exhibited by demonstrators who become riotous. The wanton destruction of public and private properties; the reckless disregard of the law; the senseless, irresponsible assault on the rights and dignity of men, including the innocent, are illustrations of violence which the church cannot tolerate. It is good for us to become nauseated with graft and corruption, allergic to the dishonesty and inefficiency of those in public service, sensitive to the evils of bribery and similar vices. But when such anger produces similar if not worse evils, all we get is pure violence.

This type of violence is likely to be committed not only by those who are deeply dissatisfied with the Establishment, but also by those who are doggedly determined to protect the Establishment. Peace officers who become panicky in the face of a mob can be more violent, because in addition to truncheons and tear gas they also carry guns. Violence of this type is often irrational. It often leads to the indiscriminate use of force. When force is used indiscriminately, it becomes a form of madness that is most inhuman.

The second type of violence is definitely less spectacular but is equally devilish. It comes to us in the form of oppression and exploitation of the poor by the rich and the mighty. When laborers in the farms or factories are not given fair wages, when they are treated simply as tools for production and profit and not as human beings, that is violence. When their rights are trampled upon because of their passiveness or ignorance, when they are not given the opportunity to develop their talents to the fullest and to achieve some progress in their search for social betterment, they suffer from violence.

The prophets of the Old Testament speak of the oppressors as full of violence. In Micah 6:11 and 12, the prophet says, "Shall I count them pure with the wicked balances, and with the bag of deceitful weights?" (Here, the prophet is referring to practices now rampant in our own market places where a ganta of rice is actually less than a ganta; and a kilo of sugar is actually less than a kilo, hence, their balances are "wicked" and their weights are "deceitful.") Then the prophet continues, "For the rich men thereof are full of violence, and the inhabitants thereof have spoken lies, and their tongue is deceitful in their mouth."

In chapter 22 of Jeremiah, the prophet laments saying, "Woe unto him that buildeth his house by unrighteousness, and his chambers by wrong; that useth his neighbour's service without wages, and giveth him not for his work." Is that not exploitation? According to the prophet, such exploitation is a form of violence. In verse 17, he says: "For thine eyes and thine heart are not but for thy covetousness, and for to shed innocent blood, and for oppression, and for violence, to do it." In the same manner, Zephaniah identifies fraud with violence. He says, "on that day I will punish every one who leaps over the threshold, and those who fill their master's house with violence and fraud" (1:9).

The students are right: the glaring inequalities in our society today, the apparent advantages of the influential and the wealthy over those who have no political connections, the injustices created by feudalism, are definitely a form of violence. Such violence may not be as spectacular as throwing Molotov bombs at the American Embassy or the breaking of window glasses or burning parked cars. Nevertheless, it is violence just the same, which God-fearing people must not allow to spread.

The third kind of violence takes the form of indifference and non-involvement. This one looks very innocent and very harmless. It is perhaps the most prevalent in our society. When we do not do anything about the spread of evil, when we retreat into the privacy of our homes while the agents of wickedness roam around the streets, when we prefer to see no evil, hear no evil, and speak no evil so as not to get involved in direct confrontation with evil, we become the silent instruments of violence. This is what theologians call the sin of omission. When public servants behave as if they own the state, when they serve themselves in ways that offend our sense of decency, when immorality is being committed by those who are expected to set the example — when these and similar expressions of moral bankruptcy glare before our eyes and we prefer not to lift our finger lest we get involved, we tolerate the spread of violence by our eloquent silence.

Jesus' parable of the sheep and the goats underscores this point poignantly. To the goats the Master said, "Depart from me, you cursed, into the eternal fire prepared for the devil and his angels: for I was hungry and you gave me no food; I was thirsty and you gave me no drink; naked and you did not clothe me; sick and in prison and you did not visit me." In short, those people were condemned because of their sin of omission. They did not do what they should have done. They went to hell not because they oppressed the poor, not because they did not pay their income taxes, not because they padded the vouchers, not because they indulged in worldly pleasures, but because they failed to get out of their comfortable homes to give aid to the hungry and comfort to the suffering.

Then there is the parable of the good Samaritan. A man fell among robbers on his way from Jerusalem to Jericho. He was stripped of all his belongings and badly beaten up, and left behind half-dead. A priest passed by and saw the dying man, but hurriedly went to the other side of the road and did not even bother to see if the man had a chance to survive. Likewise, a Levite passed by and did no better than the priest. Then a Samaritan, who was looked down upon by the Jews, came to where the dying man was and with all the compassion he had, carefully bound up his wounds, pouring on oil and wine. Then he helped the man to mount his own horse, brought him to an inn, and hired the inn-keeper to take care of him.

The priest and the Levite in this parable may well represent the so-called religious people who are often in the precincts of the church and have developed the habit of saying their prayers, but somehow have not truly understood that religion calls them to participate in setting at liberty those who are oppressed and in extending a helping hand to those who are in trouble.

When Christians keep silence in the midst of a deteriorating social order, their savor has been lost and their light is actually hidden under a bushel. In a situation like that, the prince of darkness will have his day not only because of the persistence of the evil doers, but also because of the complacency and the indifference of the supposedly good men who are not brave enough to be involved.

The fourth kind of violence which has redemptive effects can be described, for lack of a better term, as calculated or regulated violence. It employs a discriminating use of force. It is a rational exercise of power, designed to correct wrong, or rectify mistakes. Indeed, this type of violence hardly looks violent and, therefore, we would rather call it by another name. In the family, and in some organizations, we may call it discipline. When a child misbehaves, we spank him with either belt or rod. When an employee does something wrong, we suspend him without pay, for a short period of time. When a student is often tardy, we give him a conditional grade which can be changed to a passing grade when he makes up for his tardiness. In all these cases, the use of power is dictated by love and concern.

When Jesus in the Temple turned the tables of the money changers upside down, did He not commit a violent act? Call it violent, but He did not destroy the tables. He did not touch the altar, did not break the chandeliers, if there were any. But His act was spectacular enough to get the attention of the crowd. He put His message across, and drove the money-changers out.

Righteous indignation — that is what we mean by regulated violence. In the words of the Apostle Paul, it is being angry without sinning. It is hurting our children when they go wrong, not because we are such strict disciplinarians but because we love them. It is suspending our employees when they misbehave not because we enjoy punishing them but because we want them to realize the need for order and the value of discipline.

This type of violence will oppose the practice of corruption, bribery, and oppression. It will resist the pressure of vested interests. It will fight colonialism and feudalism and imperialism. In the process, it will not become an oppressor, a colonialist, or an imperialist. It will avoid the very evil it seeks to eliminate. If and when it uses force, it will be very cautious and judicious.

People who resort to this type of violence are angry, but will avoid sinning. They will denounce the malpractices of men in power, but their denunciations will not be vulgar. They will not mince a word in their criticism, but they will not be arrogant in their role as critics. They will relentlessly attack the perpetrators of corruption, but they will refuse to be discourteous or impolite. They will engage in demonstration, but they will not approve of riots.

It is this type of violence, inspired by Christian love and concern for justice, that we need to master if we are to restore decency in our public life and instill discipline among our people. To do this requires a certain amount of maturity of mind and emotion. In fact, it requires maturity of faith and a sense of mission.

How, then, can we achieve such maturity which makes us sober in trying circumstances? I suggest that first of all, we must recognize the magnitude of our problems. The evils which lurk in almost every corner of the land cannot be destroyed by human ingenuity alone. The flaws in our social and economic set-up have spiritual undertones, and the answer to such a problem should necessarily touch the human spirit. If our problems were technical in nature, perhaps we could hope to solve them overnight. When we deal with the depraved nature of man and the selfishness of the human heart, even the best of moral armament is insufficient. What we ardently need is a genuine sense of dependence on the spiritual forces that are waiting to be harnessed. Such an attitude can save us from the arrogance which makes us blind to our own inadequacy. This is to say that we must look at our situation as a predicament in need of supernatural help.

In the second place, to be an agent of divine love and to achieve spiritual maturity, we must welcome and benefit from the chastenings of God which come to us. The chastisements of the heavenly Father may appear quite violent, but the pain inflicted is, from the perspective of faith, a warning for us to avoid a greater danger that may come upon us. It is the experience of chastening, which is an aspect of love, that will teach us to be sober and firm in our approach to the excesses of our fellow men. It will keep us human in the use of force, and responsible in the exercise of power.

30

"Righteousness Exalteth a Nation"

Righteousness exalteth a nation; but sin is a reproach to any people. — Proverbs 14:34

This verse succinctly summarizes the experience of men, both as individuals and as tribes or nations. Sin (whether it be in the form of pride or greed or immorality) is a reproach to any people, but righteousness (call it honesty or uprightness or spirituality) has saving power. It can rescue us from shame and death, and lead us to glory and greatness.

The destructiveness of sin is abundantly illustrated in the Holy Scriptures. Adam and Eve's disobedience in the Garden of Eden and their subsequent banishment from Paradise is described by Bible scholars as "the fall." Anyone who sins, who openly defies the clear mandate of the Creator, is falling. Samson fell when he revealed his secrets to Delilah. David fell when he sent Uriah to war in order to have Uriah's wife, Bathsheba. Peter fell when he denied his Lord. The prodigal son fell when he indulged in riotous living.

This simple but dreadful phenomenon is even more conspicuous in the life of nations. The fall of nations and empires can often be traced to the moral decay of the people, to their internal corruption rather than to the external forces of the enemies. Even the strongest nations are not immune to the corroding effects of their arrogance and self-sufficiency. They may defend themselves against the foreign military aggression, but their avid materialism and wanton disregard for morality can reduce them into helpless slaves and captives of their own carnal appetites.

We must, therefore, see the obvious interrelatedness of our mundane problems and the life of the spirit. The floods that occasionally visit us with ferocious effects are somehow related to the avarice of men who carelessly denude our hills and forests without doing an adequate job of reforestation. The spread of *El Tor* in the city can be traced to the inefficiency and lack of vision on the part of public servants, and also to the indifference and lack of coop ration on the part of the citizens. The senseless killings and bloody bickerings in Cotabato and ther places can be attributed to the selfishness of men who are determined to have their own way at any price. The terrible mess we find in Philippine society these days is surely related to the system of graft and corrupt practices that have become endemic in public and private sectors.

In other words, the evils we find flourishing around are the consequences of moral lapses and spiritual deterioration. If we are to free ourselves from the shackles of socio-economic stagnation, from the scourge of tribalism and racism and denominationalism, we simply should not overlook the urgent need for the renewal of the inner man. Of course, renewal should be total, and for this reason we also need the expert guidance of the economists and educators and sociologists and politicians. In the final analysis, our greatest need is to change our sinful, wicked ways and be the men and women God has destined us to be.

How, then, can we acquire that righteousness which can purify our life and can exalt us as a nation? Well, one of the practical things we can do is to sedulously cultivate honesty in and among ourselves. This must begin in our homes, the basic units of our society. The little children in the formative stages of their life must be taught the virtue of honesty not only as something socially desirable but also as realization of the self. Young people must imbibe the love of truth until they discover for themselves the thrilling romance of a godly life and the lasting satisfaction of all honest labors. The adults must set the example of honesty and rectitude, and must constantly resist being tainted by moral compromises.

May I briefly remark, at this juncture, that there are certain situations where absolute honesty may not be the ethical demand. But this is the exception rather than the rule. A doctor, for instance, may discover that his patient is suffering from cancer. If, in his best judgement, telling the truth might do more harm than good, the doctor may not reveal to his patient the condition of his health. This penumbra, if we call it, does not seem to encourage honesty nor does it seem to condemn concealing some secrets. In human life, there are times when we have to face such similar moral dilemmas where Christian guidance is not very clear. In times like that, we need both the sympathy of our friends and the determination to be sincere in our convictions.

As a rule, honesty is a good policy. Honesty increases revenue for the government, inspires more accurate figures on our income tax returns, dictates better quality of work in everything we do. Honesty prevents infidelity between friends, between husbands and wives, between brothers and sisters. It creates a pleasant atmosphere for a happy relationship. It gives no room for cheating and bribery.

Speaking about bribery, we are reminded of the biblical reference condemning it. In the book of Exodus we read: "And you shall take no bribe, for a bribe blinds the officials, and subverts the cause of those who are in the right" (23:8). This is the same admonition we find in the book of Deuteronomy (16:19). The prophet Isaiah, denouncing the princes of Israel, declared that because they took bribes, they could not defend the cause of the fatherless and the widows (1:23). In the book of Amos, those who take bribes afflict the righteous and turn the needy at the gates (5:12). Every sad period in the history of Israel was characterized by too much bribery and the concomitant perversion of justice.

When people give up the virtue of honesty, they often fall into taking bribes. And bribery leads to injustices, and injustices can breed revolution. The cry for a bloody revolution which we hear nowadays is basically a reaction against the injustices which seem to be almost unbearable. And the eruption of that violence cannot be stopped by arming the special forces and the Metrocom with armalites; it can be stopped only when people become more honest and more just, and the demands of relationship are properly satisfied.

In Proverbs 29:2 we read: "When the righteous are in authority, the people rejoice; but when the wicked rule, the people groan." Today, the people are groaning in every corner of this land, and their groaning is becoming more and more alarming. We can no longer pretend we do not hear their cries, for they carry placards for all of us to see. Many of them, specially students, believe that our way of life in this part of the world has been a total failure, and that no meaningful change in our society is possible without violence. They do not even see the feasibility of the Constitutional Convention. They believe we are all victims of imperialism and feudalism, and that our Christian duty at the moment is to rise up in rebellion against the constituted authorities. In short, they are not only groaning; they are angry. They are rebelling against the insincerity and dishonesty of the economically powerful and the politically influential. Their anger cannot be subdued by guns and bullets; it can be appeased only by a radical change that will put an end to bribery and dishonesty in high and low places.

Let honesty be a shining virtue, and there will be peace within our gates. Let honest people rule the land and, in the words of the Proverbs, people will rejoice. But the big trouble is that many honest people do not get elected. (Some honest ones win and we hope we will have more of them). In many cases, honest people are not fortunate enough to win. However, the fact still remains that when we have honest rulers, they have the moral authority to expect their followers to be honest also.

So, if we are to restore righteousness in the land, honesty must be seriously cultivated. In the second place, we must have a healthy attitude towards defeat. In an honest game (like bowling, basketball, chess, golf), to lose is never dishonorable. In the same manner, if one loses in an honest election, there is nothing dishonorable in his defeat. When we are convinced that we would lose face if we don't get elected, the temptation to cheat becomes almost irresistible. When the game is an honest one even defeat can be honorable. It does not profit a man to win in any game if his victory is achieved through fraud. In this life we cannot always win. Sometimes we have to lose; and a healthy attitude towards defeat will not only prevent us from brooding but will also contribute to the propagation of righteousness itself.

Let us remind ourselves that as Christians our goal is not to succeed, but to be faithful. Of course, we all aim at success; we all pray for success; we all want to succeed. But as far as God is concerned, He will be happy if we are faithful. The image of Jesus hanging on the cross is hardly a picture of success. It is a picture of real, utter failure. But He was faithful unto the end and, therefore, He received the crown of everlasting life.

So shall it be with us. May God grant us success. May He grant us humility of spirit when we achieve victory. But above all, may we remain faithful even in defeat. May our faith grow stronger and more meaningful when the door closes before us and we find ourselves staring at the blank wall of failure. We can be grateful that in the providence of God, even the cross can be a throne.

In the third place, if righteousness is to be restored and morality revived, we need to be afraid of God. When I say **afraid** of God I really mean **afraid**. Admittedly, the fear of the Lord includes the elements of love and respect; but it also includes fear. God is love; God is kind; God is good. We know that. We believe in a loving and merciful God. But God is also the God of wrath — and that we sometimes forget. He is the God who gets angry and His anger can be worse than any human anger that we have ever known. Jesus said, "Do not fear those who kill the body but cannot kill the soul; rather, fear him who can destroy both soul and body in hell" (Matt. 10:28). God can consume us in His anger. He can destroy both our body and our soul. He can pursue us even beyond the grave. He can torment us with fire and brimstone.

In other words, we can believe that ours is a moral universe. We will reap everything we sow; we will be accountable for everything we do. The evildoers may have their way and prosper; but they cannot escape from the divine judgement. They may use their wealth and their connections to evade serving a term in prison or paying a fine in court; they may cheat and kill and get away with it; but the God of justice, we can be sure, will never allow such wickedness to go on unchecked, and for every wicked thing they do, they will pay a hundredfold. We must be afraid of God because while we can cheat our fellow men and fool ourselves, we cannot hide anything from Him.

When people truly fear the Lord, they will not likely commit immorality. They will likely behave well, lest they incur the wrath of the Almighty. That kind of fear is indeed the beginning of wisdom, because to be wise is to be good, and to be good is to be godly. The fear of the Lord begets love, and in love obedience becomes free, and in freedom we fulfill ourselves. This is why the fear of the Lord generates righteousness, and righteousness, in turn, exalteth a nation.

Finally, if righteousness is to be restored and morality regained, we need to revitalize the church. The mission of the church is to proclaim and promote righteousness. The church may not be an expert in finance, in education, in government. There is no reason why it should not be an expert in righteousness. There is no reason why the church should not be the conscience of society and the guardian of morality.

The breakdown of morality in this land must be a judgment on the church. It is an indication that the church has not done a good job of inculcating honesty and decency and purity in the hearts and minds of men. It has not resisted the onslaught of secularism and the spread of immorality. It has not produced enough leaders with character, with a deep love for God and country, with a real sense of heroism. The church must have contented itself with ceremonies and rituals, with form rather than substance, with doctrines rather than life.

Fr. Jaime Bulatao, that beloved Jesuit priest, raises serious questions in one of his articles. He writes, "How is it that the Philippines, which according to statistics is so Catholic and is the only Catholic country in the Orient, is so filled with graft and corruption in its government, is so much more dishonest, say, in its customs service than even a pagan country like Japan? Even the ordinary Japanese storekeeper can be much more trusted to do an honest transaction with a customer than a Catholic businessman. How is it that the murder rate in Manila is so high?"[1]

Charito Planas of Quezon City, in one of our CNEA meetings, said: "In Red China, there is no religion, but there is morality. Here in our country there is religion, but there is no morality. Miss Planas, I am sure, intentionally said it the way she did to underscore the sad fact that while in our country we find Christian churches at almost every street corner, our way of life is far from being Christian. The churches must wake up before it is too late, and make up for the lost opportunity by helping set things right, beginning with ourselves.

In the context of the Christian faith, when I say church I mean you and me [and not just the church in the third person]. The revitalization of the church, the body of Jesus Christ, can come about only when we in this congregation and the brethren in other congregations resolve with firmness and humility to be the instruments of God's peace. This means we the people of the church should be honest ourselves, should nurture a healthy attitude towards defeat, should strive to be faithful, and should learn to fear the Lord. It means taking seriously the ministry of the church and the cause of the Christian movement. In fact, whether we like it or not, it means giving more of our substance, our time and talents to enhance the work of the church — so that with our gifts and through our labors more and more people may learn to be righteous. Let everyone be on fire for God, for the church, and for the gospel, and righteousness will flow like mighty streams.

I pray to God that this church which we love so dearly may continue to do its share in moulding Christian character among men and in sowing the seed of righteousness through our corporate worship and through our witness in our homes and in our places of work. If we have that determination, we may yet envision a bright future for the Philippines and for the world.

---

[1] *Moral Value,* Vol. III, p. 1.

31

How to be Sober

Scripture Reading: II Corinthians 4:1-18

The happenings in our country today are very upsetting — nationwide drivers' strike, student unrest, riotous demonstrations, the threats of martial law, etc. Understandably, civic and religious leaders are appealing for sobriety to avoid acting carelessly in the face of mounting crises.

The question is, "How do we become sober?" Sobriety is not something that can be mechanically generated. It is essentially a spiritual condition of the heart and mind which refuses to be uncontrollably excessive or unreasonably extravagant. Sobriety cannot be legislated; it can only grow out of a disciplined character that receives nourishment from the transforming influence of the Holy Spirit.

How do we become sober? While there is no sure formula for sobriety, we should mention at least three things which can help us to become sober. One is prayer. To pray is to stand before the throne of grace, and in the presence of God we can relax and be at peace.

Prayer is a kind of spiritual tranquilizer; it calms us down, cools off our rising temper, and gives us a better perspective. When things go wrong and we are either enraged or frightened, prayer will control our anger and dispel our fear.

The story of great men in the Bible is often the story of their victory in difficult circumstances through prayer. Moses, for instance, was destined to be a leader of a great nation in search of freedom and a place they could call their own. They were in a foreign land as slaves of the Egyptian Pharaoh. How to get away from the yoke of bondage with almost nothing in their hands was a crucial test on his leadership. Dealing with a capricious king required more than political acumen, and escaping from the blood-thirsty Egyptian soldiers was simply beyond his wits.

Day and night he called upon God, asking for wisdom and courage. One time, he almost gave up because he could hardly deliver a speech in public; a task he could not avoid as a public servant. But the mighty hand of God was upon him, and while he did not live long enough to reach the Promised Land, he became immortal in the hearts of his descendants.

Of course, our supreme example is Jesus Christ himself. Criticized for going about and doing good, hated for dining with publicans and sinners, maligned for healing the sick and for preaching the Word, He sought refuge in the sanctuary of prayer. And because He lived in constant fellowship with God, He died with a prayer on His lips. That is why He rose again from the dead: the purity of His Life cannot be contained in the grave, and the power of His love cannot be frustrated by human wickedness.

The same testimony of victory and blessing is what we hear from those who follow in Jesus' train. Paul, for instance, was suffering from what he called a thorn in his flesh and was always threatened with a sword over his head. Many times he was imprisoned; several times he thought it was the end of the road for him. But a portion of his letter to the Corinthians eloquently reveals the abiding peace he possessed, that peace that made him more than a conqueror. He writes, "We are troubled on every side, yet not distressed; we are perplexed, but not in despair; persecuted, but not forsaken; cast down, but not destroyed." Only a man of prayer can give such mighty testimony. Only a man of faith can know that serenity of soul.

Does not our own experience confirm the efficacy of prevailing prayer? When the going is rough and the world looks dreary, when enemies laugh and friends deride, when nature frowns and the light of hope flickers, we find solace and peace in the presence of the Eternal. Prayer gives us strength. Prayer gives us health. Prayer enables us to transcend ourselves and to look at life from the perspective of eternity. When we are betrayed or cheated or persecuted or simply ignored, prayer can open up the way to the source of Power, so that we can say with the Apostle Paul that though we be cast down, we will not be destroyed.

At this juncture, we should quickly point out that if prayer is to fulfill its ministry, it should not be an expression of human disappointment but a vehicle of divine forgiveness. When prayer is the voice of anger, we will likely become deaf to the "still, small voice." We will likely convince ourselves that because we are the friends of God, therefore, our enemies are also God's enemies.

Are there not people today who pray as if the present administration has become completely godless? And there must be some friends of the administration who pray as if the critics and the rebels are completely misguided. Very often our prayers reveal the fact that while we can see the beams in our brother's eyes, we cannot see the speck in our own eyes.

But once this tendency is guarded against, prayer can be the window of the soul through which the fresh air of God's forgiveness can enter and drive away the suffocating fumes of excessive pessimism. Prayer becomes its own answer, for it is the cry of our hearts for divine companionship. Men of prayer know the secret of sobriety.

In the second place, if we are to be sober we must try to be rational. In the words of a newspaper editorial, we must try to reason together. Negatively, it means we should refuse to be emotional or carried away by passion and feelings. Positively, it means we should keep an open mind and be willing to listen to the arguments of all sides.

Such an attitude is a prerequisite to any meaningful dialogue. Participants in a dialogue must be prepared to articulate their position. More importantly, they must be willing to yield to reason and truth. This is why a dialogue becomes a sheer *palabas* when the participants, from the very beginning, are already set in their thinking and that their decision is already predetermined.

God, whose thoughts are higher than our thoughts and whose ways are not our ways, bids us to reason with Him with the assurance that though our sins be as scarlet, they shall be as white as snow. We negate the very nature of our being if we refuse to reason together among ourselves. In the bivouac of life, there is need for us to be rational. Sobriety can be our reward for reasoning together.

Finally, if we are to be sober we must constantly remind ourselves that God is the Lord of history. If we truly love Him, we can safely believe that all things will work together for good. History is moving towards the final consummation of His will. No amount of human freedom, which is often turned into a license, can ever defeat the purposes of God which He had laid even before the foundation of the world.

This is what it means to believe in the almightiness of God: no matter what we do, and no matter what we do not do, His will will reign supreme. The dictator may have their day, the vandals may roam around with utter impunity, but they can never defeat the forces of truth and goodness. Ultimately, they will wither like grass and reap shame and infamy. God alone is omnipotent, and those who trust in Him will never know the sting of failure. In the words of a popular hymn:

> Though the cause of evil prosper,
> > Yet 'tis truth alone is stronger.
> Though her portion be the scaffold
> > And above the throne be wrong,
> > Yet that scaffold sways the future;
> > And behind the dim unknown
> Standeth God within the shadow,
> > Keeping watch above His own.

Our Christian faith is firmly established on the assurance that God will overcome. And He will work through men of His own choosing. He will not forever ignore the boasting of arrogant men. He will not let man prevail. Because of that assurance we need not be afraid. In the words of Martin Luther, "Though this world with devils filled should threaten to undo us, we will not fear for God hath willed His truth to triumph through us."

Today, when crisis after crisis shakes the very foundation of our faith, we would do well to remind ourselves that "God is our mighty Fortress, a Bulwark never failing." We would do well to scan the pages of the Scriptures and meditate on the Words of truth and life. When the angry words of men chill us to the bones, the living Word of God will keep us from falling.

"Trust in the Lord with all thine heart and lean not unto thine own understanding. In all thy ways acknowledge Him, and He shall direct thy paths." "They that wait upon the Lord shall renew their strength. They shall mount up with wings like eagles; they shall run and not be weary; they shall walk and not faint."

"God is our refuge and strength, a very present help in trouble. Therefore will not we fear, though the earth be removed, and though the mountains be carried into the midst of the sea."

"Come unto me, all ye that labour and are heavy laden and I will give you rest. Take my yoke upon you, and learn of me; for I am meek and lowly in heart; and ye shall find rest unto your souls."

" In the world ye shall have tribulations; but be of good cheer: I have overcome the world."

32

The Golden Rule

"So whatever you wish that men would do to you, do so to them; for this is the law and the prophets" (Matthew 7:12). This is what is popularly known as the golden rule. It is golden in that it has "inestimable value and utility." It is a rule not that it is a legal regulation but that it is "an ideal principle." Some people call it the capstone of the whole Sermon on the Mount. One scholar calls it the Everest of all ethical teaching.

Prof. William Barclay tells us that the golden rule has many parallels, although mostly in the negative form. A Jewish teacher by the name of Hillel said to a proselyte: "What is hateful to yourself, do to no other; that is the whole Law, and the rest is commentary." In the *Book of Tobit*, an apocryphal book, Tobias speaks to his son saying: "What thou thyself hatest, to no man do." In another Jewish document, called *The Letter to Aristeas*, we read the story of an Egyptian king who gave a banquet at which he asked his guests some very difficult questions. For instance, he asked, "What is the teaching of Wisdom?" One scholar stood up and said, "As you wish that no evil should befall you, but to be a partaker of all good things, so you should act on the same principle towards your subjects and offenders, and you should mildly admonish the noble and good."

Tsze-Kung asked Confucius: "Is there one word which may serve as a rule of practice for all one's life?" To which Confucius replied, "Is not reciprocity such a word? What you do not want done to yourself, do not do to others."

The Greeks and the Romans were familiar with the golden rule in the negative form. King Nicocles is said to have advised his subordinate officials by saying: "Do not do to others the things which make you angry when you experience them at the hands of other people." We remember the Stoics for their basic maxim: "What you do not wish to be done to you, do not do to anyone else." In short, many teachers have said, "Do not do to others what you would not have them do to you," but Jesus says, "Do to others what you would have them do to you." Certainly, the golden rule in this positive form is richer and more meaningful.[1]

---
[1] Barclay, *Commentary on Matthew*, pp. 277-278.

But the golden rule, taken in itself or taken out of context, is not always true. Our own experience reminds us that sometimes our acts of goodness are not reciprocated by acts of goodness. There are cases where our goodness to other people is rewarded with ingratitude or even meanness. It is not always true that when we do good to others they will do good to us in return. Jesus is the classic example. He went about doing good, but He ended up hanging on the cross.

Of course, there are people with a sense of gratitude. There are those who will treat us fairly because of the fair treatment we are giving them. The fact is that it is not always true that what we do to others will also be done to us.

In the second place, taken out of context the golden rule is sub-Christian, if not unchristian, in its motivation. If I want you to send me Christmas greetings, then I must send you Christmas greetings. If I want you to praise me, I must praise you to the highest heavens. If I want you to do me some favors, I should first do you some favors. In the same manner, if I don't want you to criticize me, I will not criticize you. I will not attend your birthday party, so I don't have to invite you to my birthday party. If this is the rule, it does not look golden at all. At best, it is no more than calculating justice. How, then, are we to understand the golden rule?

Well, one of the first things we have to do is to understand it in the light of the context. And its context is not just chapter 7 of Matthew but the entire Sermon on the Mount. You will notice that the golden rule begins with the word **So** — "So whatever you wish that men would do to you, do so to them..." In the King James Version, the word used is **therefore.** "Therefore, all things whatsoever ye would that men should do to you, do ye even so to them..." "This is because Jesus had said so many things which constitute a premise, and now He concludes by saying **therefore.**

Briefly, the Sermon on the Mount is a discourse on the new law that should govern the community whose members expect to be in the Kingdom of God. There you have the beatitudes, a sermon on the relation of the disciples to the world, new interpretations of old laws on murder and anger, adultery and lust, divorce, oaths, hatred and love, etc. It also speaks about prayer and fasting, about anxiety and trust, about the censorious spirit and prayer — and then the golden rule, as a general rule for behavior. In short, the new law is the law of love. But it is love that does not abolish the law. And it is law which is an expression of love.

Now, both love and law and the golden rule itself explicitly remind us that one basic problem we have in life is the problem of relationship. Dr. D. Martyn Lloyd-Jones, in his *Studies in the Sermon on the Mount*, contends that the great problem of the twentieth century is that of relationship. He writes, "Sometimes we foolishly tend to think that our international and other problems are economic, social or political; but in reality they all come down to this, our relationships with people...it is what I myself want, and what the other person wants; and ultimately all the clashes and disturbances in life are due to this."[1] Think of whatever problem you have right now, and see if it does not affect your relationship with some people.

In a world where a certain degree of harmony in the relationship of people has to be maintained, law must be enriched by love. The law can compel us to drive safely, but love will cause us to give a lift to someone who has no ride. The law can compel us to serve people, but love will cause us to give our best in serving them. The law can fix the taxes we have to pay, but love can cause us to give without counting the cost.

"Therefore, whatever you wish that men would do to you, do so to them." The central idea is not to get the services we want from other people, but to serve them the way we would want to be served. In other words, the best that we want for ourselves should be the basis of our service to others. This is parallel to what Jesus said about loving our neighbors: "Thou shalt love thy neighbor as thyself." We love ourselves, don't we? In fact, the root of our problems sometimes is that we love only ourselves. But Christianity demands that our love of neighbors should be no less than our love of self. In like manner, the service we render to our fellow men must be no less than the service we ourselves would want to enjoy.

Quite clearly, Jesus did not intend to tell us that if we do good to others they will do us good also. The fact is that human goodness is not possible apart from the work of the Holy Spirit, for only God is good. What He teaches is that those who have known the presence of God's spirit will somehow manifest some qualities of goodness by giving their best service, not because they want to be served in return, but because they are citizens of the kingdom.

Understood in this light, the golden rule is indeed the capstone of all ethical ideals. It has practical value because some people do appreciate the deeds of kindness we do to them; and it also has spiritual value because it is the expression of Christian love which fortifies us against ingratitude

---

[1] Lloyd-Jones, *Studies in the Sermon on the Mount,* Vol. II, p. 208.

and envy and arrogance and insolence. Because it is the rule of love, the practice of the golden rule is never motivated by any selfish desire to be served.

Now, to those who have pledged their loyalty to Christ, the golden rule means at least three things. First, it inspires us to act positively. The urge to do some things as a normal compulsion will naturally refrain us from doing some things. After all, living a Christian life always requires us not to do certain things. But essentially, Christianity is doing and being. It is not enough that we don't steal or commit adultery; we must also promote honesty and work for peace. It is in this aspect of doing where we authenticate the dynamism of the Christian faith.

There are some churches in the United States which require their people to be members of at least one service organization either in the church or outside the church — either in the Women's Club or Choir or Sunday School or in the YWCA or Rotary or Boy Scouts. The idea is to be directly related to a service organization in order to give flesh to our creeds and beliefs. A man may have memorized the Apostle's Creed and the Lord's Prayer and the Ten Commandments, but if that is all he has got, we may well doubt the authenticity of his faith. A follower of Christ cannot remain in the ghetto of his narrow interests. He has to be in the world where the action is. The golden rule is a call to involvement — to a life of witness and service. It is a call for us to act positively.

Second, the golden rule is a solemn confirmation of the infinite value of man, every man. When we serve people in obedience to the will of God, we acknowledge their importance. Admittedly, some men are more important than others; the general manager is more important than the janitor; the president than the barrio captain; the Pope than the parish priest. But this is only in the hierarchy of men. There is no question that in the sight of God all men are equally precious. Jesus did not say, "Whatever you wish that certain men would do to you. . ." He said, "What you wish that men" — all men without distinction; the men and women who are the objects of God's love and the crown of all creation.

The death of Christ upon the Cross is an eloquent tribute to the worth of men. He died that we may live. He left the throne of glory and dwelt among us to rescue us from the clutches of sin and death. He is the Good Shepherd who leaves the fold to look for the missing soul. We are important because God created us in His own image.

It is this conviction in the value of the human personality which leads us to cultivate a deep reverence for life itself. Take away this conviction from our scale of values and men will not be afraid to kill and to plunder. The ambushes and murders which we witness almost everyday are unmistakable signs that our belief in the worth of the human life is being eroded by our neurotic propensity to cannibalism. They are signs that the churches have failed to instill in the hearts of men that reverence for life is a central tenet of the Christian faith. Wanton killing even in broad daylight is a disgrace especially to the churches which are supposed to be the moral guardians of our society. For it to happen in a supposedly Christian country is to betray the naked fact that Christianity in this land of ours is more of a label rather than life; and all the pomp and splendour of our worship services are more of a ceremony rather than experience.

Teaching men to practice the golden rule will revive our lost reverence for life. It will radically improve the services in public and private offices. It will bring out the best we have as a people and as believers. Those who follow in the footsteps of the Master are sure to be the instruments of God in redeeming our world from irresponsibility and suicidal tendencies.

Finally, the practice of the golden rule will entail some suffering. This is the unavoidable concomitant of service which is rendered in the spirit of love. One of the characteristics of love is its ability to suffer. In the words of the Apostle Paul, "love suffereth long." But it has redemptive effects. It helps us to bear the sting of bitterness and to face the fact that in this world of sin, even our best services could be ridiculed or purposely frustrated. When people mock us for our sincerity, when they deride our honesty, when they hate us for our love and crucify us for our loyalty, only patient suffering can prevent us from getting the guns and shooting them to death. When friends forsake us and loved ones fail us and the world looks dark and dreary in spite of all our faithfulness and purity and concern for them, only suffering love can hold our peace and keep us from falling.

Suffering is involved in the practice of the golden rule because the golden rule is a call to bear the cross. To do good to those who revile us, to serve those who hardly notice our presence, to love the unloving and the unlovely — that is the golden rule. It is a cross of discipleship that we must shoulder without murmuring, if our world is to know something about the beauty of God's saving grace. It was through the cross that Jesus saved us from sin; and it is through the cross that we can save our homes, our church, our world from total failure or disintegration.

"So whatever you wish that men would do to you, do so to them; for this is the law and the prophets." If we obey this rule, we will experience the greatest joy of the Christian life, the joy that can convert our sufferings into an act of love. If we practice the golden rule, we will obey the will of God and find fulfillment of our deepest yearnings.

33

Mission Possible

Scripture Reading: Matthew 24:3-13

One of the most popular TV programs we have these days is titled "Mission Impossible." Often it is the story of a man, or a few men, commissioned to do a certain task for their government, a task that often looks impossible but somehow, in the end, the objective is achieved either through sheer luck or through some marvelous human ingenuity. Of course, the plots vary, as they should, but every plot is a gallant tribute to the discipline and sense of mission of the main characters.

It occurs to me that if the discipline and sense of dedication of those people could be imbibed by us, the mission of the church cannot be impossible. The fulfillment of the Christian mission will be service rendered not only to our God, but also to the peoples of this world. It is the greatest, noblest mission in which mortals can achieve immortality.

The glorious message of the gospel is that all of us, members of the church, are called upon to carry out that mission. It is a humbling fact that in spite of our unworthiness and natural inadequacies God has called us to carry out His mission. This is also a sobering thought for the privilege carries with it a most solemn responsibility. We would do well to remember that our discipleship is a serious business.

I presume we are resolved to do our best in the service of the Lord and therefore we would welcome being reminded of our supreme duty as agents of God's mission. If we are to do a good job, we should always be clear on the nature of our mission. This is why we must inquire about what our mission is. Just what is our mission? What does God want us to do these days? What must we do as a church, as a part of the Body of Christ?

At the risk of over-simplification, may I suggest that our mission is to spread the love of God in Jesus Christ by meeting human needs. It is to help meet the needs of men, in the name and in the spirit of Christian love. Our mission is to be the instruments of God in saving His people from famine and hunger, from sickness and ignorance, from slavery, from corruption, from avarice and vindictiveness.

Of course, our mission is also to preach the Word of God, the good news, that men may come to the saving knowledge of Jesus Christ. Our mission is to persuade our fellow men to grow within the fellowship of the church. We aim to teach them to worship, to pray, to give, and to do good to their fellow men. There is a need for us to emphasize today that mission is mission to the whole man, including his nonspiritual needs. In other words, it is helping men to become more human.

To understand this in our own context, we must know the needs of our own people. We do not have to look too hard to see that, among other things, we have nagging economic needs. Many do not have enough to eat. Millions have no jobs. The prices of gas and oil go up; jeepney and bus drivers go on strike. We are told we do not have enough facilities in the fire department. The inmates at the national penitentiary are half-naked. We do not have enough trucks to collect the garbage. We do not have enough money to pay government doctors. This litany can be kilometric, and it is a litany of ardent economic needs.

I know there are Christians whose doctrinal orientation does not allow them to meddle in anything that is clearly the responsibility of the government. They will confine themselves to the so-called spiritual concerns of the church and leave the question of garbage collection and fire fighting facilities to the proper civil authorities. They are right in that the church should not meddle with the government, just as the government should not meddle with the church. They are right in delineating the church from the state to avoid any unholy alliance between the two and the temptation of one to lord it over the other. But they are wrong if they think that the church is isolated from the state as if the members of the church are not also citizens of the state. They are wrong if the missionary spirit is confined only within the religious activities of the congregation.

What we need to stress here is that the church has a mission in meeting the economic needs of men, and that mission is a spiritual undertaking. If one is hungry, we must give him food. If he is thirsty, we must give him something to drink.

After all, when we talk of the relevance of the church to the world, we mean the ability of the church to touch the very core of life. Relevance is hardly seen when poverty walks like rags in every corner of the land and all that the church can offer is a word of prayer. Relevance is not manifest when people have empty stomachs and all the church asks them is whether they are saved. How often has the church betrayed its mission by conveniently engaging itself in purely spiritual pursuits?

A courageous reassessment of our Christian mission should embolden us to consider projects that will provide employment for the unemployed. We need to realize that the economic sphere is a vital area of Christian witness.

The church must also think of training people for certain jobs. This is now being done, in a small scale, by the Manila Community Services, a service arm of our churches. Job-seekers are interviewed to discover their interests and those who show promise in such vocations as driving, typing, auto mechanics and the like are given help to acquire those skills. They are also helped to get employment after their training.

In fact, we are encouraging our church-related schools to offer vocational courses, if at all desirable. The idea is to gear our educational ministry to meeting the country's needs and in a slowly industrializing society like ours, vocational schools have a role to play.

Surely, we have other needs that are not basically economic. Those needs can be generally described as social, political, cultural, moral and even religious. Sometimes the need is distinctly social, or political, or moral, but often it is a mixture of the three. The principle remains the same, namely, that wherever human needs exist we have a mission to accomplish. We must, however, confess that in the political field the mission of the church is a little delicate. There are highly technical issues on which the church, as an organization, does not have the competence to judge and in which Christians are apt to differ in their judgments. Issues of that nature are better left to the conscience of the individual Christian.

Furthermore, the church must avoid getting mixed up in partisan politics, unless the issue at stake involves a basic moral decision in which the church is sure of its stand. By all means, the church must cooperate in promoting clean elections, in clarifying political issues, in safeguarding the sanctity and sacredness of the human personality. Above all, Christians and the churches must be the vanguards of righteousness and justice and must take the lead in providing leadership in moral reformation.

Impossible? Not to men of faith, for they can be more than conquerors. Mission-minded Christians become civic-minded citizens, and their zeal for the Kingdom of God can spell blessings for the country of their birth. Therefore, if we are to fulfill our mission, we must grow in spirit.

Here we come to the crux of the problem. Spiritual growth is our basic need, therefore, it is a basic part of our Christian mission. Hence we must ask ourselves: How do we cultivate the life of faith? How do we achieve spiritual maturity?

This, admittedly, is a big question. But in the light of our present concern, that mission is meeting human needs. We must suggest that stewardship is one discipline that can contribute to spiritual growth and it is in this area of stewardship where many of us are sadly wanting.

If only to underscore the gravity of our shortcomings as stewards, we must recall the strong words of the Bible against those who neglect their commitments. In the book of Malachi, the people of Israel ask, "Will a man rob God?" The answer comes ringing, "Yet you have robbed me." The question is asked again, "Wherein have we robbed you?" God's reply is straight to the point, "In tithes and offering."

Every now and then we read in the papers about robberies here and there sometimes in broad daylight. As civilized people we feel sick in the stomach to read about those ugly things. We even pray that somehow such wickedness may end and that the peoples of this earth may live in harmony and peace. But let us ask ourselves: Do we feel embarrassed when God Himself is robbed? Have we ever thought that we ourselves are the robbers?

"Bring ye all the tithes into the storehouse, that there may be meat in mine house, and prove me now herewith, saith the Lord of hosts, if I will not open you the windows of heaven, and pour you out a blessing, that there shall not be room enough to receive it." (Malachi 3:10) Here is one of the greatest challenges for us: that we prove God and see if He would not open the windows of heaven.

One big blessing we receive from faithful stewardship, aside from the dedicated resources with which to meet the obligations of the institutional church in carrying out its mission, is the abiding peace of soul which we experience especially in times of stress and strain. It is peace that comes from the indwelling presence of the Spirit. It is peace that keeps us together when the world is breaking to pieces. It is this inward peace of soul which we most ardently need if we are to help meet human needs and fulfill the deepest yearnings of our hearts. I pray that we may know something of that peace, for it will be a source of hope in times of despair and a source of strength in times of trouble.

34

"Be Not Anxious"

Do not be anxious about your life, what you shall eat or what you shall drink, nor about your body, what you shall put on. Is not life more than food, and the body more than clothing? — Matthew 6:25

In order to understand the word **anxious** in this verse, a brief review of the other translations will be helpful. In the King James Version, the word used is **thought:** "Take no thought for your life, what ye shall eat, or what ye shall drink; nor yet for your body, what ye shall put on." William Barclay uses the word **worry:** "Do not worry about your life. . . ." Wycliffe had it: "Be not **busy** to your life." Tyndale, Granmer and the Geneva Version all had: "Be not **careful** for your life." Here the word **careful** is in the literal sense: full of care. It appears, therefore, that by anxiety Jesus means excessive concern, extreme worrying, magnified fear, persistent brooding, morbid uneasiness.

In other words, Jesus is not advocating a careless, thoughtless attitude in life. He is not ignoring the value and necessity of planning for our future. In fact, some of His parables underscore the importance of good planning. He tells us that if we are to build a house, we must be sure we have enough materials to finish it, otherwise a certain segment may remain incomplete. What Jesus is forbidding is that anxious worrying which takes a lot of joy out of our life, creates unnecessary tensions detrimental not only to our souls but also to our bodies.

To be sure, anxiety is a much more complex subject and our definition of it is woefully inadequate. It is, in fact, a technical term in theological and philosophical discussions as well as in psychological and psychiatric studies. The psychoanalyst, for instance, will distinguish between neurotic anxiety and erotized anxiety, between the free-floating anxiety and basic anxiety, between instinctual anxiety and manifest anxiety, between organic anxiety and primal anxiety. Perhaps, our common anxiety today is the "free-floating" one. This and the other types of anxiety have their peculiar characteristics. But we just wonder whether Jesus had in mind these technical descriptions of anxiety when He said, "Do not be anxious about your life." Jesus was not speaking as a professional psychoanalyst, although He certainly knew the fickleness of the human heart. He was speaking as a Teacher of human nature who knew the utter futility of wasting life in needless brooding. Surely, the message He wants to convey is that we can overcome the tragic difficulties of the human situation and that life can be meaningful and satisfying even in chaotic and perilous circumstances.

Perhaps, it should be pointed out that, in a real sense, anxiety cannot be completely removed. It is what the theologians call existential anxiety and is primarily understood as the threat of nonbeing. It can be overcome only by affirming our being. Since the threat is always there, there is always a need for self-affirmation. This existential anxiety "is the natural anxiety of man as man," and its object is often vague. Prof. Paul Tillich observes that "it expresses itself in loss of direction, inadequate reactions, (or) lack of intentionality."[1] To live is to face anxiety with courage and to transcend the threat of nonbeing by relating ourselves to the Ultimate Being.

This is why, strictly speaking, our concern is not to eliminate, but to overcome, anxiety. This means not allowing ourselves to be anxious even if anxiety is a part of our human existence. We are to face the unavoidable anxiety and, therefore, must mobilize the spiritual forces that will save us from despair. The question then is: How do we do this?

First of all, it will help us to remember the sheer pointlessness of being anxious. In the words of Jesus, we do not add one cubit to our height, or one year to our life, by worrying about it. One cubit is 18 inches and, perhaps, it is more than what we want when we really wish we were a little taller than we are. But the point is that anxiety cannot perform a miracle or produce the very things we need. On the contrary, it can be injurious because it makes us desperate and such despair can be a foretaste of hell. Reinhold Niebuhr is regarded as the author of the following prayer:

> "Lord, grant us the strength to change what should be changed; and the courage to accept what cannot be changed; and the wisdom to distinguish one from the other."

Anxiety is the lack of courage to accept what cannot be changed, and any rebellion against anything that cannot be changed can affect our appetite and destroy our hopes. We save ourselves from needless suffering

---

[1] Paul Tillich, *The Courage to Be,* p. 36f.

when we remember that being anxious does not in any way contribute to our physical and spiritual well-being.

In the second place, it will help us to remember that anxiety is the opposite of faith. It is a form of distrust in the goodness of God. Jesus says, "Look at the birds of the air, they neither sow nor reap nor gather into barns, and yet our heavenly Father feeds them." Of course, we may ask: why compare us with the birds? The birds are not anxious, not because they have faith in the goodness of God, but simply because they are not capable of being anxious. Perhaps, if the birds could be anxious, they, too, would be anxious.

A re-reading of the Sermon on the Mount will reveal that the point is not whether the birds are susceptible to anxiety. Jesus, I believe, has enough knowledge about birds to know that they are not capable of being anxious. What He wants us to see is that if God is good enough to feed the birds, He is good enough to feed His children who are more valuable than the birds.

Actually, the crucial question that is not easy to answer is this: If God really cares to feed His children, why are there so many who die of hunger everyday? Why are there millions who go to bed every night without a decent meal during the day? The phrase "go to bed" is not entirely accurate when we realize that the hungry millions do not have beds. They are "floor leaders" — they sleep on the floor. Why is there massive poverty on the face of this earth when God is supposed to be good?

We cannot treat this question properly without diverting from our main subject. We must at least point out that the goodness of God can be thwarted by the selfishness of men. It is not fair to doubt the reality of divine goodness just because poverty walks like rags. In the same way, it is misleading to identify material abundance with the graciousness of heaven. In many parts of the world the prevalence of hunger is not due to the lack of goods, but due to the consuming greediness of those who have more than what they need but are not willing to share.

Thirdly, we can overcome anxiety by reducing it into fear. As stated above, the object of anxiety is vague — it cannot be easily pinpointed. But fear has a definite object and, therefore, can be analyzed, attacked or endured. This conversion of anxiety into fear is possible because they have the same ontological root. Once it is reduced into fear, we can marshall our strength and courage and face the object of our fear. Once we know where our enemy is, we can position ourselves at a place where an encounter with him gives us a fair chance of victory.

Admittedly, such victory is not easy to achieve. Fear is our enemy number one. As far as the biblical record is concerned, fear was the first enemy which attacked man. When Adam and Eve broke God's commandment by eating the fruit of the forbidden tree of life, they became afraid, and hid themselves among trees. In the New Testament, the Apostle Paul calls death our last enemy, and since we fear death, fear is, therefore, our first and last enemy. .

It is not surprising, therefore, that the Bible has much to say about fear. In most cases, however, the biblical injunction is "Fear not," "Be not afraid," "Be of good courage," "Be of good cheer," "Let not your heart be troubled." The Psalmist, who knew the sustaining presence of God, wrote, "I sought the Lord and He heard me, and delivered me from all my fears."

Fear is a stark reality that can ruin our spirits, but it may be no more than a shadow and an imagination. It will be wise to ascertain the authenticity of our fears before we spend our vitality on mastering them. We know the case of a man who was greatly terrified when he saw in the distance what he thought was a monster. When it came a little closer, he realized it was not a monster, but only a man. When that man came still closer, he saw that the man was his brother.

Alexander the Great was said to have waged military campaigns from Macedonia to India riding upon a beautiful black horse called Bucephalus. The horse was so vicious he would kick at anyone who came near him. Alexander discovered that the horse was afraid of his shadow, and so he took him "by the bridle and turned his head towards the sun." The horse leaped to his back and galloped up and down, and became more popular than Alexander's right-hand man. His story reminds us that, at times, what frightens us is only a shadow.

And what do we read about the disciples who were caught by the storm one dark night on the Sea of Galilee? They saw Jesus walking over the sea and they were terrified, thinking He was a ghost. He was not a ghost, but their friend and master. Their fear vanished when they heard Him say, "It is I, be not afraid."

Once we are able to eliminate our imaginary fears, we can concentrate our efforts on fighting our real fears. We will try to preserve our health as best as we can so our knees may not tremble, not too much anyhow, when we are afraid. We may try to cultivate the habit of positive thinking so our minds need not be confused by the conflicting claims of falsehood. We may secure our gates and doors so that burglars may not easily break into our homes or offices. Whatever else we do, one thing is most needful in order to overcome fear; and that is to fear God. As the book of Proverbs says, "The fear of the Lord is the beginning of wisdom." This is the same message of an old hymn which says,

> Henceforth, the majesty of God revere.
>
> Fear him, and you have nothing else to fear.

Now, the fear of the Lord is not the same fear which is the child of anxiety. It is not an emotional reaction to someone who capriciously wields authority and power. Rather, by fear of God we mean that reverent attitude which inspires obedience and love. "God has not given us the spirit of fear, but of love, and of a sound mind." This is the wonderful mystery, that fear, which is our first and last enemy, can be overcome by the fear of God!

Now we return to our text: "Do not be anxious about your life." And, precisely, our problem is how not to be anxious. We have noted its futility. We have unmasked its nature which is the opposite of faith. We have suggested that it be reduced into fear and overcome it with our fear of God. But whatever else we do, Jesus' direct suggestion should never be overlooked. He says, "Seek ye first the Kingdom of God and His righteousness." The Kingdom of God is a mighty fortress which can withstand the onslaughts of anxiety. It is a citadel of power where the sense of transcendence over earthly cares can be fully experienced. It is the kingdom of love where fear cannot survive. To seek that kingdom first is not only to overcome anxiety, it is to be assured that our basic needs in life will be adequately met.

Can we believe that glorious promise? Can we really believe that when we seek the Kingdom of God, all the other things shall be added unto us? Can we believe? That, in essence, is a question of faith. The tragic shortcoming of our generation, like many other generations in the past, is that we are men of little faith. The pitiful meagerness of our faith is certainly one of the factors which account for an increasing demand for tranquilizers. We still need to discover that the Christian life is a thrilling spiritual adventure, and that our search for the Kingdom of God and His righteousness is, in fact, a search for the real answer to the deepest yearning of the human spirit.

Today, let us resolve not to allow anxiety to rob the joy out of our life, lest our struggles for existence become a sordid and trying experience.

God is the God of light and can dispel the darkness in our souls. He is the God of glory and can rescue us from the tangled webs of confusion and meaninglessness. Those who trust in Him will not be afraid. They shall run and not be weary. They shall walk and will never faint. They shall tread the path of duty with confidence, being assured that throughout their pilgrimage God is their refuge and strength.

35

From Suffering to Hope

Scripture Reading: Roman 5:1-11

Our text is taken from Paul's letter to the Romans, chapter 5, verses 3 and 4: "More than that, we rejoice in our sufferings, knowing that suffering produces endurance, and endurance produces character, and character produces hope." This is the rendering in the Revised Standard Version. In the King James Version, the translation runs this way "...we glory in tribulations also: knowing that tribulation worketh patience; and patience, experience; and experience, hope." William Barclay, the New Testament Greek scholar, puts it this way: "Let us find a cause of glorifying in our troubles; for we know that trouble produces fortitude; and fortitude produces character; and character produces hope."

Whichever translation we use, the metamorphosis of hope is the same. The starting point is suffering (or tribulations or troubles), but suffering produces endurance, and endurance produces character, and character produces hope. Paul is saying that we may begin with sufferings, but we can end up with hope.

It is important to note this because of a prevalent impression that hope is dependent on hopeful circumstances. Often, we are hopeful because things are hopeful. In like manner, when things look bad, we lose heart. To Paul, when things look bad, he begins to hope. Hope to Paul is not just a matter of attitude which is conditioned by outward circumstances. It is a quality of character which learns to endure in adverse conditions, which is called out when most needed, that is, when things look bad.

It will be a pity if our hope vaporizes when things go wrong or when our hope is simply a mere creation of outward circumstances. For then we will be at the mercy of external forces, and our hope will be just as good as the condition of the weather. The true character of a man is revealed when he is hopeful, not due to hopeful circumstances, but in spite of extreme adversities.

We can also admit that hopeless situations make people hopeless.

But the deeper truth is that hopeless people make the situations hopeless. This is one thing we need to remember during these days of social upheavals. There are militant groups who would like to believe that the situation in this country is a hopeless one. Even if we grant that their analysis is accurate (but, of course, there are those who do not believe that our case is hopeless), and even if we finally discover that our situation is indeed hopeless, that need not make us hopeless people. The real tragedy in the life of a nation is not when the situation is hopeless, but when the people themselves are hopeless; for hopeless people are bound to make the situation hopeless.

This last sentence is a little redundant, but the intention is to impress upon us the fact that people are meant to be masters of circumstances. This is a central theme in the Holy Scriptures. The Valley of Weeping can be a place of springs. Sufferings can be redemptive. Calvary can be a throne. Death itself can be an entrance into that life which is beyond the touch of earthly cares. Let there be more people of the calibre of Paul, and our difficult situation, however hopeless it may seem, can be the initial stage in the coming of the Kingdom of God!

At this point, let us look a little more closely at what we mean by hope. We use the word so often that its meaning has become quite loose. Sometimes, it is used primarily as a term of politeness: "I hope I didn't disturb you," we would say to someone we like to see without a previous appointment. Sometimes, it means a mere wish or desire: "I hope it doesn't rain." Harry Emerson Fosdick, the great American preacher, tells us that many people regard hope as "a mere matter of idealism, lovely and comforting, a realm of alluring dreams to which one turns for solace from the realistic facts." This is similar to the observation of Voltaire who, in his *Philosophical Dictionary,* defines hope as "a Christian virtue which consists in our despising all poor things here below in the expectation of enjoying it in an unknown country, unknown joys which our priests promise us for the worth of our money."

Most certainly, this is not what the Apostle Paul means. In the New Testament, the ground of hope is the resurrection of Jesus Christ. That resurrection is God's mightiest act, and while the fullness of His saving act is still to come, it can be experienced now. The future is so sure that it becomes a part of the present. In Romans 8:24, Paul says we are saved by hope — not that we are saved by hoping, but saved by that hope which is grounded on the resurrection of Jesus Christ. In other words, hope is not a matter of idealism, is not a realm of alluring dreams to which we turn for solace from the sordidness of the present. Hope, in the New Testament, is a present possession. Surely, it is hope for the future, but it is a future that is already present, and it is a present possession which is at the same time a promise of the future. In the words of the theologians, hope is an eschatological reality, a present-future and future-present reality, a reality that expresses itself in history yet cannot be contained in history. It is eternity that concretizes itself in the present and in the now.

The reason why hope is a certainty is that it is hope in God. Paul, in Roman 5:5, tells us that "hope does not disappoint us." God is faithful, and His promise can be depended upon.

Today, we suffer from many disappointed hopes because they are hopes in man. The politician is probably the best example of a universal human weakness of arrogating unto ourselves what really belongs to God. Especially during election time, the politicians talk with eloquence about the precariousness of the situation, about poverty, ignorance and disease that oppress life itself and then, in equally eloquent words, they project themselves as the hope of the land who can save us from total failure. They project themselves as political messiahs who can give fulfillment to our fondest dreams.

Of course, some of them do. Some of them are really instrumental in saving us and our people from the mighty grips of a rotten system. Such men and women deserve to be elected. They deserve our cooperation and support, but what we still need to learn is to give our ultimate trust to God, and that is the cultivation of the faith that will save us from despair when our trusted men fail; the conviction that God is not made helpless by the tyranny and the inhumanity of those corrupted by power. We need that hope in God which alone can bind our broken hopes in men, which can rebuild our broken faith, which can heal our broken spirit. We need that hope which can sustain us in our confrontation with miseries and sufferings.

When we speak of sufferings, we mean not only social maladies like poverty, fascism, corruption and the like. We also mean personal misfortune like losing a finger or an arm or a leg, loss in business, failure in a career, or even the loss of a loved one. These are grim realities if not in our own life, at least, in the life of those very dear to us. The likelihood is that if we don't have them right now, we are sure to have our own share of sufferings one of these days. It belongs to the very nature of the Christian life to have a Calvary to climb and a cross to bear. Jesus says, "In the world ye shall have tribulations . . ." And given such a case, what are we going to do?

St. Paul says, "We rejoice in our sufferings." Now, this does not mean that if we have ulcers or cancer or conjunctivitis, or when we are suffering from a severe toothache or stomach pain, we will play our favorite records and exclaim, "*Mabuhay*! Come and dance and eat! Let us celebrate. Let us rejoice in our sufferings." Once that happens, it is time to examine our heads. That is not the kind of rejoicing Paul had in mind. That is not what Jesus had in mind when He said, "In the world ye shall have tribulations, but be of good cheer." Rejoicing in tribulation is only the product of the knowledge that suffering produces endurance; and endurance, character; and character, hope. In Romans 5:2, Paul says, "We rejoice in our hope of sharing the glory of God." It is in that sense that we can rejoice in our sufferings.

To be sure, suffering in itself does not necessarily lead to fortitude or strengthen character. In fact, it can only break and embitter a man's spirit. The same experience of tragedy can be the destruction of all hopes in a man; but to another, it can be a means of God's revelation. And Paul is telling us that to those who truly put their trust in God, suffering can make us real men. It is an experience in which we become more pure.

This is the meaning of the word tribulation in the original Latin. The verb ***tribulare*** means "to press, to oppress, to afflict." The noun ***tribulum*** originally refers to a "threshing sledge which separated grain from chaff. It consisted of a wooden platform studded underneath with sharp flints or iron teeth. As this instrument passed over the pile of grain, the wheat was separated from the straw."[1] In other words, tribulation separates men from the children. It produces endurance or fortitude. It expels the elements of cowardice and fear and cynicism. Just as gold becomes more pure when it goes through the fire, so man develops a stronger character when he experiences the purifying fire of suffering.

Now, suffering produces endurance or fortitude. The Greek word for this is ***hupomone*** which means more than endurance. "It means the spirit which can overcome the world, it means the spirit which does not passively endure but which actively overcomes and conquers the trials and tribulations of life."[2] When Job lost his children and his properties, he said, "Though He slay me, yet will I serve Him." That is ***hupomone***. When a certain businessman failed in his undertaking, he said, "I will not despair.

---

[1] Barnhouse, *Exposition of Bible Doctrines*, Vol. IV, p. 73.
[2] Barclay, *Commentary of the Romans*, p. 73.

God will give me another chance and I will start all over again." That is *hupomone*. When a missionary lost his son on their way to the Philippines, he said, "This tragedy will not stop us from going into the mission field." That is *hupomone*. When a politician almost lost his life at Plaza Miranda, he said when he regained consciousness, "I will continue to fight for the cause of justice in this land." That is **hupomone**.

In the King James Version, *hupomone* is translated, patience. Patience, said Cabesang Tales in one of Rizal's novels, is what we need when things are most upsetting. A poet, who probably did not have it, wrote the following verse:

> Patience is a virtue,
>
> Possess it if you can;
>
> Seldom found in woman
>
> And never found in man.

If I were to rewrite this verse, I might say: Seldom found in men and never found in women, but even in this proposed revision, the veracity of the verse is open to question. It is safer to say that patience is among the rarer virtues. It is one of the fruits of the Spirit which Paul mentions in his letter to the Galatians (5:22).

Endurance or patience produces character. The word Paul used for character is *dokime*. "*Dokime* is used of metal which has been passed through the fire so that everything base has been purged out of it." Prof. Barclay says that the word *dokime* "describes something out of which every alloy of baseness has been eliminated. When affliction is met with fortitude, out of the battle a man emerges stronger, and purer, and better and nearer God."[1] And that is character.

Are not men of character the ardent needs of our time? We may have a perfect constitution, we may produce enough to overcome every shadow of poverty in this land, we may have all the roads and bridges we need and drive the imperialists away from our shores, but if our people have no character in the Pauline sense of the word, all our gains in the political and economic fields will be of no use. The Con-Con may come up with a good constitution, the students and the peasants may succeed in fighting fascism and colonialism, the government may sell more rice and build more roads, but if the churches and the schools do not produce men of character, our society, including the churches, will go down the river.

---

[1] Barclay, *op. cit.*

Remember the Great Wall of China? It was a gigantic structure built at the great expense of labor. When it was finished it looked like an excellent way to gain security. Dr. Fosdick tells us, "within a few years of its building it was breached three times by the enemy... It was breached, not by breaking down the wall, but by bribing the gatekeepers. It was the human element that failed. What collapsed was character, proving insufficient to make the great structure men had reared really work."[1]

This is why, in the development of our country, we should not forget the supreme importance of developing character. We may put up big and massive walls, but if the gatekeepers can be bribed, destruction and decay will always be closer than we think.

A Christian character nurtured by sufferings and endurance cannot but lead to hope. And in that hope character becomes even stronger. Men of such character will never yield to the blows of defeat or failure because underneath them is the everlasting arm of God.

Let it be our prayer that whatever troubles we may have right now, whatever sufferings may be in store for us in this life, we may still have the power to rejoice in them, knowing that by the grace of God, we can endure and we can overcome. Let this be our hope and let this be our faith, and we will find ourselves equipped for the living of these days.

---

[1] Fosdick, *A Great Time to be Alive*, p. 46.

36

Water and Wine

Scripture Reading: John 2:1-11

The first miracle wrought by Jesus was the conversion of water into wine at a certain wedding feast in the village of Cana. Some students of the Bible maintain that the wine mentioned in this story was unfermented grape juice—very much similar to what we drink during communion Sundays. A number of Bible scholars contend, however, that the good wine at the wedding feast in Cana was fermented grape juice—very similar to what we now call, *"Ang inumin ng tunay na lalaki."*

One Bible commentator tells us that in ancient Palestine, "The wedding ceremony took place late in the evening, after a feast." This interests me because here in our country, as in many other places, the wedding reception takes place after the wedding ceremony and the result is that there are more people at the reception than at the wedding ceremony. Friends of the newlyweds may miss the ceremony, but they will seldom miss the reception. The ancient Palestinians were apparently smarter. They had the wedding ceremony immediately after the reception, presumably in the same place where people gathered for the feast and I imagine the guests stayed for the ceremony. It would have been quite impolite to leave immediately after eating.

Of course, in ancient Palestine, the wedding celebrations lasted more than a day. In fact, they could last for a week, depending on the groom's financial ability. To us these days such extravagance could be very alarming, but most probably, except for the main feast, the food was very, very simple, and that the only thing they had in abundance was wine.

To understand this story of a wedding feast in Cana, we need to remember that the author of the Fourth Gospel was a Jew and, therefore, some of the details in his story are intended to convey a message to the Jews. For instance, in verse 6 of our Scripture lesson, we read that there were six stone jars standing in one corner of the house "for the Jewish rites of purification." More particularly, the rite of purification was the cleaning of feet upon arrival in a Jewish house and the washing of hands before meals. In a more formal gathering, like wedding receptions, the hands should be washed after every course. Hence, the need for jars for storing water.

To the Jews, seven was the complete, perfect number. Six, therefore, means incomplete or imperfect. The Gospel of John specifically mentions that there were six stone jars. John, therefore, is understood to be saying to the Jews that their imperfections and even their inadequacies can be met by Christ and that in Jesus, men can overcome their incompleteness and their shortcomings.

This is the same message we need to proclaim these days: that Christ is the answer to the longings of the human spirit. Before Him we realize our helplessness and yet that realization is, at the same time, an assurance of His unfailing grace. Thus, we can rejoice that though we are beset by a nagging sense of imperfection, Jesus can give us sufficient grace and adequate strength.

The other thing to note is that the Gospel of John is also for the Greeks. This is obvious from the very first chapter of the Gospel, where the author speaks of the Logos, or the Word of God — a concept popular among the Greeks. And the Greeks happen to have stories strikingly similar to what we have in chapter 2 of John. Dionysos was the Greek god of wine. They had stories about people visiting the sanctuary of Dionysos. Somewhere at the altar they could deposit no more than three empty kettles, and on the following day those kettles would be full of wine. In other words, John was saying to the Greeks: You have your god of wine, but he is only a legend. Our Jesus is not a legend; He is the true God who makes good wine. That message is worth re-echoing, for many of us today are being tempted to indulge in fantasies and in illusions. We need the realism which Jesus gives, the realism that can save us from daydreaming and sluggishness and irresponsibility.

At this point, let us observe that the realism which Jesus gives is essentially the realism of joy. This is a central emphasis in the Gospel of John. This is particularly illustrated in the story of the wedding feast. The wedding feast is the symbol of jubilation, of happiness. Nothing can be more exhilarating than to be at a wedding feast. In other words, the evangelist is telling us that to be with Jesus is to be happy, to be alive, to be inspired. It is divine, it is blissful, it is heavenly. To be a Christian is to be characterized by an abiding cheerfulness.

This should be stressed because there are some religious people who seldom smile and they very seldom laugh. To them, piety means to be serious all the time. They will not see a movie. They will not play games. They do not go to parties. They would rather go to church even when it is not a Sunday. They read the Bible regularly (which is good), but frown upon those who turn to the comic section of the newspapers. People like that are what our young people call KJ — kill joy. They radiate gloom instead of joy. Their presence makes us feel inhibited, formal, cold. To them, to be happy is almost sinful.

That is not what the Gospel of John recommends. The evangelist declares that the Christian life has a definite place for laughter, for social fellowship, for recreation, for having a good time. That does not mean we should be smiling all the time — if we do that, people will think we should be in a mental hospital. It means we can be happy, whole and secure under the canopy of God's love. It means being assured that "though the wrong seems oft so strong, God is the Ruler yet." C. H. Spurgeon, the famous preacher, gives the following advice to his students in the ministry: "I commend cheerfulness to all who would win souls, not levity and frothiness, but a genial, happy spirit. There are more flies caught with honey than with vinegar, and there will be more souls led to heaven by a man who wears heaven in his face than by one who bears Tartarus in his looks." The Apostle Paul, in his letter to the Galatians, tells us that joy is one of the fruits of the Spirit. Our own experience with Jesus should enable us to testify that life in Him is, indeed, a glorious life.

Now, we must hasten to add that the felicitous Christian life is not necessarily free from miseries and embarrassments. On the contrary, it is a life full of trials and difficulties. The Gospel of John clearly points this out by saying that the wine at the wedding feast had run out, and that was a supreme embarrassment because the celebration would not be complete without wine. We may not pay too much attention to this particular incident in the story, but to John it is an important element in the entire narrative precisely to remind us that life in Christ is still exposed to all sorts of unpleasantness. Jesus himself once said, "If anyone will come after Me, let him deny himself, take up his cross, and follow Me." He does not deceive us into thinking that discipleship is all sunshine and fair weather. Storms do come and rains descend and strong winds blow, and all of these will continue to be a part of our experience even when we believe in Christ.

So, they ran out of wine in Cana, and the hosts were exposed to a great humiliation; but Mary, the mother of Jesus, was there and she understood what the embarrassing situation meant. Thus, she approached Jesus and said, perhaps in a whisper, "There is no more wine. Would you please do something?" Perhaps, Mary was expecting Jesus to answer, "Well, then, I will go to the nearest grocery store and buy a case or two and I will ask Peter and John to come along with me," but that was not what he said. Instead, he said: "O Woman, what have you to do with me? My hour has not yet come." To us, that answer sounds very shocking. We don't dare call our mother, woman, do we? The Tagalog translation sounds even more repulsive. It says, *"Babae, anong pakialam ko sa iyo?"* In modern parlance, Jesus was saying, So what if there is no more wine!

Here we must recall that when Jesus was hanging on the cross, He called His mother woman. "Woman, behold thy son." We must also recall that in the writings of Homer, the Greek Poet, Odysseus addresses his beloved wife (Penelope), woman. Augustus, the Roman Emperor, called Cleopatra, the famous Egyptian queen, woman. In other words, the word "woman" was a title of respect. It was not a rough or discourteous address. On the contrary, it was a title of endearment and respect.

Now, how do we interpret the words, "what have you to do with me?" Very briefly, the phrase means that Mary need not worry, that she could leave the problem in the hands of her son. It should not bother her a bit. The sentence was the colloquial way of giving loving assurances to one who has complete confidence in you. In effect, Jesus was saying: "Don't you worry Mother, just leave it to me. I will take care of it."

The point is that it was the host's responsibility to take care of the situation. If there was no more wine, the groom must get some — somehow, somewhere. Jesus was only an invited guest. He should not even know that there was no more wine and that is exactly the point: Jesus the invited guest acted as if He was the host. Hence, the evangelist is telling us that when we invite Jesus to be our guest in our homes, somehow we will discover that He is the host; somehow we realize that even the house we built is really His and we His guests.

Remember that incident on the first Easter day? Two travelers were on their way to Emmaus. They were talking about the tragedy that took place on Calvary two days before. Suddenly, a third man joined them in their journey and participated in their conversation. It was getting dark when the travelers reached their village, and they invited Jesus, whom they did not know was the risen Christ, to stay with them for the night. Jesus accepted the invitation. They had supper together, but it was Jesus who broke bread, and it was in the breaking of the bread that they recognized Him to be the risen Lord. The hosts, who invited Jesus, should have broken the bread and should have served Jesus, the guest, but in that glorious Easter story, the Visitor broke bread and acted as the Host. Always in the gospel the message is clear, that when Jesus is invited into our homes as our guest, we are led to the thrilling discovery that He, in fact, is our Host. That He owns not only our house, but also us. He has a claim upon our hearts and hands; He has a claim upon our life. The miracle which John proclaims in chapter two of his gospel is not the miracle of turning water into wine, but the miracle that happens in the life of those who ask Jesus to come into their hearts and homes, the miracle of discovering that Christ indeed is our Lord and King, the real Owner of what we possess.

"O Woman, what have you to do with me? My hour has not yet come." Let us explore the meaning of the words, "My hour has not yet come." In John, chapter 7, the word **hour** has reference to Jesus' emergence as the Messiah. But in chapter 17, the word hour has definite reference to His crucifixion. His prayer begins with the words, "Father, the hour is come, glorify Thy Son, that Thy Son also may glorify Thee." In Matthew 26, Jesus instructs His disciples to see the owner of the Upper Room where Jesus wanted to institute the sacrament of the Lord's supper. He tells His disciples saying, "Go into the city to such a man, and say unto him, The Master saith, My time is at hand; I will keep the passover at thy house with My disciples." In short, when Jesus says, "my hour has come," or "my hour has not come," that hour has reference to His crucifixion. The Gospel of John is therefore telling us that the works of Jesus must be viewed in the light of His saving act upon the cross.

This is to say that the newly-married couple in Cana were saved from embarrassment not just because Jesus miraculously turned the water into wine, but because Jesus was willing to be crucified. And this means that if we of today are to be God's instruments in saving our homes, our loved ones, and our fellow men from humiliation and disgrace, we, too, must be willing to be crucified. If our family is to be saved from total disintegration, if we are to win the love and confidence of those who are beginning to abandon us, we must be willing to be crucified. And to be crucified means to go through certain forms of suffering even when we think we are innocent.

Of course, this is difficult to do. When we know we are right, we don't care what happens to those who are wrong. If they do not speak to us, we do not speak to them either. If they do not greet us, we do not greet them. Such attitude, nurtured by a wrong kind of righteousness, cannot redeem life from disharmony and failure. Only the willingness to be crucified can. This means speaking to our brother even when he does not like to speak to us. It means greeting him when he does not want to greet us. In short, it means taking the initiative in putting up a new beginning and in tearing down the wall that sadly separates us from one another.

Can we do that? On our own strength we cannot. But Christ is our strength, and with His help and by His grace, nothing is impossible. Surely, we can turn water into wine — by denying ourselves, by taking up our cross, and by putting our confidence in Him who said, "In the world ye shall have tribulations, but be of good cheer."

37

"It Is Finished"

(A Good Friday Sermon)

"It is finished." "It is consummated." The Tagalog translation is *"Naganap na."* And we wonder what Jesus meant by that. What was finished? Well, in the eyes of Jesus' enemies, nothing was finished except Jesus Himself. They finished Him. But the Greek word translated **finished** does not mean to put an end, but to bring to completion: hence, to be consummated or accomplished. And so we ask again: What was it which Jesus said was consummated?

Apparently, Jesus was referring to His mission. He came into this world to reveal the very nature of God. Such revelation had its climax upon the cross. Jesus taught that God is a loving, heavenly Father; such loving God can go into the depths of human sufferings and pain. Jesus came to set at liberty those that are oppressed — oppressed not only by the cruelty of their fellow men and by the ugliness of outward circumstances, but also by our own inherent weaknesses; by our sinful tendency to indulge in riotous living. Jesus came to give us life abundant — and that means a certain degree of material comfort as well as spiritual growth. This glorious mission of the Son of God to redeem mankind from infamy and perdition had been consummated. His death was for our salvation. And so He said, "It is finished."

But is it? Until now, the church, which is the body of Christ, has a long way to go in proclaiming the saving message of the Saviour. In fact, many of those who profess to believe Christ have yet to show the marks of Christian discipleship. Corruption in our midst is so rampant that we sometimes wonder whether what we have got is nothing but paganized Christianity or Christianized paganism. When we look only at the present, we cannot say, " It is consummated."

To be sure, Jesus Himself teaches that life is a constant warfare with the evil forces in the world. To follow Him is to take up our cross daily. In one of His parables He says that the tares grow together with the wheat.

He reminds us that there shall be false prophets, that friends will betray friends and nations will rise up against nations. In short, He does not deceive us into thinking that once we believe in Him everything will be fine and pleasant. On the contrary, Christians will be persecuted. He says, "In the world ye shall have tribulations." In the words of the Apostle Paul, our calling is to fight the good fight. Therefore, the task of mission is far from finished.

If this is so, why did Jesus say, "It is consummated"? Here we are face to face with a central paradox of the Christian faith. Admittedly, we still have to evangelize many parts of the world, yet from the divine perspective such mission is already consummated. We still have to work for the cause of brotherhood and righteousness and peace, but even that is already consummated. We still have to give our full share in the task of liberating men from anything that dehumanizes, but in Christ such a task is already a foretaste of future fulfillment.

Such assurance of ultimate victory is what we ardently need these days, especially when we are overwhelmed by the seeming uselessness of our efforts in preserving our national and personal decency, in promoting goodwill and understanding, in building a more just society. Very often when we get involved in a crusade for good government, for moral or spiritual regeneration, for uprightness and fair play in every sector of life, we just find ourselves crucified, and the anguish and pain of our crucifixion can do damage to the human spirit. But the remembrance of Jesus, who on the cross could triumphantly say, "It is consummated," can revive our hopes and renew our faith, and such renewal can generate strength equal to our task. It can enable us to transcend jealousies and mockeries, and to carry on with the conviction that even our failure can be a necessary part of that ultimate victory promised by the omnipotent God. Such confidence in the ultimate reign of goodness and truth can give us courage and hope. It can make us victorious even in defeat; it can make our crown of thorns into a crown of honor.

In the gospel of John, the author connects Jesus' thirst for water with His word, "It is finished." Here is how the Evangelist puts it: "After this, Jesus, knowing that all was now finished, said (to fulfill the scripture), 'I thirst.' A bowl full of vinegar bottle stood there, so they put a sponge full of the vinegar on hyssop and held it to His mouth. When Jesus had received the vinegar, He said, 'It is finished' and He bowed His head and gave up His spirit." (19:28-30) John the Evangelist makes it very clear that it was only after Jesus received the vinegar that He said, "It is finished." Jesus could not say, "It is consummated" until after receiving the vinegar.

Now let us emphasize that the vinegar was given in response to Jesus' word, "I thirst." To be sure, it was not a loving response to the humble cry of a suffering man. It was more of a comedy, perhaps for the entertainment of the Roman soldiers and the scribes and the others who thought that the Man on the center cross was a great Pretender. Nevertheless, it was a response to the plea of an agonizing soul, and immediately after that, Jesus said, "It is finished."

The message which the gospel writer wishes to underscore is that the accomplishment of Jesus' mission cannot be divorced from our attempts to meet the crying needs of the suffering people. The thirsty Christ is the symbol of mankind in want, and if men can be moved to do something to help alleviate human suffering, then the mission of Christ is indeed consummated.

This is why we cannot fully understand Jesus' word, "It is consummated," apart from the giving of vinegar in response to His cry, "I thirst." We cannot really appreciate the fullness in His saving act unless we see it evoking some human compassion. And we cannot meaningfully celebrate Good Friday without resolving to do our part in making life a little better especially for those who have much less in the world. The Christian celebration of Good Friday is not just to pray, not just to bear listening to long sermons on the seven last words, but to renew our resolution to be God's instruments in giving water to the thirsty and help to the needy. Remember the parable of the sheep and the goats? The sheep were gathered on the right side and the goats on the left. And to those on the right-hand side the master said, "Come, inherit the Kingdom that was prepared for you even before the foundation of the world." Greatly amazed, the people asked, "But sir, what have we done to deserve such an honor?" And the master replied, "I was thirsty and you gave me drink; I was hungry and you gave me food, I was sick and you visited me; I was lonely and you comforted me." The people asked again, "Sir, when did we see you thirsty and give you drink, or hungry and give you food? When did we see you sick and pay you a visit, or lonely and give you any comfort?" The master replied, "Inasmuch as you have done it unto the least of these my brethren, you have done it unto me."

When we give jobs to the jobless, justice to the victims of injustice, dignity to every man however underprivileged he may be, we are contributing to the fulfillment of Jesus' mission. To plant rice, raise chickens and catch fish; to make soap, toothpaste and face powder; to clean polluted rivers and air; to promote efficiency and honesty in the government and in private business — all these are a part of God's redeeming work. When we do these to meet the needs of men, somehow we will hear Jesus say, "It is consummated."

It is interesting to note that the man who gave the vinegar was not a disciple; and that it was vinegar, and not water, which was given to Jesus. In fact, as we have already said, the giving of vinegar was not really a loving response to the thirsty Jesus. And yet Jesus used that man and accepted his gift. And if unbelievers can be instruments of God's grace, can we imagine the tremendous goodness there will be if believers themselves respond lovingly and faithfully to pleading for help and friendship? If a sponge full of vinegar could evoke Jesus to say, "It is finished," can we imagine the boundless blessings a cup of water can create?

The tragedy of our age is that while the forces of evil are gathering all around us, the forces of goodness are not being consolidated. The so-called good men, especially the so-called Christians, are not around when people cry "I thirst." We come out only during special occasions, like Good Friday or Easter or Christmas. But when terrorism mars the sanctity of the ballots, when the marijuana peddlers make a killing in their business, when hoarders keep the milk in their *bodegas*, when vested interests clash at the expense of the public, we somehow become invisible.

Today, we can be truly grateful that by God's grace we can redeem our lost opportunities. The fight is still on, and the need for good Christian soldiers is most urgent. We need not be daunted by the overpowering strength of falsehood and darkness. We need not be dismayed by our own inadequacy. We only need to know that Christ is the captain of our souls. With Him we can conquer. And with Him we too can say, "It is consummated."

38

The Regnant Christ

Scripture Reading: Luke 19:28-44

Jesus' entry into Jerusalem, as described in all the four gospels, was a dramatic announcement of His Kingship. In the olden days, when prophets wanted to stress the importance of their message, they would act it out. For instance, in the book of Kings, the prophet Ahijah wanted to tell King Jeroboam that the twelve tribes of Israel would be divided, ten would be delivered to Jeroboam and only two would remain (I Kings 11:29-31). So the prophet, in the presence of the king, rent a new garment into twelve pieces and said, "Take thee ten pieces; for thus saith the Lord, I will rend the kingdom out of the hand of Solomon, and will give ten tribes to thee."

In the book of Jeremiah (13:1-11), we read about a linen girdle which the prophet hid in a hole of a rock, only to find a few days later that the girdle was marred and therefore useless. Jeremiah was commanded to show that girdle to the people and to tell them that they, like the girdle, would become good for nothing because of the hardness of their hearts.

The prophet Ezekiel used much drama in his prophetic ministry. He used a plumbline to tell his fellow men that they were under divine judgment. He cut his hair with a barber's razor to dramatize the desolation that was to come if the people did not repent. In short, he not only spoke but also used some visual aids in his preaching.

That method of proclaiming something was what Jesus employed on the first Palm Sunday. He rode upon an ass. He could have walked. In fact, He and His disciples had been walking all throughout their journey. But not upon entering the city of Jerusalem. The disciples walked, but He rode. It was a dramatic enactment of the words of the prophet Zechariah who said, "Rejoice greatly, O daughter of Zion; shout, O daughter of Jerusalem: behold, thy king cometh unto thee, he is just and having salvation, lowly and riding upon an ass, and upon a colt the foal of an ass."

In other words, on the first Palm Sunday, Jesus was publicly announcing His Kingship. Before that time, He did not want the people to spread the news. Remember that blind man in Bethsaida who was brought to Jesus? Jesus restored his sight until the man could see clearly. And after that, Jesus advised him to go home and not to go into town, and not to tell it to anyone.

On the Mount of Transfiguration, Peter, James, and John witnessed the appearance of Moses and Elijah. They also heard a voice coming out from the clouds saying, "This is my beloved Son: hear Him." But as they were coming down from the mountain, Jesus charged them not to tell anyone about the things they had seen and heard.

Now the time had come. The time had come for Jesus to proclaim publicly that He was indeed the Messiah, the King, the Lord whom God promised to send to Israel. His entering the city upon an ass was a public declaration that He was the Savior His people had been waiting for.

Now, let us review the people's reaction. Undoubtedly, they gave Him a royal welcome. Matthew says, "Most of the crowd spread their garments on the road, and others cut branches from the trees and spread them on the road" (21:8). That was exactly what the people did when, many years before that time, Simon Maccabeus entered Jerusalem after one of his notable military victories. That was also what they did to King Jehu (II Kgs. 9:13). It was, therefore, a tumultuous welcome reserved only for a king.

Here let us note that while they welcomed Him, they welcomed Him on their own terms. They welcomed Him as a political leader and as a military man. That was what they wanted Him to be. They had hoped for the coming of the Messiah who would set them free from the oppression of a foreign power. They had hoped that Jesus would be a king like their father David, a great military figure. They had hoped that Jesus would establish an army powerful enough to destroy the fortresses of Roman colonialism.

As a matter of fact, His own disciples shared that kind of an expectation. While they were on their way to Jerusalem, James and John made the request that they be seated on Jesus' left and right sides in the Kingdom. The rest of the disciples got mad not because of the two brothers' self-preferment, but because they too wanted the places of honor for themselves. In other words, even the disciples thought that the kingdom Jesus wanted to establish was a military, political kingdom; therefore, they wanted to become members of the new cabinet who would advise the king on matters of national importance.

That is the same tendency we often have these days. We welcome Jesus on our own terms. The radicals welcome Jesus as patron saint of the radicals. Those with communist leanings proudly declare that Jesus was a communist. The revolutionaries insist that Jesus was revolutionary. Those who advocate violent revolution welcome Jesus as the violent man who drove the temple money changers out. The pacifists picture Jesus as the meek and lowly person whom everyone should imitate. Those who champion the cause of the peasants and the laborers welcome Jesus as the Master Carpenter. Those who cannot withstand clerico-fascism welcome Jesus as the enemy of the scribes and the chief priests. We want Him to be our king, not because we will obey Him, but because we want Him to sanctify our own brand of pacifism or radicalism; because we want Him to dignify our own concept of communism or fascism or democracy; because we want Him to bless our own liberalism or conservatism. So we welcome Him on our own terms.

But Jesus says, "My kingdom is not of this world." We cannot just force Him to be on our side. We cannot monopolize Him. We cannot manipulate Him. And unless we surrender and submit to His claim, we, too, may be tempted to participate in His crucifixion.

Notice, further, the clamour of the people as recorded in Matthew and in Mark. They shouted, "Hosanna! Blessed is the one who comes in the name of the Lord! Blessed is the kingdom of our father David that is coming. Hosanna in the highest" (Mk. 11:10). Today, when we say "Hosanna," we often use the word only as a greeting — perhaps we mean something like "*Mabuhay.*" But this was not what the people meant when they cried out to Jesus, "Hosanna." The word means **save now**. In other words, they were pleading to Jesus, "Save us now!" They were so eager for salvation that they wanted it at that very moment, "now." Not tomorrow, not hereafter, but now. They had been political prisoners in their own country. They wanted deliverance now. They had been suffering from poverty and disease. They wanted release from such miseries right away. They had been waiting for the appearance of the Anointed One, the promised Messiah. And here the Messiah comes, riding upon an ass. So they shouted, "Hosanna! Save us! Blessed are you in the name of the Lord for coming now!"

"Save Now" or Salvation Today is a favorite subject of conversation among the churches. And there is value in stressing the present aspect of man's salvation. The New Testament teaches salvation being now. We can have it today. But let us not forget that the present is only one dimension of salvation. Salvation is also past. In fact, it is also future. Salvation is God's work, to whom our thousand years are but a day. Therefore, we must allow God to work the way He wants. His ways with us today may not be His ways with our grandchildren years from now. We cannot make our practices today binding upon the succeeding generations. Today, we may be content with the presidential form of government. Tomorrow, we may have a parliament. Today, church facilities may be exclusively for worship and Bible studies. Tomorrow, we may allow socials and square dancing. Today, we may bar women from becoming ministers or government officials. Tomorrow, we may allow them to become bishops or Presidents or Prime Ministers. But whatever it may be, let it be the will of God. Let God save us in the way He wants. Let God be God!

The trouble with the Jews was that they wanted Jesus to save them and, at the same time, they wanted Him to adopt their own method of salvation. They wanted political independence, so they wanted Jesus to be their political leader. They wanted freedom from Rome, and they wanted Jesus to establish an army which could drive the enemies away. They wanted Jesus to save them the way they liked.

Is that not what we also see in ourselves? When we feel that the Establishment is rotten through and through and we want to change the system by overthrowing it and putting up a new one, we pray that God may bless our plans of subversion or rebellion or insurrection. When we are nauseated with the evils of capitalism and the free enterprise, we want God to save our people by endorsing our socialism or modified communism. When we are deeply touched by the helplessness of those whose thoughts and ways of life are very much controlled by their supposedly infallible spiritual leaders, we convince ourselves that their only salvation is to become like us, Protestants. But the truth is, we cannot prescribe the method of salvation for God to follow. We cannot ask Him to save us unless we are willing to allow Him to save us in any way He wants. It is one thing to ask for guidance; it is another thing to ask God to put His stamp of approval on a course of action we have already decided upon.

And so, as we pray for salvation today, let us listen to what God wants us to do in order to make His salvation real. Such listening may cause us to change the plan of action we have already made. It may cause us to modify our plan. Or it may convince us that the very plan we have is consonant with His will. But, by all means, let us be ready to obey. God's thoughts are higher than our thoughts. And let our actions be tempered by the knowledge that even our best judgement can be tainted by our sin.

Finally, Jesus' entry into Jerusalem was a declaration of war against corruption. This He dramatized by turning upside-down the tables of the money changers. He would not allow the house of prayer to be converted into a den of robbers. He denounced the hypocrisy of those who were supposed to be the moral guardians of the people. And this is why a fitting observance of Palm Sunday is not the making of long prayers, however important that may be; not the carrying of palm branches, though that lends color to the celebration. We truly observe Palm Sunday by resolving in our hearts to be God's people in combatting corruption — in the church, in the government, in every sector of society. Indeed, to welcome Jesus as our King is to join Him in His crusade of cleansing the nation and the human hearts of all greed and pride, of all ugliness and unrighteousness. If this country we love so dearly is to know something of Jesus' blessings, we the citizens must put a stop to corrupt practices. We must be willing to give our share in combatting the evils of corruption, even if in so doing, our enemies nail us to the cross. After all, we cannot hope for the salvation of our people and for the cleansing of our nation unless we are ready to be crucified. If Jesus shed His blood, His followers cannot do any less.

If the celebration of this day is a mere ceremony, then this celebration will not in any way minimize corruption in our midst. Bribery and cheating and dishonesty will go on as usual — except perhaps during Palm Sundays and Maundy Thursdays and Good Fridays.

But if our celebration is a daring attempt to equip ourselves for the conquest of greed and sin, the world can never be the same. The forces of goodness will prevail, and we may yet save mankind from planetary death.

Today, in a very special way, Christ is marching into the cities and hearts of men. May God grant us the courage to welcome Him as our Lord and King.

39

The Joy of Easter

Scripture Reading: Mark 16:1-10

Easter is rightly regarded as the Queen of the Christian festivals, for it is the festival of life, love, and power. It is the festival of the resurrection, of Christ's triumph over the grave, of God's power over man's stubbornness. So it is fitting that we gather on this Easter Sunday and, in an appropriate ceremony, celebrate Christ's glorious victory over the grave.

We begin with the incontrovertible fact of Christ's resurrection. The scripture says He rose again from the dead. Or, more accurately, God raised Him from the dead. He is risen! This is the central theme of the New Testament. It is the dominant note in the writings of the Apostle Paul.

Today we sing with the rest of the Christian world: Hallelujah, Christ is risen! He is no longer crucified; He is no longer in the grave. He has conquered death, and today He is the living Lord.

But after all this is said and sung, what is next? Do we play the same old game which lulls our sense of duty, which relaxes our moral idealism, which slackens our spiritual sensitivity - *sapagka't tayo'y tao lamang?* Do we go back to the dirty business of name-calling, of spreading lies, of fomenting disunity? That will be a contradiction of the resurrection faith. That will be a desecration of the Easter festival. And yet, is that not the very scandal we make?

Let us confess we are caught in the web of embarrassing self-contradictions. We say one thing on Sunday and declare the opposite the following day. Today, we affirm our faith in the risen Christ; tomorrow, we live as if we are the captains of our soul. Today, we approach the throne of God through worship. Tomorrow, we live as if there is no God at all. No wonder the world finds it hard to believe in the resurrected Christ, for we who profess to believe in Him are a bundle of obnoxious contradictions.

Perhaps, the present mess in our society today is largely due to this appalling lack of consistency in our Christian convictions. We call on God as our heavenly Father, but we hit each other below the belt; we preach love as the most excellent way, but we cannot suffer long; we call ourselves Christians, but we are strangers to the ways of Christ. It is not surprising, therefore, that in this so-called Christian land, death looms even in broad daylight; graft and corruption are rampant, immorality and vandalism are the order of the day. What can save us from this messy contradiction which looks like disaster?

The joy of Easter can. The certainty of God's power can dispel the clouds of pessimism. For Christ's resurrection is the guarantee that God is not dead; that He is the Spirit who guides the destinies of men and nations. And when we are assured that in the divine economy the last word is not tribulation but triumph, and that the ultimate reality is not death but life, then our hopes can be revived and our faith can be renewed.

But now let us ask: In the light of our present situation how can we know the reality of Easter joy? How can the resurrection faith become a living power in the hearts of men?

One answer is that we must go to the tomb of Christ. This is what the early Christians did. Mary Magdalene and the other women, Peter and John and the other disciples, and possibly many other faithful believers, captured the blessed joy of Easter because they went to Jesus' tomb. So shall it be for us. If we are to discover the wonder of Easter we too must go to Jesus' tomb.

But where is Jesus' tomb? His tomb today is wherever men lay him. It is wherever truth is suppressed and justice buried. It is wherever love is withheld and brotherhood is crushed. It is wherever morality is effaced and freedom is destroyed.

The tomb of Christ may be in an industrial set-up where people lose their personal identity and become mere tools of production. It may be in a socio-economic framework where opportunity is reserved only for a chosen few. It may be in a political system which has no place for the poor and the *mahina*. It may be in religious institutions where bigotry and intolerance usurp the place of Christian charity.

In other words, to go to the tomb of Christ is to involve ourselves in the struggles of the human race. It is to see for ourselves the deadly sting of prejudice which mars human relationships. It is to touch the sarcophagus of freedom, to bewail the eclipse of righteousness, to decry the exploitation of the masses.

We will never know the fullness of Easter joy if we shy away from the vital issues of the day. For Easter cannot be divorced from the tomb of the crucified Lord. We miss the message of the Resurrection if we think we would do well without bothering ourselves with the problems of mankind.

It is for this reason that we must resolve to face the difficulties we have before us. Easter is a summons for us to restore morality in all places and to destroy whatever system perpetuates indolence and irresponsibility. We must determine to go wherever men bury Christ today.

But how? — we may ask ourselves. How can I, a common factory worker, a small businessman, an ordinary housewife, an unknown citizen? Who am I to stop the rampant traffic of narcotics, the highly efficient smuggling of bills and blue seal cigarettes, the flagrant abuse of police officers?

What if Mary Magdalene, Salome, and Mary, the mother of James, allowed themselves to be overwhelmed by the sullen thought of their smallness and weakness? Probably, they would not have gone to the tomb. But they went, though they were wondering how they could roll away the stone from the door of the sepulchre. They were determined to do what they could, and thereby discovered the most glorious fact of all history: **Christ is risen**.

Easter, therefore, is a solemn tribute to the possibilities of the common man. Mary Magdalene was not a senator. She was a woman out of whom Jesus cast seven devils. And who was Salome? Even Bible scholars are not very sure who she was. And we do not know much about Mary, the mother of James, either. And what about the disciples? Peter was a fisherman and so were the rest of them. They did not have any college diploma. They did not have any political connections. But, they discovered the blessed joy of Christ's resurrection. And because of that, they went out into the world as ambassadors of righteousness, determined to snatch the world from the clutches of death and put it under the dominion of God.

So, let us not be discouraged by our lack of power — be it economic, social or political power. Let us not be daunted by our smallness. Easter is an assurance that ordinary people — the *common tao* — can, by God's grace, handle extraordinary tasks. We can be instruments of God's peace so that, in the words of St. Francis of Assisi, "we may sow love where there is hatred; pardon, where there is injury; hope, where there is despair."

Again, to possess the fullness of Easter joy we must have a personal experience of the risen Lord. It is not enough that we go to Jesus' tomb; we must also feel His presence there. It is not enough that we involve ourselves in the complex problems of communal life; we must also realize that God is truly with us. The disciples and their friends not only went to the tomb; they also apprehended within themselves the living presence of the Master. And if they crossed the borders of Jerusalem, and Judea, and Samaria, and went unto the uttermost parts of the earth, it was because Christ indeed was a living presence in their life. That is the same experience we need to acquire if we are to possess the fullness of Easter joy.

Unfortunately, there are those who enjoy going to the tomb of Christ but are not quite eager to apprehend His living presence. They are in the midst of the fight for a good cause — defending the rights of the underprivileged, ministering to the needs of the socially ostracized and physically handicapped, zealously guarding the sacredness of individual freedom, protecting the sanctity of the constitution, and doing all kinds of humanitarian works for the good of the people and for their own satisfaction. But that is all. The awareness of Christ's presence is very dim; they are hardly persuaded of their need for divine companionship. The result of such venture, from the perspective of the Christian faith, is never spiritually satisfying.

I am sure you know some people of this kind. They are involved in the complex problems of our time. They are at the forefront of all social crises. They are experts in preventing serious conflicts between management and labor, between the rich and the poor, between the Nacionalistas and the Liberals. They see to it that justice is properly administered, that truth is not suppressed, that morality and decency are upheld, that integrity and freedom are respected. Yet, they are strangers to prayer, allergic to the Bible, and they consider worship as something optional. How can such people say with sincerity: Hallelujah, Christ is risen?

The misfortune of such people worsens when their humanitarianism becomes a form of religion; so that their work or profession — whether it be social work or politics, business or teaching, farming or scientific research — becomes a substitute for God. How many have told us that it does not matter whether you go to church or not, whether you pray or not, provided you do good things to your fellow men? How often does good work become a substitute for Christ?

I submit that our urgent need, especially on this day of Resurrection, is to experience in our life the sustaining, empowering presence of the risen Lord. It is the joy of Easter. It is the joy which the world can never give.

40

Christmas and Crisis

Scripture Reading: Matthew 2:1-12

There is something beautiful in the tradition that makes the Christmas holidays a very special season of the year. In many schools and universities, the Christmas vacation is good for no less than two weeks and to both students and faculty that is something to be happy about. In many offices, the last working day before Christmas is usually spent in Christmas programs and all sorts of Christmas parties. In many places, the spirit of goodwill can really be felt. In war-torn areas, whenever military leaders agree, a cease-fire is observed. Many voices join in the singing of the Christmas songs and somehow the world looks a little different.

In a culture like ours which loves to exalt the day of Jesus' birth as a red-letter day in the Christian calendar, three things should be underscored. First, Christmas, with all of its redemptive meaning, should never be divorced from the ordinary life of man. The gospel account of Jesus' birth is a simple account of a common human experience. What is so extraordinary in the birth of a child? True, He was born of a virgin. But the virgin birth was not the central fact which attracted the shepherds and the three wise men. The uniqueness of Christmas is not established by whatever doctrinal pronouncements the church makes on the so-called virgin birth. While we believe in the virgin birth, it is not the basic reality that inspires us to celebrate the coming of our Lord.

The gospel account, therefore, is a simple story of a child born in a lowly manger. The gospel of Luke, in giving us the background of Jesus' birth, speaks of men and women going about their ordinary duties. Joseph and Mary, for instance, were on their way to the city of David to be enrolled. In ancient Palestine such enrollment or census was for the purposes of recruitment for military service and of taxation. Since the Jews were exempted from military service, Joseph and Mary's enrollment was for the purpose of taxation. In other words, they went to Bethlehem to file their income tax returns. They were exercising their civic responsibilities in accordance with the decree issued by Caesar Augustus.

Then, there were the shepherds keeping watch over their flocks. They were on routine duty when the angels suddenly appeared to tell them of the good news. The scene suggests that common, ordinary life of man is the background of the incarnation.

Any attempt, therefore, to make Christmas an out-of-this-world affair is a misunderstanding of the clear intention of the gospel. We do not object to Santa Claus if he can give added emphasis on the relevance of Christmas to our day-to-day life. But when our children are taught that Santa Claus comes in the middle of the night, riding in a flying saucer from outer space and then quickly vanishes after filling up with candies and toys the stockings (of only the good children) placed hanging at the windows precisely in anticipation of Santa's coming, then Christmas comes close to becoming fictitious. The element of moralism which is the basis of Santa's generosity may later on become the opiate which will destroy religious faith itself.

We are not against Christmas trees and all kinds of Christmas decorations — the lanterns and the colored lights, the stars and the camels. But we should not use them as our means of escaping from the reality of our world. The Christmas season is not a period of retreat from the drab ordinariness of life. Rather, it is a time for spiritual replenishment so we can perform our duties with a sense of mission and achieve self-fulfillment in our daily work.

Once this becomes our attitude, we will go back to our work after the holidays are over with a deepened sense of dedication. Instead of mildly forcing ourselves to face once again the pressing demands of our world, we will see meaning in the ordinary and the common and we will behold wonders in the familiar experiences of life.

In the second place, Christmas should not be detached from reality itself. And this includes the reality of man's inhumanity to fellow men. Indeed, Christmas cannot be truly appreciated unless we bravely face the issue of sin and evil. This was the issue lurking behind the event of Jesus' birth. Herod was the governor of Judea and he was a very wicked leader. Throughout all history only a few could equal his perfidiousness and shameless lust for power. He was a perfect personification of greediness and immorality.

On the national scene, the people were burdened by foreign domination. They had no liberty to speak of; they were slaves of the Roman emperor. Poverty walked in every corner of the land and grief was deeply written on the faces of everyone. With the exception of a few, life was hard and miserable.

It is, therefore, legitimate that today we make an honest reappraisal of the harsh facts of life — without rancor or bitterness. We must face the fact that we have not been always treated the way we think we should; that our achievements and abilities are not always appreciated; that our loving-kindness and generosity are sometimes rewarded with ingratitude. In short, we have been victims of disloyalty and injustices and the world has not been kind enough to us.

Or, it can be the other way around. We may have wounded the feelings of our friends; we may have caused them unnecessary troubles; we may have said something unkind; we may have been cruel to our neighbors and unforgiving to our loved ones. Either way, whether it is because of us or because of other men, we cannot get away from the reality of evil and we cannot overcome it by pretending it does not exist.

And yet, we have been wrongly taught that Christmas is the time to forget the miseries of life, the time to ignore them as if they do not exist at all. Such approach to the problem is actually an escape from it. Such an escape mechanism cannot hold for long, and very often, immediately after the Christmas holidays are over, the problems come back with horrifying ugliness that can drive us to madness.

Certainly, if the Christmas season is to serve its purpose, it must be a time of heroic struggling with our fears, with our uncertainties, with our disappointments, and even with our bitterness. This is a time to acknowledge the real magnitude of our prejudice and pride. Christmas is a summons for us to meet face to face the many trials that touch our nerves and test our faith.

Here comes the central point: namely, that while Christmas bids us to face the forces of sin and loneliness and wickedness, it also bids us to remember the abiding power of love over hatred, of joy over sadness, of goodness over evil. The God who came to us in the person of Christ is the Lord of the world, and no amount of inhumanity can ever alter His divine purposes. The type of forgetting which we should cultivate in connection with the many crises that come our way is that forgetfulness generated by the solemn remembrance of God's humility. The assurance of His love and care which Christmas mightily instills in every human heart is all that we really need to emerge victorious from our daily encounter with the devilish schemes of our fellow men. In the end, therefore, we will not be alarmed by the awful ugliness of evil because we know that by the grace of Christ our Lord, we can overcome it with good.

Thirdly, we should not hastily conclude that the Christmas season is especially conducive to the life of the Spirit since it is during the Christmas season when more Christians participate in church activities when they are not wont to do so at other times of the year. The fact is, people exhibit mixed reactions to the claims of Christ even on the day of His birth. The story of the Nativity is in a real sense still the story of contemporary Christmases as far as our reactions to the claims of Christ are concerned. There is, for one thing, the attitude of rebelliousness as exemplified by Herod. His act stemmed from a morbid jealousy that the newborn child might take away the royal throne from him.

But Herod had great possibilities. From available information we have about him, the Romans trusted him in the civil wars of Palestine. He was a veteran military and political leader. Truly, he deserved the title of Herod the Great. At least in his province of Judah, peace and order should be credited to him. He helped in the rebuilding of the Temple of Jerusalem. During difficult times, he remitted taxes that made things easier for the citizens. During the famine of 25 BC, he bought corn from neighboring places for his starving subjects. He could be very generous.

But unfortunately, he could also be insanely suspicious. Even in his old age, he was called "a murderous old man." Anyone whom he suspected to be a threat to his crown was promptly eliminated. He murdered his wife, Mariamne, and her mother, Alexandra. He assassinated three of his sons — Antipater, Alexander, and Aristobulus. Augustus, the Roman Emperor, made the remark that it was safer to be Herod's pig than to be Herod's son. When he suspected that no one might shed tears when someday he died, he arrested the most distinguished citizens of Jerusalem on fabricated charges, and kept them behind bars. He instructed his guards that at the time of his death, those prisoners should all be killed so that many would cry. Only such a man could order the execution of children two years old and below, in order that no rival would disturb his security.

But note that Herod did not reveal his consuming jealousy in open negativism. On the contrary, he expressed conformity with the wise men who wanted to worship the newborn child. "Go," he said to the wise men, " and search diligently for the child, and when you have found him, bring me word, that I, too, may come and worship him," You and I know the truth: Herod did not really want to worship Christ. Deep within his heart, he only wanted to exterminate him.

Where else can we find a more eloquent proof that worship can be a camouflage of revenge and enmity with God? Did not Jesus say that not all who call him, "Lord ,Lord," would enter the kingdom of heaven? This is why we suggest that a seemingly surprising interest in the worship of Christ which we see suddenly exhibited during the Christmas season is not necessarily a guarantee that more have learned to honor our God; it may be just a front to hide their irreligion or otherwise patent agnosticism. Like in the days of Herod, we have people in every generation who are crafty enough to know that an open defiance of Christ's claims will not do them any good; but at the same time, they succeed in worshipping only themselves by pretending to take interest in the celebration of the birth of the Saviour. But God who knows the deepest secrets of the human heart will never honor the pretended piety of such hypocrites.

Then, there is the reaction of complete indifference. This was the case with the scribes and the chief priests. When asked where the Anointed One of God was to be born, they knew the place: in Bethlehem of Judea. Displaying their thorough knowledge of the Old Testament, they quoted from the prophet Micah and said, "And you, O Bethlehem, in the land of Judah, are by no means least among the rulers of Judah, for from you shall come a ruler who will govern my people Israel." In other words, they knew the Scripture. Ask them any question about religion and theology and with lightning speed they will give you the correct answer. But did they ever bother to seek the Holy Child? No, because Christ did not make the slightest difference to them. They were so engrossed with the affairs of the Temple that they simply disregarded Christ. To them, Jesus did not matter at all.

And so, we must reserve our praise for people who can recite the *Magnificat* and sing Handel's *Messiah*. Singing Christmas carols and intimate acquaintance with the Christmas story are not to be identified with Christian devotion. Indifferent people are often knowledgeable people and people of means and influence. In the language of the Bible, they are scribes and chief priests. Christmas may come and go, and to them it does not make any difference.

Of course, as Barclay notes, there is also the reaction of adoring worship as exemplified by the three wise men. They too were men of wisdom and perhaps also kings in their own rights. Like the simple shepherds, they took time out of their busy schedule and their magnificent spirit in paying homage to the Holy Child lends untold beauty to the story of Jesus' birth.

That spirit of adoring worship is what we seek to express today. For we are here to pay homage to the Holy Child. We are not escaping from the tumults of our world, and we have our own concerns that demand our time and our attention, but we dare not resist the urge to seek the newborn King.

Let us, therefore, exert extraordinary efforts to make this Christmas a meaningful, spiritual experience in our ordinary life. Let Christmas present the very reality of our world, both the reality of human suffering and the reality of God's saving grace. Let us not be dismayed by the crises which come even at the height of our Christmas celebrations, because the Christ of Christmas is our Strength, a very present help in times of trouble. Let crisis come and go, but let us keep Christmas everyday. That is the secret of victorious living.

41

Invitation to Live

Scripture Reading: Matthew 22:1-14

This passage contains two parables: one is the parable of the wedding feast, and the other is the story of a man without a wedding garment. The first gives us a picture of a gracious God who welcomes into His banqueting chamber peoples from all walks of life. The second portrays the scrutinizing character of that same God who would not allow the unrepentant soul to stay forever in the royal chamber.

The wedding feast in Matthew is described as a great supper in Luke (14:15-22). The host, who is a **king** in Matthew, is simply a **man** in Luke. In Matthew, when the invited guests did not show up at the wedding reception, the king was furious and "he sent his troops and destroyed those murderers and burned their cities." At first glance such an act appears quite drastic, but not when we remember that the guests, aside from insultingly turning down the king's invitation, also killed the king's messengers. This is why Matthew uses the word **murderers**.

To be sure, the king's act in the light of our own culture can be criticized as betraying his facism and his strong instinct to retaliate. He did not wait for a congressional investigation of the case and for a report from the department of justice. But certainly, we can appreciate his readiness to act on the case. He did not have any helicopter to transport his troops. Perhaps he knew the big politicians who tried to protect the murderers. With lightning speed he got them and, who knows, because of that he might have been reelected.

Actually, Matthew's account has some allegorical elements. The king in this parable stands for God, and the wedding feast is the symbol of life in the Kingdom of God. The king's messengers were the heralds of the good news who were killed for prophesying and for calling the people to prepare for the coming of the Saviour. The invited guests were the Jews who refused to acknowledge the Lordship of Christ. The destruction of the murderers and the burning of their city must have reference to the destruction of Jerusalem by the Roman army in 70 A.D., when the temple itself was burned. The writer probably believed that God used the Roman army to execute His judgement.

The interjection of this historical event into the parable does not affect the image of a wedding feast as a symbol of life in the Kingdom of God. The Great Supper in the Lucan account approximates a wedding feast, and the same parable seeks to illustrate what the Kingdom of God is like. The picture we get is that of plenty, of joy, of festivity: Life in the Kingdom of God is above all things a life of happiness.

Perhaps our immediate reaction to this reminder is that it does not speak to our present situation: in the kingdom there is plenty, but what we now know and have is appalling poverty; in the kingdom there is joy, but only God knows the gripping sadness in our hearts; in the kingdom there is festivity, but here in this part of the world people do not have enough to eat. Should we not, therefore, regard life in the kingdom as a dream which does not touch reality?

In answering this question, we must admit that the abundant life Jesus offers to all includes material blessing sufficient for our needs. However it should not be equated with economic prosperity *per se*, otherwise those who have everything in the world would have no reason to be unhappy. For the same reason, abundant life is not negated by the absence of material security, otherwise, those who have nothing cannot be happy. The abundant life which Jesus offers is something which is more than mere earthly life. It is a quality of existence that enables us to overcome both the misery of material want and the great dangers of economic prosperity. Jesus Himself had no place to lay His head on; He had to borrow an ass when He entered Jerusalem. When the utter sinfulness of men caused His death upon the cross, He had to be buried in a borrowed graveyard. Yet, in Him we see the fullness of a happy life which though troubled on every side cannot be distressed.

Jesus' invitation is for us to live a happy life, and that life is not necessarily free from want and sufferings and misfortunes. In fact, the Christian life is a life with a cross, and to follow Christ is to face our own Calvary. To be happy is to be blessed; and to be blessed is to be sustained by the everlasting arms of God. And that is why a truly happy, blessed life does not cower in the face of gloom, darkness, and death because in darkness it can see the light of God and in death it is assured of life beyond the grave. It is a triumphant, victorious life not because it can laugh when the enemies fail but because it can sympathize with the enemies' failure. It is a strong, radiant life not because of its own strength but because in its weakness it can experience the sufficiency of God's grace. It is a happy, merry life not because the day is bright and the going is nice but because it has confidence in the Lord of history, a confidence that cannot be shaken by the ugly turns of events and by the heavy storms that make the going rough.

This, then, is Jesus' invitation: that we enter the Kingdom of God where life is like attending a wedding feast. But the trouble with us is that, like the invited guests in our parable, we turn down the invitation. In the gospel of Luke, the excuses offered are patently flimsy. One of them said, "I have bought a field and I must go out and see it; I pray you, have me excused." Does he mean to tell us that he bought a field without seeing it first? He must have trusted the seller or the agent so much. There might be nothing in the field but rocks and stones; it might not be a good piece of property for whatever purpose he had in mind. And if he was a smart fellow, and he must be since he was a friend of the king, he should better see the field first before signing his check. Perhaps he really felt that to go to his field was a better use of his time than attending a wedding reception.

Another man said, "I have bought five yoke of oxen, and I go to examine them; I pray you, have me excused." Again we would say, why buy the oxen without examining them first? Suppose upon examination, he discovered that one or two of them were hopelessly sick or badly deformed, then what? At any rate, could he not wait until after the reception? Well, perhaps he thought that since he was not a *ninong,* he was not one of the sponsors or witnesses, he might just as well preoccupy himself with his new tractor or car.

And still another said, "I have married a wife, and therefore I cannot come." What a romantic excuse; he would not leave his wife. Of course under the law, a newly-married person was exempted from work and military service for one year so he could be with his bride. Could it be that his wife did not want him to go? Was he that understanding?

By the way, we must point out here that in ancient Palestine the custom was to invite the people to a wedding feast a few weeks in advance. The invitation, however, did not specify the exact time of the reception. The custom was to remind the invited guests through messengers of the exact time of the feast just a few hours before the reception. In other words, those to be reminded were only those who accepted the invitation extended to them a few weeks before.

In studying this parable, I was wondering why the guests were not invited to the wedding ceremony. They were invited to the reception. Perhaps the reception was more important than the wedding ceremony. In our country, like in many other places, is not our invitation, to the wedding itself? Very often the invitation reads:

> You are cordially invited to the wedding of
>
> so-and-so to be solemnized at
>
> Cosmopolitan Church or Malate Catholic Church

Then somewhere below the card, we read the words: Reception will follow at the Aristocrat or perhaps at the Wack Wack Club House. My experience is that very often there are more people at the reception than at the wedding ceremony. Sometime ago a young man who was to get married in this sanctuary asked me what he should do to see to it that his invited guests come to his wedding. Taking my advice seriously, he printed at the bottom of the invitation the words, "Reception will follow at the place to be announced immediately after the wedding ceremony."

But the men in our parable are different: they did not go to the reception. Maybe they did not even send their wedding gifts. Yet, we cannot blame them for being so devoted to their business, so concerned about their properties, so faithful to their families. Their major mistake was that they divorced their work and their leisure and their homes from God. That was their tragic mistake.

Certainly, we in this congregation would pray that more and more people may have more land and buildings and other sources of livelihood. We must have a high respect for people who attend to their work and business with the fullest measure of their devotion. But when such people find no time for the Kingdom of God, a fatal spiritual famine cannot be too far away.

O that God would give us not only five yokes of oxen but also a brand-new stereo or a car which we have been dreaming of, but what a pity if such passing joy over a newly-acquired thing crowds out the king's invitation to a wedding feast.

And what can be lovelier than a home where husband and wife, parents and children find time to be together? Yet it is these lovely things in life that sometimes take us away from God. A family without Christ is no more than a mere social unit.

And so the men in our parable refused the invitation to a wedding feast not because they were wicked. On the contrary, they were very decent people. They refused simply because they were preoccupied with the good things of the world. If the first man did not attend to his field, it could mean financial difficulty for his family. He was so busy making a living he forgot to live. Deeply concerned with the needs of the body, he ignored the deeper needs of his spirit.

We have here a parable which gives us some explanation why many people take spiritual matters of secondary importance. By nature, our tendency is to attend first to our own private concerns and interest. We rebel against anything that will alter this pattern of life, because we love ourselves more than we love God. The Christian gospel teaches us that true self-love is not possible unless we love God first. In His other parables, Jesus tells us that the Kingdom of God is like leaving the plow in the field to follow Him. The Christ who teaches us to honor our father and mother is the same Christ who says that unless we leave our father and mother, unless we leave our homes and our lands, we are not worthy to enter the Kingdom of God.

Now, when the invited guests did not show up, the master said to his servant, "Go out to the highways and hedges, and compel people to come in, that my house may be filled." Long time ago, Augustine used this text to justify religious persecution. It was used as a defense for coercing people into the Christian faith. It was used as a justification for the inquisition and for the bloody campaign against the so-called heretics. Such interpretation cannot be supported by the parable itself. It is very unlikely that one servant (and in the gospel of Luke the word servant is in the singular) could have fulfilled his commission. What the writer wants to emphasize is that when the stalwarts of the church and of the Christian tradition fail, God turns to the nobodies; when the expected supporters of the church and the expected defenders of the faith walk out and descend into petty moralism, God turns to the new converts to carry out His will.

Now when the king came in he looked at the guests and saw one who had no wedding garment. "Friend" he said," how did you get in here without a wedding garment? You are not properly attired. Your hair is long, you did not shave, your necktie is too wide, your pants are too tight, your sunglasses are too big." The man was speechless. He could have said. "Sir, I had no time to change. I was just recruited in the streets by your servant. I did not even have time to take a bath. By the way, sir, why are you so meticulous about my garment? Are we not supposed to come to you as we are? Is not the heart more important than the clothes?"

Several years ago at the Yale Divinity School, the faculty and the students were having some differences of opinion on the proper attire of ministerial students. The faculty felt that the informal, sometimes sloppy attire was out of place in the Divinity School. But the students felt that there was nothing wrong with their casual apparel. The debate took the form of posting scriptural texts on the bulletin board. The faculty quoted Isaiah 52:1, which says, "Awake, awake, put on your strength, O Zion; put on your beautiful garments, O Jerusalem, the holy city." The students replied by quoting Matthew 6:25, which says, "Therefore, I tell you, do not be anxious about your life, what you shall eat or what you shall drink, nor about your body, what you shall put on."

The central point of the parable is that we cannot be in the wedding feast without a wedding garment; we cannot be in the Kingdom of God and at the same time continue having our old unregenerated character. If we are in Christ, we should become new creatures, and the old things must pass away. The robe of hypocrisy and pride must be replaced with the new garment of honesty and reverence and faith. Otherwise, we would be cast into outer darkness and there reap shame and infamy.

That is what it means to live in response to Jesus' gracious invitation: it is to have our will purified by the purpose of God, to have our imagination cleansed by the love of God, to have our temper controlled by the Spirit of God. It is to offer up our burdens and our sorrows to Him who knows our secret fears. It is to be happy, in the deepest meaning of the word, and to be sustained by the conviction that God is our refuge and underneath are His everlasting arms ready to uphold us.

42

Tension and Peace

Scripture Reading:
Matthew 10:34; John 14:27

In Matthew, Jesus says, "Think not that I am come to send peace on earth: I came not to send peace, but a sword." In John, Jesus says, "Peace I leave you, my peace I give unto you: not as the world giveth, give I unto you."

At first glance, these two verses seem to be conflicting: they even suggest that Jesus is contradicting Himself. However, the students of the Bible tell us that Jesus is not contradicting Himself. The word peace in Matthew is to be understood in the context of the entire chapter (Chap. 10) where Jesus speaks of the Gospel as the proclamation of the Christ event which is, at the same time, a demand on the people to decide for or against Him. In fact, the language Jesus uses here is perfectly familiar to the Jews, who believed that the Day of the Lord would be characterized by the division of families. Here is a well-known passage from their Rabbis: "In the period when the Son of David shall come, a daughter will rise up against her mother, a daughter-in-law against her mother-in-law. The son despises his father, the daughter rebels against the mother, the daughter-in-law against her mother-in-law, and a man's enemies are they of his own household." This is why when Jesus said, in Matthew 10, that He came not to bring peace but sword, and to set a man at variance against his father, and the daughter against her mother, He was practically saying that the Day of the Lord had come, and that His coming was a fulfillment of the Rabbis' teaching. It is in that sense that He came not to bring peace, but a sword. Some members of the family will believe in Him; others will not — and in a situation like that there is no peace. Furthermore, the stringent demand of Christian discipleship is that a man must love Jesus more than he loves his family. Jesus says, "He that loveth father or mother more than me is not worthy of me; and he that loveth son or daughter more than me is not worthy of me."

By the way, both in the writings of the Rabbis and in the gospel of Matthew, we find no mention about the son-in-law being at variance against his father-in-law. We read that the daughter-in-law will be against her mother-in-law and vice versa but nothing of this sort is mentioned about the son-in-law in relation to his father-in-law or mother-in-law. Perhaps, this is because men seldom give any problem to their in-laws.

At any rate, our Scripture lesson establishes the fact that there will be division among men, and Christ is the instance of that division. "His doctrine is either true or untrue, His Cross is either a pathetic and ironic tragedy or a very redemption. Neutrality is not possible. We are either for Him or against Him, and between the two camps there is inevitable clash".[1]

Jesus experienced this in His own life. At least during the early part of His ministry, the members of His own family did not believe in Him.

The point we should stress is that our Scripture lesson, when read in the light of Jesus' teaching about life, underscores the fact that as pilgrims on this earth we are bound to have tensions, conflicts, and strifes. "In the world ye shall have tribulations." And the reality of that experience is perhaps most acute during this century. Someone has suggested that just as there were periods in history which were labelled "the age of enlightenment" and "the age of reason," so our present time may well be termed "the age of tension." The demands on us are so terrific that, if we are not careful, our hearts may not be able to take them.

Apparently, one of the sources of tension is our own internal world. There is, for instance, our inability to accept what we are. We find it difficult to accept ourselves and such ugly feeling is a fertile ground for all kinds of evil thoughts.

Then, there is our lack of courage to face our failures and to wrestle with our fears. Defeat is a painful experience and sometimes we cannot take it with integrity. Even when it leads us to a hospital, we find ourselves thinking of revenge.

Tension is sometimes caused by the crushing weight of a heavy schedule. The anxiety over what to do at the next hour or on the next day may deprive us of a much needed rest. We lose control of ourselves and we become slaves of time and victims of circumstances.

The external sources of tension can be equally mortifying. Natural calamities that cause great havoc on lives and properties can generate fear.

---

[1] George A. Buttrick, *Interpreter's Bible,* Vol. 7, p. 374

They can really make us tremble and make us feel very helpless. One external source of tension which we will always have until the end of time comes from our relationship with other people. They may be our loved ones, the immediate members of our family. They may be our friends, including our best friends. They may be our neighbors. They may also be our enemies. In many cases, the intensity of the tension is proportional to the closeness of the relationship. They who are dearest to us can hurt us most. Their thoughtlessness or carelessness, their arrogance or immaturity, their misdemeanor or misbehaviour can rob our peace and kill our joy. They can make us miserable, they can tear us to pieces.

Yet, it is useless to break down and to resign from life itself. In moments of sobriety, we know it will not profit us to waste our life just because there is so much disappointment. Deep within our hearts we know that a greater power can sustain us through the night and enable us to rise above the storms. The question, therefore, is how do we overcome? How do we transcend the tumults of life? How do we acquire that peace which the world can never give? How do we maintain quietness and confidence when the billows are raging and the world looks so cruel?

Before we mention some specific suggestions, we must remind ourselves that withdrawal from this world cannot solve the problem. For wherever we go, we still have ourselves and for as long as we live we must live with ourselves. We may run to the hills, or dwell in the uttermost parts of the seas; we may even fly to the moon or to the farthest star, but those places do not have the final healing touch and we still have to wrestle with our pains. The Christian life is a life with the cross; it is a life with Calvary. A life which has no problems or suffering cannot be Christian; it cannot be even human.

We must, therefore, resist the temptation to run away from the conflicts and trials of life. We would do well to meet them face to face and to overcome them in the regnancy of Christ's spirit. There is wisdom in the words of a poet who said, "No peace, except I struggle; No struggle, except I have peace."

So we go back to the question: How do we acquire that peace which we ardently need in handling the stress and strain of modern life? Well, one advice from a certain Capt. Eddie Rickenbacker, a very busy man, is for us to collapse physically. And by that he means to let go of every muscle in our bodies. It is the art of relaxing by just lying down or by sitting in your chair as comfortably as you can. Maybe Elizabeth Ramsey says it more graphically: *Relax lang,* she says. And *relax lang* means more than her Marvel detergent advertisement suggests. It means: Take it easy; don't let your worries get into your nerves. Be confident that Someone [meaning God] not something [meaning Marvel] is ever beside you to give you courage and strength. *Relax lang.*

Dr. Norman Vincent Peale, that famous preacher in New York's Marble Collegiate Church, tells the following story in one of his articles: "I went to a certain city on a lecture date and was met at the train by a committee. I was rushed to a bookstore for one autographing party and then on to another. After that I rushed to a luncheon, rushed back to the hotel where I was told I had 20 minutes to dress for dinner. While I was dressing the telephone rang. 'Hurry,' the voice said, 'we must get down to dinner.' 'I'll be right down,' I said. I was about to rush from the room when suddenly I stopped. 'What is this all about?' I asked myself. I telephoned downstairs and said, 'If you want to eat, go ahead. I'll be down after a while.' I took off my shoes, put my feet up on the table and just sat. Then I had a little talk with myself: 'Come on now, slow down. God is here and His peace is touching you.' I shall never forget the sense of peace and personal mastery I had when I walked out of that room 15 minutes later. I had the glorious feeling of having taken control of myself emotionally. And all I had missed was the soup."

I am sure Dr. Peale will agree with Elizabeth Ramsey and say: *Relax lang.*

Dr. Peale himself, in his book on *Positive Thinking,* strongly recommends positive thinking as a means of relieving tension and acquiring serenity of mind. He believes that the mind can be drained of all irritation, resentment, disappointment, frustration, annoyances. He says, "To do this, think of the most beautiful and peaceful scenes you know — a mountain at sunset, a valley filled with the hush of early morning, a lake by moonlight." In other words, forget the garbage once in a while. Think of Rizal Park instead, of the Cultural Center, of the play, *"Walang Sugat."* Something of this advice, in a deeper sense, of course, comes from the pen of the Apostle Paul. He says, "Whatsoever things are true, whatsoever things are honest, whatsoever things are just, whatsoever things are pure, whatsoever things are lovely, whatsover things are of good report; if there be any virtue, and if there be any praise, think on these things." This type of positive thinking is certainly worth cultivating.

Then, there are tensions caused by grief over the loss of a loved one, or by miseries inflicted by the injustices and greed of our fellow men. Dr. Joshua Loth Liebman in his book *Peace of Mind* prescribes that we must give way to as much grief as we actually feel. We must not be ashamed of our emotions, he believes. It is essential that we express, rather than repress, our griefs, and heartaches and resentments. The ancient teachers of Judaism as we see them in the Bible, encouraged open and unashamed expression of sorrow and pain by wearing sackcloth, rending their garments, and engaging in fasting. Such a custom has a curative function and can save us from a tragic abyss. So we must let it out, so to speak. Cry, if you must. Our tears may prevent a more serious damage in our heart.

Now, let us turn our eyes and ears from Elizabeth Ramsey and Vincent Peale to the Master Workman of the race and see what He has to say. And immediately His words in the Sermon on the Mount come to us with revitalizing freshness. He says, "Love your enemies, bless them that curse you, do good to them that hate you, and pray for them which despitefully use you and persecute you."(Matt 5:44). Perhaps, our first reaction might be: My goodness, bless those that curse us? Do good to them that hate us? No sir. Not I. I will curse them that curse me and hate them that hate me. An eye for an eye, and a tooth for a tooth!

But again, the gentle voice of the Master speaks with convincing authority: "Whosoever shall smite thee on thy right cheek, turn to him the other also. Whosoever shall compel thee to go a mile, go with him twain." How in the world can such formula give us peace?

Well, let me put it this way: In the New Testament, we do not obtain peace by seeking it. We obtain it only by being concerned that God's will is done. Peace is not the main object in the Christian life. It is only the fruit of our having received the Holy Spirit. "Seek ye first the kingdom of God and His righteousness, and all these things" — including peace of mind and peace of soul — "shall be added unto you."

Peace, therefore, is the result of our obedience to God's will. Jesus, who lived in perfect harmony with God's will, is the picture of absolute peace even when the mighty forces of evil were conspiring against Him. He died upon the cross with wonderful tranquility because He knew it was God's will. He frontally and fearlessly met the onslaughts of His enemies with confident faith in the sovereign will of God. He towered above the storms and crossed the bar with quietness.

That is the same way it should be for us. We will not achieve peace of soul by concocting psychological formulas and prescribing saccharin methods of attaining peace. It can be ours only when God's will becomes also our will.

This is why those who are really at peace with God are seldom peaceful in the secular meaning of the word. They are often the objects of the world's scorn, of malice, and of hate. Being obedient to the will of God, they get involved in the cause of justice and brotherhood. Being obedient to the will of God, they cannot help but participate in the building of a world where men may know something of love, compassion, and forgiveness. But the mysterious thing about them is that while they are troubled on every side, yet they are not distressed; and while they are being persecuted, yet they are not forsaken.

Today, let us resolve not to be impoverished by the nagging pains caused by life's bitterest disappointments. Let us not allow tensions to erode our faith and spoil our future. God had meant us to be masters of circumstances, and to emerge victorious from every situation. If we will but do His will with gladness and patience, we may yet see some guiding star as we walk through the dark or as we sail on the rough sea of life. The storms may come and the winds may blow, but we will not be afraid because we know that the Prince of Peace is with us and is able to keep us from falling. And who knows, the people of this world may turn to us and ask, "What is the secret of your peace?" Then we may be led to answer, "What else but the doing of God's will as revealed to us in Jesus Christ our Lord."

43

"Only Believe"

Scripture Reading: Mark 5:21-43

This passage in Mark is about a man named Jairus who came to Jesus for help. This narrative is found in the first three gospels in the New Testament — Matthew, Mark, and Luke. In the book of Matthew, however, no name is given to the man. He is simply described as "a certain ruler." In both Mark and Luke, that man is known as Jairus. In Matthew, the ruler's daughter was already dead when he sought for Jesus. He said, "My daughter has just died; but come and lay your hands on her, and she will live." In Mark, the daughter was still alive but very ill ("My little daughter is at the point of death"). Luke follows Mark in saying that the daughter was at the point of death, but adds that she was Jairus' only daughter and about 12 years old. In Matthew, the story is related in only 9 verses; Mark is more detailed and relates the same event in 23 verses; Luke has 17 verses.

In all three accounts, the story of that woman suffering from hemorrhage is inserted. Mark, however, says that she "had suffered much under many physicians, and has spent all that she had, and was no better but rather grew worse." We don't find this reference to the physicians in the gospel of Luke. Perhaps, it is because Luke himself was a physician, and therefore would be reluctant to say that the woman had spent all her money consulting many doctors and yet she became worse instead of better.

At any rate, we actually have in this passage two related stories: the story of Jairus who asked Jesus to heal his daughter, and the story of the beleaguered woman. We will see the relationship between those stories as we try to see what the passage as a whole is trying to tell us.

Regardless of how we approach this passage, it seems that the gospel writers are telling us that in spite of the imperfections of our motives and of our faith, Jesus is prepared to help us. Let me spell this out a little further. Jairus is said to be a ruler of the synagogue. In other words, he was a very important man. He might even be a man of wealth. To be a ruler of the synagogue, one must be elected by the elders. Essentially, Jairus' job was that of general administration. He appointed people who would teach and preach in the synagogue. He must see to it that everything was fit for synagogue activities.

Now, we must remember how the synagogue authorities regarded Jesus. To them Jesus was a heretic and an anathema. Jairus' colleagues could not have encouraged him to solicit Jesus' help. Even the members of his household were quick to advise him not to bother the Master anymore when his daughter passed away. As much as possible, they did not want Jesus to have anything to do with him.

But the sick girl was Jairus' only daughter. No doubt he must have brought her to the best doctors in town. And yet she was at the point of death and, therefore, out of desperation he must look for Jesus and ask His help.

This is what I mean by an imperfect motive on the part of Jairus. He would not come to Jesus unless it was extremely necessary. It is similar to our own experience of almost ignoring God when the weather is fair and we are in perfect health, but we would storm the gates of heaven when we are in a most precarious situation. But Jairus' case reminds us that God will still have mercy even when our approach to Him is merely dictated by circumstances. He is the God who cares for us not only when we care for Him but also when we are dragged into His presence by our pressing need of His favor.

Then, there was that woman who came to Jesus with an inadequate faith. She had a bleeding problem for 12 years and, as Mark tells us, she had spent all she had for medical care but her condition did not improve. So, she said to herself that if she could only touch the edge of Jesus' garment she would get well. Such a faith, we would say, was no better than belief in magic. She reminds us of those who visit shrines to kiss the feet of the Black Nazarene, or to touch the handkerchief of saints, and be made whole. The woman's faith was no deeper than mere superstition. Yet, Jesus gave her all His attention and sought to speak to her personally. He knew someone touched His garment and she could have hidden herself in the thick multitude. In fact, when Jesus asked His disciples who it was that touched Him, they replied, almost deridingly, "You see the crowd pressing around you, and yet you ask, 'Who touched me?' " Such mild reproach did not stop Him from looking around until the woman, in fear and trembling, "fell down before Him, and told Him the whole truth." We never read about that woman again in the rest of the New Testament, but we can be sure that her most glorious experience was when Jesus told her, "Daughter, your faith has made you well: go in peace and be healed of your disease."

The point is that in spite of the embarrassing inadequacy of our faith God remains the same loving Father who responds to our needs. It is His mercy and gracious favor that nurtures our faith and delivers us from superstition. Only in His presence do we realize the bankruptcy of our faith and that solemn realization is at the same time a healing experience.

In the gospel of Matthew, the story of Jairus' daughter whom Jesus brought back to life is immediately followed by the story of two blind men who cried to Jesus saying, "Have mercy on us, Son of David." Matthew's purpose in doing this is to suggest that even those with an inadequate concept of Jesus or with inadequate theology are not necessarily pushed outside the realm of divine concern. The blind men's concept of Jesus as the Son of David clearly reveals their militaristic hope, shared by many of their fellow men, that the promised Messiah was a great military and political figure like their honored king, David. It was, in fact, a national expectation which Jesus refused to dignify because they failed to understand that His kingdom was not of this world. But when those men, both physically blind and theologically blind, cried to Him for help, He did not withhold His mercy just because of their theological inadequacy. It is not theological refinement that saves us, however important that may be; it is our honest seeking for the truth that leads us to the throne of the Saviour.

Secondly, our Scripture lesson tells us that sometimes interruptions in our life are among the greatest opportunities to serve. Mark says that "when Jesus had crossed again in the boat to the other side, a great crowd gathered about Him." Has it ever occurred to you that in the majority of cases whenever Jesus was surrounded by a crowd, He would open His mouth to teach or preach? In the gospel of Mark, before Jesus could open His mouth, this ruler of the synagogue came and interrupted both Jesus and the crowd. In Matthew, Jesus was already speaking when Jairus came. He could not wait for Jesus to finish. It might be too late. He had to beg their pardon because his daughter was very ill. And Jesus, who knew the burden in his heart, consented to go with him.

But that was not the main interruption. The main thing was the interruption of the interruption. Jairus and Jesus were walking, almost running in a hurry because the child was at the point of death. But someone touched Jesus' garment and He stopped to find out who it was who did it.

We can imagine Jairus saying to himself, "Come on, be quick. Never mind who touched You. Don't tarry anymore. We do not have much time." Perhaps, the disciples were sympathizing with Jairus when they said to Jesus that they would not know who touched Him as there were so many people around Him. In effect, they were saying, "Sir, it is useless to find out who touched Your garment. We cannot ask these people one by one. We may just as well proceed." But Jesus wanted to know who touched His garment and began looking around. Can you imagine the mounting tension in Jairus? Jairus broke all rules of courtesy and interrupted Jesus in His teaching because his child was very ill, but now an irresponsible person had caused this delay in their trip by touching Jesus' garment. Perhaps, he politely came near Jesus to plead that they proceed and before he could say a word, there came a woman who knelt before Jesus, trembling with fear. Then, she began her speech saying, "Lord, please forgive me. I have been wanting to see You but because I am sick I decided to wait until you pass this way. You see, Lord I have been suffering from this disease for twelve years now and somehow deep in my heart I know that if I could only touch the hem of your gown I will get well. Please pardon me. Please forgive me. And please have mercy upon me." We don't know how long her confession was. And she must have paused a great deal to sob. Maybe Jesus also asked a few questions. But while all of that was going on, we can just imagine the burning tension in every blood vessel of Jairus who probably was now eager to push the woman. But he held his peace, and that much was his contribution to the woman's healing.

How is it with you and me? How many times have we been tried with some unexpected interruptions which turned out to be golden chances to serve in a very special way? It will be a great blessing if, in all our planning, we allow a certain degree of flexibility in order to convert needed interruptions into an asset for the soul. That requires some maturity of judgement. We cannot just give way to any interruption, but those that cannot be avoided can make us and our world richer.

In the third place, our Scripture lesson suggests that faith is possible even when we have reached the end of our wits. Remember that Jairus' daughter was very ill. He said that she was at the point of death. Then, while Jesus was talking with the woman, messengers came to inform Jairus that his daughter had just died and there was no more need to bother the Master. But Jesus, ignoring what they said, spoke to the ruler of the synagogue, saying, "Do not fear, only believe."

Could the messengers be right? Now that the daughter was dead, why bother the Master? It was all right of Jairus to see Jesus when his daughter was still alive. At least there was some hope. Jesus could still do something for her. But now she was dead. Why bother Him?

On the other hand, Jesus' words cannot be taken lightly. When He overheard what the messengers said ("ignoring" in some translations), He gave Jairus the assurance: "Do not fear; only believe." Believe when the possibility of help is intellectually impossible? To have faith when it is too late? Yes. The answer is yes, even when it is intellectually incomprehensible.

Two things must be said in connection with this kind of believing. First, faith is not something that begins at the end of reason. It is a mistake to say that we believe or have faith when we can no longer understand. Jairus came to Jesus when he knew there was still hope for his daughter. His faith, in other words, had a rational basis. Faith and reason go together; reason is the foundation of faith, and faith is the expression of reason. Today, it is necessary not only to believe but also to understand. To understand is not to lose faith; it is to enrich faith. Secondly, faith is not necessarily limited by reason because faith is transrational. Jairus continued to believe even when his daughter was already dead. Faith is not only an intellectual assent to something we can understand. It is also the surrender of the will, a bold abandonment of self to the wisdom of Almighty God. It is trust; it is commitment; it is self-surrender.

This is not to say that we can just fold our arms and be secure in the thought that God will take care of us. As I have already stated, discipleship demands that we love God with all our mind, and that means being willing to pay the cost of knowing what can be known. However, when we can no longer understand, either because of the finiteness of our mind or because we have understood everything that could be understood, let us not say that God is helpless at a certain situation because that would be limiting the possibilities of God. The central point in this story of Jairus is not that his daughter was brought back to life, for that is just one of the many miracle stories we have in the Bible; the central point is that Jairus was able to believe when believing was almost ridiculous. His faith was a glowing tribute to the Almightiness of God whose thoughts are higher than our thoughts. He demonstrated that a human predicament can be a divine opportunity. And it was that faith that enabled him to live triumphantly.

Finally, and this is just a summary of all that has been said, our Scripture lesson teaches us that Jesus can give peace to a sin-sick world and to a troubled heart. The passage before us is simply a picture of a disturbed and despairing people on the one hand and the confident, comforting Christ on the other hand. We have described the mighty anguish Jairus had to struggle with. We have noted the pitiful condition of that woman who touched the hem of Jesus' garment. We must also include the pandemonium of grief which accentuated the acute loneliness in the household of Jairus.

Three mourning customs characterized every Jewish household of grief. One was the rending of garments. It was the symbol of great despair. Something like that was going on in Jairus' house when Jesus reached the place. The other was the wailing for the dead. This was done by professionals, mostly women. They were paid to cry, to mourn, to express deep sorrow. To us that might look no more than drama, perhaps a funny drama. But to them it was a touching experience, a moving way of expressing the desolation of their souls. Thirdly, there were the flute-players. Like the wailers, the flute-players were paid to play all kinds of music that would evoke sadness. The more players, the better. But a Roman law limited the number of flute-players to ten because to have more might produce too much grief which the people might not bear. All these: the rending of garments, the wailing, and the flute-playing must have been employed in the household of Jairus because he could afford to have all of them. The picture that we get is that of unspeakable sadness, of indescribable grief, of untold anguish.

All that is marvelously overcome by the holy presence of Christ, whose appearance suddenly introduced life, instead of death; hope, instead of despair; joy, instead of sorrow. The Scripture says that Jesus put those tear-jerkers out, and when He caused the little daughter to walk, everybody was overcome with amazement.

That is the same blessing that can be ours today. If your household has been made desolate by the death of a loved one, Jesus can give you the strength to smile. If you are in the valley of spiritual loneliness, being forgotten by your friends and being mocked by foes, Jesus can give you hope. If you are in the dungeon of sin and shame, imprisoned by the past and embittered by the present, you can touch the hem of Jesus' garment through faith, and thus find yourselves again in the company of believers. If you are at the end of your human resources and at the moment cannot see how you can make a go out of your life, do not be afraid; only believe, and Jesus will be a real presence in your life to give you peace and strength and light.

44

The Living Water of Life

Scripture Reading: John 4:1-24

Jesus' conversation with a Samaritan woman beside Jacob's well is one of the most familiar stories in the New Testament. Once we read it, it lingers in our memories — not only because it is a touching story of a wretched woman who became a missionary, but also because the rottenness of her life has some affinity with our own moral depravity. She was the talk of the town for her notorious popularity. People would not talk too much about women who had been married twice or thrice — that is not really sensational. But for a woman to be married five times, and presently to be living with a man who was not her legal husband — that is sensational enough to provoke gossip. In fact, she had to fetch water at noontime — at a time when most probably no one would be at the well. She wanted to avoid the piercing, scornful stare of her neighbors. The embarrassment would be just too much for her to bear.

But that noonday someone was by the well. First, she perceived that He was just a Jew. Then she realized that He was a prophet. And finally, she discovered that He was the Messiah. We know the rest of the story — how she showed her knowledge in polemics, how conversant she was in religion, and how, finally, she became a magnetic witness to the transforming grace of the Saviour of men.

Now let us see how this story of Jesus' redemptive influence is unfolded in the gospel of John. First, let us note that Jesus began with human needs. "Give me a drink," He asked. He and His disciples were on their way to Galilee from Judea. The shortest way was through Samaria, and after hiking the whole morning they were tired and hungry. The disciples went to buy some food while Jesus was left waiting by the well. It was hot and humid, and a cup of cool water would be a natural desire. That is why when the woman came around to fill her pitcher, Jesus requested, "Give me a drink."

Why did Jesus begin that way, we wonder. He could have started the conversation by saying, "Woman, I am the Messiah mankind has been waiting for. I am the living water of life which I freely give to all who follow me. I will give you some of it, if you quench my thirst by giving me some water to drink." But that was not what He said. He began by revealing the true nature of His need — He was thirsty, and He was asking the woman to give Him some water. In other words, He began with human needs.

This is one basic approach which the churches have often overlooked. In our desire to preach the good news, to make Jesus known, to convert people to the Christian fellowship, we build churches and organize prayer meetings and conduct worship services. Of course, we do believe in church buildings and prayer meetings and worship services. There is no doubt about that, but how often have we neglected to find out the basic needs of the people we seek to evangelize? We teach them how to pray, when the more urgent need is to teach them how to plant *camote*. We give them chapels, when the more urgent need is a toilet or a classroom. We give them sermons when they need sympathy. We give them used neckties, when their need is employment. How can we justify the building of huge, airconditioned cathedrals and palatial residences for ecclesiastical leaders when people languish in *barong-barongs* and struggle for existence by scavenging? Why speak of the bread of life when their ardent need is bread?

I submit that one of the basic aims of Christian mission is to help meet human needs. Unfortunately, there are some Christian leaders who insist that the church should have nothing to do with rice production, family planning, university education and other forms of social concern. They insist that the main business of the church is to preach the gospel and to administer the sacraments. Such position cannot be biblically justified. Jesus healed the sick and fed the hungry. The salvation He offered is not only for the soul but also for the body.

Therefore, if mission is to be Christian, we must consider the situation of the people and understand their needs. Our mission is to play our role, with the limited resources given to us by God, in meeting their needs. Christian mission begins when we respond to the needs of men. The living water of life becomes more meaningful when we have drinkable water (*Nawasa water*).

In this connection, let us note that in our Scripture reading, it was Jesus, and not the Samaritan woman, who was thirsty. It was He who needed a cup of cool water. It was He who asked, "Give me a drink." In the gospel of John, where the deity of Christ is very much emphasized, Jesus is also projected as a very human person. In fact, He can be the symbol of mankind in need. The thirsty Christ knows the pains of hunger and thirst. And that is why to those who feed the hungry and visit the sick and comfort the lonely, He says, "Inasmuch as you have done it unto the least of these, my brethren, you have done it unto me." And that is why we are firmly convinced that to serve the poor and the downtrodden and the underprivileged is to serve Christ Himself, the Christ who dwells not only in the sanctuary but also in the slums.

Furthermore, we will note that Jesus asked the woman to do something for Him. Of course, as the story clearly reveals, it was she who had the bigger needs — she needed Christ's mercy and forgiveness and help. And it was Christ alone who could help her rise up from the ashes of her wretchedness. Yet, Jesus began by asking her to do something for Him. Here was a woman who became a Christian missionary because Jesus asked for a glass of water from her.

Is it not also our own experience that at times people become deeply committed to the cause of the Church because they were asked to do something for the Church? I know of a good number of people who became real friends of Jesus Christ, who grew more mature in their Christian faith, who became strong supporters of the Christian ministry, because they were asked to contribute to the building of a sanctuary, because they were asked to sign a pledge card, because their help, which, they gladly extended, was first of all solicited. A late American president, who knew the supreme blessedness of self-giving, advised his fellow countrymen to think not of what their government could do for them but of what they could do for the government.

What can we do for God? This is the question we often fail to ask ourselves because we are preoccupied with what God can do for us. While it is true that God can satisfy our deepest longings and can grant us the desires of our hearts, we should not forget that He, too, solicits what we can do, and even depends on us for the accomplishment of His will. It is when we resolve to give the best we can in response to what we believe is being asked of us that we discover that in the end we become richer and, in fact, more blessed. We discover that we receive more than we give because for giving water, we receive the living water of life.

This leads us to another point, namely, that while Jesus begins with the crying needs of men, He goes beyond the purely physical, material, and human. He reaches for the spiritual, for the fulfillment of the human spirit. Surely, He asked for water and did not hide the fact that He was thirsty. But He did not stop there; He also talked about the living water of life. In other words, it is not enough that we have something to drink and eat: man does not live by bread alone. In fact, it does not profit us to gain the whole world if in the process we lose our souls.

This is what is missing in purely secular development projects. They are designed to increase food production, to curb population explosion, to improve the lot of the laborers — in short, to give water to the thirsty. Now the business of the Church is to teach people that we are also children of the spirit. That is why we believe in prayer and in worship and in meeting regularly for Christian fellowship. We can be rich in the things of this world but sadly wanting in the things of the spirit. The abundant life which Jesus offers is not just freedom from material poverty but also growth in the knowledge of God.

In other words, every concern for man's economic and material well-being without regard for moral and spiritual education, and any excessive concern for evangelism that has nothing to do with the material needs of men are both extremes that can do more harm than good. The true Christian gospel is the gospel of bread, but also of the Bread of Life. It is good news about water, but also about the Living Water of life. It is a message about life on earth, but also about life in heaven. It is the message of salvation for the whole man — the man who is both body and soul.

This is the meaning of the Incarnation, of the Word that became flesh. The gospel says that Jesus was born in Bethlehem, and Bethlehem means the house of bread: "Beth" meaning house; and "lehem" meaning bread. Bethlehem was the granary of Palestine; wheat was its main crop. Hence, it was called the house of bread. But Jesus, in the gospel of John, calls Himself the Bread of Life, and that Bread of Life was born in the house of bread in Bethlehem. The Incarnation, therefore, is God's way of telling us that we need not only the house of bread but also the Bread of Life.

And so, in our attempts to help the squatters secure better housing, in our ministry to indigents and handicapped and the oppressed, in our participation in the task of liberating society from obsolete traditionalism, let us be sure our Christian witness is not obscured or neglected. Let us be sure that our Christian witness is clearly seen in our service, so that the people may know that as we give them water, it is also our prayer that they may somehow know the abiding presence of the Living Christ.

At this point, let us observe that the Samaritan woman, before finally acquiring that triumphant spirit which enabled her to transcend the shame of her past life and to witness with courage and power, went through certain difficulties which we still find in human life today. There was, for instance, the barrier of culture and tradition. The Samaritans were not supposed to be in speaking terms with the Jews. Furthermore, she was a woman; and the men, particularly the scribes, were prohibited from talking with women in public, particularly with women of questionable character. The whole tradition was against her, and yet because Jesus took the initiative, she received the Living Water of life.

How many of us find it difficult to completely identify ourselves with Christ because of culture and tradition? Because our companions in the house and in our places of work might look upon us with suspicion? Because our neighbor may not approve of it? Because the majority of the people around us may not endorse it? We can sympathize with those who are in that situation, for undeniably it is a difficult situation. We know that ultimately they will pass the test, but it will not be an easy one.

Secondly, the Samaritan woman had difficulty overcoming the barrier of religion and theology. In fact, for a while when Jesus' disclosure of His knowledge about her was becoming a bit embarrassing, she tried to divert His attention by engaging Him in a theological discussion. She argued that Mount Gerizim and not Zion was the place of worship. She admitted that the Messiah, when He came, would announce all things to men. On this question of the Messiah, Jesus said, "I am He," and on the subject of worship, He declared, "God is a spirit; and they that worship Him must worship Him in spirit and in truth."

Do we have that same difficulty — that because we have our religion inherited from our forebears, and because we have our beliefs and teachings which our church holds sacred, we begin to think that God can be found only in our church and that Jesus need not disturb our theological security? If that be the case, we must recall that God is a spirit — that He cannot be contained in temples made by human hands; and that He must be worshipped not in terms of our inherited dogmas but in truth.

Finally, the Samaritan woman, in order to receive the living water of life, had to go beyond the barrier of technicality and legality. When Jesus told her, "Go, call your husband, and come back here," she said, "I have no husband." Of course, she had no husband; she was living with a man who was not legally her husband. She had five husbands, and the sixth man, technically speaking, was not her husband. They did not sign a marriage contract. They had no wedding ceremony. They just decided to keep household together. And so she said, "I have no husband."

How often have we denied ourselves the gift of the living water because of technicalities? How often do we keep on sinning because legally we have a way out, because there is a way to make it appear it is not really sinful?

Today, we must resolve not to hide our sins from God. He knows us more than we know ourselves. We do not have to hide our tears, our doubts, our anxieties. We can surrender them to Christ, who promises living water that can quench our thirst for peace, for happiness, for purity.

45

When You are in Love

(A sermon on Valentine's Day)
Scripture Reading: I Corinthians 13

Today is the day of that little-known saint, Valentine. All we know about him is that he cured the blind daughter of a certain Asterius. Asterius was charged by the Emperor Claudius to win Valentine back to paganism, but somehow it was Asterius who was won to Christianity. Then for reasons we do not know, Valentine was imprisoned, tortured, and later on beheaded. It is very doubtful, however, whether this short and sad story about St. Valentine has any relation to our celebration of Valentine's day on the 14th of February.

Valentine's day is more commonly associated with the ancient Roman festival of the *Lupercalia*, also celebrated in the month of February. This festival was highlighted by a sort of a game where the names of young women were put into a box, "from which they were drawn by the men as chance directed." We are told that similar customs existed in England and France for centuries, especially among the upper classes [meaning, among the oligarchs].

It is, therefore, fitting that we today talk about love — about human love as well as divine love. We begin by briefly summarizing the various interpretations of love. Most common, of course, in literature and in daily life, is the experience of love as an emotional reality. This is suggested by popular songs like "When you are in love, it's the happiest time of the year." Love is within the sphere of affection; it has power that can be felt, for better or for worse.

The philosopher Spinoza, while affirming this emotional character of love, also suggests that love can be intellectual. Intellectual in the sense that it is the love with which we love God. Other Christian thinkers would rather use the big word **ontological** in describing love. It simply means being ourselves in relation to the Supreme Being who is God. This interpretation has some profound implications but the central point is that the concept of love cannot be contained within the sphere of emotion or feeling.

Another way of looking at love is contributed by Judaism and Christianity. In Christianity, the word love is often combined with the imperative "thou shalt." The Great Commandment, for instance, demands of everyone to love God and neighbor. This is the ethical nature of love. If love is just emotion, it cannot be demanded because emotions cannot be legislated. Emotions cannot be commanded. But love is not just emotion; it also has ethical character. Therefore, we can say, "Thou shalt love the Lord thy God with all thy heart and mind and strength; and thou shalt love thy neighbor as thyself."

For our purpose, we will limit our thought to three specific manifestations of love, namely, anger, justice, and forgiveness. Anger can be an expression of love. Perhaps, the better word is righteous indignation because anger is sometimes identified with outburst of emotion. But if the word is correctly understood, then we can describe those who love God as angry people. Were not the Old Testament prophets angry? Amos was angry because of the social injustices prevailing in Judah. Jeremiah was angry because of immorality in high and low places. Nathan was angry because his good friend, David, took Bathsheba from her husband. Jonah was angry because of the wickedness of the people in Nineveh. Such contempt for sin is actually one side of love. This is why the wrath of God, which we also read about in the Bible, is understood as an aspect of God's love. To love God is at the same time to wage war against the devil.

On the other hand, anger is not to be easily identified with love. The Egyptian pharaoh was angry when Moses and the Israelites left. Cain was angry when his offering was overshadowed by Abel's offering. The elder brother in the Prodigal Son was angry when his brother came back and there was merrymaking tendered in his honor. When Jesus was arrested, an angry crowd shouted, "Let him be crucified!"

Today, there are so many angry people and they make us believe that their anger is in the name of love — love of country or love of their fellow men. Only God knows whether their indignation is righteous or not. But always we need to remind ourselves that unless it is an expression of love, anger can lead to the graveyard of the soul. The salvation of our world cannot be achieved through anger. It can come only through love. Love is not genuine unless it is capable of being angry.

Secondly, love expresses itself in justice. In fact, in our daily course of life, justice is the nearest expression of love. But precisely because justice is not a perfect expression of love, it is not our highest goal in life. Our highest goal is brotherhood, because brotherhood transcends justice.

We made mention of the Prodigal Son, and that parable is a parable of God's love. When the elder brother refused to greet the guests who were invited by his father to a *bienvenida* party in honor of the younger son, he was, in effect, saying that his brother did not deserve such an honor. In the unrecorded conversation between him and his father, he could have said, "Father, where is your sense of justice? That son of yours has wasted your money in riotous living. He does not deserve to be given this royal reception. He deserves to be ostracized from the family, and should not be given any share of our properties." The father in the parable who symbolizes brotherly love, simply said, "My son, your brother was dead but now is alive. He was lost and now is found again. We have reasons to be happy and be thankful for."

The Christian Church is committed to work for human brotherhood under the fatherhood of God. By human brotherhood we mean the reign of Christian love. The mission of the Church is no less than to spread brotherhood among men, and we, as members of the Body of Christ, are committed to participate in that mission.

It appears that our immediate task is to work for justice. For while brotherhood transcends justice, it does not negate it. Without justice there can be no brotherhood, and without brotherhood there can be no love. There is love because there is God. Therefore, there can be justice and, therefore, there can be brotherhood. For as long as we believe in God, our struggles for justice must go on and our love for brotherhood must be authenticated.

The Church may not be the best champion of political reforms, because of some technical issues in which the Church, as an organization, is not competent. On technical issues, Christians are apt to differ in their judgment. So matters of that nature are better left to the conscience of individual Christians. The Church should be the moral leader in all crusades for justice because justice, we repeat, is the nearest expression of love. Whenever there is injustice, the Church must be seriously alarmed.

To say the same thing even more strongly, we must declare that unless there is justice in the Church, Christians have no right to expect justice outside the Church. This is the meaning of the cleansing of the Temple. When Jesus entered the city of Jerusalem for the last time, He did not first go to the Jewish *Sanhedrin*, the equivalent of our Supreme Court. He did not first go to the Governor's Palace, the equivalent of our *Malacañang*. He did not go to Congress first, or to the City Hall. He went to the temple, and when He saw that the house of prayer was converted into a den of robbers He turned the tables upside down and drove the money changers away. The point is that if righteousness is to be felt in the entire community, it must begin with the Church. It must begin in the fellowship of those who claim to believe in God. In the final analysis, unless our relationship with God is right, our relationship with one another cannot be right. And so, if we are to contribute our share in the establishment of justice in this land which we dearly love, we must be sure there is justice in the Church. We must see to it that our church workers are at least given the minimum wage. We must see to it that they deliver the goods, that they do their jobs faithfully and religiously.

Thirdly, love expresses itself in forgiveness. Why? Because love is essentially the overcoming of estrangement among people. It is reconciliation. It is reunion.

Curiously, however, before love can be forgiving, it must first be willing to listen. The first task of love is to listen. No human relation, especially intimate human relation, is possible without mutual listening. One reason we find it hard to forgive is that we find it hard to listen. Our mind is closed and, therefore, our heart is also closed. We listen only to our own reasons. We are unable to understand the meaning of a person's behaviour.

Listening can be tedious, but it is imperative. To refuse to listen is to refuse to love. When love is real, there is willingness to listen. In listening, we discover that some of our presumptions are false, that some of our information is not accurate, and that the situation is not as bad as we thought. Also, in listening, we sometimes discover that the situation is worse than we thought, that our presumptions are much too kind, that our information is woefully inadequate. In either case, the task of listening is essential. It fulfills a basic function of love.

Implicit in this task of listening is love's nature to give. People have a right to demand something from us, just as we have the right to refuse to give. When we listen to them, we at least recognize their personhood, and we give them the dignity of being listened to. Love involves intelligent giving and, in some cases, sacrificial giving.

The deepest meaning of love is expressed in forgiveness. The Apostle Paul's word for this is justification. It is here where some seeming contradiction between love and justice appears. Justification is making just the unjust. It does not sound right to make the unjust, just. Yet, this is the central message of the gospel. Nothing less than this is the fulfillment of justice. In the words of Prof. Tillich, "Forgiving love is the only way of fulfilling the intrinsic claim in every being, namely, its claim to be reaccepted into the unity to which it belongs. Creative justice demands that this claim be accepted and that he be accepted who is unacceptable in terms of proportional justice." In short, forgiveness is love transcending justice.

To forgive is hard enough, to forgive those who are not repentant is even more difficult. In the act of forgiving, we must also listen, but how can we listen to one who does not even want to talk? In the act of loving, we must give, but how can we love one who does not want to receive? These are practical problems we encounter everyday. Perhaps, we do not have a sure formula for every situation. Whatever be the case, our supreme duty is to love. Therefore, we must ask, How are we to cultivate love? How can we have that love which will enable us to overcome the barriers in our human relationship?

The answer, I submit, is that we must be close to God who is love. God is the Source of love that makes us human, the love that makes us experience His divinity because we are created in His own image. Our love of country or love of fellow men, our love of freedom and decency and honor must ultimately be nurtured by the love of God in whom we live. A true patriot cannot be an atheist. A sincere seeker of truth cannot be godless. Their love of country and their love of wisdom are gifts from the Great Lover of all mankind. To possess genuine love, we must be possessed by God. We can be confident that because God loves us, we too can be loving and lovely.

In the second place, if we are to cultivate love we must keep ourselves close to the world because God is in the world. Of course, God is in heaven too — that is why we pray, that is why we go to church, that is why we worship. But God is also in the world. We do not have to run from this world in order to find God. God is here, where we are in this world. In the words of W. Norman Pittenger, "God is in this world where we are; He is its secret life, its mystery and its meaning; and He is known to us chiefly in our own human loving."

This simply means that the God who is real to us in the prayer room and in the sanctuary is also the God present in the conflicts of life in our world, in the struggles of the masses for liberation from hunger and oppression and ignorance, in the clashes of interests among men and nations. God is present not only in the beauty of a setting sun but also in the strifes of truth and falsehood, in the feuds between the critics and the establishment, in the storms of business competition, political rivalries, and racial discrimination.

We cultivate love by being in the world because God is there. Therefore, we must be in the world, and be there as agents of God's love. When we share with the people of this world in their triumphs and tragedies, their hopes and disappointments, their joys and sorrows, love grows deeper and becomes sweeter. When love becomes more abounding, we acquire more strength.

Today, when lack of love among men, sometimes among the members of our families, makes our life on earth a foretaste of life in hell, the love of God should captivate our souls and take away our bitterness. Let us stay close to Him and to our world, and our life can be bright and gay. There is wisdom in the song, "What the world needs now is love." That is what we need. And God can give it to us.

46

Mary and Martha

Scripture Reading:
Luke 10:38-42; John 11:1-10

Martha and Mary had a brother, Lazarus, whom Jesus raised from the dead though he had been in the tomb for four days. Perhaps, Martha was the oldest, Mary came after her, and Lazarus was the youngest. Mrs. Edith Deen, in her book *All of the Women of the Bible*, surmises that Martha was a widow and Mary never married. However, Prof. E. P. Blair in his articles on Martha, believes that Simon the leper, mentioned in the gospel of Mark (Chap. 14) was either the husband or the father of Martha. Simon the leper was cured by Jesus, and it was in Simon's house that Jesus used to rest, as He apparently became quite close to the family.

That house, according to Mark and according to the gospel of John, was in the village of Bethany outside of Jerusalem. Luke gives us the impression that it was in Southern Galilee, but Bible scholars believe that Mark and John's descriptions are more accurate, because Luke's chapters 10 to 19 are clearly a collection of materials from various periods of Jesus' ministry. Furthermore, tradition has tagged Mary and Martha as the sisters of Bethany.

That the sisters were women of means is very probable. Author Edith Deen writes of them, "Their house was probably a two-storey place with a broad outer stairway leading to an upper room. The staircase…led up from a well-shaded court; and it was here that Jesus often paused to refresh Himself. Both house and garden were inviting, for Martha excelled as a homemaker."

Unfortunately, we do not have much information about these sisters. The only materials we have about them are the few verses in Mark 14, the few verses in Luke 10, and chapter 11 of the gospel of John plus the first few verses in John 12. All these, however, point up to one inspiring fact: they were friends of Jesus. The Lucan version alone gives us an idea of the quality of friendship they had. The freedom with which Martha approached

Jesus in her desire to get help from her sister was devoid of any protocol common among friends. In the fourth gospel, the sisters' message to Jesus about their brother's illness is a message to an intimate friend: "Lord, He whom you love is ill." In fact, in verse 5 of John 11, we read: "Now Jesus loved Martha and her sister and Lazarus." Look at verse 36, when Jesus openly showed His sorrow over Lazarus' death, the people said, "See how He loved him!"

Joseph Scriven, speaking from a deep spiritual experience, wrote: "What a Friend we have in Jesus; All our sins and griefs to bear!" He goes on to say that we often forfeit peace, and we often bear needless pain because in our selfishness we forget to share with Jesus the heavy burdens in our hearts.

Friendship with Jesus can make us stronger and better men. For friendship is essentially a matter of relationship, and not of speech. Today, when people tell us that they are friends of the poor or of the masses, we can almost be sure that all they want is our vote. Something of that experience was behind the words of the Marechal de Villars who, taking leave of Louis XIV, exclaimed, "May God defend me from my friends; I can defend myself from my enemies."

So, the question is: What kind of friends are we to one another? At a certain birthday service, I heard the following lines read to the celebrant:

>One whose grip is a little tighter,
>One whose smile is a little brighter,
>One whose deeds are a little whiter,
>>That's what I call a friend.
>One who'll lend as quick as he'll borrow,
>One who's the same today as tomorrow,
>One who'll share your joy and sorrow,
>>That's what I call a friend.
>One whose thoughts are a little cleaner,
>One whose mind is a little keener
>One who avoids those things that are meaner,
>>That's what I call a friend.
>One when you're gone, who'll miss you sadly,
>One who'll welcome you back again gladly,

> One who, though angered, will not speak madly,
> That's what I call a friend.
>
> (by John Burroughs)

We would do well to review the kind of friends we have; but what is even more urgent is for us to know the kind of friend we are. Our friendship with Jesus is less than sincere if our friendship with our friends is based on personal advantage.

Now, a closer look at Mary and Martha enables us to see two different, if not contrasting, personalities. Mary was the quiet type, Martha was the active type. Mary was more pensive and was inclined to be more contemplative; Martha was a dynamo of activity and very practical. We do not have to have children of our own to know that no two children are exactly alike in their character and temperament — not even twins. Our problem is that the activists are often tempted to look down upon those who are more passive in their ways; and the quiet, uninhibited people sometimes feel that their noisy, active companions are not capable of listening to the still small voice of God. The truth is that both types of people are needed by God. The Marys and the Marthas are needed in the kingdom of God.

Arthur John Gossip, in his exposition of St. John's Gospel, submits that Martha is the patron saint of our generation. The author is obviously referring to this a-go-go generation, especially the young people. This is something worth stressing even only to emphasize that Martha's busyness did not deprive her of the opportunity to listen to Jesus' words of life. It was to Martha that Jesus first declared, "I am the resurrection and the life; he that believeth in Me, though he were dead, yet shall never die." It was Martha that met and welcomed Jesus to her house. If Mary sat at the Lord's feet and listened to His teaching, it was because Martha called her. It was Martha who declared, in the presence of people who came to console with her and Mary, "Yes Lord, I believe that You are the Christ, the Son of God, He who is coming into the world." When Jesus came to raise Lazarus from the dead, it was Martha that met Him once again, while Mary sat in the house. And, as usual, it was Martha that called for Mary to meet the Master. She was indeed a very thoughtful sister and if Mary enjoyed the beneficent effects of Jesus' godly influence it was because of Martha's thoughtfulness.

The defect of our present-day activism is that often, it has no place for Jesus Christ. Such activism can be injurious to the soul if it is only a substitute for the working of the Holy Spirit. The activism we need today is definitely the Martha-type for it welcomes Jesus and gets others to listen to Him. It is this activism that brings blessings not only to ourselves but also to others.

Now, let us observe that while the Martha-type activism is greatly to be desired, it must be inspired by the thought that in the divine scheme of things, our quest for the spiritual must supersede our longing for the material. This is the central point in Luke's account of Jesus' visit with the two sisters. Mary sat at Jesus' feet and listened to His teaching, but Martha was distracted with much serving. Finally, she complained to Jesus and said, "Lord, do you not care that my sister has left me to serve alone? Tell her then to help me." But Jesus answered with the compassion of an understanding Teacher, "Martha, Martha, you are anxious and troubled about many things; one thing is needful. Mary has chosen the good portion, which shall not be taken away from her."

It must be pointed out that Jesus did not, in any way, underestimate the importance of Martha's concern. He said what He said because she complained and wanted Mary to help her serve. After all, she must have noticed that the Lord was tired and might appreciate a glass of *calamansi* juice and a ham sandwich. Perhaps, she was preparing a real big meal which in our setting could mean *adobo, sinigang, pansit,* and ice cream. That is just the point: Martha should have known that a simple meal would suffice and that, therefore, instead of spending her time baking an angel cake she should have listened to what the Master had to say.

We in the church have been proclaiming the importance of material things in the divine plan of God. We believe that the Incarnation, for instance, is the drama of that beautiful blending of the spiritual and the material. For the Word of God to become flesh in Jesus Christ is the highest tribute that God can give to what is human and what is material. Unlike the Greeks who regarded matter as evil, Christians look at it as God's creation and, therefore, even the human body is the temple of the Spirit.

We believe in the importance of social concern. Jesus' parable of the goats and the sheep inspires us to feed the hungry, to visit the sick, to comfort those who are sad — because service to them is service to our Lord. Not long ago, in our review of the missionary enterprises of our national Church, we made mention of our modest contributions in the area of food production. We declared that the abundant life Jesus promises to those who follow Him is not only spiritual security but also economic stability.

We believe in the importance of the prophetic ministry. We know that the Old Testament prophets spoke not only about prayer and worship and God and sacrifices, but also about justice and righteousness and equitable distribution of wealth. We believe that a prophetic ministry should involve us in the social issues of our day, in a campaign for the elimination of corruption in high places, in a crusade for the vindication of the innocent, in a quest for human freedom and national integrity. We affirm that our Christianity should express itself in a vigorous struggle for the reign of love in the hearts of men and nations.

But now we must remind ourselves that while our deep concern for the social and economic amelioration of our people is part of our total Christian concern, the pursuit of such objective should not hinder our growth in the love and knowledge of our Lord. In other words, the giving of ourselves, of our time, and of our talents to noble and good causes should not be a distraction in the cultivation of our relationship with God. Serving coffee or preparing a big meal even for Jesus cannot take the place of prayer and worship. For if we are to infuse the life and teaching of our Lord into a society that needs to know the blessings of His presence, we must, of necessity, be suffused with the spirit of the Lord. We believe in social work and in humanitarianism and in all works designed to bring about human betterment, but all those things should not make it impossible for us to sit at Jesus' feet.

When we are too busy campaigning for clean and peaceful elections, for a more militant citizenry to oppose vandalism and other vices, for a new constitution which is more relevant to the needs of our time — when we are too busy to sit at Jesus' feet and learn from Him, sooner or later we will discover that something vital is missing in our life, that there is a vacuum in our souls.

The story of Mary and Martha is the story of two sisters who differed in their characteristics and in their temperaments, yet, both loved and served the Lord. It is the story of a home where Jesus was a welcome guest. From the wealth of their own experience they tell us that the secret of a happy life is to have friendship with Jesus, for that friendship can give us strength which we sorely need when life tumbles down and our light begins to flicker. They tell us when we get so worried about serving meals and anxious about mundane concerns, to seek first the Kingdom of God and His righteousness, with the assurance that all the other things shall be added unto us.

47

Courage and Strength

Scripture Reading: Psalm 31:24

In the Bible, courage and strength very often go together. For instance, in the book of Deuteronomy, God speaks to Moses, saying, "Be strong and of a good courage. .. for the Lord thy God, He it is that doth go with thee; He will not fail thee, nor forsake thee." (31:6). "Be strong and of a good courage. . ." These were also said by God to Joshua (1:6).

In Psalm 27:14, we read, "Wait on the Lord: be of good courage, and He shall strengthen thine heart." This is the same message we get from Psalm 31:24, "Be of good courage, and He shall strengthen your heart, all ye that hope in the Lord." In all these verses courage and strength go together: he who has courage has strength, and he who has strength has courage.

In philosophical writings, however, courage is often understood as the affirmation of one's essential being. To affirm one's being requires courage, but to know our essential being requires wisdom. This is why in the early days courage and wisdom were clearly distinguished from each other.

In the medieval period, the soldier became an outstanding example of courage — the soldier who was ready to make sacrifices, even the supreme sacrifice of his life. By and large, this was the connotation of the Greek word for courage, *andreia* (which means manliness) and the Latin word *fortitudo* (meaning strength). However, the disintegration of the so-called aristocratic tradition led to the convergence of courage and wisdom, and courage was understood as the "universal knowledge of what is good and evil."

In the writings of Thomas Aquinas we have duality in the meaning of courage. "Courage is strength of mind, capable of conquering whatever threatens the attainment of the highest good. It is united with wisdom, the virtue which represents the unity of the four cardinal virtues (the two others being temperance and justice) . . . Courage, united with wisdom, includes temperance in relation to oneself as well as justice in relation to others."[1]

Thomas Aquinas contends that perfect courage is a gift of the Divine Spirit. "Through the Spirit, natural strength of mind is elevated to its supernatural perfection… Courage listens to reason and carries out the intention of the mind. It is the strength of the soul to win victory in ultimate danger, like those martyrs of the Old Testament who are enumerated in Hebrews 11."[2]

Prof. Paul Tillich, in analyzing the concept of courage, discovers that it is simply the name of a virtue. He suggests, however, that courage is the child of faith. Therefore, an analysis of courage is no less than an inquiry about faith.

I am not sure at all whether I have the competence to analyze courage, but I am sure that courage is what we need in times like ours. If we are to rise above the tumults of our age, if we are to affirm the orderliness of life and of the universe in the midst of chaos and fratricidal strifes, if we are to believe in the ultimate reign of love and justice even as we witness the nauseating spectacle of greed and corruption, we have to have courage.

If we are to transcend the corroding effects of partisanship and petty bickerings, the treachery of character assassinators, the perfidy of those who have no regard for virtue, righteousness and decency, the vulgarity of the vicious and the immaturity of the irresponsible, we have to have courage.

If we are to remain sober in the face of major crises, the crises which shake the very foundation of our life as a people and as a nation, if we are to remain unaffected by the mounting charges and counter-charges going on in our midst so that we can do our work and produce good results, we have to have courage.

Courage is what we need when things go wrong not only in our world, not only in our land, but also in our immediate family and in our personal world. When we become the object of scorn and mockery, when we are gravely misunderstood or ignored, maltreated or cheated, when for the good we do we are rewarded with ingratitude, and for the loyalty we give we are crowned with thorns, we need courage to keep our heads unbowed and our spirits high.

When our loved ones writhe in pain as they struggle for their lives, when the shadow of death itself is lurking behind; when the light of hope begins to flicker and darkness engulfs their souls, we need the strength of

---
[1] Tillich, *The Courage To Be*, p. 7.
[2] *Ibid.*, p. 8.

faith that will sustain us through the night.

When we ourselves are in the valley of weeping — forlorn, forsaken, persecuted; or when the prospect of losing an eye or an arm horrifies us beyond description and makes us feel as if the whole world is breaking to pieces and God seems to be very far away, we need the courage to believe that things will work together for good, and that God Himself can feel the very pains we have.

In short, when life tumbles in and the storms of doubts threaten to undo us, when the winds blow and the rains descend and the floods of miseries come rushing on against us, we need courage and strength to live above the storms with quietness and confidence, and to run the race with patience, with hope, with honor.

Surely, that kind of courage is the child of faith — the faith which is a gift from God. It is the gift which Jesus offers. It is the gift of courage and strength we need for the living of these days.

48

Belief and Unbelief

Scripture Reading: Mark 9:14-29

Our Scripture lesson is about the healing of the epileptic boy. To appreciate the meaning of this passage we must recall that the incident took place immediately after the Transfiguration. In the gospel of Mark, the first part of chapter 9 describes that glorious experience on the mountain top where Peter, James, and John witnessed the appearance of Moses and Elijah. Peter was so inspired that he suggested to Jesus that they build three booths there — one for Moses, one for Elijah, and one for Jesus. Of course, they had to come down again, and the first incident that claimed their attention was the pleading of a father whose son was suffering from epilepsy.

Some of us may have seen Raphael's painting, "The Transfiguration." The upper part of the canvas shows the glorification of Christ, and in the lower part is the scene of a father begging Christ to have mercy upon his son. And that is how we are to understand this incident narrated in our Scripture lesson. This shadowed valley of human needs should be illumined by the light of the Transfiguration. In fact, the Transfiguration itself cannot be understood apart from its relation to that valley of tears. This is why Jesus did not yield to Peter's suggestion that they construct three tents on the mount. Peter had to learn that a glorious communion with God is precisely to equip us for service in the world.

Here is a poem by an unknown writer:

> I sought to hear the voice of God.
>
> I climbed the highest steeple;
>
> But God declared, Come down again:
>
> I dwell among the people.

Like Peter, we are inclined to stay in the steeple, on the mountain top. During the medieval period, the monasteries became tents which Peter wanted to build. Monks and hermits very seldom came down to the valley of men. They spent their time in communion with God, forgetting the fact that such communion was meaningless unless it equipped them to become channels of God's grace in meeting the crying needs of men.

In the New Testament, worship and service are intimately linked. This is why in Evangelical Christianity, the act of coming together for prayer and meditation is often called "worship service." Worship ends when the benediction is pronounced, but the end of worship is the beginning of service.

While the medieval monks were too busy communing with God to have time with people in the valley, today many modern Christians are too busy in the world to have time with God. They are busy preparing their briefs or writing their reports or doing this and that. In their scale of priorities, service first and worship last.

Perhaps, we need to recapture the spirit of primitive Christianity. We need to rediscover the truth that worship is a preparation for service and never a barrier to it. If there is so much dissatisfaction with the kind of service we render and receive, if there is so much discontent particularly with the kind of public service we have, it may be because something vital is missing in our worship life. When the cultivation of the spiritual life is neglected, even our best service cannot be more than mere humanitarianism.

So from the Mount of Transfiguration, Jesus comes down to the valley of human needs. Here is how Mark puts it: "And when they came to the disciples, they saw a great crowd about them, and scribes arguing with them. And immediately all the crowd, when they saw Him, were greatly amazed, and ran up to Him and greeted Him. And He asked them, 'What are you discussing with them?' "

Note that the disciples were not able to heal the epileptic boy and the scribes took advantage of their failure to embarrass them. Perhaps, the scribes were also questioning the authenticity of Jesus' power because if He was really the Messiah, His disciples should prove themselves equal to the task. At any rate, when Jesus came He found them deeply engaged in discussion.

Two things can be said about this episode. First, discussion can be a sign that nothing has been done. The disciples might not be able to drive away the evil spirit, but certainly they were able to debate with the scribes. We may even imagine that they tried to make up for their failure by being at their best in the discussion. Now, this is not to say that discussion has no merit. On the contrary, it can be very necessary. In the book of Isaiah, God says, "Come, let us reason together. If your sins be as scarlet they shall be as white as snow." Discussion can enrich our knowledge and improve our plans. It can clarify certain points and thus eliminate certain misunderstanding. But it can also be an exercise in futility. It is this kind of discussion which Paul, in his letter to Titus, advises us to avoid.

Second, when church leaders disappoint us we must fix our eyes on Jesus. Imagine the disciples and the scribes engaged in heated discussion. In fact, according to the record, a big crowd had gathered around them to witness the discussion. What if Jesus did not come? And what if the father of the boy did not have the courage to ask Jesus for help? He and the rest of the crowd might have gone home greatly disappointed, not only with the leaders of a new religious movement but also with the authorities of the religious establishment. The scribes might have gone home to celebrate their empty victory and the disciples might have gone away with bitterness and resentment.

"What are you discussing?" asked Jesus, and one of them answered, "Sir, I brought my son to you for he has a dumb spirit; and I asked your disciples to cast it out, and they were not able." Such disappointing report elicited Jesus' sighing remark: "O faithless generation, how long am I to be with you? How long am I to bear with you?"

Such lamentation reveals Jesus' agonizing struggles in making His disciples into men of faith and power. They had been with Him for quite sometime now, and they still had a long way to go to acquire that faith which could move mountains. But that was not the last time He would be with them. His mission was to make them whole, and His ultimate goal was to save men from faithlessness. Thus, even before His last word of sigh faded in the air, He resolved to do something and, with daring confidence, He said, "Bring him to me." And they brought the boy to Him.

William Barclay, commenting on this passage, writes: "When we cannot deal with the ultimate situation then the thing to do is to deal with the situation at the moment it confronts us. It was as if Jesus said, 'I do not know how I am ever to change these disciples of mine, but I can at this moment help this boy. Let me go with the present task, and not despair of the future.' "

We, too, have our own despair. We do not know how we can ever change our society, how the present system can be changed to insure better opportunities for those who have less in life. We do not know how national discipline can be instilled in us, and how this land of ours and the world in which we live can become a haven of peace and plenty. Such concerns for the future well-being of our children and our children's children can so absorb us that we fail to do what can be done in the present. If we cannot change the world where we are, if we cannot revive the Church, we should at least renew that part of the Church in which we find ourselves. In the words of an Oriental proverb, "It is better to light a candle than to curse darkness."

Jesus asked, "How long has this boy been this way?" The father answered, "Since he was a little child." And then, mustering enough courage to ask for a favor, the father said, "If you can do anything, have pity on us and help us." But Jesus replied, "If you can believe." In effect, He was saying: "It is not a question of what I can do; it is a question of what you can do." Then underscoring this very point, Jesus said, "All things are possible to him who believes." In other words, Jesus was saying to the father of the boy, "To approach anything in the spirit of hopelessness is to make it hopeless. To approach anything in the spirit of faith is to make it a possibility." (Barclay)

When we are cursed with the spirit of the impossible, miracles do not happen. When we are clothed with a sense of hopelessness, the situation becomes hopeless. When we are gripped by a sense of futility and defeat, we become helpless, and baffled and ineffective. To transcend such wretchedness is not a question of God's ability, which is always sure; it is a question of our trustfulness and courage, which we often lack. We need the assurance that "all things are possible to him who believes."

The father's reply is a revelation of our own condition and need. He said, "Lord, I believe; help my unbelief!" Like him, we are a sorry mixture of faith and lack of faith, belief and unbelief. We try to hide this sad state by being very sure, only to discover that life is often assailed by the onslaughts of doubts.

Let me put it this way: Everybody doubts. There are times when we are not sure. We are in doubt. By the way, we are talking here about the genuine doubt which is "the reverse side of genuine faith." We are not talking about the "phlegm that follows shabby conduct." We are not talking about that "impatience with coercive or stultifying form of religion," not the airing "of brilliant denials" which is conceit. The opposite of faith is not doubt, but cynicism. Doubt, I repeat, is the reverse side of genuine faith, a lack of faith that seeks to be satisfied and overcome. We find this a very common experience in our life.

But that is not the whole truth. The other side of the truth is that everybody believes. If not in God, at least in something that takes the place of God — in nature, in the universe, in justice, in goodness. The Christian life is always a life of tension between faith and doubt. We believe, but we also doubt. This is why the man's prayer is also our prayer: "Lord, we believe; help our unbelief." That is why even when we are lacking in faith, we need to pray. This is what the man in our Scripture lesson did. He confessed his unbelief. He confessed it to Jesus. Jesus' answer not only cured his unbelief, but also healed his boy.

So, in the faith-doubt tension, we can still make our choice. We can choose to say, "Lord, I believe." We can choose faith. And when we choose faith, we can fling our doubts on God and ask Him to help our unbelief.

The boy was healed. When Jesus and His disciples had entered the house, His disciples asked Him privately, "Why could we not cast it out?" Jesus answered and said, "This kind cannot be driven out by anything but prayer." Did Jesus mean that while other cases could be cured with aspirin or penicillin, the case of that little boy could be cured only by prayer? If God can do that, why doesn't He teach us the kind of prayer that works, so that our patients suffering from cancer and high blood pressure and epilepsy need not go to the hospital?

Let us not pursue this kind of reasoning. Many theologians have wrestled with that nonsense. What we need most is not explanations about God but God Himself. Of course, we cannot solve unemployment by prayer alone. We cannot cure an acute appendicitis with prayer alone. However, there are cases which only prayer can save and we have not been trusting enough to bring everything unto the Lord in prayer. Our prayerlessness is the sin behind sin. It is a blockade to the flow of power that comes from above, cutting the vital contact between the world of grace and the world of human needs.

Let us, therefore, renew our faith in prayer. It can do miracles in our world. It is the channel through which God imparts His healing grace for our sick bodies, His transforming influence for our tired spirits, His redemptive presence for our troubled world. Let us believe in Jesus Christ who comes to us when we are in need, who gives us faith when we are in doubt. Let us also believe in ourselves: that we can do something for our own little world, that our good works cannot be in vain, that our humble services can be a blessing to our neighbors. Let us believe that God is good, that He knows us more than we know ourselves, and that the future is secure in His hands.

49

Love is Involvement

Scripture Reading: I John 4:7-21

That love means getting involved is tantamount to saying what is obvious. Love is not love unless it gets involved. For love is the mainspring and the foundation of a relationship — be it a relationship between man and God, or between man and man. Our Christian faith affirms that the relationship between man and God cannot be divorced from the relationship between man and man. In First John we read: "Dear friends, let us love one another, because love is from God. Everyone who loves is a child of God and knows God, but the unloving knows nothing of God. For God is love; and his love was disclosed to us in this, that he sent his only Son into the world to bring us life. The love I speak of is not our love for God, but the love he showed to us in sending his Son as the remedy for the defilement of our sins. If God thus loved us, dear friends, we in turn are bound to love one another" (1 John 4:7-10).

Surely, the essence of the Christian religion is love, and love means getting involved.

Now this business of getting involved because of love inevitably leads us to the issues of justice. When Jesus described the nature of His mission, He quoted from the prophet Isaiah and said, "The spirit of the Lord is upon me because he has anointed me; he has sent me to announce good news to the poor, to proclaim release for prisoners and recovery of sight for the blind; to let the broken victims go free to proclaim the year of the Lord's favour" (Luke 4:18,19). When we minister to the poor and the prisoners and the broken victims of society, we get involved in the issues of justice. In the words of Reinhold Niebuhr, "Love makes our consciences more sensitive to the needs of others, especially to the needs of those who have been neglected or exploited."[1]

Those of us who have heard Jaime Cardinal Sin must have noticed that his favorite theme is love. In fact, it has become his habit to conclude

---

[1] Kegley & Bretall, ed., *Reinhold Niebuhr*, p. 59.

his speech by telling his audience, "I love you." A few years ago, he invited some outstanding Catholic lay people to his palace (he was gracious enough to invite me too). After dinner, he began telling us about the purpose of our meeting. He said he was receiving so many letters everyday from people who suffer from what they believe to be gross injustice, people who are crying for help so they could put an end to their difficulties. After giving some more details, the Archbishop said, "Well, ladies and gentlemen, I have decided to create a Committee on Justice and Peace, and I hope you will consent to serve on that Committee."

The Archbishop (he was not yet a Cardinal) made it clear that as leaders in the church we should not do anything that might displease or antagonize anybody, particularly government authorities. At that point, a learned, respectable retired justice of the Supreme Court (JBL Reyes) remarked, "Monsignor, in my experience, when you work for the cause of justice, some people will be displeased or antagonized."

Whether we like it or not, Christian involvement may lead to confrontation with those who are in the seat of power. Such confrontation, however, need not be violent; in fact, it does not have to be violent. It can be on the high level of dialogue and discussion of issues that affect the welfare of the people.

At the height of martial rule, the National Council of Churches in the Philippines issued a statement on church-state relations. The Council declared that its member churches were not prevented or prohibited from "some measure of involvement in matters affecting the life of the human community in the Philippines, especially if that involvement is deemed as a necessary exercise and expression of faith in God and love of fellow men and will result in the good and benefit of this same community." This belief, said the NCCP, was based on the following:

1. The member-churches of the NCCP exist to promote the worship of God, as well as community among people through the practice of freedom, love, justice, and brotherhood.

2. The member-churches of the NCCP believe that the God they worship cares actively for the welfare of persons and uses the initiatives of men and women and institutions of society in achieving His will in human history for the good and welfare of the people... Thus, human institutions may be used by God to secure and promote human welfare. But, whether in theory or in practice, no political institution exists so perfectly as to leave no room for

criticism and improvement.

3. In view of this conviction that no form and initiative of the state is so perfect as to be beyond criticism and improvement, they [the member-churches] may have to express their cooperation with the state precisely through rational criticism and prophetic judgment.

In other words, criticism against certain government programs need not be construed as subversive. It is not necessarily designed to agitate the people to rise up in rebellion. A government that has no room for constructive criticism cannot know the pulse of the people. And the suppression of such criticism may only lead to the illusion that the rulers have achieved perfection. It is the prophetic function of the church to call the people's attention to what is evil in society, and to proclaim God's stringent demand for righteousness and justice.

Months before the assassination of Ninoy Aquino, the Catholic bishops issued a joint pastoral letter entitled "A Dialogue For Peace." It described the fact that "Legitimate dissent is all too easily construed as rebellion and treason, as subversion in its conveniently amorphous definition." It criticized the government's "heavy reliance on multinationals and its favoring of their needs over those of the people; its attention to tourist facilities and services, like lavish film festivals." It called upon the people to be ever vigilant in safeguarding their God-given rights.

Martin Luther, the sparkplug of the Reformation, teaches us that the preachers who proclaim God's Word are "executors of God's sovereignty over history." He says the preacher of God's Word "is the authorized critic of secular government. Rulers are subject to the judgment of God and of His Word, and it is the duty of the preacher to criticize the rulers boldly and openly. . ." Luther reviles the preachers "who, out of laziness, flattery, or fear fail to carry out this mission."[1]

The prophet Isaiah, the messenger of God's love, was also a preacher of social justice. Listen to his words in the opening verses of Chapter 10:

"Woe to the legislators of infamous laws,

to those who issue tyrannical decrees,

who refuse justice to the unfortunate

and cheat the poor among my people of their rights."

If we did not know it was Isaiah speaking, we would suspect the speaker was Jose Diokno or Ninez Olivares.

---

[1] Quoted by Roger L. Shin, *Christianity and the Problem of History*, p. 79

Prof. Wafford T. Duncan, in his book *The Preacher and Politics,* tells us that "the extent to which the church has prophetically related itself to public affairs has been the measure of advance in government."[1] That is precisely what the NCCP wishes to achieve in offering constructive criticism: some measure of advance in government. Such ministry is beneficial not only to the state but also to the church. Prof. Duncan says, "The days of spiritual power have been those of combat with wickedness in high places."[2]

Admittedly, the church may not be the best authority on economic development, on foreign policy, on education, on business and finance. The church may not be competent to answer questions about the ideal political structure in society or about the preservation of peace and order. But it is the business of the church to be a champion of human rights, to be the guardian of morality, to be a defender of freedom and justice and truth. The church should be a leader in the preservation of the dignity of man. It is the business of the church to minister to the poor and the hungry and the prisoners and the broken victims of oppression.

Fr. Horacio de la Costa, a respected name inside and outside the circle of history scholars, in his book *Asia and the Philippines,* gives us a summary of Confucius' teachings on the government. When one of his disciples asked him what an efficient government must have, Confucius replied: "An effective government must have sufficient food, sufficient weapons, and the confidence of the common people."

The disciple asked further, "But suppose one of those three has to be dispensed with, which should it be? Confucius answered, "Then let weapons go."

The disciple pursued his question: "And suppose one of the remaining two must go, which should it be? Confucius, without any hesitation at all, said, "Let the food go. For, from of old, death has been the lot of all men; but if the people have no confidence in the government, the state cannot stand." Then adding his own words of advice, Fr. de la Costa writes: "All government, as Belloc has pointed out, is by persuasion; the moment the people refuse to be persuaded, no government on earth, no matter what its resources for coercion, can stay in power. For power in the last analysis resides in the people. A president is powerful, a congress is powerful, a dictator is powerful, only if, and only as long as, they can persuade the people of their necessity. Power independent of the people or against the

---

[1] Wafford T. Duncan, *The Preacher and Politics,* p. 15.
[2] *Ibid.,* p. 29.

people is an illusion made possible by the boundless patience of the people."[1]

Now the question is: How are governments to persuade the people? Is it by laws or decrees? Is it by threats of punishment? Is it by the secret police? No, says Confucius; it is by virtue. Here are his exact words: "If one tries to guide the people by means of rules, and keep order by means of punishment, the people will merely seek to avoid the penalties without having any sense of moral obligation. But if one leads them with virtue, and depends upon propriety to maintain order, the people will then feel their moral obligation and correct themselves."

This is what the Confucian scholars consider to be the essence of Confucius' political philosophy, his most original contribution to the science of government: the importance of good example in society. Government "is impossible unless the people correct themselves, and the only way a ruler can persuade the people to correct themselves is not by telling them to, but by showing them how." Or, to use the words of Fr. de la Costa, "if virtue shines forth in the ruler, the people will follow his example; and the more virtuous he is, the less he will need to depend on force."[2]

Well, now, someone may ask: But Pastor Rigos, why talk about the government and politics and the state? Why don't you just talk about prayer and heaven and salvation? The answer is: Salvation is meaningless if it does not include the state. God is dead if He does not care for those in government. Love is an illusion if it has no politics of its own to offer.

This is why the question we have to ask ourselves is: How can we love to the point of getting involved in securing justice and promoting brotherhood? How can we overcome the fear of getting involved in matters that may demand our time, our courage, and our commitment? How can we cultivate the love that can enable us to make some sacrifices whenever necessary?

Perhaps we can never answer these questions exhaustively, but we must affirm the need for a closer fellowship with God, for God is the source of love. That is why we worship; that is why we pray. In spite of all our shortcomings, deep within our souls we wish to be more loving, more holy, more trusting. And only God can satisfy that longing. Therefore, we must keep ourselves close to God.

But we also need to keep ourselves close to the world, for God is in

---

[1] Fr. Horacio de la Costa, *Asia and the Philippines*, p. 162-163.
[2] *Ibid.*, p. 163.

the world. This is the world which He has made. He is active and working through the affairs of men. He is the God not only of the church but also of the world. It is, therefore, in this world where we are called to witness to His love; it is in this world where we must exercise our discipleship. We are not meant to be of this world, but we are in this world; it is here where the action is. And what this world needs is love. The world will never know that love unless we Christians get involved.

Let us thank God that through the grace of His Son, Jesus Christ our Lord, we can be a little more loving and a little more involved.

50

The More Excellent Way

Scripture Reading: I Corinthians 13

One of the best known passages in the Bible is the 13th chapter of the Apostle Paul's first letter to the Corinthians. It is often referred to as the hymn of love. It was written by one who has been deeply concerned with faith. In fact, the theme "Justification by Faith" is the great theme we find in the writings of Paul. But now in this chapter he speaks to us of love.

But first, a word must be said about the context of this passage. In chapter 12, Paul is talking about the various spiritual gifts, such as the gift of speech, the gift of healing, the gift of prophecy, the gift of ecstatic utterance of various kinds and the ability to interpret it. Paul admits that those gifts are greatly to be desired. But he concludes by advising the Corinthian Christians to covet the higher gifts, and to consider the more excellent way, which is the way of love. That is what he discusses in chapter 13.

The question that we may ask is: Why does Paul make a contrast between love and faith, and between love and hope? Can there be faith without love and can there be love without hope? Are they not the great spiritual virtues which all of us must possess? In a time like ours when many are not sure whether they can hold on to their jobs, when life as it has always been is a survival of the fittest, is not our greatest need either faith or hope?

The answer to these questions should candidly admit that as Christians struggling for existence we cannot really separate love from faith or faith from hope. The fact is that the essence of a truly Christian experience is a mixture of love and faith and hope. Indeed, it is an experience of love in constant conflict with hate, of faith in opposition to unbelief, of hope versus despair. At any rate, it is an experience where love is not divorced from faith and hope, and vice versa.

Yet there is no glossing over the record: Paul says, "So faith, hope, love abide, these three; but the greatest of these is love." In what sense is love the greatest?

You will recall that Paul is speaking in the context of time. He says, "Love never ends; as for prophecy, it will pass away; as for tongues, they shall cease; as for knowledge, it will pass away..." In verse 12, he writes, "Now we see in a mirror dimly, but then face to face. Now I know in part, then I shall understand fully even as I have been fully understood." In other words, he is saying that love has the quality of absolute permanency. But not faith and hope. Here on earth we trust God whom we cannot see; therefore, we need faith. As we read it in the letter to the Hebrews, "Faith gives substance to our hopes, and makes us certain of realities we do not see." But Paul tells us that in heaven we will see God face to face, and therefore, we will not need faith anymore.

Likewise, on earth we hope for things still to come. But in heaven, all hopes are fulfilled. Therefore, in heaven there will be no need for hope.

However, in heaven love will continue. Only in heaven can we love God more perfectly. On earth our love for Him is always imperfect. This is why Paul says that while faith and hope and love abide, the greatest of them is love.

In the King James Version, the word used is not love but charity. This word is borrowed from the Latin Vulgate which translates the Greek agape into *caritas*. The reason for the use of this word is that love is ordinarily understood as selective — it is aroused by the virtue or merit in the object of one's love. Charity on the other hand is not selective. It is all-embracing. It does not discriminate.

However, in the Revised Standard Version and the Good News Bible the word used is not charity, but love. And perhaps, it better be that way because in our country charity is very much associated with the charity wards in the hospitals. In our case, therefore, the word charity does not convey the exact meaning of Christian love.

Today, as we reflect on the nature of love, we have to remember that, among other things, love expresses itself in giving. This is what we have often emphasized. What we have not emphasized enough is that love is also receiving. In the words of John Burnaby, "Love cannot fulfill itself in a one-way process; unless there is both giving and receiving, love must remain unsatisfied."[1]

This means that while God loves us without any thought of being

---
[1] *Christian Words & Christian Meanings*, p. 52.

loved in return, nevertheless, His love is not satisfied unless we respond with gratitude. In a similar way, a mother cares for her child and will not mind getting up in the middle of the night to attend to his needs. But such mother will be disappointed if her child does not grow up to return her love for him.

So it is not enough for us to give; we must also receive. While it is more blessed to give than to receive, yet not to receive (especially when being given) can be a sign of pride. It is good to give and, in fact, we encourage giving; but when we refuse to receive that which is in response to our love, we may well suspect that something might be wrong with us.

Man is a social being. Self-sufficiency is a negation of our humanity. We can be self-sufficient in terms of money, in terms of the material things of life. But we cannot be self-sufficient in terms of affection. Our personhood can be realized only in our personal relationships with one another, and such relationships, to be deeply satisfying, should be characterized by both giving and receiving.

This element of receiving is very often overlooked in our concept of Christian love. And the result is that when a marriage, for instance, is on the rocks we hastily conclude that one or the other does not have enough love. A simple love ethic will not solve the complexities of life. Love, which is the basic law of life, is not just giving. It is also receiving. A man or a woman who loves and loves without being loved in return will most probably stop loving someday. It may take quite sometime before such love fades away, but it will surely fade away if it does not receive love.

This is why in the Bible the anger or the wrath of God is an aspect of His love. The Bible does not tell us that God is always smiling and kind and gracious. He is capable of getting angry. The story of Sodom and Gomorrah is the story of a people who did not respond to the love of God. Consequently, God allowed them to perish in their own folly. And what do we see in the New Testament? Not just the Christ who said, "Come unto me, all ye that labor and are heavy-laden, and I will give you rest," but also the Christ who said, "Depart from me, ye evil doers. I never knew you," and "Woe unto you, scribes and Pharisees, hypocrites!"

And so we affirm that love is both giving and receiving. The love which only gives cannot live forever. To sustain itself and to continue giving, it must also receive.

Another point to note is that to express the love of God is not as easy as giving our love indiscriminately; it requires us to make moral choices. When we give, we do not just give; we first study whether the cause to which we want to give is really worth our support. I know of a number of deeply committed Christians who refuse to give to beggars (except during the Christmas season) not because they do not like to help but because they believe giving to professional beggars only encourages them to perpetuate mendicancy.

Another misconception which results from a too simple love ethic is the tendency to give way to group interest over self-interest. It is the tendency to confer special moral virtue on a larger group, so that the interest of the community is supposed to be higher than the interest of a family, and the interest of the nation is supposed to supersede the interest of the community. The fallacy here is the presumption that the group interest is always higher than self-interest, and that self-interest has no place in the Christian life. The fact, however, is that self-interest can be legitimate and group interest can be illegitimate. We know from experience that the claim of the nation is not always paramount, and that the demand of the family is not necessarily secondary. It is only when the claim of a bigger group is legitimate that it can expect priority consideration over the smaller groups. Christians should remember that the majority is not always right; the voice of the people is not always the voice of God.

Finally, may I submit the nearest expression of love in human life is justice. Perhaps, we should suggest that love should be the spirit of justice. We may even say with Reinhold Niebuhr that without the grace of love, "justice always degenerates into something less than justice."

I am not saying here that if there is justice, therefore, we can forget love. For Christians, justice is the expression of, and not the substitute for, love. But if there is to be love in our society and in our world, our immediate step is to work for justice.

In practical terms, this means that our prayer for peace and love and brotherhood needs to be complimented by social action for the cause of justice. Our concern for the Kingdom of God should involve us in the plight of the underprivileged, in the struggles of the sugar planters, in the misfortune of the coconut farmers. To work for justice is a Christian imperative. It will require not only our courage but also the best abilities we have. In a world where justice is in travail, to work for its cause is to be an instrument of God in the salvation of men.

But of course, while we glory in the possibilities of righteousness even in our time, many of us may be suffering from the pain of our wounded hearts. We may be the victims of injustice ourselves, and we find it difficult to hold our peace. Therefore, we need to be sure that our passion for justice is not just a form of revenge. We should not carelessly equate our vindictiveness with the quest for justice. The Bible does not allow us to forget that vengeance belongs to God. Only He is the ultimate Judge of all mankind.

For the meantime, if we are to transcend the pain in our hearts caused by the perfidy and ingratitude of our fellow men, we need the experience of God's suffering love, the love that equips us for the bitterest tears in life. It is that love which can make us conquerors, and it can be ours if we ask for it in faith.

51

The Saving Love

Scripture Reading: Luke 15:1-10

In chapter 15 of the gospel of Luke, we have a grouping of three parables: the parable of the Lost Sheep, the parable of the Lost Coin, and the parable of the Lost Son (often called the Prodigal Son). These parables are sometimes called a trinity because of their common theme — God's concern and love for the lost. In the first 10 verses, we have the twin parables of the lost sheep and the lost coin; the rest of the chapter is devoted to the story of the prodigal son and his elder brother. Although our Scripture reading covers only the first two parables, we intend to include in this meditation the parable of the prodigal son.

These parables describe three ways of getting lost. One is through our own deliberate will. That was the case with the prodigal son. Nobody forced him to go to a far country and waste his life in riotous living. Talking with his father one day, he said, "Father, give me the portion of goods that falleth to me." That was actually a demand — an imperious demand. He did not have the courtesy to say "please." He knew that legally a portion of the family assets belonged to him. He knew that sooner or later his father had to divide the property equally between him and his elder brother. So, he felt that he might just as well have his share now. Perhaps, the father remarked, "But Sonny, you are still too young to go away. Why don't you wait a few more years and you can do as you wish?" If he had said that, the lad must have replied, "No, Daddy, I'm not too young anymore. I want my share now, and I want to be on my own." So the poor father obliged: he yielded to his son's demand. And the young man went his way, happy in the thought that at last he could have a good time. But we know he only made a mess of his life. The phrase "he wasted his money in reckless living" is a vivid description of wildness and irresponsibility. He plunged himself into the abyss of moral degradation. His father could not stop him. He did it quite deliberately.

Second, one can get lost unintentionally, that is, one does not wish it deliberately. This was the case in the parable of the lost sheep. The sheep did not want to get lost, and the shepherd did not want any of his sheep to go astray. But the poor animal perhaps just enjoyed the green grass. It was so absorbed eating the best leaves it did not know it was already by the precipice, so it fell into the ravine. The animal could not extricate itself from such a perilous situation.

Is this not what many people would claim to be the reason for their being lost? They do not mean to forget God. A deliberate defiance against God is most unthinkable for them. They just drifted a little bit, perhaps with the thought of making up for it someday. Their failure to say their prayer was not deliberate; they were just too tired. But the following day, they were again tired and so they did not pray. For several days, they did not pray because they were tired. And before they knew it, the urge to pray was no longer there.

Thirdly, there are those who get lost not because of any deliberate design, nor because of any carelessness on their part, but because of some circumstances not of their own making and beyond their control. This was the case with the lost coin. In fact, the coin itself did not know, as it was not capable of knowing, that it was lost. The point is that separation from God is not always the result of willful disobedience or relative carelessness; it can be caused by other factors beyond our control. For instance, we hear of cases where some young people are forced into drug addiction against their will. We can be forced to do certain things against our conscience. We can only hope that in such conditions, God will be more merciful.

At this point, let us note that in the parable of the lost sheep, the sheep got lost when separated from the flock and was not found in the fold. As long as it was in the fold, it was safe. But in the parable of the lost coin, the coin got lost in the house. One does not have to leave his home to get lost. And what about the prodigal son? He went to a far country where he wasted his money in riotous living. His older brother, however, stayed at home and continued helping his father in the farm; but he was equally, if not more, prodigal. One does not have to leave his house before he can indulge in prodigality. Perhaps, there are more prodigals in the homes than in any other place.

Here we appreciate the wisdom in the song which says, " A house is not a home, a home is not a house." A home is not just a roof, a kitchen, bathroom, chairs. It is a relationship of people in the house. Like the elder brother in the parable, we may not leave our house. We may be with our father, or mother, or wife or husband or children — but we are worlds apart. There is an air of bitterness and resentment and antagonism that suffocates the soul. The situation may be tolerable and bearable, but we know it can be a foretaste of hell.

Now, what does Luke 15 tell us about the consequences of being lost? First of all, except for the lost coin, Luke 15 depicts the lost sheep and the lost son in misery. In the case of the lost sheep, the sheep could not by itself come back to the fold. It had to be rescued by the shepherd and the rescue was at the price of leaving the ninety-nine. In the case of the prodigal son, he had to repent and resolve to come home. Of course, his father met him while he was yet at a great distance, but he had to come home. For him to eat the feeds intended for the swine was a supreme insult to whatever little dignity he possessed. Both the sheep and the son were miserable because they got lost.

In the second place, when a soul gets lost, God is the first one to suffer. When the sheep got lost, the shepherd could not rest at ease. Perhaps, he asked a fellow shepherd to watch over the ninety-nine so he could look for the missing one. Perhaps, there was no one left to watch, and he had to risk the safety of the ninety-nine for the sake of the missing animal.

In the case of the missing coin, the owner was obviously distressed. She took a lamp and diligently looked for the coin under the table and in every corner of the house. It was not a big amount; it was worth about a day's work but to her it was a precious coin, as she was not a wealthy person.

In the case of the lost son, who can ever imagine the agony and gripping sadness of the father? Day in and day out he was praying for his son, asking God to touch his heart that he might be led to come back home.

The message is clear: God suffers when a soul goes astray. The wayward man or woman may not realize it, but God is the first one to feel the pain of separation. He is the heavenly Father whose will is that we stay with Him in His home and, therefore, is greatly grieved when we get lost one way or the other.

Thirdly, when we sin, human relationship is also affected. The ninety-nine sheep were left so the shepherd could look for the missing one. They were exposed to danger because one was not careful enough. The lost coin, if not found, would lessen the value of the necklace or headdress that should have 10 coins, for it was probably a part of coins that normally should have 10 coins. And what about the lost son? He had to deal not only with his father but also with his brother. Sin destroys not only the sinner but also his relationship with a host of other people.

Think of any problem you may have in life and see whether it does not affect human relationship. A businessman may have committed something highly irregular; that affects his family and also his employees. A husband may be tempted to fool around with another woman; that may affect not only his wife but also the other woman's husband, if she has a husband. A young man may not be diligent in his studies; that may cause headaches to teachers, friends, and relatives. One basic problem we have in this life is the problem of human relationships. Sin is a destroyer of good relationships.

Now, the parables tell us that whenever the lost is found, there is great rejoicing among the angels in heaven. This is how important we are in the eyes of God. The Bible is full of stories about celebrations. When a king comes home as a victor in a war, the kingdom celebrates his victory. When a shepherd finds his lost sheep, there is rejoicing in his community. When a woman finds her lost coin, she summons her neighbors and friends for a celebration. But those are all on the human level. Jesus says that when a sinner repents, the hosts of heaven rejoice. To be sure, God is happy when we pass the school examination, when we get promoted in our work, when we are given a salary increase, when we get over our flu or ulcer. But the greatest joy in heaven is when a sinner repents. That is what makes God truly happy.

At this moment, let us not think of the black sheep in the family that needs our special prayers today. Let us think of ourselves, for all of us have come short of the glory of God. Let repentance begin with ourselves, without waiting for one who is a greater sinner than we think we are. Let us make this worship an experience of God's redeeming grace in our lives. That will make us and the angels above happy.

And how do we do it? How shall we come to the Father to receive His forgiveness? Well, there is one thing the prodigal son did which we can also do. We recall that when the prodigal wanted to leave his home, he said to his father, "Give me the portion of goods that falleth to me." But when he decided to go back, he said, "Make me as one of thy hired servants." In other words, he changed his "give me" to "make me." Unless we allow God to make us into what He wants us to be, unless we say, "Lord, not my will, but Thine be done," unless we say, "Make me," there is no true repentance. Unless we say, "Make me a captive, Lord," or "Make me more holy, make me more loving, make me more humble," in short, unless we allow God to make us and mold us, we can never be found again.

And when God releases us from the prison cell of sin, when we experience the freedom of a truly forgiven soul, we will be God's own instruments in the redemption of others still in darkness and in sin. God may use us in looking for one who belongs to our home but is not at home. It is not enough that we be forgiven; we must also be forgiving. And that means we must also be loving.

And so, if there is a lost soul in our home, and we want him back to the fellowship of his family and of God, let us love him. Let us love him with a love that will cause us to pray for him, to look for him with a love that will understand him and will forgive him when he comes back. Let us love him with a love that will make us courageous enough to leave the ninety-nine to look for him and to rescue him from the thick forest of moral entanglements and spiritual lapses. Let us love him because only love can save him. Revenge will only add more fuel to the fire. Vengeance is the weapon of the weak. Indifference can lead to a greater destruction. But love can heal and redeem.

That was exactly what Jesus did: to save us from eternal death, He gave Himself as ransom for us. He became obedient even unto death, in order that He may open for us the gate to an abundant life. And unless we learn to walk in His steps, we cannot hope to remove the stains which cause so much unhappiness. But when by His grace we too become more like Him, when by His grace we become more loving, we will see more beauty in the hearts of our fellow men, and will discern more meaning in our struggle for brotherhood on earth, and for peace in our homes.

52

The Other Prodigal

Scripture Reading: Luke 15:25-32

Luke 15 contains three parables: the parable of the Lost Sheep, the parable of the Lost Coin, and the parable of the Lost Son. On several occasions I preached on the parable of the lost son (or the Prodigal Son) where I made passing mention of the older brother. This sermon is largely on the older brother, with passing references to his younger brother.

It is not difficult to imagine the strained relationship between those two brothers. The older one is apparently meticulous and efficient in the performance of his duties, but his younger brother is undeniably carefree and irresponsible. One is hard-working and even thrifty; the other is an impossible, irritating character.

We can, therefore, understand the feeling of the older brother, for we too find it extremely trying to live with people who lack concern, who have no sense of duty, who are wanting in many respects. It is hard enough when such people are our associates in business, in school, in church, in the club or fraternity. It is unspeakably difficult when they are with us under the same roof, and dine with us at the same table or even sleep with us in the same room. The pain is most acute when such people are members of the same family — husbands and wives, brothers and sisters, parents and children.

It will help us who have prodigal brothers and sisters or prodigal children, or even prodigal parents to remember that one cannot give what one does not have. Common sense tells us that if I have no silver, I cannot give silver; if I have no love, I cannot give love; if I have no understanding, I cannot give understanding. It is as simple as that. And yet, we sometimes forget this in our eagerness to get what we want. It would have helped the older brother in the parable if he had resigned himself to the fact that his brother could not be depended upon because he had no sense of responsibility. And it will help us to remember that we cannot ask for tokens of thoughtfulness from those who are thoughtless, of love from those who are loveless, of concern from those who have no concern. They simply cannot give what they do not have.

So many people suffer morbidly because they do not get what they want from those dear to them. There are husbands who spend sleepless nights brooding over the fact that their wives do not mend their socks and their underwears. And there are wives who grieve for days and days because their husbands do not notice their new dress or new hairdo. But how can husbands notice a new dress when they cannot even distinguish a midi from a *bata de baño*? When people do not have the virtue of mending torn clothes or cooking your favorite *sinigang*, it will be quite unreasonable to expect them to excel in that virtue.

Sometimes, parents openly expect their children to be versatile with the piano or the violin or the guitar. Naturally, they cannot hide their disappointment when they discover that their children are not musically inclined. They buy expensive Yamahas from Tokyo and beautiful accordions from Germany, but the children prefer to tinkle their Cebu-made yukelele. They expect them to become lawyers and engineers and doctors, but their children prefer to dance or act or repair run-down cars.

We, ourselves, cannot give what we do not have. How can we be charitable when our hearts are bereft of charity? How can we trust God when we have no faith? How can we show goodness when there is none of it in us? Surely, a lot of our disappointments will vanish into thin air when we truly realize that one cannot give what one does not possess. We will be more kind to ourselves and to other people when we become reasonable in our expectations.

Secondly, we would do well to accept people as they are. Some people have five talents, others have two, still others have only one. By nature some people are most charming, just as some are rather simple. It is not right to expect the two-talented man to live as if he had five talents. It is not profitable to be angered by the coldness of the loveless or by the atheism of the infidel. This is the problem of the older son in our parable. He wants his brother to be as good as he is, to work daily in the farm, to be judicious in the use of his money. But, somehow, the brother is a spoiled brat. Perhaps, he gallivants too much, goes out with his *barkada* too much and drinks too much. He loves to stay up late in the evenings, to hibernate in the casinos. And his older brother cannot accept him as he is.

Of course, it would be nice if our brothers and sisters and the members of our clan were all cultured and well-mannered and most thoughtful. It would be great joy if they were loving and appreciative and generous. It would be heavenly if they were always courteous and diplomatic and outgoing. But alas, some of them are shy and quiet. Some are stingy and unappreciative. Some of them do not think and live the way we do. And we wish they would pack up and go into a far country. Indeed, when they pack up and go, we feel very much relieved, but when we see them trekking back home again after two or three days, we feel very much upset.

When we cannot accept people as they are we create something detrimental to our own health. Aside from the air of pride and arrogance we unconsciously betray, we nurture hate and resentment in our hearts. And such kind of an attitude will eventually affect our health.

But God gives us the key to a glorious and meaningful existence by accepting us as we are. The doctrine of justification, in the annals of our creeds, simply means that God accepts us as we are. And if we become as we ought to be, it is not because it is a precondition of our fellowship with God but because His accepting us in spite of what we are leads us to discover the way to our self-fulfillment.

So shall it be with us. When we learn to accept people as they are, we remove the string of prejudice which disturbs our serenity, and we create an atmosphere conducive to the development of some tolerable relationship with them.

At this point, let us candidly admit that one terrible problem we have in life is that of selfishness. We can excuse those who do not give because they have nothing to give. But what about those who have something to share but are not willing to share? There are those who do not care, not because they have no concern, but because they are preoccupied. They do not notice your hairdo not because they are blind but because they do not feel they should express their appreciation.

Selfishness is a basic human problem. The prodigal son ended up with nothing because he was spoiled, easygoing, and greedy. His older brother had everything he wanted but his greed made it hard for him to forgive. Selfishness is one of the root causes of prodigality.

And this is the same evil that besets us everyday. Not only those who have something but also those who have nothing can be victims of consuming selfishness. There is little giving and little sharing and little loving because there is too much selfishness. Only the love like that of the father in the parable can save us from vanity and death.

Fortunately for us, while greediness saps the very life blood of the soul and disturbs the harmony of life, we can be grateful that in the providence of God people can change for the better. The wicked, wretched, prodigal son who wasted his life in riotous living did not remain forever irresponsible. When he realized the filthiness of his being, he repented of his sin and went back to his father. And his coming home was reason enough for the grand celebration.

And what about the older brother? The parable does not tell us whether he heeded his father's plea, but I would like to believe that he was finally prevailed upon to come up the house and meet the guests. I can imagine him embracing his long lost brother and that they were reconciled. I would not be surprised if, in the end, they lived happily ever after.

The Bible abounds with stories of men and women who experienced the transforming influence of God's redemptive grace. Jonah, for instance, was a stubborn prophet who wanted things done his way. God wanted him to go to Nineveh, but instead he went the opposite direction. Yet, in the end, he yielded to God's divine sovereignty. Matthew and Zacchaeus were notorious tax collectors who could be the patron saints of the *tong* collectors. But both became followers of Christ and strong supporters of the Christian movement. Paul of Tarsus was a fierce enemy of the early Christians and a zealous persecutor of the church, but the church never produced a greater saint and a more profound theologian than Paul. Mary Magdalene was the woman from whom Jesus cast out seven demons, but it was she who washed Jesus' feet with oil. In all these cases it was their spiritual encounter with the living God which liberated them from bondage into newness of life. The solemn awareness of God's holy presence removed their pretensions and drove them to repentance.

And this is the same glorious possibility that is open before us. By God's grace we can become new creatures. We can be more trusting, more loving, more faithful. For God can make our heart of stone into a heart of flesh. It is His pleasure to give us a new beginning.

53

The Good Samaritan

Scripture Reading: Luke 10:25-37

Luke 10:25-37 is more popularly known as the parable of the Good Samaritan. The adjective **good** is not to be found in the parable itself. Jesus did not call the Samaritan **good.** But the readers of this parable all through the centuries, have been so impressed by the goodness of the Samaritan that the title **good** was spontaneously conferred upon him. Today, when we speak of the Good Samaritan, we have in mind this beautiful parable preserved for us in the Gospel of Luke.

We should note at the outset that the parable was related as part of Jesus' reply to a rather theological question. The story of a businessman taking time to help someone badly beaten up by brigands is not what we would call a theological treatise, but it was the story used by Jesus in answering a theological question. Verse 25 says, "Behold, a teacher of the Law came up and tried to trap Jesus. 'Teacher,' he asked, 'what must I do to receive eternal life?'" (Here, the teacher of the Law is an expert in Jewish laws, the Torah — one whom we today would call a theologian.) And his question was, "What must I do to receive eternal life?" To that theological question, Jesus' answer was a very practical one.

Let us recall a similar story — the story of the rich, young ruler in Luke chapter 18 who asked the same question. He started by calling Jesus good Teacher. Then he asked, "What must I do to inherit eternal life?" Again, Jesus' answer was thoroughly non-theological: Obey the commandments — Thou shalt not kill, Thou shalt not commit adultery, Thou shalt honor thy father and thy mother.

In other words, Jesus has a subtle way of telling us that all our theological sophistication, the highly technical language of our creeds, the abstract ideas in church doctrines and encyclicals should never remain up in the air, but should find their true expression in the concrete life of the people. Theology will fail in its mission if it does not grapple with the real problems of the faithful. Even God would have remained meaningless if

He did not become flesh in Jesus Christ. He who dwells in the highest heavens chose to dwell among men, and became one of us. Divine salvation must be relevant to human experience.

Let us go back to our Scripture lesson. When the teacher of the Law asked, "What must I do to inherit eternal life?" Jesus replied, "What do the Scriptures say?" The man answered, "Love the Lord your God with all your soul, with all your strength, and with all your mind, and love your neighbor as you love yourself." Then Jesus said, "You are right. Do that and you will live." But the man pursued the question by asking, "Who is my neighbor?" And in answer to that question, Jesus related the parable of the Good Samaritan.

The distance between Jerusalem and Jericho is about 17 miles. Jerusalem is 2,300 feet above sea level and Jericho is 1,300 feet below sea level. The road was "notoriously dangerous." Josephus describes it as "desolate and rocky." Prof. William Barclay says, "It was a road of narrow, rocky defiles, and of sudden turnings which made it the happy hunting-ground of brigands."

A veteran preacher, in his study of this parable, submits that the characters can be classified into three. They are those who are wounded, those who wound, and those who heal. And we see them not only on the road to Jericho but also on the road of every life.

Let us look more closely at those who are wounded. They are represented by the half-dead man in the parable. We do not know his name, his social standing, his religion. We do not know whether he was a college graduate or a school dropout. We do not know whether he was young or middle-aged or a senior citizen. All we know is that we see him on the road of human life — mortally wounded, dying, in pain, in need. We see him in our own life, for we, too, have been wounded. In some of us the wound will probably remain for as long as we live.

The wound may be in the economic sense. Once there was affluence, now the traces of need cannot be concealed. Once there was a comfortable elbow room for leisure and recreation, now there is an apparent tightening of the belt. The wound may be our pride and self-respect. We may be the victims of an empty promise or of disloyalty and unfaithfulness. Our dignity has been violated, and the lingering pain is robbing us of sleep. The wound may be on our soul — we have done what should not have been done, and a sense of guilt is building up into despair. Whatever be the nature of that wound (be it physical, emotional, financial, spiritual) we bear it in our life. Surely, we can say we belong to that great company of the wounded.

Then there are those who wound, those who cause others to suffer, those who inflict the bitter wounds that make life ugly and miserable. This group is divided into two: first, those who wound aggressively. They are typified by the brigands in the parable. Those highway bandits, seeing that a man was coming alone, emerged from their hiding places and ganged up on him, beat him up mercilessly and divested him of everything he had. Such form of violence is present in many parts of the world; we see it in our own society. It is the method of earning a living by forcibly taking from others their livelihood and their property. Whatever be the social causes that make it necessary, it cannot be condoned. Every civilized society must do everything within its power to stop it.

Second, those who wound passively. They use no guns, no bombs, no clubs. Someone has said that you can break heads with a club, but you can break hearts with neglect. Those who break hearts with neglect are represented in the parable by the priest and the Levite. They did not steal from the dying man; they did not participate in robbing him. But they did nothing to help him. That type of indifference is actually a form of violence, however innocent or harmless it may appear. It is, perhaps, the most prevalent form of violence in our society. When we do not do anything about the spread of evil, when we retreat into the privacy of our homes while the agents of wickedness roam around the streets, when we prefer to see no evil, hear no evil, and speak no evil, so as not to get involved in a direct confrontation with evil, we become the silent instruments of violence. This is what the theologians call the sin of omission. When people abuse their authority and treat those under them as if they were mere chattels, when they behave in ways that offend our sensibilities, when immorality is being committed by those expected to set the example, when these and similar expressions of moral bankruptcy glare before our eyes and we prefer not to lift our finger lest we get involved, we actually tolerate the spread of violence.

Jesus has another parable that underscores this point — the parable of the goats and the sheep. To the goats the Master said, "Depart from me, ye cursed, into the eternal fire prepared for the devil and his angels; for I was hungry and you gave me no food; I was thirsty and you gave me no drink; I was a stranger and you did not welcome me; naked and you did not clothe me; sick and in prison and you did not visit me." In short, they were condemned because of their sin of omission. They did not do what they should have done. They went to hell not because they oppressed the poor, not because they indulged in riotous living, not because they padded the vouchers, but because they failed to get out of their comfortable homes to give aid to the needy and comfort to the suffering.

If there are those who wound aggressively, there are those who wound passively. And of these two groups the Lord seems to have regarded the latter as the more dangerous. In another parable, when the one-talent man hid his talent in the ground and did nothing with it, the Master ordered that he be cast out into outer darkness, and that his only talent be taken away from him. No wonder the Apostle James could say with boldness, "To him that knoweth to do good, and doeth it not, to him it is sin." (James 4:17).

So there are the wounded, and those who wound. But thank God, there are those who heal, represented by the Samaritan in the parable. When he saw the half-dead man, he got off his beast, gave first aid to the robbery victim, set him on his animal, brought him to an inn, and took care of him.

How beautiful this world will be if we had more people of his calibre! The good Samaritan may not know much about religion — he was just a layman outside the pale of orthodox Judaism. The teacher of the law who asked the question, "Who is my neighbor?" was certainly more informed and more knowledgeable. But it was the Samaritan's deed of kindness that makes the story both moving and immortal. The works of love and mercy are the final answers to the most perplexing theological questions.

Who is our neighbor? The story of the good Samaritan answers the question. Our neighbor is anyone in need. And need recognizes no religion, no culture, no nationality. To help those in need is to be neighborly to them. That is what the Samaritan did. And today, Jesus is telling us, "Go and do likewise." Be neighborly. Compassion is not enough. You must do something. You must give part of yourself. You must really care. Our calling is not just to drop something into the offering plates, not just to send something to the Community Chest. Sometimes, the giving of financial contribution is the easiest thing to do. But neighborliness demands more. It asks for our love and for our concern.

To be sure, neighborliness can cause us some inconvenience. It may give us some headaches we are not asking for. It may even lead us to troubles and difficulties. But that seems to be the way God wants it to be. Jesus did not save mankind by sitting on a swivel chair. He saved us by bearing the cross and giving His life freely. He did not tell us what to do by sending some imperial decrees from His throne in heaven; He came and dwelt among us, and became hungry and thirsty as we are. In the words of the prophet Isaiah, "He hath borne our griefs and carried our sorrows." In short, it is through the bearing of the cross that we save a half-dead marriage, a half-dead church, a half-dead economy, a half-dead fellowship. It is through sacrificial loving and caring that we bring life to a dying spirit.

The real tragedy of our time is not the mounting highway robberies we hear of every now and then, not the exploitation of people by those with guns and goons. The real tragedy is when, in the face of such wickedness, no one is willing to do something for fear of getting involved.

But God who is more than equal to our difficulties is not rendered helpless by our cowardice or complacency. He uses the Samaritans — those whom we consider to be outside the gates of heaven because they do not dress the way we do, they do not think the way we do, they do not act the way we do. God uses them to show us that divine help is available with which to meet every human need. That is why we pray for the multiplication of the good Samaritans. And that is why we pray that we too may go and do likewise.

And when we go and do likewise, somehow we will see for ourselves that human complacency can be overcome by Christian commitment, and that "earth has no sorrows which heaven cannot heal."

54

The Nature of Hope

Scripture Reading: Luke 13:10-17

Here is the story of a woman who had been sick for eighteen years and finally received healing grace from Jesus the Christ. We cannot ascertain the kind of infirmity she was suffering from. The evangelist Luke, himself a physician who often described the kind of sickness people had, did not, in this instance, give us a detailed description of the woman's infirmity. In several translations of this passage, she is simply described as having the spirit of infirmity or weakness.

At any rate, a British preacher, analyzing this story, suggests that the woman's infirmity robbed her of her physical beauty. That, I believe, cannot be far from the truth, for we read that she was bent over and could not fully straighten herself. When she acquired such infirmity we do not know, but she had it for eighteen years, and those years must have included the prime period of her life.

This picture of a woman — bent over and ugly and weak — is, in our generation, a sad symbol of misfortune and despair. For ours is an age of cosmetics which makes beauty possible for almost everyone. Of course, beauty is relative. What may be beautiful for me may not be beautiful for others. But the fact is that we are becoming more and more beauty-conscious, as evidenced by the increasing sales of lipstick and deodorant, and by the growing popularity of beauty contests. Many women today, both young and the not-so-young, would rather not come to church if they fail to complete their make-up. They would rather stay home than show themselves to their friends in their natural simplicity.

In an era which has a growing appreciation of beauty, a bent and weak woman is a symbol of despair. And the healing of that woman in our Scripture reading is Luke's way of telling us that Christ can rescue us from despair and can enable us to see some meaning in our life. That is what our generation has to learn. Nothing can be more tragic than to see beautiful women and handsome men with empty souls and wasting their life in riotous living. Such people may have the form of vitality but are actually sinking into death because they do not know the beauty of God's peace. In the words of a song, they are laughing at the outside but crying in the inside.

The beauty we ardently need is not the beauty which we can acquire in the beauty parlor, however important that may be. It is the beauty of character which only Jesus can create. It is the beauty which saves us from needless brooding and makes us radiant personalities. It is the beauty which surpasses the ugliness of our human situation and makes us masters over circumstances.

In the second place, our Scripture lesson tells us that the woman who had the spirit of infirmity was also robbed of her physical strength. According to the record, she could not even straighten herself. She was that weak. To be robbed of beauty was bad enough. To be deprived of strength was to compound her tribulation. And in this age of rockets and high-powered guns and atomic energy and vitamins, a weak body is a symbol of utter dejection. In an age of instant vitality and, sometimes, instant marriages, to be weak for eighteen years is to experience grave disconsolation. The healing of that woman in the gospel story, therefore, is Luke's way of telling us that Christ is the true source of power — the power which enables us to straighten out the many crookedness and wickedness in the corridors of our life.

Unfortunately, there seems to be an imbalance in our strategy for growth. While many of us patronize that power "which puts a tiger in our tank," the practice of prayer and the contemplative life is becoming optional. Such imbalance is not healthy for the soul because power — whether it be political, economic, or technological — becomes a highly dangerous weapon in the hands of the spiritually irresponsible. We need Jesus to save us from such predicament.

And so, the woman who had the spirit of infirmity was robbed of her beauty as well as of her strength. But that is not the central feature in her life. The central, inspiring feature in her life is that she did not allow her infirmity to rob her of her hope. Although she was not strong enough to straighten up herself, she managed to go to the synagogue. Who brought her there, we do not know. But she was there, listening to Jesus' teaching. If we know the Jewish custom, then we can be sure the synagogue was terribly crowded, for it was Sabbath. Yet, to that holy precinct, bursting with people from all walks of life, this infirm and sickly lady found her way.

In other words, we see in her the quality of hope that sustained her in her infirmity. She had no beauty, but she did not become bitter. She was pitifully weak, but she was not helpless. For eighteen years she struggled with her sickness but she did not become impatient. The moving story of her healing would not be a blessing for us today had she given up hope after seventeen years of praying and waiting.

We could do well to take a close look at the nature of that woman's hope, since it is the kind of hope we must covet for ourselves. Almost immediately we see that it is hope borne by the reality of suffering. The lady had been suffering for many years but, at the same time, she had been hoping for the coming of a brighter day. Bishop Gerald Kennedy of the Methodist Church says, "There is a sense in which Christian hope is impossible unless one has faced the despair in the human situation. . . Until a man has looked at the abyss which looms in front of every human soul, he can never know Christian hope." In other words, the hope of getting well is related to the condition of being sick; and the hope for victory is an illusion if it is dissociated from the experience of conflict.

John W. Vannorsdall, in his article on *The Shape of Hope*, writes: "This is one of the most profound insights of the gospel: that the shape of hope is the experience of failure." So it is not just suffering and conflict that give birth to hope; failure itself can be the gate to the fountain of spiritual power. Prof. Vannorsdall says, "It is when we have tried our best to be like God and failed that we are open to the One who comes to proclaim that He alone is God. It is when we have tried to be good and righteous and failed, that we are open to the Christ who bestows the gift of righteousness. It is when we have blasted the heavens with our prayers and fall dry and empty that the Holy Spirit fills our lives with the assurance of His presence." Concluding his discourse on human failure as God's good opportunity, Prof. Vannorsdall says, "Out of the failure of the grave, God brought forth a new people. . . Out of the failure of the monastery, God brought forth a reformation of His church. . . And we also shall run and fail, and out of this failure God will show us the shape of hope."[1]

In brief, hope is meant for all of us because all of us, without exception, are in varying degrees involved in the mighty conflict of life. Our experience tells us that life itself is the arena where the conflict between truth and falsehood, between good and evil, between love and hatred, takes place. To live is necessarily to be involved in certain conflicts.

---
[1] Quoted by Edmund A Steimle in *Renewal in the Pulpit,* pp. 196f.

But the overriding fact is not that we are in the midst of conflicts or perhaps, already at the brink of failure, but that in the midst of all our difficulties and even in failure we can have hope.

In the second place, our hope must be nurtured by a constant search for the truths of God. In our Scripture lesson the bent lady was healed in the synagogue while listening to Jesus' teaching. Of course, her healing could have taken place in the hospital or in her home or in the streets, as God after all is not confined in the synagogue or the temple. But if we are to understand the nature of Christian hope, we must emphasize that it is always hope in God, and that, in fact, our God is the God of hope. And if that hope is to equip us for the fierce storms that come upon us from every direction, it must be nurtured in fellowship with Him who chooses to meet with us in the house of worship.

In the third place, our hope should be manifested in our faith. Hope is our response to the promises of God. To hope is, in a sense, to have a foretaste now of what is yet promised, or to appropriate now that which is stored for the future. In this sense, hope and faith are twin virtues, for faith is also our response to the graciousness of God. We cannot really divorce hope from faith for as long as God grants us to live.

The gospel we proclaim, which is the gospel of God's love which comes to us through faith in Jesus Christ, is also the gospel of hope. It is the gospel which we are called upon to spread. In a world of sickness and poverty and greed, of war and famine and meaninglessness, the message of hope can replenish our strength and sharpen our vision.

However, we need to remind ourselves that our Christian hope should not be perverted by making light of the serious problems we have. Bishop Kennedy classifies those who do much harm into two groups — the professional optimists and the professional pessimists. The optimist is always sure that "everything will be all right." He cries, "Peace, peace," when there is no peace. "He is the man who does not see reality but always blurs the unpleasant with pretense. He believes that wishing will make it so . . . that if we pretend everything is well, things will actually turn out that way." We need to guard ourselves against such extreme optimism.

On the other hand, the professional pessimist is one who cannot see anything right or hopeful. Kennedy says, "Whenever there is one promising possibility, he (the pessimist) can see a hundred things which may prevent it. He helps to create the very thing he fears. His mood of helplessness encourages evil."

A true Christian is neither a professional optimist nor a professional pessimist. His hope is not a bloated optimism, and his despair does not degenerate into hopeless pessimism. The Christian hope bravely recognizes the element of despair in the human situation, but at the same time realizes the sufficiency of God's grace in coping with the situation. This is why in proclaiming the gospel of hope, we must not speak only of the golden roads in heaven; we must also face squarely the problems that shake our nation, that disturb the peace of our homes, that poison our love for one another. Our hope, in other words, must bring into focus not only the acuteness of our difficulties but also the glory of God's abiding faithfulness.

This is why I say to those who are laboring under the heavy weight of life's crushing burdens: Hold on to God and hope for His mercy. Wait upon the Lord and believe in His goodness, and He shall renew your strength.

55

The Angry Prophet

Scripture Reading: Amos 5:14-24

Amos, until the beginning of his prophetic ministry, was a layman with no professional training for a religious office. He did not go to a seminary and was never ordained to perform the priestly tasks. His was a very humble background, coming as he did from the village of Tekoa, some 10 miles south of Jerusalem. Although in Jewish tradition Amos is considered as a well-to-do shepherd, many Bible scholars believe that the size of his flocks could not have been large. Indeed, Amos himself took care of his sheep which, like the sheep of other shepherds, were small and medium-sized because their village was not the best place for sheep-raising. We have reasons to believe that shepherding alone was an inadequate source of livelihood for Amos and his family. He had to supplement his earning by dressing Sycamore trees, the insipid fruits of which were the food of the poor.

Amos has an intimate familiarity with nature which is reflected in his writings. He speaks of the lion roaring over its prey, the plague of locusts that eat up the pasture, the seven stars and Orion that decorate God's heavens. And his own experience of being exposed to the heat by day and to cold winds by night makes him aware of the sterner aspects which the world of nature can display.

But this *provinciano* is equally familiar with the sights of the city. He is aware of the shocking ugliness of the nation's life in the capital city of Jerusalem. He must have travelled much, for he knows the situations obtaining not only in Israel but also in the neighboring countries.

The opening verses of his book are enough to convince us that the prophet has no soft words to say. His marvelous literary skill and particularly his poetic ability do not detract, but powerfully emphasize, the divine punishment which God will inflict upon those who remain in sin. The Edomites, the Temanites, the Ammonites, the Moabites, and the people of Judah and Israel — all of them cannot escape divine punishment because of their blatant disregard for the laws of God and the welfare of their fellow men. Unlike the prophet Hosea who is known as the preacher of God's mercy and love, Amos is universally considered as the prophet of doom who speaks of God's wrath in no uncertain terms. He is the angry prophet, but he is angry for God. He is angry at the crooked ways of his fellow men, at the merciless oppression of the poor, at the rampant bribery in high places, at the lavish display of religious piety by no less than the perpetrators of injustice and slavery.

Listen, for instance, to his mordant indictment in chapter 6:

> "Woe to those who lie upon beds of ivory, and stretch themselves upon their couches, and eat lambs from the flock, and calves from the midst of the stall; who sing idle songs to the sound of their harp and, like David, invent for themselves instruments of music; who drink wine in bowls, and anoint themselves with the finest oils, but are not grieved over the ruin of Joseph! (vss. 4-6)."

This is to say that while they can afford all luxuries in life, while they have all the time for leisure and enjoy the best steaks and the best wine and the best entertainment, they are not in the least concerned with the plight of the underprivileged and the underfed! They are living only to themselves, unmindful of the gnashing poverty and the abject misery which is the lot of many.

Such lack of social concern is not their only shortcoming. What is even more atrocious is their uncontrolled greediness, particularly among the merchant class — greediness which has no regard for the rights of others and has no sense of decency. In chapter 8, Amos says:

"Hear this, you who trample upon the needy, and bring the poor of the land to an end, saying, When will the new moon be over, that we may sell grain? That we may offer wheat for sale, that we may make the ephah small and the shekel great, and deal deceitfully with false balances, that we may buy the poor for silver and sell the refuse of the wheat?"

In chapter 2, Amos exposes their sin of selling into slavery "honest men who cannot pay their debts, poor men who cannot repay even the price of a pair of sandals." In verse 7 he says, "They trample down the weak and helpless and push the poor out of the way." In chapter 5, he accuses them of tampering their scales and balances so that a cavan of palay is less than a cavan and a kilo of sugar is actually less than a kilo.

In chapter 3, Amos criticizes his nation's stand on the question of national defense. He reminds his government not to put their ultimate trust in military power. In effect, he is saying, "Might is not necessarily right." He is suggesting that the foreign policy of Israel or of any nation should not be determined by what the nation can do, but by what the people ought to do.

The opening verses in chapter 4 may sound like a vulgar expletive for here Amos calls the women of Samaria cows. But we must remember that Amos is angry at the shameless greediness of those women who push their husbands into doing things that will insure their comfort even at the price of committing injustice. Even Jesus, who got fed up with the artificial righteousness of the scribes and Pharisees, called them serpents and a generation of vipers who could not escape the damnation of hell. When men forget the high purposes of life and become preoccupied with the "tawdry business of personal display and social ambition " they are reduced into mere animals bereft of any concern for fellow human beings.

The life of Amos is not a happy one, especially when he finds it necessary to say uncomplimentary remarks about the women of his country. Oriental culture is such that we may engage in a hot verbal war with men, but as much as possible we should avoid having any clashes with women. There are times, however, when we can no longer hold our peace, especially when the vanity of women has reached a certain limit where silence is no longer respectable. In the case of Amos, he has to say his piece and, in the process, he fulfills a prophetic ministry.

Amos' story, therefore, clearly illustrates the kind of anger which God's people should cultivate. It is the kind of anger which Jesus Himself manifested when the temple, a house of prayer, was converted into a den of robbers. Christians should have that kind of anger, especially in the face of immorality and dishonesty and oppression and injustice.

In our Scripture reading, we have a clear intimation that in spite of all the social wrongs prevailing in Israel, the public services of religion were also flourishing. In verses 21 to 24, God, speaking through Amos, says: "I hate, I despise your feasts, and I take no delight in your solemn assemblies. Even though you offer me your burnt offerings and cereal offerings, I will not accept them, and the peace offerings of your fatted beasts I will not look upon. Take away from me the noise of your songs; to the melody of your harps I will not listen. But let justice roll down like waters, and righteousness like an ever flowing stream."

Scholars tell us that the temple in Jerusalem was never busier than it was in the days of Amos. The priests were busy officiating at the altar and performing all kinds of ceremonies. But the moral life of the people was low, and spiritual decay was apparent in every segment of society.

Is that not a timely reminder that activism in the church is not necessarily a sign of spiritual vitality? The truth is, activism can be a substitute for the working of the Holy Spirit. A church bustling with people is not necessarily sensitive to the needs of men, and the people who frequent the precincts of the church are not necessarily looking for God. They may be looking for some fulfillment of a personal need or simply performing a mechanical duty.

Some years ago, a survey was conducted in Metro Manila on the motives of people in going to church. The survey revealed that the majority of our people go to church to ask favors from God. Now, we are not against making petitions to the Lord. Jesus told us to ask great things from God. Petitionary prayers have a place in our life. But when worship is motivated by what we can get from God, we have not truly understood what it means to worship Him.

If Amos were to speak to us today, I am afraid he will ask us why we go to church. Do we go to church to see someone who may not be found in his home on Sunday morning? Do we go to church because the time for worship suits well with our schedule? Do we go to church because we like the singing of the choir? Do we go to church because of the preacher? These reasons may be valid at some points and should be legitimately considered; but if these are the primary motives of our churchgoing, then perhaps God will take no delight in our assembly, however solemn it may be. He will not look upon our offerings, however generous they may be; He will not listen to the melody of our songs. What He wants is a genuine renewal of our determination to let justice roll down like waters, and righteousness like an ever flowing stream. He wants us to worship Him, which means not only praising Him with our lips but also obeying His will for ourselves and the rest of mankind.

It is good to see our church almost always full of people, and we should be grateful for good church attendance. But we must always remind ourselves that our church is not the place to study the art of public speaking — Congress is a better place for that. This is not the place to enjoy great music — the Cultural Center of the Philippines can offer much better musical presentations. Our church is a place of worship, and if we go to church to worship God, we will find that even the stammering words of the preacher are a medium of God's message and that even the occasional mistakes of the choir are a vehicle of that divine grace which takes away our fears, our loneliness, our worries, and our pride.

Amos is a prophet who encourages us to be angry for God. Such anger can be cultivated in our experience of worship. There is one thing more which Amos advocates: he advocates the kind of religion which is deeply concerned with the affairs of our world.

Unfortunately, there is a prevailing concept of a religious man which is incongruous with the biblical concept. To many people, a religious person is one who prays, who goes to church regularly, who attends prayer meetings, who reads the Bible faithfully. Furthermore, a religious man has nothing to do with political conflicts and will not associate with publicans and sinners. He seldom goes to parties; in fact, he is often aloof. Well, if that is what we mean by a religious person, then that person's religion falls short of Amos' standard.

To Amos, a religious person is not only prayerful, church-loving and a devout Bible student, but also vitally concerned with the issues of justice and peace, deeply interested in the dissemination of the truth, in the liberation of people from anything that dehumanizes. A religious man, therefore, gets angry with bank robbers and with abusive police officers, with those who are chronically inefficient in the performance of their duties, with those who make promises but do not intend to fulfill them. A religious man is civic spirited, is a passionate lover of social justice and a crusading advocate of nationalism and patriotism. In short, a religious man, according to Amos, imparts God's presence to the people in his home, in his community and in his nation and will oppose every form of unrighteousness that contradicts the will of God for men.

That is also the kind of religion which Jesus wants us to embrace. It is a religion where intimate fellowship with God is the very reason for our enthusiastic participation in the affairs of men. It is a religion where the end of worship is the beginning of service.

And that is the kind of religion that I covet for all of us. It is my prayer that as we come to church Sunday after Sunday, as we read our Bible and say our prayers and sing hymns of praise and adoration, we may also be moved to give our share in alleviating the suffering of the poor and oppressed, in improving the lot of our neighbors, in defending the cause of truth and freedom. It is also my prayer that as we guard the sacredness of our rights and the sanctity of our homes, as we contribute in our own humble ways to the economic and social and cultural development of our nation, we may also find time for worship that we may find prayer a much-needed spiritual discipline, and that we may find the Holy Scripture a great source of guidance when we are bewildered and a source of strength when we are discouraged.

56

Youth and Discipleship

Scripture Reading: Matthew 19:16-22

The story of the rich young ruler appears in the gospels of Matthew, Mark, and Luke. In Matthew, he is described as a young man. In Mark, he is a rich man. In Luke, he is a ruler. This is why Bible scholars speak of him as the rich young ruler. When one has wealth and youth and social respectability, what else can he ask for? As a ruler, he must be a member of either the local synagogue or the Jewish Sanhedrin. If he was a member of the local synagogue, then he was the equivalent of a member of a local church council. In other words, he was a religious man. He might even be a pious man. Or, if he was a member of the Jewish Sanhedrin, he was more or less like an associate justice of the Supreme Court. That is why I said he had social respectability. And to be a member of the Jewish Sanhedrin, he should have some formal education. He should be conversant on the laws of the Jewish people. With all those admirable credentials, what else could he ask for?

The answer is quite obvious: to that young man life is not complete without Christ. And that must be the message the gospel writers had wanted to convey, for they themselves were young when they enlisted themselves for Christian discipleship. In effect they are telling us that the greatest adventure of the youth of any generation is to be in the company of Jesus, to be the agents of his love that can set men's hearts on fire for God. Youth is life's summertime. It is the period of time when one feels strongly the tender throbs of life. But without Christ, it can be an empty desert, a wasteland in the dark wilderness which cannot be made alive by the wildest bacchanalian revelries.

The rich young ruler had great enthusiasm with which he sought Jesus — he was running. Surely, it was because he had the vigor and the strength of youth, and also because he was quite eager to meet the Master. And then kneeling before Jesus, he asked, "Good Master, what must I do to inherit eternal life?" No doubt it was a polite salutation. Every Jew knew that only God was good, and here the young man was greeting Jesus as the good teacher. Jesus' reply cannot be construed as a denial of His own goodness. It was more of a reminder to the young man that flattery can be injurious to the soul, and therefore, one must always guard against it. At any rate, the young man's question betrays the notion prevailing at that time that salvation could be earned by doing something. And since that was what he knew, Jesus answered him on that level and said, "Obey the commandments — thou shalt not kill, thou shalt not steal, thou shalt not commit adultery." But the young man said, "I have done all these things since I was a little boy." He excelled in the "thou-shalt-nots." He got a good mark on negative righteousness. It was not surprising, therefore, that he felt some strange emptiness within himself, for all that he had was empty legalism.

Such situation gives us a mixed feeling of pity and gladness: pity because his punctilious observance of the law had not brought him an inch nearer the Kingdom of God; and gladness because the realization of his emptiness had brought him face to face with Christ. Some people would succumb to an utter failure, but this young man knew where help could be available.

So this confession of absolute helplessness, in spite of much effort on his part, drew that most loving look from Jesus. As St. Mark puts it in his gospel account, "Then Jesus beholding him loved him." It is the same saving look which Jesus gives us today. We don't have to be perfect, for we can't be; we don't have to be good first; all we need is some courage to confess our weakness and our inadequacy.

Now, the final testing comes. Jesus tells the young man, "If thou shalt be perfect, go and sell thy property, give the proceeds to the poor, then come, and follow me." The young man must have said to himself, "Where is the logic, Lord Jesus? I have acquired all my properties honestly. Why should I sell them now? And if in order to follow you, I have to sell my properties, what about those who will buy them? Do they have to sell the same in order to follow you? And if all people were to follow you, then who will buy their possessions?" These could have been the thoughts in the mind of that young man, but apparently, he did not entertain them. His reaction was rather swift and negative. In the words of our Scripture reading, "But when the young man heard that saying, he went away sorrowful, for he had great possessions."

Clearly, what Jesus means in this instance is to get rid of anything that hinders us from following him. If our right eye causes us to stumble, he says, pluck it off; it is better to have one eye and be sure of the Father's welcome in the Kingdom of God than to have two eyes but miss the boat altogether. If our right hand causes us to stumble, says Jesus, cut it off. In like manner, if possessions become rigid barriers to Christian discipleship, get rid of them or share them with those who have less in life. Nothing, absolutely nothing, should stand between Christ and us.

Today, we need to ask: What is it that hinders us from complete discipleship? Is it wealth? Is it popularity? Is it pride? Is it laziness? Is it complacency? Is it a sinful habit? Is it religiosity? Whatever it is, let us put it away. It does not profit us to gain the whole world if, in the process, we lose our souls.

Today, many of our young people have become victims of certain circumstances that prevent their full development. One of those unhappy circumstances is poverty. As a result, many of them are forced to do what should not be done. Almost everyday we hear of young people getting involved in carnapping, thieveries, shoplifting, and the various forms of hooliganism. Delinquency is so endemic that we wonder whether some kind of a moral catastrophe has descended upon our land. The problem becomes more perplexing when we remember that even millionaires steal. The unparalleled plundering of the nation's wealth by those who were entrusted to secure it for the benefit of the people offends us no end. It may well be the symptom of a morbid spiritual cancer eating up the flesh of our society today.

In the second place, the influence of movies which depict violence in gory details is now known to be a contributing factor to the moral degeneration of our youth. Furthermore, beta films which portray lasciviousness and barbarity are now available in every nook and corner of the land. They can be viewed within the privacy of our homes, and they can wreak havoc on the moral development of our youth.

Another cause of delinquency among the youth is their broken homes. We need not ask for statistics to understand this. Delinquent parents are lucky to have well-behaved children. But that is the exception rather than the rule. In many instances, the maxim holds true — like father, like son. Or, like mother, like daughter. It is important, therefore, that young people be guided in the choice of their life partners. Christian parents should take it as their sacred duty to instruct their young ones on the things to be considered before getting married. This is a most delicate task because, for one thing, it requires utmost understanding on the part of parents whose common temptation is to make decisions for their children even when said children are already of age. The church should be a place where problems on boy-girl relations are freely discussed to enable our young people to draw some guidance from the resources of the Christian faith.

Furthermore, the youth of today, as with previous generations, have to deal with environmental influences, particularly the company or *barkada* with whom our young people associate. Mr. Abraham Manalo, the leader of the famous Apache gang in Pampanga some years ago, in an interview with a newspaper writer, said: "Our parents should not be blamed for our deeds. We just can't help going out with the gang. When the gang calls, we respond. We had to find ways of leaving our homes at night." Our dilemma here is that even if young people come from good families, if they happen to get involved with wild and irresponsible company, they will always find ways of leaving their homes at night to respond to the call of the gang.

There are, of course, other causes of delinquency which we cannot discuss now, but the ones I have just mentioned are, perhaps, the most common. Those are problems we should not ignore if our youth and people of all ages are to be helped in overcoming such difficulties. Those are barriers to full discipleship that must be addressed with all seriousness.

The rich young ruler did not have the disadvantages I have just enumerated. He was a man of means; he did not have to steal other people's money. He was a leader in his community, and did not have any desire to be in the front pages of the local newspapers. But he and the young people of our time have a similar need — the need to come face to face with Jesus for the fulfillment of their deepest yearning. But in the case of the rich young ruler he was not willing to pay the price. And though he had the joyous privilege of meeting Jesus face to face, he went away sorrowing.

Here, two things need to be noted: (1) Discipleship requires some sacrifice; and (2) To meet Jesus personally is not always a glorious experience; it could be an unsettling confrontation that disturbs the lifestyle we have learned to love and which we are not willing to give up.

Many Christians today are Christian only by name. Their Christianity is no more than a religious tradition inherited from their parents and grandparents. They go to church out of habit; worship to them is a perfunctory observance of an empty ceremony. Many of them can sincerely appreciate a good anthem or a moving sermon. When the offering plate is passed around, they dig into their pockets in order that they may put something in it. But if that is all that they do, Christianity is not really a living experience; it is only a veneer of a cultural heritage and not the foundation of a lasting faith.

Today, we need to remind ourselves that discipleship is costly and requires some sacrifices; that no one comes to Jesus without, at the same time, denying himself. Discipleship cannot be divorced from cross-bearing, and any attempt to do that will only lead to dissillusionment.

The thrilling romance of the Christian life is not guaranteed to all who come to Jesus; it is only for those who will heed His call and obey His command. Those who come to Him without any sense of self-surrender will, like the rich young ruler in the gospel account, go away with gripping sadness in their hearts.

May it be our prayer that all of us, especially our youth, may have the courage to cast our lot with the Savior of mankind without reservation of any kind. It will be an adventure in Christian discipleship that can lead us to the very gates of the Kingdom of our God.

57

The Stewardship of Health

Scripture Reading: I Corinthians 6:9-20

One of the key words in our religious vocabulary is the word **salvation.** Yet we sometimes forget that it means health, or wholeness, or healing. In the Bible, Savior means healer. In fact, the image of the Savior as healer is quite prominent in the Bible. When John the Baptist sent his disciples to Jesus to inquire whether He really was the Messiah, Jesus answered, "Go and tell John what you have seen and heard: the blind receive their sight, the lame walk, lepers are cleansed, and the deaf hear" (Luke 7:22a). In other words, Jesus cited his acts of healing as signs of his saviourhood. And when He sent the twelve disciples to the towns and cities of Israel, He sent them not only to preach the good news but also to heal the sick, to raise the dead, to cleanse the lepers and to cast out demons. Matthew records in chapter 10 of his gospel that Jesus called His disciples and gave them authority over unclean spirits, to cast them out and to heal every disease and every infirmity (10:1). And when He visited Nazareth — the place where He grew up — He went to the synagogue on a Sabbath, as was His custom; and when He stood up to read from the book of Isaiah, He read that portion which says, "The Spirit of the Lord is upon me, because he has anointed me to preach good news to the poor. He has sent me to proclaim release to the captives, and recovery of sight to the blind" (Luke 4:18f). After reading, He said with dignity and authority, "Today this scripture has been fulfilled in your hearing."

To appreciate more deeply this New Testament emphasis on salvation as health and on the Savior as a healer, we should review the Old Testament provisions on the subject. For in the Old Testament, we can trace the early beginnings of the Hebrew attitude towards health and the sanctity of the human body. In Ecclesiasticus, an apocryphal book found in the Roman Catholic Bible, health is regarded as the greatest of all earthly benedictions. But it is the Psalmist who is most vocal in ascribing to God the healing of man's afflictions. For instance, the Psalmist says, "The Lord healeth the broken in heart, and bindeth up their wounds. . . Bless the Lord, O my soul. . . who healeth all thy diseases, who redeemeth thy life from destruction" (147:3, 103:2,3,4).

Prof. R. K. Harrison, writing on health and healing in the Old Testament, observes that "In the earlier phases of Hebrew thought, disease was regarded as a divine visitation consequent upon disobedience or sin, and this penal theory persisted in the popular mind throughout the entire biblical period...Because of the consistent spiritualizing of pathological phenomena, the general biblical view of the incidence of disease related it more or less directly to divine interposition. Since God was the physician of his people, it followed that healing constituted a manifest token of his forgiveness."[1] Also in the Old Testament, there is a concept that health can be maintained by a meticulous observance of the divine laws. Indeed, material prosperity may be added to physical and mental health if one is consistent in disciplining his spiritual life. In Exodus 15:26, we read: "If you will diligently hearken to the voice of the Lord your God, and do that which is right in his eyes, and give heed to his commandments and keep all his statutes, I will put none of the diseases upon you which I put upon the Egyptians; for I am the Lord, your healer."

At this point, let us note that the Mosaic code in the Old Testament has a strong emphasis on prophylaxis. Because of the theory that the incidence of disease ultimately proceeded from the Omnipotent Lord, fellowship with God was understood to be the surest safeguard against sickness. Therefore, the emphasis was on the prevention of disease rather than its cure. In fact, when disease arose and someone attempted to cure it, he was trespassing upon the Divine Physician and was interfering in the functions which solely belonged to God. And because of this exceptional concern for prophylaxis, Moses may well be spoken of as the Father of preventive medicine. Prof. Harrison maintains that "In the medical enactments of the Pentateuch, social hygiene was elevated to the level of a science, and the precepts of the Mosaic era survive to the present as a model of sanitary and hygienic insight."

This emphasis on prophylaxis and sanitation is also dominant in the other Mosaic laws. The Sabbath observance, for instance, was, among other things, for the specific purpose of physical rest. The religious aspect of the Sabbath was to provide opportunities for mental and spiritual recreation. But the Sabbath was also for the maintenance of physical vigor and functional efficiency by regular, periodic rest. In Exodus 23:12, even

---

[1] *Interpreter's Dictionary of the Bible*, E-J, p. 542.

domesticated animals should relax from work. In the book of Leviticus, the concept of the Sabbath was extended to the land in order to ensure the continued fertility of the ground.

The laws on edible foods were also intended to maintain health and vigor. Scholars believe that the "dietary rules of the Pentateuch (are) by far the most scientific of their kind to be found in the ancient Near East."[1] In Deuteronomy 14:21, we have the provision that no one should eat the flesh of an animal which had died from a natural cause. Under normal circumstances, the flesh may be eaten if all the blood had been drained from the tissue and then properly cooked. In Leviticus 11:31-38, food and water should be protected from being polluted by unclean objects.

The Mosaic law on cleanliness required that when lepers were declared ceremonially clean, the clothes and the bodies should be thoroughly washed. Leviticus 14:2-32 is a purification ritual. Even the priests had to go through an ablution ceremony before they could exercise their priestly office.

The Mosaic legislation also covered the sanitary practices among the Israelites. In Deuteronomy 23:12-13, the armies were required to dispose of all excreta by burial to avoid fly-infestation. In Numbers 31:7-24, we read how the victors were isolated from the vanquished before they could go through their ceremonial ablutions.

Thus, we can safely say that the prophylactic approach was the special contribution of the Hebrews to medical theory, and the principles embodied in the Pentateuch are surely in harmony with the basic precepts of contemporary preventive medicine.

In the New Testament, we will not find any passage supporting the Old Testament concept of disease as punishment sent by God. On the contrary, Jesus' ministry is closely bound up with the frail and feeble of body and soul. While He was primarily concerned with man's spiritual well-being, He never underestimated the value of physical health. The gospel abounds with stories of His healing ministry. He was touched by the sight of suffering men and women. He responded to their crying need for wholeness and healed them of their diseases. His methods may not be an adequate clinical demonstration of therapeutic techniques — and they should not be taken as such — but His compassion for the sick assures us that disease is not an established part of the divine order of things. In some instances, He attributed the incidence of illness to the work of evil in human life (Luke 13:16); and because His mission was precisely to destroy evil,

---
[1] *Interpreters' Dictionary of the Bible*, E-J, p. 543.

it therefore followed that He would exert every effort to fight disease.

Also basic in the thinking of Jesus is the unity of body and soul. He did not subscribe to the teachings of the Greeks who maintained the duality of the human personality. Nor did He regard the body as evil as the Greeks thought. His mission was to the whole man and to the wholeness of life. While He noted the temporal and mortal quality of the human body, He did not consider it as a seat of evil. Instead, He pointed at Himself as the Word made flesh, as the Incarnation of God Himself. No wonder His passion was for the salvation not only of man's soul but also of man's body.

This emphasis on the sacredness of the human body was so pervading in the mind of the early church that the Apostle Paul, in his letter to the Corinthians, speaks of the body as the temple of the Holy Spirit. And he asserts that the misuse of Christian liberty which is consequently detrimental to health is a sin not only against God but also against the body. He strongly exhorts his readers to avoid immorality because, he says, "the immoral man sins against his own body." The body, says Paul, "is not meant for immorality, but for the Lord, and the Lord for the body." Rebuking his Corinthian brethren for their association with the harlots, he says, "Do you not know that your bodies are members of Christ? Shall I therefore take the members of Christ and make them members of a prostitute? Never! Do you not know that he who joins himself to a prostitute becomes one body with her?" And reminding them that they were bought with a price, he appeals that they glorify God in their bodies.

Such concern for the body as a sacred gift of God is also brilliantly expressed in his appeal to the Roman Christians. He says, "I beseech you therefore, brethren, by the mercies of God, that you present your bodies as a living sacrifice, holy and acceptable to God, which is your spiritual worship" (Romans 12:1). In other words, Paul is saying that the adroit care of the body to preserve its health or to deliver it from the pain of sickness should be inspired by the conviction that it is a divine imperative. That means that a daily and constant watchfulness to protect the body from moral and physical blemish is in itself an act of spiritual worship.

Actually, one does not have to be a Christian to believe in the supreme value of health care. The Buddhists, the Hindus, the Muslims and even the pagans also believe in health care. But for the Christians, health care is a matter of stewardship. There is a saying: Cleanliness is next to godliness. For Christians, cleanliness should be an expression of godliness. This is not to negate the fact that cleanliness is not necessarily an expression of godliness. To be sure, it can be a mask to cover up one's godlessness. But if we are in Christ, we need to believe that the body is the temple of the Spirit, that salvation means health, that Savior means healer. The Bible does not allow us to forget that worship is not just coming together on Sunday and singing the doxology and putting something into the offering plates; it is also the constant care of our bodies that we may present ourselves as a living sacrifice. A Christian, therefore, should want to have and maintain good health because he believes it is the will of God.

Let us, therefore, cultivate the consciousness of God's presence in our life because from it will issue the kind of health consciousness our nation truly needs. To be aware of God is to crave both for physical health and spiritual strength. It is a blessing of great value because even when our physical health fails, we can still hope to live triumphantly.

58

Stephen: A Model Layman

Scripture Reading: Acts 6:1-15

In the book of Acts we have a brief account of the progress and the problems of the early church. In spite of the unfriendly and even hostile attitude of the Roman empire toward the early Christians, the church grew by leaps and bounds. The high cost of belonging to the Christian community did not deter Jesus' followers from preserving and propagating the Christian fellowship.

In the case of the Jerusalem church as related in our Scripture lesson, their increase in number led to a problem raised by the Grecians or the Hellenists. In verse 1 we read: "In those days, when the number of the disciples was multiplied, there arose a murmuring of the Grecians against the Hebrews because their widows were neglected in the daily ministration." Here, murmuring is a concomitant of numerical growth: the two seem to be twin realities in the life of the church. When we grow in number, as indeed we do, there are those who will feel that the fellowship becomes less intimate — the person next to us is a stranger, and even when we try to know him as much as possible, the growing size simply makes it difficult, if not impossible, for us to really know each other. So deep within our hearts we are murmuring. In the Jerusalem church, the Grecians felt their widows were being neglected in the daily ministration. Apparently, the distribution of relief and aid to the poor and needy was a day-to-day activity of the church, and somehow a particular group of widows were not getting what they should. So the twelve Apostles called the congregation to a meeting for the purpose of electing seven deacons who would help distribute the relief goods or money, so that the Apostles could continue giving themselves to prayer and to the ministry of the Word of God.

The lucky seven are chosen because they are men of good repute, full of the Spirit and of wisdom. And they all have Greek names — Stephen, Philip, Prochorus, Nicanor, Timon, Parmenas and Nicolas. Now, while we know something about Stephen, we do not have much information about the other six. Of course, tradition says that Nicolas, or Nicolaus, who is number 7 on the list, is the founder of the heretical sect the members of which came to be known as Nicolaitans. Irenaeus, one of the early church fathers, asserts that the Nicolaitans were followers of Nicolaus, one of the seven appointed by the Apostles. "Hippolytus supports Irenaeus and adds that Nicolaus departed from correct doctrine." Tertullian speaks of the lust and luxury of the Nicolaitans. Clement of Alexandria describes the followers of Nicolaus as "lascivious goats" who believed that it was necessary to abuse the flesh. And the author of the book of Revelation condemns three of the seven churches for having been influenced by the Nicolaitans.

If tradition and the church fathers I have cited are correct, then Nicolaus is another sad example of a man with a good beginning but with a tragic ending. And yet, his story is not an exceptional one, for even today we have friends and acquaintances who were once pillars of the church but are now outside any Christian fellowship.

Our consolation, however, is that in every generation there are always men and women like Stephen whose Christian testimony is a source of courage and inspiration. They do not shirk from their Christian commitment even at the risk of their life. They are the real heroes of faith who have found abiding strength in the sure promises of God.

As a layman, Stephen is among the finest the church has ever produced. We read that he is a man of honest report, a man of good repute. His record is not tainted by any shady deal. He has never been accused of immorality or recklessness. He has a clean conscience.

I wonder why the twelve Apostles, in their search for those seven men, placed good reputation on the top of the list of qualifications. Can it be because they were living at a time when the thought of accumulating wealth was debilitating the character of men? Such thought, indeed, was so endemic that many would not mind getting involved in some ticklish moral compromises provided they got some material benefits. Jesus asks rhetorically, "What does it profit a man to gain the whole world but lose his soul?" It is a question which betrays the sordid materialism that often makes man poor towards God. In the book of Proverbs we read that "A good name is to be chosen rather than great riches, and favor is better than silver or gold" (Prov.22:1). In the Bible a good name is often associated with victory over the seductive allurements of wealth. Today, as in the days of Stephen, we need people of good repute.

Stephen, furthermore, is a man full of the Holy Spirit. To him God is real. That is one experience I covet for all of us — to be filled with God's Spirit, to experience the reality of God's presence.

Today, there are those who claim that the supreme manifestation of God's indwelling presence, the presence of the Holy Spirit, is the ability to speak in tongues. Such a claim is a bit overboard. Speaking in tongues is a gift of the Holy Spirit, but it is not the only manifestation of the Spirit.

The Apostle Paul, in his letter to the Corinthians, declares: "The Spirit's presence is shown in some way in each person for the good of all. The Spirit gives one person a message full of wisdom, while to another person the same Spirit gives a message full of knowledge. One and the same Spirit gives faith to one person, while to another person he gives the power to heal. The Spirit gives one person the power to work miracles, to another, the gift of speaking God's message; and to yet another, the ability to tell the difference between gifts that come from the spirit and those that do not. To one person he gives the ability to speak in strange tongues, and to another he gives the ability to explain what is said. But it is one and the same Spirit who does all this "(1 Cor. 12:7-11).

In other words, we have different gifts and those gifts come from one and the same Spirit. There is, however, one gift which all of us must seriously strive for, and that is the gift of love. This highest of all gifts is what Paul develops in I Corinthians 13 which we now refer to as the hymn of love.

In Chapter 14, Paul concludes his discourse on the subject by saying, "It is love, then, that you should strive for." In this chapter, he says that the gift of proclaiming God's message is, in fact, better than the gift of speaking in tongues because "one who speaks in strange tongues does not speak to others but to God, because no one understands him" (v.2). Paul says, "I would like for all of you to speak in strange tongues, but I would rather that you had the gift of proclaiming God's message. For the person who proclaims God's message is of greater value than the one who speaks in strange tongues . . ."(vs.5). The person who is full of the Holy Spirit will know what special gift God has given him.

Stephen, a man full of the Holy Spirit, is also full of wisdom. Indeed, he has more: in verse 8 we read that he is full of faith and power (or, as we have it in the RSV, he is full of grace and power). To have faith is to know the deepest peace of soul and that is indeed power of the highest quality.

If, in the fierce controversy with the Libertines, Stephen is able to remain sober, it is because deep within him is the staying power of faith. And if, at his death, he prays for the forgiveness of his murderers, it is because his heart is big enough to overcome the perfidy of his adversaries. His faith has made him a conqueror.

What a blessing it will be for us to be full of faith and grace for then we will have power to resist the corrupting influence of society. Without those gifts we can never hope to live victoriously; we will only be swayed by the winds of avarice and greed.

At this point, we need to note that to be filied with the Spirit and wisdom and grace and faith is not to be exempt from trials and tribulations. The truth is that one's faithful services even to God may only provoke some to jealousy or envy. This was the case with Stephen. His enemies bribed some people to accuse him of blasphemy against Moses and against God. Moses was the symbol of their nationalism, and they made it appear that an attack on their nationalism was tantamount to the desecration of God's holy name.

Today, we make the same serious blunder: the blunder of trying to contain God within the shallow pitcher of nationalism, or within the walls of the denominational church. But we cannot imprison God within our creeds. He is above the state, He is above the church — and we need not be saddened by the erroneous feeling that a criticism of either institution is a blasphemy against God. We should avoid committing sins in the name of patriotism or of religion.

And so for his faithfulness, Stephen was stoned to death. That was the cost of his discipleship. That is why Jesus does not allow us to forget that to follow Him is to take up the cross. Jesus Himself faced the mighty forces of persecution and He ended up hanging on a cross. The lesson is clear — we need not be intimidated by brutal and wicked power. For, in the words of Martin Luther,

> A mighty Fortress is our God,
>
> A Bulwark never failing;
>
> Our Helper He amid the flood
>
> Of mortal ills prevailing.

> The Prince of Darkness grim,
> We tremble not for him;
> His rage we can endure,
> For lo! his doom is sure,
> One little word shall fell him.

When Stephen was brought to the Sanhedrin, an ecclesiastical court, for the trial, they that sat at the council, gazing at him, noticed that his face "was like the face of an angel." We may interpret that to mean that his was a picture of poise, gentleness, and kingly dignity. There was no trace of strain or hate on his countenance; his face was radiant with peace and faith. Moses had the same experience when he talked with God on Mt. Sinai. His face shone like the face of an angel and the people noticed it. On the mount of Transfiguration, Jesus' face shone like the sun and three of His disciples saw it.

Even today we see people who reflect the light that they have caught. For nature is such that we simply catch the light of the things that we live with and, quite naturally, we radiate the glory and the joy which dwell within our souls. Of course, if within us there is nothing but gloom and hate and despair, we cannot help but create a gloomy atmosphere, for we can give only that which we have. In the beautiful words of Theodore P. Ferris, "If our inner life is a mass of merging shadows, those shadows are projected into the world around us until they finally hide the sun. If our inner life is illuminated by a light caught from the perpetual Light, that light is thrown upon the world we live in until even a cross is circled with glory. If the fashion of our countenance is a twisted pattern of gloom mingled with resentment, the burden we are bearing will not only be heavy but unbearable. If the fashion of our countenance is altered so that it becomes the image of bravery and beauty, the burdens will somehow be altered into things bravely and beautifully borne."[1]

Stephen's message is that every crisis in life can be an opportunity to radiate the beauty of God's peace; and the trying moments of our souls can be the occasions for others to see in us the face of an angel.

There is one interesting lesson in the life of Stephen which we should not overlook. He began as a server of tables, as one of the humble relief distributors. But he ended as a great Christian martyr whom the world will long remember. That is usually the story of great men. "Jesus began as a

---

[1] *Interpreters' Bible,* Acts, p. 96f.

teacher in the local synagogue. He ended as the Savior of the world. Paul began as a man struck blind on the Damascus road. He ended as the man who turned the world upside down. Wesley began as a single convert who saw the light of God in Christ. He ended as the man who took the world for his parish."[1] In the business world and in the other areas of life, do we not find many similar cases?

So Stephen began as a table server. There was a need in the church of Jerusalem, and Stephen rose to meet it. Had it not been for that emergency which required the assistance of seven men, Stephen's potentialities might have remained dormant within him and the church would not have discovered a saint and a martyr.

I find this episode in the life of Stephen particularly significant because it can be applied in our congregations. Because of the nature of our ministry, we, every now and then, are in need of some people who can help in some humble ways — in ushering, for instance, or in presiding over the service. Sometimes, the need is for help in folding the bulletins or in distributing the same as worshippers come.

And yet, in many cases, those little opportunities for service become the gateways to great and lasting service in the Kingdom of God. We just can never tell how far our people can go once they are challenged to meet the need of the church and to make their help available in times of emergencies.

Certainly, we can learn much from the example of Stephen. Like him, we can be full of God's Spirit and grace and faith, so that the lowly needs of the church and of the country may lead us to the wide avenues of self-giving and self-fulfillment. Then we shall have courage for the living of these days — the courage which will never leave us even in the face of danger and death.

---

[1] *Interpreters' Bible*, Acts, p. 92f.

59

O Man Greatly Beloved

Scripture Reading: Daniel 10:10-21

In the King James Version, Daniel 10:19 reads: "O man greatly beloved, fear not: peace be unto thee, be strong, yea be strong..."

These were the words of an angel to Daniel who came to him in one of his visions. The angel here is God's special messenger, and his message is therefore a message from God. Said message was of course intended for Daniel, but it may well be the message for the men and women of every generation. In fact, the same message comes from the heart of the gospel and has a special relevance for us these days.

Consider first of all God's reassuring love for man. In the words of our text, "O man greatly beloved . . ." This theme is the peculiar note not only in the book of Daniel; it is the ringing message of the entire Scriptures. Man is greatly beloved of God. Our God is a loving God.

This assertion becomes more arresting when we remember that there is nothing lovely in man that deserves the love of God. In fact, the Bible is equally uncompromising in its emphasis on the sinfulness of man. The story of Adam and Eve, for instance, is the story of a couple who did not truly appreciate the goodness of their Creator. They were given everything they needed in Paradise, they had no reason to doubt the ultimacy of God's Word, and yet they gave in to the serpent's seductive promises. And their fall has become the lot of all mankind.

Or take the case of Cain and Abel. Abel was a shepherd while Cain was a tiller of the soil. One day the two brothers worshipped God with their offerings. Abel brought the firstlings of his flock and Cain offered the best fruits of his farm. But when jealousy and envy got hold of Cain, he struck his brother Abel to death, and thus became the father of all murderers.

The utter sinfulness of man is graphically illustrated in the story of Ahab who grabbed the land belonging to Naboth, and in the story of David who sent Uriah to the battlefield so he could possess Uriah's wife,

Bathsheba. And in the story of Herod who was so consumed by insecurity that he ordered the mass execution of children two years old and below.

And what about the rivalry and bickering among the disciples? We will recall that while Jesus was talking about His impending death, His disciples were debating on who among them would be on His right and left sides in the Kingdom of God. Even the physical presence of our Lord did not prevent them from engaging themselves in the pursuit of selfish interests.

Then of course there is the church herself. Who can deny that the church has the marks of sin and pride? She who is called to be the body of Christ is often torn by internal politics and fanaticism; she who is called to be one is sadly divided; she who is called to be apostolic is often remiss in her missionary endeavors; she who is called to be holy is sometimes scandalized by the moral laxity of those who manage her affairs.

Actually we need not go too far to see the sinfulness of man. We only need to look at ourselves and, when we are honest enough, we will not deny the ugliness of our souls and the impurities of our thoughts. Even our best motives are tainted by our prejudices and colored by our interests. The things we ought to do we do not, and the things we should not do, we do. At times our spirits might be willing but our flesh is weak, or our intentions may be good but our approaches are not. And sometimes even as we worship God we are actually only worshipping ourselves.

And yet the gospel emphatically declares that God loves us. He loves us as we are. We are His children and the people of His pasture. He cares so much that He sent His only begotten Son to assure us that we belong to Him not only by virtue of our creation but also by virtue of our redemption. Unmistakably, the nature of God is love.

"O man greatly beloved." How we need to know that truth. When friends and loved ones forget us, and our enemies heap their hatred upon us; when circumstances conspire to make our life a foretaste of hell; when the light flickers and the sun and the moon and the stars seem to disappear in the sky, it helps us to know that God cares and that He loves us with an everlasting love.

Now, the certainty of God's love has some very vital, helpful effects. For one thing, it delivers us from fear. It enables us to be courageous. One of the immediate results of God's presence is the banishment of fear. When the angel appeared to the shepherds to announce the birth of Jesus, he said,

"Fear not, for behold, I bring you glad tidings of great joy." In the gospel of Mark, we have the story of Jairus whose daughter was very sick. He asked Jesus to come to his house so that the damsel might be healed. But before they could reach the house, they were met by the servants who said that his daughter had just died. No one could ever imagine the terrible sense of loss that gripped Jairus' heart. But Jesus told him, "Be not afraid, only believe."

The disciples were out in the sea fishing. Suddenly, they saw a man coming their way, walking on the water. They were greatly terrified "and cried out for fear" (Matt. 14:26). Whereupon Jesus said, "Be of good cheer; it is I; be not afraid." Fear is our number one enemy. In the book of Genesis we read that when man broke God's commandment, he was afraid and hid himself among the trees in the garden. The Apostle Paul calls death as our last enemy, and since we are afraid of death, fear is therefore our first and last enemy.

Dr. Basil King, in his book *The Conquest of Fear*, has a paragraph that may well describe our own situation. He writes:

> When I say that during the most of my life I have been the prey of fear, I take it I am expressing the case of most people. I cannot remember a time when dread of one kind or another was not in the air. In childhood it was the fear of going to bed; later it was the fear of school; still later it was the experience of waking in the morning with a feeling of dismay at the amount of work that had to be done before night. In some form or other fear dogs every one of us. The mother is afraid for her children; the father is afraid for his business; most of us are afraid for our job. There is not a home or an office, a school or a church, in which some hangdog apprehension is not eating at the hearts of the people who go in and out. I am ready to guess that all the miseries wrought by sin and sickness combined would not equal those we bring on ourselves through fear. We are not sick all the time. We are not sinning all the time. But most of us are always afraid—afraid of something or somebody.[1]

Let us recall that legend about a peasant who was driving into town.

---

[1] *Treasury of Sermon Illustrations*, p. 123.

He was hailed by a woman who asked for a ride. Along the way, he asked her who she was, and she answered she was the plague, Cholera. She further told him that she was going to town to kill ten people. The peasant had wanted to push her out, but she assured him that she would not kill more than ten, and that should she break her promise, he then could kill her. When they reached town, they parted ways, and after some time the peasant heard that 100 people died. When he met the woman on the street, he drew his dagger to kill her, but she lifted up her hands and said, "I did not break my promise, did I?" The peasant said, "I heard one hundred people died." "That's correct," replied the woman; "but I killed only ten, the others died of fear."

We know from our own experience that fear has a crippling effect. It can prevent us from witnessing to the truth. It can numb our spirit and paralyze our will. It can spell our death. But the men and women who know the love of God can rise above the tumults of life, for God has not given them the spirit of fear, "...but of power and of love, and of a sound mind" (II Tim. 1:7).

"O man greatly beloved, fear not: peace be unto thee..." That is another blessing that comes from the love of God — peace. God surrounds us with His love. He also grants us His peace.

This is not to say that those who know the love of God will be spared from life's miseries and difficulties. Jesus speaks of the cross, of the storms and the winds and the rains that come upon our life. The peace, which Jesus gives, is inward peace, the strength of character that equips us to face the most terrifying experiences. It is peace of soul that cannot be disturbed by pain and suffering. It is peace of mind that cannot be destroyed by perplexities and uncertainties.

That is the peace we must covet for ourselves and for the world — not just the absence of war, not just the prevalence of order, but also the experience of spiritual tranquility. The peace that God gives transcends human understanding.

Finally, when we experience the love of God we will also become strong. In the words of our text, "O man greatly beloved, fear not; peace be unto thee, be strong, yea be strong." This is the same assurance given by the Apostle Paul in his first letter to the Corinthians. He writes, "Be watchful, stand firm in your faith, be courageous, be strong. Let all that you do be done in love." (1 Cor. 16:13-14).

How do we become strong? The answer is hinted in our text. Love makes us strong. Strength is neither generated by positive thinking nor affected by tranquilizers. It is produced by love. To be sure, there can be no strength, in the biblical meaning of the word, apart from love. In the words of Prof. Paul Tillich, "Without love he who is strong becomes a law for the weak. And the law makes those who are weak even weaker. It drives them into despair, or rebellion, or indifference. Strength without love destroys, first others, then itself. . . One cannot be strong without love... Strength without love leads to separation, to judgment, to control of the weak. (But) love reunites what is separated; it accepts what is judged; it participates in what is weak, as God participates in our weakness, and gives us strength by His participation."[1]

In other words, the strength we are longing for is not the kind that is derived from might, for that kind of strength can be brutal, merciless, vindictive, and even unjust. The strength we need can come only from a compassionate heart, from the faith that love is stronger than hate. It is the strength that builds human relationships, that transcends animosities and petty rivalries, that preserves the dignity and beauty in the family of mankind. It is, in the words of Martin Luther King, the strength to love.

Today, we need to be reassured that God truly loves us. Let there be no doubt about that. Once we realize that fact, we need not be afraid though we walk through the valley of the shadow of death. Because God loves us, we will have peace even when the storms come and the rains descend and the winds blow. Because He loves us we will have strength — the strength to live with courage and conviction, the strength to hope even when the odds are against us, the strength to give and to forgive, and the strength to love even the unlovely. "Fear not, peace be with you; be strong, and of good courage."

---

[1] Paul Tillich, *The Eternal Now*, p. 153f.

60

Heroes or Villains?

Scripture Reading: Mark 2:1-12

Ellinwood-Malate Church was part of an inter-congregational group called *Paglingap* Ministry, a ministry to political detainees. This program was phased out when we were told there were no more political detainees, but I was quite active in the implementation of that ministry. Every time we visited those detainees, many of whom were the top leaders of the communist movement in the country, we would cheer them up with some canned goods and cigarettes and with our prayers, hoping to break what we thought was the nagging monotony of their life in jail. Ironically, every time we visited them, they cheered us up instead. With all the pride they could muster, they would show us the pictures they had painted, the things they had made out of wood, the surroundings they had improved. They would even recite with feelings the poems they had written and sing the songs that they had composed. Each visit we made became a source of inspiration.

And after each encounter, the question that often haunted us was: What is it that enables them to transcend the sordidness of their situation? What enabled their faith in their cause to be so strong that it cannot be crushed by even the harshest treatment? Sometimes, I feel that if we in the church had even only half of their commitment, Christianity in this land will be unrivaled as a revolutionary movement that seeks to win people to Jesus Christ.

From where does the power of insurgency come? Dr. Feliciano Cariño, Professor of Christian Ethics at the Philippine Christian University and now General Secretary of the National Council of Churches in the Philippines, reflecting on this very question, writes: "The power of insurgency, first of all, comes from the manner in which it is able to identify and then grasp the depth of the inhuman condition under which the masses of people in our society have suffered through the ages . . . Insurgency is an icon of the intolerable and violently dehumanized condition in which so many of our people live, whether in the urban sectors or in the countryside, and mirrors in a very profound way the essential heartlessness of our social order in regard to their plight. It grasps the grinding poverty, the ignominious material condition of the life of the masses, the inhuman quality of their existence, and the manner in which they have been prevented from realizing their full development as human beings amidst the scandalous luxury and opulence in which a few are permitted to live." In short, the root cause of insurgency is social injustice. And when its victims decide to put an end to their miseries, they will face even the mightiest army in the world to uphold their human dignity, and to demand for their rightful share in the fruits of the land.

Prof. Cariño further states: "What insurgency signifies is the conviction that the power for redemption comes from those who have been the victims of oppression themselves. The power of insurgency is the power of the dispossessed and the disinherited. It is the power that comes from centuries of suffering and deprivation. It is the power that comes from those who have little else to give except their bodies and their lives. It is the power that comes from those who have no armies to command and to protect except the armies which they themselves could put up and command. It is the power of those with no way of ventilating their views or problems, or controlling opinion about them. It is the power of those who have little or no wealth with which to buy or peddle influence."[1] Hence we can call it the power of intense desire to liberate themselves from the bondage of oppression and suffering.

In our Scripture reading, four men who brought a paralytic to Jesus did something which society would not easily approve of. Jesus was healing so many people in a private home, and when those four men could not go through because of the crowd, they went to the roof. How they did it we are not told, but they went up there, directly above where Jesus was. They made a hole in the roof big enough to let down the pallet on which the paralytic lay. Vandals — that's what we would call them. They destroyed the roof and they probably would not repair it. The owner of the house had every reason to go to the police and to report that act of vandalism. In a civilized society you cannot just rip off somebody else's roof.

But, of course, we know that to Jesus, what the four men did was not vandalism at all — it was an act of faith. It was their faith that Jesus saw, and it was their faith that moved Jesus to heal the paralytic.

---

[1] *Kalinangan,* December 1986, pp. 4ff.

The point is that an act of faith can be mistaken for pure vandalism. What may look like simple rebellion may actually be an act of liberation. It takes Christian understanding to realize that what we hold to be true may be tainted by some errors, and that the errors of our enemies may yet contain some truths.

Let us recall what happened when Jesus healed a man possessed with evil spirits (as recorded in Mark, chapter 5). Jesus asked him, "What is your name?" He answered, "My name is Legion" — or Mob. Meaning, there were so many spirits possessing the man. Now there was a large herd of swine in the region — about two thousand pigs in all — and when the spirits left the man they entered the pigs; and the pigs were so frightened they ran to the precipice, rushed down the side of the cliff into the lake and were drowned. And how did the people in the community react? They did not even notice the man who got healed. They were so worried about the economic implication of Jesus' healing ministry that they asked him to leave. To them preserving economic stability was infinitely more important than the healing of the devil-possessed man.

To complete the picture, let us also recall the cleansing of the Temple where Jesus turned the tables upside down. He charged the people of converting the house of prayer into a den of robbers. He drove the money-changers out, and thus created a commotion seldom seen in Jerusalem. That must have made him a marked man in the eyes of the military for being a threat to the peace and order of the city.

Thus, the Christian faith may sometimes appear quite radical. For the truth is that it is a radical faith. Its author and founder was considered anathema by the religious establishment because he would not allow himself to be circumscribed by their empty traditionalism and their cold legalism. Finally charged as a rebel who had wanted to become the King of the Jews, Jesus ended up hanging upon the cross.

The Christian faith has a certain dynamism that can defy even the spectre of death. It was that dynamism which propelled the great missionary movements in history. For how else can we explain the courage of those missionaries who left the comfort of their homes to live with peoples of different and sometimes hostile cultures? How can we explain their supreme eagerness to witness to the love of God even at the cost of their lives? We see it as the work of their faith, as the happy result of commitment and dedication to the highest purposes of life as revealed by God through Jesus

Christ our Lord. In the words of the Apostle Paul, it was faith that made them more than conquerors.

We must long for the same experience in our day: an experience of liberation from the hold of traditionalism and fanaticism and fear. It is the experience of venturing in faith unto the highways of life, of giving ourselves to the building of an enduring brotherhood based on love and justice and service. It is the joyous experience of bringing the sick in mind, body and soul to the healing touch of the great Lover of mankind.

But now we must also point out that while acts of faith can be mistaken for vandalism and radicalism, radicalism and its various expressions, including vandalism and even rebellion, should not be too easily identified with faith. It is like love which expresses itself in giving, and yet giving is not necessarily an expression of love. If faith can be radical, Satan can also be radical. In fact, Satan can be even more radical. Vandalism can be a symptom of a sick mind or a distorted sense of values. Christians do not have a monopoly of dedication. The enemies of God can be equally dedicated to the pursuit of their devilish schemes. Their success is often due to their admirable spirit of commitment.

This is what Nehemiah is telling us in the book that bears his name. He undertook the rebuilding of the walls of Jerusalem. He led a group of civic-spirited men in the restoration of the precious walls. But some of the citizens became insanely jealous. They invited him to come down from the hill where work was being done in order that they might have some kind of a dialogue. But Nehemiah perceived that they were intending to do him harm, and he refused to go. Four times they invited him to come, and four times he refused to go. So they decided to send him the following letter which read: "It is reported among the nations. . . that you and the Jews intend to rebel; that is why you are rebuilding the wall. You also wish to become their king . . . and that you have set up prophets to proclaim that you are a king in Judah. So now come, and let us take counsel together."

Can we imagine Nehemiah, one of the Old Testament prophets, being charged with rebellion? That he was planning to stage a coup? That he wanted to become the president of Judah? But let us forget that for a while. The point is that Nehemiah's enemies were very patient: they would not easily give up. They went to the extent of fabricating charges against an innocent man to stop him from rebuilding the walls. Many of us Christians do not have that kind of patience, that spirit of persistence in accomplishing the goals that we have set. The conflict between right and wrong, between truth and falsehood, between good and evil, is often a test on which of them is more persevering. There are times when the victory of evil and falsehood can be attributed to the persistent courage and determination of the evil doers as compared with the faltering commitment and lack of consistency on the part of the pious. We would do well to remember that the destroyers of our peace and the agents of exploitation can be more aggressive and more patient than many Bible-carrying and church-going people.

Going back to the story of the paralytic who was brought to Jesus, Jesus, upon seeing the faith of his friends, told him, "My son, your sins are forgiven." Well and good, his sins were forgiven. But he was brought there not for the forgiveness of his sins, but for the healing of his body. Eventually his sickness was also cured, but it was preceded by the forgiveness of his sins. Jesus wanted him to realize the priority of his spiritual needs over his physical and material needs.

Today, we have the opportunity to bring to Jesus not only our own personal needs but also and especially the needs and agonies of our fellow men. Because of our eagerness to be of help to them, we may, in the process, be tempted to destroy somebody else's roof — not because we love to do it, not because we are vandals, but because it seems it is the only option left. In order that such an act may not be construed as rebellion without a cause, it is important that we cultivate our faith in the sufficiency of Jesus' grace and in the boundlessness of His mercy. For after all, it is only Christ who can rescue us from the abyss of cynicism and bitterness. His healing touch can mend our broken hopes and revive our broken spirits. It can nurture the seeds of love in our hearts and make us more daring.

61

God's Patience and Ours

Scripture Reading: Jeremiah 12:1-6

The prophet Jeremiah is very much upset by the flourishing wickedness in society. Although he admits the righteousness of God in dealing with his complaints, he cannot help but complain some more. For instance, he asks, "Why are wicked men so prosperous? Why do dishonest men succeed?" Obviously, Jeremiah is getting impatient with the workers of iniquity. He is scandalized by their continuing prosperity. And in his desire to cleanse society of such kind of people, he prays to God, saying: "Drag these evil men away like sheep to be butchered; guard them until it is time for them to be slaughtered" (Jer. 12:3b). In fact, Jeremiah is getting a bit impatient with God who does not seem to mind what is happening in the land.

The case of Job is perhaps even more telling. He is known to be courageous and persevering. We will recall that after losing his wife and children he still has the courage to say, "Though he slays me, yet will I trust in Him". But he seems to have reached the bottom of his resources when, in Chapter 6, he cries out and says, "Why won't God give me what I ask? Why won't he answer my prayer? If only he would go ahead and kill me! If I knew he would, I would leap for joy, no matter how great my pain" (vss. 8 & 9). Here is a man who wants to end his suffering, and death seems to be the only way left. In deep anguish he says — and his words are loaded with hopelessness — "What strength do I have to keep living? Why go on living when I have no hope? Am I made of stone? Is my body bronze? I have no strength left to save myself; there is nowhere I can turn for help" (vss.11-13).

These experiences of Jeremiah and of Job may have some relevance to us because they reflect our own experiences in this world of sin and greed. We too grow impatient, perhaps more easily, when things do not come up the way we expect them. Moments of despair, pain or disappointment may give way to destructive thoughts and evil plans unless, by God's grace, they are overcome by long-suffering love.

This long-suffering love, a phrase which appears in the 13th chapter of First Corinthians, is, in the Revised Standard Version, translated as patience. We are, of course, aware that the word **patience** in the New Testament, has at least two meanings: one is the ability to endure, or to stand firm in the face of difficulties and sufferings, to hold on until the end. The other meaning is used in relation to time — to wait faithfully and calmly, trusting that God will bring his purposes to pass, and knowing that to worry about anything will not solve it any quicker. In the Old Testament, the word **patience** acquires a deeper meaning when used to describe the nature of God. In Exodus 34, there is a verse which speaks of God as "merciful and gracious, slow to anger, and abounding in steadfast love and faithfulness" (v.6). Here the words "slow to anger" are a translation of the Hebrew word for patience. God is all-powerful and can destroy the sinners anytime, but He does not do it because, in the words of Exodus, He is slow to anger. He is not in a hurry; He waits for the appointed time.

Bishop Stephen C. Neill, in his book on being a Christian, has this very interesting paragraph:

> God is not in a hurry in working out his purpose for mankind. He was prepared to take two thousand years, from Abraham to John the Baptist, to prepare the people of Israel for the coming of His Son. There were long periods in which nothing at all seemed to be happening. There were nearly four hundred years between the Old Testament and the New. Important things were happening in history, but not one new prophet spoke until John the Baptist appeared. And still God waited; and "when the time had fully come, God sent forth his Son" (Gal. 4:4).[1]

The modern man, however, is often in a hurry. He forgets that God created a world in which things move at their natural pace. When he is unable to accept this fact, he develops high blood pressure and becomes difficult to get along with. We need to remember it takes years to grow a tree, that every man should pass through every stage of childhood and boyhood before becoming a man; that great harm is done to a child when he is forced to grow more quickly than he really can.

To live victoriously and fruitfully, we need the virtue of patience. This is what the Bible strongly recommends. In the parable of the weeds (Mat. 13:24-43), the servants are in a hurry, and they want to pull up the

---
[1] Stephen C. Neill, *The Difference in Being a Christian*, p. 60.

weeds. But the Master is wiser. He advises them to wait until harvest time when they can easily distinguish the good grains from the bad. Jesus is like that. He gives us time to repent. How patiently He deals with His disciples. They are sometimes slow and cannot comprehend His words. But He is patient with them.

Certainly, we need the virtue of patience. For one thing, we need it in relation to ourselves. St. Peter, in his Epistle (2 Pet 3:18), encourages us "to grow in grace." But it takes time to grow in grace. Bishop Neill says, "Many Christians make the mistake of thinking that they can arrive at the end of their journey almost before they have begun it." There is wisdom in the words of the prophet Isaiah, "He that believeth shall not make haste" (Isa. 28:16). This means that he shall not "get in a flurry of excitement." The late President Quezon meant the same thing when he told his driver one day, "Please drive slowly because we are in a hurry."

Let us emphasize here that to be patient with ourselves is not to become lackadaisical and to succumb to the mediocre. To be patient with ourselves does not mean we should allow any rationalized form of laziness. On the contrary, we have to keep our integrity and subject all our acts to the scrutiny of Christian love. This means we have to do our best, and then wait for the result of our act. In the book of II Samuel, chapter 18, there is a verse (vs. 24) which says, "Now David was sitting between the two gates." Have you ever wondered what he was doing there? Well, he was waiting. He had sent his army against Absalom. He had done his best in that great war. And now he had to wait for word from the battlefront. Hence he sat between two gates and waited. Like David, there are times when we have to wait, and we must learn to be patient with ourselves.

Secondly, we need to be patient with those about us. In I Thessalonians 5:14, Paul admonishes us "to be patient with them all." The pronoun **them** in this verse refers to the weak, the idle, and the faint-hearted. To be patient with them can be very trying, and yet this is the test to which we are exposed everyday. Paul further reminds us that this virtue is to be sedulously cultivated in the family.

In his letter to the Colossians he says, "Wives, be subject to your husbands, as is fitting in the Lord. Husbands, love your wives, and do not be harsh with them" (3:18,19). The dilemma that we see right away here is that if in the first place the wives do not subject themselves to their husbands, the husbands will find it difficult not be harsh with their wives, and vice versa. In fact, when husbands are harsh with their wives, the wives fight back like tigers and refuse to be subject to their husbands.

Now, this patience with those about us should be applied on our prospective church members. There are some church members who pray almost everyday for the conversion of a friend or a loved one. They want him or her to become officially affiliated with the church. But such conversion, let us note, cannot be hurried up. For one thing, it is the work of the Holy Spirit. And, as we have already noted, God always takes His time. But some earnest Christians are sometimes too anxious to bring others into the fellowship of the church. In their desire to effect a quick decision for Christ, they sometimes resort to intimidation. They tell their prospects that if they don't decide for Christ now, they may have no more chance tomorrow because they may die tonight or meet an accident early in the morning. Would it not be better to allow the seeds of the gospel to sink deeper into the hearts of those prospects and wait for God's own time to harvest? Is it not our experience that when people decide for Christ out of their own volition and not just to please anybody, their conversion is generally more lasting and meaningful? In my hometown, there was a doctor who took 17 years before he submitted himself to baptism, and when he became a church member he even supported me in my seminary studies. I am not saying that we should be easygoing and complacent in evangelism. We should not be haphazard in our duty to witness. In the words of the Apostle Paul, we should be constant in season and out of season. But when our efforts do not bear fruits immediately, when our prayers are not answered favorably, there is no need for us to become impatient and discouraged.

Bishop Neill, in his book I already cited, tells us of the "Lone Star" mission in South India, so named because for 30 years of mission work it won only one convert. Some missionaries suggested that they give up and go somewhere else, but the majority felt they should go on a little longer. They did not succeed with the high caste people, but the so-called outcastes became interested in the gospel and, within a few years, thousands of them joined the church and a strong Christian community was born. Had the missionaries failed in patience, the time for reaping in that area would not have come.

Corollary to being patient with other people is being patient with the world itself. Because of sin, tensions prevail. Nations rise up against nations. Friends betray friends. Graft and corruption abound in high places. Immorality is rampant, and poverty is in every nook and corner of the land. In times like ours, Psalm 37 is a source of comfort: "Fret not yourself because of evildoers...Trust in the Lord and do good... Be still before the Lord and wait patiently for Him." This Psalmist wishes to assure us that history is in God's hands, that "though the cause of evil prosper, yet 'tis truth alone is strong." We can trust that in the final reckoning, righteousness will triumph and wickedness shall perish. In the words of Martin Luther, "Though the world with devils filled, should threaten to undo us, We will not fear for God hath willed His truth to triumph thru us."

Finally, we should be patient with God. Not because He does not seem to care, but because He knows us more than we know ourselves. When we get impatient with God, He reminds us that His ways are not our ways and that His thoughts are higher than our thoughts. He has a different view of things in the world. To Him, a thousand years are but a day, and we would do well to look at life with the eye of our faith in Him.

And when we do that, we realize that to be patient with God is actually to be patient with ourselves, with those about us, and with the world itself. And we realize that in truth, it is God who has been patient with us. He knows the weaknesses of our spirits, He knows the waywardness of our hearts. We cannot hide the impurities of our thoughts, the ugliness of our motives, the devilishness of our ways. Very often, God is afflicted by our willful disobedience to His will, by our slowness of perception, by our indulgence in riotous living. And yet God gives us time, hoping that somehow, someday, we would turn a new leaf, give up some of our consuming selfishness, and take up the shield of faith, humility and love.

62

Come, Everyone

Ho, every one that thirsteth, come ye to the waters, and he that hath no money; come ye, buy and eat; yea, come, buy wine and milk without money and without price.

Wherefore do ye spend money for that which is not bread? and your labor for that which satisfieth not? hearken diligently unto me, and eat ye that which is good, and let your soul delight itself in fatness. — Isaiah 55:1-3

Notice some of the things mentioned in this passage — water, wine, milk. Apparently we have a choice — the children may prefer milk, the young people may just go for plain water, and the more mature people (the *gurang*) may have what we call *inumin ng tunay na lalaki*. But the picture in this passage is not just that of a drinking spree. The mention of bread indicates that there is some eating too. And we hope it is not just bread, but also something that goes along with it — such as Dairy Creme which tastes like butter, bacon, ham, eggs, liver spread, etc. In fact, I think this is what is meant by the phrase *let your soul delight itself in fatness*. People at the time were not yet cholesterol-conscious; they were fond of fatty foods. Hence, we may conclude that God's invitation in this passage is an invitation to a reception, or a fiesta, or a banquet. It is an invitation for us to eat and drink to our heart's content.

We will recall that in the New Testament, Jesus uses this image of a banquet to describe what life is like in the kingdom of God. There is, for instance, the parable of the Great Supper in the gospel of Luke (which is a wedding feast in Matthew). The gospel of John does not have such a parable, but it has an account of Jesus attending a wedding feast (chapter 2). Then there is the sacrament of the Last Supper, where the principal elements are bread and wine. In the resurrection narrative, we have the story of Jesus standing at the shore and shouting at the disciples who had gone back to fishing, "Have you got any food to eat?" In the book of Revelation, Jesus is portrayed as standing at the door, knocking and saying, "If any man hear my voice and open the door, I will come in to him, and will sup with him, and he with Me" (Rev. 3:20). In other words, drinking and eating in the Bible is a symbol of the kind of life we will have in the Kingdom of God — a life of joy, of happiness, of abundance. God's invitation is for us to eat and drink.

Now this invitation is for free. In fact, it is addressed to those who have no money. But here, one may ask: How about those with money? Are they not invited too? A closer look at our text can lead to more questions. Take, for instance, the wording in verse 1— "he that hath no money, come ye, buy and eat." If a person has no money, why ask him to buy? It would be more logical to say: You who have no money, come and get it. Of course, one may remark: Are we not being too impertinent? Is it not enough to presume that God's invitation is for those who have no money? Well, if we accept such presumption — that God is talking to those who have no money — then we must also accept the presumption that in verse 2, the question is addressed to those with money. Verse 2 says, " Wherefore do ye spend money for that which is not bread?" Mere common sense tells us that we cannot spend money if we don't have it.

The question, therefore, is: How do we interpret Isaiah 55? What is it trying to tell us? Part of the answer is to remember that Isaiah 55 is actually a poem. In the King James Version it is written as a prose, but in other modern translations, like the Good News Bible, it is written as a poem. Of course, in the English translation, things like rhyme and meter, present in the Hebrew original, no longer exist. But it is a faithful translation of a Hebrew poem. At any rate, we know that some poems defy logic: a poetical work does not have to be logical. It can be translogical. This is true even in our own literature. We recall, for instance, a favorite Tagalog ballad where a lady, after hearing the supplications of her suitor, tells him:

> *Kung talagang tunay na ako'y mahal mo,*
>
> *Magtanim ka muna ng niyog sa bato;*
>
> *Ngayon din bubunga, ngayon din bubuko,*
>
> *Ngayon din kukuha ng igagata ko.*

We can plant coconut seedling now, but how in the world can we expect it to grown instantly and bear fruits and give us coconut milk right away? Even in this age of instant coffee and instant marriage, we cannot have instant coconut milk according to the prescription of the poem I have just quoted.

In other words, Isaiah 55 is not to be interpreted literally. It is not really talking about water and wine and milk and bread and fatness. Those are but symbols of something deeply spiritual. Isaiah 55 should be understood as God's invitation to a life of fellowship with Him, to the high adventures of living, to a spiritual banquet that can quench our thirst and satisfy our purest longings. The question is not whether we have money or not. That is not the question at all. Isaiah 55 is simply saying that however important money may be, there are things in life which money cannot buy. It can buy books but not wisdom. It can buy tranquilizers and medicines but not peace of soul. It can buy a house but not a home. It can buy chandeliers and pews and candles and church buildings but not salvation. The grace of God cannot be bought, but God offers it to us for free.

The tragedy of our age is the same all through the centuries: we do not always appreciate the free grace of our God. Jesus underscores this point in His parable of the Great Supper. In that parable, the host had invited many guests, but when the day of the feast came, his guests began making excuses. One said he had bought a field and wanted to see it; therefore, he could not come. Another said he had secured five pairs of oxen and wanted to try them; therefore he could not come. Still another said he just got married and therefore, would rather stay home with his wife. Sometimes it is the good things in life that hinder us from coming to God. For what can be more exciting than to have a farm and five pairs of horses or carabaos? What can be lovelier for a person than to be with his or her family? Yet, it is these beautiful and lovely things that sometimes prevent us from having fellowship with God.

But today, we are gathered to honor His invitation. We are here for a spiritual banquet. We are here because we are hungry for the Bread of Life and thirsty for the living water. We are here to delight ourselves in spiritual fatness.

Verse 3 is an important part of God's invitation. It says, "Incline, your ear, and come unto me: hear, and your soul shall live." In the Bible, to incline one's ear or to hear or to listen means to obey. The Bible speaks of those who have ears but cannot hear, referring to those who listen but do not obey. But without obedience, one has not really listened. To hear, in the biblical sense, is also to obey.

Is this not also our problem today? Many Christians are content with mere listening, forgetting the fact that Christian hearing is not complete without action. The Apostle James has words of advice on this regard. He says:

> But be ye doers of the word, and not hearers only, deceiving your own selves. For if any be a hearer of the word, and not a doer, he is like unto a man beholding his natural face in the glass: For he beholdeth himself, and goeth his way, and straightway forgetteth what manner of man he was.
>
> (James 1:22-24)

Hearing and obeying — these are the twin aspects of Christian discipleship. We have not really heard unless we obey. We have not really come unless we go — to wherever God leads us, which is where the action is. Coming to God in worship is not complete unless we go into the world where we are called to witness for Him.

Admittedly this is a tall order. To be doers of the word will require courage and strength. It will demand the best that we have. It will require constant spiritual replenishment. But Jesus has another invitation which is music to our ears. He says, "Come unto me, all ye that labor and are heavy laden, and I will give you rest." Those who labor and are heavy laden are those who are "exhausted and weighted down beneath their burdens." They are those with a crushing weight upon their shoulders, those who are saddled with loads of cares. Perhaps they have difficulties dealing with people, especially with those whom they find to be morbidly insincere, contemptible, arrogant, selfish, ungrateful. Perhaps they have difficulties with themselves — they cannot help but be censorious, bitter, unforgiving, and even violent. Those who labor and are heavy laden may be those who have to live with a prodigal husband or wife, those who are victims of disloyalty or unfaithfulness, those who are being assailed by life's miseries and tribulations. In short, they are those whose problems are sapping their energies and giving them a hell of an experience, causing them to develop ulcer and headaches and tensions.

To those people — and that means all of us — Jesus offers rest, if they will but come to Him. Jesus, in effect, is saying that He can wipe away our tears, can heal the wounds in our hearts, can banish the fears in our souls, can revive our zest for life. Of course, the rest which Jesus offers is not exemption from the fierce battles in life, not the absence of struggles and strifes. It is the recharging of our vitality and strength and the rekindling of our determination so that we may continue to fight the good fight and run the race. It is the refreshment and relief from weariness, so that we may carry on our appointed tasks.

And so, if we are to honor God's invitation, let us make this worship a hallowed time for the reconsecration of our life, and resolve, with God's help, to forgive those who have hurt our feelings; to forsake our own wicked ways and evil thoughts. We should incline our ears to the marching order of the Lord, and face the crises of our age with courage and confidence, believing that they who obey His bidding will never know the pang of failure. Our God has promised that the Word which goeth out of His mouth shall never return unto Him void, but will accomplish that which He pleases.

63

In the Hour of Trial

Scripture Reading: Matthew 4:1-11

Matthew 4:1-11 describes one of the most important events in the life of Jesus. We are inclined to believe that since no one was with Him when He was tempted in the wilderness, the story must have come directly from His lips. The experience was so real that He shared it with His disciples. He was about to enter the public ministry, and He had to decide on how best He could fulfill His mission.

The Scripture says that the temptation of Jesus occurred immediately after His baptism at the River Jordan. Does that not suggest that a great spiritual struggle may come up after a replenishing spiritual experience? To be sure, temptation, like a thief, may come anytime, as it in fact does regardless of our spiritual condition. But the trouble is that we are often unprepared for it during periods of spiritual ecstasy. When inspired and uplifted by our communion with God, we think we are already in heaven where Satan is not present; and we sometimes get annoyed when such ecstasy is suddenly interrupted by anything irritating. But life is such that even our most solemn moments are open to the attacks of the evil one, because communion with God which lifts our souls to heaven does not eliminate the fact that we are still on earth.

Therefore, we must drop the idea that when one becomes a Christian, one becomes free from temptation. Closeness to God does not exempt us from being tempted. As John Bunyan said, "There is a way to hell even from the gates of heaven."

Our Scripture lesson says that immediately after Jesus' baptism He was led by the spirit into the wilderness to be tempted by the devil. And we wonder why the spirit led Him to be tempted. Did not Jesus teach us to pray, "Lead us not into temptation?" How are we to understand the spirit leading us to be tempted?

Perhaps we should recall that in the New Testament, **temptation** meant "trial" or "testing". In John 6:5, we read that Jesus asked Philip where to buy bread for the 5,000 people who followed them, only to prove the disciple. Here the word **prove** (KJV) is often translated as **tempt** (as in the Good News Bible). Again, in II Corinthians 13:5, Paul admonishes us to examine ourselves whether we are in the faith. **Examine** here is also rendered as **tempt** in the newer translation.

Temptation, therefore, is also testing in a real sense. Just as a teacher tests her students at the end of the semester to examine the student's grasp of the subject matter, so God allows us to be tempted by the devil in order to test the strength of our character and the depth of our faith.

Let us look at the first temptation and see how Jesus handled it. The tempter came to Jesus and said, "If thou be the Son of God, command that these stones be made into bread." We must remember that Jesus was thinking of how He could win men to the Kingdom of God, and the thought of winning them over through their stomachs was a very tempting thought. The people were hungry; poverty stalked every nook and cranny of the land, and grief was written clearly on the face of everyone.

Hence, the temptation attacked Jesus along the line of His love for men. Why not, in the name of compassion, turn the stones into bread? That would relieve men of their anxiety about food and clothing, and thus enjoy a happy life. After all, He came that we may have life and have it more abundantly. Would it not be sheer cruelty to allow the people to go hungry when it was within His power to give them bread and to give it soon? Should He not prove His divinity by showing himself the Saviour not only of the soul but also of the body?

It was a very subtle temptation — satanically subtle. But the problem was not as simple as that. Jesus' mission was to win men into the Kingdom of God, but not through their stomachs. If that was the case, what would happen if the harvest is poor and the barn is empty? What if the storm destroys the crops and the well goes dry? Would that be the end of men's loyalty and of divine reality? Is not history itself the graveyard of all movements inspired only by the prospect of material gain?

And what about those who are wallowing in wealth, and whose barns are full? The great and the affluent, the capitalists and the businessmen and those who have enough to keep body and soul together? What will attract them to the Kingdom of God if it is nothing but a program of economic sufficiency? They may even taunt Jesus and say: What do we care, we have enough and more than enough; and, if we only want to, we can also give people not only bread but also lots and houses.

Thus, in the first temptation, we see that material prosperity should not be easily identified with divine favor. It is not necessarily a proof of God's blessing or a sign of godliness. We only need to look at those who have gained economic security through wicked schemes to understand that to have bread is not necessarily to have Christ. But he who has Christ has something more than bread, for Christ is the Bread of Life.

Now, the second temptation. Having brought Jesus to the highest point of the Temple in the Holy City, the devil said, "If you are God's Son, throw yourself down, for the scripture says: God will give orders to his angels about you; they will hold you up with their hands, so that not even your feet will be hurt on the stones." Clearly, this is the "lure of the spectacular." For what can be more startling than jumping from the pinnacle of a temple without getting hurt because the heavenly hosts were there to bear Him up? That would draw people into Himself and, capitalizing on their awe and admiration, He could sweep them all into the Kingdom of God. But Jesus' answer was brief and to the point: "It is written again, Thou shalt not tempt the Lord thy God."

Spectacularism therefore was out of the question. And that is why Jesus, after healing some people of their malignant diseases, advised them not to tell anyone about it. For if people followed Him because He could heal the sick and raise the dead, what guarantee was there of their constancy in faith when the show was over and the curtains had been put down? And what about those who would grow tired of seeing the same miracle over and over again? Certainly, spectacularism was as unstable as the sand. Anything built on it would not withstand the storms of competition. For there are those who don't believe in angels but can jump from a cruising aircraft with their parachutes. No, said Jesus. Men should not be won into the Kingdom of God by luring them with something spectacular.

But there is something more in the second temptation, and that is this — the desire to put God to a test. If Jesus was the Messiah, should not God protect Him from falling? The argument sounds logical and betrays the cleverness of the tempter. It also betrays our own weakness. Sometimes we ourselves cannot resist the desire to test God. We justify it by saying it would clear our doubts, but at the back of our mind we only wish to force God to act. And we even prescribe the way God should act.

Let me illustrate this. A devout Christian knows that in a certain area of the country, rough citizens and die-hard criminals are on the loose. Yet, he goes there just the same to test his belief that righteous people are sure of God's protection wherever they may be. It is not until he goes home without his pocket book and with bruises on his face that he begins to realize that stupidity can be mistaken for Christian courage. Or take the case of an adventurous, independent missionary. He feels called to preach the gospel in a foreign land, but all he has is a one-way plane ticket and a bundle of clothes. He goes with the hope that God will supply his needs, but somehow through hard lessons he discovers that God's mission deserves more planning and more common sense. Or take the case of a local church that engages in a building project. The people feel that because it is the house of God that they are building, God will somehow send the bricks and the lumber and the cement. But to their disappointment, God seems to be taking time, and although at long last the bricks and the lumber and the cement come, God does not do it the way they want Him to.

How often do we dare test God in similar ways? Is it not appallingly presumptuous of us to pretend we have enough wisdom to put God to the test? And yet this is what we often do — we pray not that we may hear God's voice, but that we may hear ourselves speak. We worship not that we may be equipped to resist temptation, but that we may be exempted from the fight. We come to God not that He may test us, but that we may test Him. Such religion which is bent on testing God rather than trusting Him is most definitely a perversion of Christianity.

Now let us examine the third temptation — the temptation for Jesus to win men into the Kingdom of God through political power. The devil took Him to the highest mountain and showed him all the kingdoms of the world, and said: "All these I will give thee, if thou wilt fall down and worship me." In other words, the thought crossed His mind that if He only had all the kingdoms of this world, He could unite all people under His leadership and thus win them into the Kingdom of God.

It was a tempting idea because, after all, the people were looking for a king like David who would free them from the yoke of Roman domination. Their concept of the Messiah was that of a political and military leader, and their deepest national aspiration was to gain political independence.

Thus, the third temptation attacked Him along the line of His patriotic spirit. He knew that God has not willed that men should rule over other men, that one nation should be the slave of another nation. Would it not be fulfilling the will of God by giving independence to whom independence was due? Another very subtle temptation. But Jesus dismissed it because He understood the deceptiveness of the idea. Men's loyalty cannot be guaranteed by political power. On the contrary, political power, if not subordinated to God, can only lead to moral bankruptcy and spiritual nihilism.

There is something more in the third temptation and that is the desire to compromise. Of course, to compromise is not necessarily objectionable. Christian ethics speaks of legitimate compromises. Our daily life is characterized by compromises. Many labor disputes are settled by compromises. Business transactions are often forged through compromises. The formation of the United Church of Christ in the Philippines was effected through compromises. Surely, there are legitimate and necessary compromises we have to make.

But when our faith in God is being challenged, when we cannot secure a cup of stew unless we give up our birthright, when we cannot marry unless we renounce our religion, when we are asked to forget our principles in exchange for some political favors, then certainly, such kind of compromising is diabolical. It has no place in the Christian life which is a life of total commitment to the sovereignty of God. Jesus would not want us to compromise that way.

This is why when Jesus appeared in Palestine, Rome girded herself to fight Him to death. Rome could tolerate other gods and goddesses, but not the God of Jesus Christ. When the religions of Cybele and Osiris and the other gods and goddesses came to Rome, Rome welcomed them with open arms because they were content to live together and share the honor. But when Jesus came, He preached about the purity and perfection of God, about the high quality of discipleship that condemns every form of wickedness and greed and pride. Jesus did not want His followers to compromise in that sense, even at the cost of their life.

To many of us, the third temptation may not come in such gigantic fierceness, but it does come to us in various and milder forms. When we try to serve both God and mammon, when we want to please Satan and at the same time keep our friendship with God, when we aspire for power but run away from responsibility — in short, when we use the label of a Christian but refuse to carry the cross, we are actually reducing Christianity into a cobweb of illegitimate compromises. To guard against such an evil, we must constantly bear in mind that Christ demands our all and that friendship with Him means total war against His enemies.

And so Jesus, in the wilderness, was tempted — but He did not yield to temptation. In our case, the test is still going on, and we pray we may not fail in the hour of trial. Jesus gives us a clue as to the secret of His strength — His ultimate acquaintance with the Holy Scripture. So if we are to experience the abiding strength which can withstand the lure of sin, we, too, must be nurtured in the Word of God. But being nurtured in the Holy Scripture is not just knowing the Bible from cover to cover; it is knowing in our life the sustaining presence of Jesus Christ, who is the living Word of God. With Him, we can conquer. With Him, we will overcome.

64

Poor Man, Rich Man

Scripture Reading: Luke 6:20-26

In the Lucan version of the Sermon on the Mount there seems to be some discrimination against the rich and an apparent preferential treatment of the poor. In verse 20, Jesus says, "Happy are you poor; the Kingdom of God is yours." But in verse 24 He says, "But how terrible for you who are rich now; you have had your easy life! How terrible for you who are full now; you will go hungry! How terrible for you who laugh now; you will mourn and weep!" Is the gospel apathetic to the rich?

We will recall that on another occasion Jesus says, "How hard it is for those who have riches to enter the Kingdom of God! For it is easier for a camel to go through the eye of a needle than for a rich man to enter the kingdom of God" (Luke 18:24,25). That figure of speech — a camel going through the eye of a needle — is used in the first three gospels (Matthew, Mark, and Luke) to emphasize the difficulty, nay the impossibility, for rich people to enter the Kingdom of God. The three evangelists must have been impressed by the vividness of such language that all of them recorded it in their gospel accounts.

Furthermore, in the *Magnificat*, Mary, mother of Jesus, praises God "for he has filled the hungry with good things, and the rich he has sent empty away" (Luke 1:53). Is Mary rejoicing over the disappointment of the rich?

The Apostle James, in his Epistle, does not withhold his uncomplimentary remarks on the wealthy. He says, "Listen, my beloved brethren. Has not God chosen those who are poor in the world to be rich in faith and heirs of the kingdom which he has promised to those who love him? But you have dishonored the poor man. Is it not the rich who oppress you, is it not they (the rich) who drag you into court? Is it not they (the rich) who blaspheme the honorable name by which you are called?" (James 2:5-7). Certainly these words are a tirade against the rich. The rich are singled out as oppressors who cause the poor to suffer, and who desecrate the holy name of God. And to complete the humiliation of the rich, the Apostle James, in the final chapter of his Epistle, declaims, "Come now, you rich, weep and how for the miseries that are coming upon you. Your riches have rotted and your garments are moth-eaten. Your gold and silver have rusted, and their rust will be evidence against you and will eat your flesh like fire" (James 5:1-3a). These are strong words which should make the rich tremble.

Before we jump to the wrong conclusion that the Bible has a bias against the rich, we should now cite some passages that speak of wealth as a reward for a person's piety. The first Psalm, for instance, likens the man who walks not in the counsel of the ungodly to a tree planted beside a stream which bears fruit in due season and prospers in all that he does. In Psalm 112, we read: "Blessed is the man who fears the Lord, who greatly delights in his commandments…Wealth and riches are in his house and his righteousness endures forever." This thought — that material prosperity is a sign of God's favor — was quite popular among the Jews in the Old Testament and in the early part of the Christian era. It is possible that even the disciples held fast to this doctrine because when Jesus told them it was easier for a camel to go through the eye of a needle than for a rich man to enter the Kingdom of God, they were so astonished that they asked, "Who then can be saved?"

We must therefore submit that Jesus does not condemn the rich because they are rich. There is no record in the New Testament of Jesus' indifference toward the rich because of their wealth. On the contrary, there is the moving story of Zacchaeus who became rich by cheating the people in taxes and in whose house Jesus lodged. We may imagine that that was the beginning of a lasting friendship between Jesus and the tax collector.

There is also the story of Nicodemus, a doctor of laws who must have done well in his law practice. It was he who came to Jesus by night and the two became good friends. Furthermore, there is the story of Joseph of Arimathea, certainly a man of means. It was he who provided the place for the burial of Jesus' body. The owner of the Upper Room where Jesus and the disciples instituted the Lord's Supper was obviously a rich man. In other words, Jesus also had wealthy friends. We can be sure that whenever He speaks sternly of the rich people, it is not because they are rich; it is because they tend to serve mammon rather than God.

Prof. William Barclay, my favorite New Testament commentator, attaches at least two meanings to the possession of riches: (1) It is an acid test of a man. "For a hundred men who can stand adversity only one man can stand prosperity. Prosperity can so very easily make a man arrogant, proud, self-satisfied, worldly. It takes a really big and good man to be worthy of prosperity." (2) Possessing wealth is a responsibility. We are to give account for the way we secure our possession and how we use it. When wealth becomes the controlling power in our life, when it becomes the master rather than the servant, it will lead to egocentricism and spiritual bankruptcy. It will destroy the citadel of our souls.

In his exposition of the parallel passage in the Gospel of Matthew, Prof. Barclay spells out the perils of wealth in the following terms:

(1) Wealth encourages a false independence. He submits that "If a man is well supplied with this world's good, he is very apt to think that he can well deal with any situation that may arise." In fact, there are those who believe that they can buy happiness as well as their way out of sorrow. And the logical result of such cynical attitude is the illusion that they can get along without God. But, as Dr. Barclay observes, "there comes a time when a man discovers that there are things which money cannot buy, and things from which money cannot save us." It is not until we come to our senses that we realize that in this moral universe we cannot get along without God.

(2) Riches can shackle a man to this world. In Jesus' words, "Where your treasure is, there will your heart be also." If our treasure is in this world, we tend to forget that our true home is one not built by human hands. When wealth shackles us to this earth, it becomes a liability to our souls.

(3) Riches tend to make a man selfish. As someone has observed, "Enough is always a little more than what one has." says Prof. Barclay:

> "Once a man has possessed comfort and luxury, he always tends to fear the day when he may lose them. Life becomes a strenuous and worried struggle to retain the things he has. The result is that when a man becomes wealthy, instead of having the impulse to give things away, very often he has the impulse to cling on to them. His instinct is to amass more and more for the sake of the safety and the security which he thinks they will bring. The danger of riches is that they tend to make a man forget that he loses what he keeps, and he gains what he gives away."[1]

---
[1] Barclay, *Commentary on Matthew*, pp. 240-241.

This emphasis on the danger of wealth, however, does not in anyway imply the undesirability of material possessions. Rather, it underscores the supreme importance of responsible management of wealth. Jesus is not against possessions; He is against possessiveness.

The fact of the matter is that there is danger not only in wealth but also in poverty. For the poor may be morbidly obsessed with the thought of wealth in their frantic effort to achieve economic security and social respectability. Poverty can be a fertile ground for the seeds of criminality and delinquency and even of communism to grow. Or it can make us feel self-righteous precisely because we are not exposed to the arrogance that often accompanies wealth.

And yet there is no glossing over the record; Jesus says, "Happy are you poor; the Kingdom of God is yours!" In what sense are the poor happy or blessed? Is there something sacred or noble in being poor?

The answer, of course, is that there is nothing sacred in being poor, although poverty can be an asset to the soul. In fact, it is not God's will that we be poor. His will is that we may have life and have it more abundantly. But the poor in the Lucan version of the Sermon on the Mount are the poorest of the poor. They have nothing in this world — no bank deposits, no bonds, no properties whatsoever. All they have is God — in Him alone do they put their trust. To Him alone do they look for mercy and help and strength.

But this kind of faith — trusting God with all our hearts and mind and soul — can be cultivated even by those who are not materially impoverished. The middle class and the rich and the super-rich can by God's grace become spiritually mature. This is why in the gospel of Matthew, the Evangelist uses the phrase, "poor in spirit." "Blessed are the poor in spirit," or, as we have it in the Good News Bible, "Happy are those who know they are spiritually poor"(Matthew 5:3). The phrase, "poor in spirit," perfectly describes the nature of a trusting faith in the wisdom of God to govern the universe. To be poor in spirit is to approach God "as penitents and suppliants, beseeching Him to supply our needs, clothe our nakedness, and enrich our poverty." It is to be aware of our inadequacy, of our utter need of God's cleansing grace, and of our absolute dependence upon His love and mercy.

And so we say that in the gospel, poverty is not in itself blessed, and wealth is not necessarily a curse. If Lazarus, in the gospel story, went to heaven, it was not because he was poor, but because he was poor in spirit;

and if Dives went to hell, it was not because he was rich, but because he was too selfish to see the suffering of a beggar at his gate. Poverty in itself is not a virtue, I repeat. There are many poverty-stricken people whose suffering is made more tragic by their inability to accept their lot, and by their rebelliousness against God. But to be poor in spirit is to transcend the advantages and disadvantages of poverty or of wealth; to be poor in spirit is to cling tenaciously to the wings of faith which enables us to have a real foretaste of the life in the Kingdom of God.

The paradox, therefore, is that to be poor in spirit is actually to be rich in spirit. To be poor in spirit is to be spiritually vigorous and strong. To be poor in spirit is the opposite of spiritual poverty or spiritual bankruptcy. It is to be humble in spirit. The Apostle Paul, in his Second Letter to the Corinthians, speaks of this paradox in the following way: "We are treated as impostors, and yet are true; as unknown, and yet well known; as dying, and behold we live; as punished and yet not killed; as sorrowful, yet always rejoicing; as poor, yet making many rich; as having nothing, and yet possessing everything" (6:8b-10).

In the New Constitution there is a pervading concern for the poor and the marginalized members of our society. Such concern is reflected in the various articles of the Constitution. In the Article on Social Justice, for instance — which is one of the new articles in the Constitution — we will find the following provisions that express strong support for the underprivileged:

> Sec. 4. The State shall by law undertake an agrarian reform program founded on the right of farmers and farmworkers, who are landless, to own directly or collectively the lands they till or, in the case of other farmworkers, to receive a just share of the fruits thereof.

> Sec. 6. The State may resettle the landless farmers and farmworkers in its own agricultural estates which shall be distributed to them in the manner provided by law.

> Sec. 7. The State shall protect the rights of subsistence fishermen, especially of local communities to the preferential use of the communal marine and fishing resources, both inland and offshore.

> Sec. 9. The State shall (provide)...decent housing and basic services . .. at affordable cost to underprivileged and homeless citizens in urban centers and resettlement areas.
>
> Sec. 10. Urban or rural poor dwellers shall not be evicted nor their dwellings demolished except in accordance with law and in a just and humane manner.
>
> Sec. 11. The State shall endeavor to provide free medical care to paupers.

This concern for the poor, now embodied in the New Constitution, may well reflect the Christian spirit of solidarity with the poor. For it is that spirit of solidarity with the underprivileged that will save us from the illusion that the solution to the nagging problem of poverty in this land is simply the infusion of agrarian, urban land and natural resources reform. Constitutional and legal remedies are admittedly necessary, but they are not enough. The poor may become rich and the rich may become richer, but if that is all they will get, it is no guarantee that our people will become happier. From the perspective of the Christian faith, our more urgent need is to be poor in spirit, for when we are spiritually healthy, improving the lot of the underprivileged becomes primarily an expression of Christian love and secondarily a compliance with a constitutional mandate.

"Blessed are the poor in spirit; for theirs is the Kingdom of God."

65

Elisha's Faith and Ours

Scripture Reading: II Kings 6:8-23

One of the well-known and beloved 9th century B. C. prophets, whose message is a constant source of strength for troubled times, is the prophet Elisha. He was the successor of Elijah and his story occupies a considerable space in the first thirteen chapters of II Kings. Bible scholars believe that he was a wealthy man, evidenced by the fact that when Elijah called him to the prophetic service, he was in his farm plowing with 12 yokes of oxen. Before leaving his place to be with Elijah, he gave a feast to his people. Ordinarily, it should be the people who should give him a *despedida* party, but obviously it was he who shouldered the expenses at that feast. That was how generous he could be.

Admittedly, the narratives concerning him may have been embellished with folkloric elements. His miracles, for instance, border between tales and history. We recall how he struck the water at Jordan which immediately parted before him; the unspent jar of oil and how such miracle saved the widow's two sons from being taken as slaves in payment of her debts. There was the incident of his staying in the home of a wealthy Shunammite woman whose child had died of sunstroke but was resuscitated by the prophet. Elisha fed a hundred men with twenty loaves of barley and some fresh ears of grain. He healed Naaman, the Syrian army commander, and refused the lavish gifts of his patient. He trained young men to become prophets and when one of them lost an axe head while cutting timber, he caused the axe head to float on water. Not even death could stop Elisha from doing miracles, for when a dead man was put into his grave, the man was revived by the touch of Elisha's bones. As to how much of these was legendary we do not know. But the historical fact which emerges out of these narratives is that Elisha was a great and beloved leader, and that he was lovingly remembered by the members of the prophetic guilds.

The passage covered by our Scripture reading is typical in that whatever legendary elements there may be in the story serve to underscore the historical greatness and the uprightness of the prophet. The passage speaks of how the king of Israel carefully avoids the ambushes prepared for him by the Syrian king, so much so that the Syrian king begins to suspect that someone in his court is spying for the king of Israel. The Syrian couriers deny this and inform the king that it is Elisha who, by some miraculous power, discovers the king's secrets and transmits the same to the Israelites. Whereupon the Syrian chief sends an army to capture Elisha. Elisha's servant is so afraid of the coming Syrian soldiers that he exclaims, "We are doomed, sir! What shall we do?" Elisha tells him to look up, and there he beholds the hillside covered with horses and chariots of fire ready to protect them. The Syrians are smitten with blindness and then led to Samaria. The king of Israel wants to slay them but Elisha objects to such mercilessness. Instead, the prisoners are fed and sent back to their king.

This narrative, which mixes history and legend, gives some insights into the nature of life. Here Elisha may well be the personification of Israel's spiritual foundation or the people's faith in the wisdom of the one sovereign God. We may take him as the symbol of the nation's belief in God as their mighty Deliverer — the faith confirmed in the covenant between Israel and God. Such covenant did not make Israel secure from physical danger from foreign aggression. In fact, her history is replete with wars and threats of war. Her faith in God did not exempt her from being attacked by her enemies. Furthermore, there were times when Israel was besieged by unbelief and her prophets bemoaned the savage godlessness in the land. And yet even when godlessness was rampant and the temples were being desecrated, there were always a few who remained steadfast in their faith and did not lose their confidence in God. They constituted the conscience of the nation and would not be daunted by the wanton paganism in their midst.

Most probably, Elisha belongs to that age when his country was not too helplessly sunk in moral laxity. His greatness may well symbolize the healthy spiritual condition of the people at that time. The readiness of the king to follow his advices may reflect the people's strict loyalty to God's holy commandments. Perhaps that was the secret of their strength — the dominant note in the story of their national survival was not the personality of their king, but the leading of God's Spirit as manifested in the practice of their religion in their daily life. Theirs was a time of peace in spite of the Syrians' attempts to conquer them.

Now, the Syrian king wanted to capture Elisha because to get rid of him was to get Israel into his hands. In other words, the Syrian king knew that by shaking Israel's spiritual foundation he could conquer Israel. Once the people's faith in God was shattered, it would be easy to destroy their fortress.

Is that not the story of many nations? Nations are beset not only by possible attacks from the outside, but also by the decline of their inward spiritual resources. The fall of the Roman Empire is a sad example of how a nation can fall to pieces as a result of internal moral disintegration. Earl Warren, former chief justice of the United States Supreme Court, said that a nation can lose its freedom not only through a direct assault by the enemy but also through erosion.

This slow but sure attack on man's spiritual fortress may come in the form of organized propaganda. For instance, the charge that religion is the opium of the people is not a mere passing criticism, but a deliberate, well planned propaganda to undermine the people's religious faith. And because much of the free world to which the propaganda is directed is populated predominantly by Christians, the propaganda in effect is an attempt to destroy Christianity itself, as a strategy of destroying the free world. The communist leaders may have learned from the Syrian king that by creating a spiritual vacuum, the people may perish from their own folly.

It should be pointed out that this kind of strategy is undertaken only by those who believe, with some sincerity, that military power can subdue man's spiritual strength. In the case of the Syrian king, he sent a large army to capture Elisha. He did not send his priests or his chaplains, if he had any, in the belief that an itinerant preacher like Elisha would easily yield to a battalion of soldiers. The Syrian king must have felt very insecure; otherwise he would not have sent a big contingent just to arrest an unarmed preacher. But history teaches us that when a ruler's cause is no longer valid, even the entire armed forces will find it hard to defend it.

This particular lesson from the history of Israel can be applied to our individual and family life. Take away the spiritual foundation of the family and it will not stand the tests of life. Take away faith from the heart of a man and he will be like chaff which the wind driveth away. Economic security cannot take the place of morality and love in the home. Loyalty cannot be bought. Stoicism is a poor substitute for faith. The strength we need for troubled times can come only from God, for God is the Ground of all being.

This leads us to the second insight into the nature of life. Elisha and his attendant woke up early in the morning to find that things were lined up against them. They saw a great host of horses and chariots, the seemingly endless line of soldiers marching towards them. The servant said, "Alas, my master! What shall we do?" Indeed, what could they do against the great army of cavalry men? The situation looks very much like ours. There are times when we wake up to find many things lined up against us — no water in the faucet, the telephone is out of order, the car is not working, the maid has left, the child is sick, the jeepney drivers are on strike. A host of big and small problems come upon us like rain and we feel terribly helpless. Sometimes we wake up to find our own fears lined up against us, and so we meet the day with trembling courage, unable to do anything constructive and productive. Like Elisha's servant, we can only sigh and say, "What can we do?"

Well, I believe we can do what Elisha did. When the servant did not know what to do, Elisha said, "Fear not, for those who are with us are more than those who are with them." In other words, we can believe that God can supply us the strength equal to the task, and even more. We can have a healthy attitude towards the storms of life. Instead of running away like cowards from the issue, we can face it with serenity. Instead of murmuring and cursing the darkness, we can hum a song and light a candle. Instead of brooding over our inadequacy and limitations, we can rejoice over the boundless goodness of Him who can make us strong. And, like Elisha, we can pray — not only for ourselves but also for our companions — so that their eyes may be opened and thus behold the multitudes of horses and chariots of fire round about us. Instead of seeing only the aberrations of our time, we can affirm the ultimate victory of righteousness and the unfailing mercy of the Lord.

Such abiding faith in the almightiness of God has a double effect: first, it keeps us calm in the face of a gathering storm, like Elisha who was calm in the face of an approaching army; second, it influences other lives precisely at a time of danger or difficulty. We do not know Elisha's servant. History does not preserve his name for us. But it may well be that way, for that unknown servant may be anyone around us. The question therefore is: Have we, by virtue of our faith in God, influenced anyone to trust in the power of divine love? Has there been anyone in our company, at home, in school or anywhere, who has been led to a vital encounter with God because of the witnesses of our life and the effectiveness of our prayer? This is the question of Elisha. It is the question of Christian evangelism. The Bible clearly suggests that the task of witnessing is not just the verbal proclamation of the word of God. Elisha's servant was converted not because Elisha preached a sermon. Elisha simply manifested the faith that could not be disturbed by the sight of an impending doom. The servant was so impressed that before he knew it, he too could feel within himself the heavenly assurance that everything would be well.

So we see, it is not only by preaching we impart the richest treasures of the Christian faith. In fact, some Christians should not preach at all — they may do more harm than good. But all Christians are called to witness — through the way we deal with people, the way we do our job, the way we conduct ourselves, the way we handle our trials and difficulties at the crossroads of life.

The latter part of our Scripture reading describes how the Syrians were smitten with blindness and then led captive to the very center of Samaria. They were, therefore, at the mercy of the Israelites whose first impulse was to liquidate them. But Elisha opposed the plan and instead suggested that the prisoners be given food and then sent home. And that was done.

Is this not an Old Testament illustration of throwing bread when you are hit with a stone, or walking the second mile, or turning the other cheek? To forgive someone who has done us wrong, to help someone who has sought to destroy us, to serve someone who has entertained evil thoughts about us — how can we do that unless our faith is as great as Elisha's? But that is the order we have to obey, if we are to experience the thrilling romance of the Christian life.

Elisha's faith is something we must covet for ourselves. It is the faith that can make us equal to the challenges of our time. It is faith in the abiding goodness of our Lord and in the sufficiency of His grace.

66

The King and the Prophet

Scripture Reading: I King 22:1-14

Jehoshaphat, king of Judah, is the guest of the king of Israel, Ahab. The author of this account leaves to our imagination the kind of welcome given the state visitor. We should not be surprised if it was a pompous welcome. People must have lined up from the city gates to the royal palace; bands of musicians must be hard at work; and shouts of *"Mabuhay"* must have reverberated all along the way. After all, King Ahab planned to ask a favor from his guest, and he may just as well give him a very warm reception.

And now the time has come for the big state dinner. In an occasion like that, they probably had no corn mixed with the rice. And, if Jehoshaphat is like the other kings of Judah, he must have asked for the *"Inumin ng tunay na lalaki."* A chamber orchestra and possibly a famous choral group must have provided the music. Happily, they need not worry about any blackout during the reception because they had no electricity yet.

Then at the most opportune time — when the atmosphere is most conducive — Ahab tells Jehoshaphat that he has a special favor to ask. Jehoshaphat must have said something like: "Go ahead, *compadre*, don't hesitate to tell me what you want." And that is the moment Ahab has been waiting for. So he tells his guest that he wants to conquer Ramoth-gilead from the king of Syria, and that he needs some military assistance from Judah. Jehoshaphat's answer is swift and firm: "I am as thou art, my people, as thy people, my horses as thy horses."

But Jehoshaphat is a religious man. It is his custom to seek the Lord's guidance before making any decision like that. Perhaps he should not have committed himself so hastily to Ahab but he has given his word, and now he feels bound to honor it. But it is not yet too late . Almost falteringly, he tells the king of Israel, "Inquire, I pray thee, at the word of the Lord today."

Apparently, Ahab is prepared for that kind of a request. He has four hundred prophets waiting to be summoned and gathering them is no problem at all. In no time they are assembled, and the big question comes ringing to their ears. The king's question is: "Shall I go against Ramoth-gilead to battle or shall I forbear?" Shall I assert myself as the ruler of Ramoth-gilead, or shall I not? That is the simple question they have to answer. And they have to answer yes or no, although they are free to give further comments on their answer.

And we know the result of that consultation. With one mind, with one voice the prophets answer, yes — a big resounding yes. Not just 80%, not just 90% but 100% yes. They say, "Go up; for the Lord shall deliver it into the hand of the king."

Perhaps, Ahab turns to his guest to say, "You have heard the answer. Have you got anything more to ask?" For a while, poor Jehoshaphat is dumbfounded. He cannot believe his eyes and ears; the entire barangay voted yes. He must have said to himself, *"Siguro, lutong-makaw ito."* But he cannot say that. He has seen the orderly and honest election. Yet the very unanimity of the voters without a single dissenting vote makes him suspect that perhaps there is something fishy behind that consultation. So he turns again to his friend and asks, "Is there not here a prophet of the Lord besides, that we might inquire of him?"

Ahab, the king of Israel, says, "There is yet one man, Micaiah the son of Imlah, by whom we may inquire of the Lord: but I hate him; for he doth not prophesy good concerning me, but evil." Very frankly he tells his guest that he hates Micaiah — that prophet always contradicts him; Jehoshaphat simply replies, "Let not the king say no." In effect, Jehoshaphat is saying: "Don't feel so bad. That prophet whom you hate may just be telling the truth."

Arrangements are made to invite the prophet Micaiah. And the king, with admirable magnanimity, decrees that the appearance of Micaiah will be open to the public. Verse 10 says that the meeting place is the entrance of the gate of Samaria, a place where many people pass by and is easily accessible. The two kings have their special places built, and they now sit on their thrones with their royal garments on.

The ceremony begins with a reenactment of the four hundred prophets' endorsement of the king's plan. Zedekiah, their chief spokesman, dramatizes their decision by running around the meeting place with horns of iron he has made to illustrate how the kings will emerge victorious in the battle. He says, "With these shalt thou push the Syrians, until thou have consumed them" (vs.11). And then all the prophets, repeating their verdict chant, "Go up to Ramoth-gilead, and prosper: for the Lord shall deliver it into the king's hand" (vs.12).

The man who carries the message to Micaiah says to him, "Behold, the words of the prophets declare good unto the king with one mouth: Let thy word, I pray thee, be like the word of one of them and speak that which is good. "Look, brod," he says, "the prophets are completely unanimous. Why don't you just agree with them and learn the art of *pakikisama*? I am sure that will please the king." Micaiah's reply should be the motto of every Christian preacher. He says, "As the Lord liveth, what the Lord saith unto me that will I speak."

So Micaiah speaks as he is guided by the Lord. He tells the king that his martial venture will not prosper, and that God is not on the king's side in his projected conquest of Ramoth-gilead. Zedekiah smites him on his face, and upbraids him for being so courageous. Then the king orders the arrest of Micaiah saying, "Put this fellow in prison and feed him with the bread of affliction and with the water of affliction until I come in peace." Micaiah has one more word before he is taken away. "If you return at all in peace," he says, "then the Lord has not spoken by me."

The king goes to war disguised as an ordinary soldier. One of the Syrians shoots an arrow into the air without aiming at anyone in particular. But behold, that deadly arrow lands on the side of Ahab, and he is hurriedly brought back to his camp with a bleeding wound. Early in the night he dies, and dogs lick up his blood in the chariot.

I have to summarize this tragic story because the weaknesses of Ahab may be a part of our own personal experiences. Ahab had no use for any criticism, however constructive it might be. He would hear only what was good about him, and he had surrounded himself with people who would say what he wanted to hear. He had made up his mind to get hold of Ramoth-gilead, and anyone who would go against his plan was likely to be in trouble. The consultation with the four hundred prophets was a mere ritual. He knew what those prophets would say. He knew they were not being true to their honest feeling.

But Ahab is not the only man who likes to be lied to. Many of us are quite susceptible to that same weakness. That is why liars are encouraged to lie; they often find customers that patronize their trade. Rev. Clovis G. Chappel has a paragraph on this subject. He writes:

> One reason for the popularity of the liar is that

he flatters us. He compliments us recklessly and we like to be complimented. I make that confession for myself. You like to be complimented, too. If you say that you do not, the only difference between you and me is that I am telling the truth about it. We like to believe that they are given sincerely. But we like them so well that none of us scrutinize them too closely to altogether kill their delicious flavor.[1]

All of us need to struggle against the mighty forces of lies, lies that nevertheless appeal to us. And when we reach the point where we deliberately make people say what we want to hear, it is time for a thorough spiritual reconditioning.

We must appreciate the efforts of Ahab in seeking the mind of God before going to Ramoth-gilead. We can be sure that even without any prodding from Jehoshaphat, Ahab had a talk with his spiritual advisers. And he must be quite intent on getting the Lord's blessings on his expansion plan; otherwise, he would not have employed four hundred prophets in his court. But the ugliness of his designs is betrayed in his stubborn attempts to bend the divine will to his whims; he even tried to convince himself that his aspirations were the manifestations of the Spirit working through him. It is the same tendency we often fall into when we cannot clearly distinguish our human ambitions from the purposes of God. This does not mean we should not make any petitionary prayers. Jesus says, "Seek and ye shall find; knock and it shall be opened unto you; ask and it shall be given." But petitions are only petitions, and always subject to the higher will of God. And when we bend heaven and earth to get God's will to conform to ours, we commit a most serious blunder that borders on spiritual suicide.

And what about the four hundred prophets? In fairness to them, should we not at least presume their sincerity? What if they really honestly felt that Ahab should take possession of Ramoth-gilead, and that such a plan in their honest opinion was not against the will of God? And what was wrong with their being unanimous? Why should we expect a few of them to cast a dissenting vote when in fact they were of the same mind? This may be just the kind of reasoning they might have advanced in the presence of Jehoshaphat. But nowhere in the story does Jehoshaphat question their sincerity. He only asked Ahab if there was any other prophet from whom they could inquire about God's will.

And the answer of the king of Israel reveals not only the kind of man

---

[1] Clovis Chappel, *Familiar Failures*, p. 20.

he was but also the caliber of the prophets in his court. He said, "Yes, there is another prophet: Micaiah the son of Imlah, but I hate him because he does not prophesy good concerning me but evil." The implication is that he liked the four hundred prophets because they always agreed with him. Of course it is good to find people who agree with us. We will get along with them very beautifully. But to hate those who do not agree with us is to betray the poverty of our character and the narrowness of our vision. We can disagree without becoming disagreeable. We can criticize without becoming censorious. We can differ without becoming dogmatic. We can oppose without becoming obnoxious.

Then look at the prophet who escorted Micaiah. He said to Micaiah, "Do you see how enthusiastic those four hundred prophets are? They highly commend the king's plan to take Ramoth-gilead. Why don't you just go along with them, and say that you too agree?" We always have people who think that way. Their philosophy is, "If you can't lick them, join them." What's the use of being in the minority? You may just as well join the majority.

But Micaiah is our man. He has the courage of conviction which every prophet and every leader and every citizen must sedulously cultivate. He will speak the truth in so far as God enables him to see the truth. He will speak it in obedience to the heavenly vision. And that is exactly what he did. At first he jokingly sided with the four hundred, but Ahab knew that he was only joking. And when at last he stated his opinion, he did not mince a word in predicting the failure of the king's military venture. Zedekiah was quick to slap his face as if the dissenting view of a solitary person was a major threat to the unanimity of the king's advisers. And the king himself, who hated the lonely oppositionist, consigned Micaiah into prison.

But the truth of God cannot be suppressed. In spite of all the precautions that Ahab made, the arrow of an archer found its way into his body and he did not live to see Ramoth-gilead. The prayers of all his four hundred prophets did not save him from such a tragedy, and we are not even sure whether they attended his funeral.

This is why the church relentlessly proclaims that obeying God's will is the secret of a triumphant life. For when we obey His will, we acquire the humility to subject our judgement to the scrutiny of His Spirit and we become keenly aware that even our best decisions may be tainted by our sin. When we obey the will of God, we gain strength equal to our tasks, we perform our duties with a sense of mission, and we experience that tranquility of spirit which cannot be disturbed by the cruelty of men and nature.

Let us therefore resolve to keep ourselves close to God, for He is the Source of light and love and hope. And let us be charitable to those who do not think the way we do, always bearing in mind that they may not always be completely wrong and we are not always completely right, without relaxing our determination to act in the light of our best judgement. And let us resolve to remain faithful to our God, even if such faithfulness may entail some difficulties. After all, true happiness and peace comes about not by acquiring more Ramoth-gileads but by being true to our conscience that depends on the guidance of the Holy Spirit.

67

A Poor Man's Vineyard

Scripture Reading: I Kings 21:1-16

Once upon a time, in the city of Samaria, there lived a king by the name of Ahab. He was a man of great wealth and worldly ambitions. He was the epitome of political power and military strength. By snapping his fingers he could move an army. His word was law. His decrees were irrevocable.

Seven miles north of Samaria, in another city called Jezreel, was the king's summer residence. Its magnificent architecture and lavish ornaments gained the title of "the king's ivory palace". It became a wonder of ancient Israel and a shrine to many tourists.

Somewhere beside that summer residence, not far from the gates, was a green, fertile vineyard owned by a private citizen. It was a good ground for planting herbs and its contour was exquisitely natural. The owner, whose name was Naboth, had his heart and soul in preserving the beauty of the place.

King Ahab wanted to have Naboth's vineyard. It would add color to his ivory palace, if properly cultivated. So one day he drove to Naboth's place and, in a friendly, courteous way, told Naboth, "I like your vineyard very much. And if it pleases you, I will give you a better vineyard for it, or pay you in cash at any price you want."

But Naboth softly and politely answered, "I am sorry, your majesty, I cannot sell this piece of land. I inherited it from my father, and it has a sentimental value to me. It means so much to me that I cannot part with it." So the king went home very much disappointed.

In the royal chamber, Jezebel, the king's wife, noticed that her husband could not eat or sleep. She sensed that something was bothering him. So with all tenderness and gentleness, she asked him, "Darling, is there anything wrong? You look so downhearted and disturbed. Please tell me what is bothering you."

So the king told her the story. "You know, dear," he said, "I went to see Naboth about his vineyard. I wanted to buy it from him but he refused to sell it."

"Ah...," said the fabulously lovely queen, "should that petty little thing bother you? Come on, your majesty, take your breakfast and be happy. Let me handle the matter myself and the vineyard will be yours."

Jezebel wrote letters to her subjects at Jezreel, telling them to make a fast or to put on sour faces, as though to avert some public calamity. She told them to exalt Naboth in the midst of their assembly, and that two sons of Belial should stand before Naboth and accuse him of blasphemy against God, which was punishable by death, and blasphemy against the king, which meant royal confiscation of his property. And, without giving Naboth a chance to be heard in a fair trial, they should drag him out of the city and there stone him to death. With almost unbelievable speed, the order was followed to the letter. Before sunset of that day the news reached the palace that Naboth was dead.

"Cheer up," chanted murderer Jezebel to the king, "Naboth is dead, and the property is yours." We can just imagine the joy of Ahab, and on the following day he rode in his golden chariot and went to Naboth's place. Perhaps on the way he was merrily singing to the hills and valleys, "It is mine, it is mine, this land is mine. . ."

But, lo, in the distance, beside the gate to Naboth's vineyard, the king saw a man who looked like he was waiting for his coming. And as he came closer to the man, Ahab noticed it was Elijah the prophet, whose countenance was radiant with the sharpness of a divine judgment he was about to pronounce. Ahab exclaimed in trembling tone, "Have you found me, O mine enemy?" And Elijah, with the courage of a prophet, firmly replied, "Yes, the Lord has found you. You have sold your soul to do evil in the sight of the Lord. Therefore, He will bring evil upon you, and cut off your posterity. Behold, in the place where dogs licked the blood of Naboth, there shall your blood be licked also. And your wife Jezebel shall be eaten by the dogs by the walls of Jezreel." And that was the beginning of a terrifying restlessness in Ahab's household.

Here is the story of a man whose covetousness paved the way to his own destruction. He was the king of Israel with an ivory palace, but was very restless until everything belonged to him. Of course, his system of getting what he wanted was seemingly legal. He was willing to pay for

Naboth's vineyard at any price the latter might ask. His approach was businesslike and his offer was reasonable. But underneath that proposed business transaction was the inordinate desire to have Naboth's vineyard. So that when Naboth sturdily refused the offer, the greedy poor king could not take his breakfast. That was starvation in the midst of plenty.

There is a great number of people today who are acutely afflicted with this inward and mortal sickness called covetousness. To them there is no lasting joy except the joy of having more vineyards. In spite of the many things they have already acquired, they cannot really say, "We have enough." To such kind of people, to have more and more of the things of this world is all that matters.

Certainly, Ahab typifies a colossal restlessness that is ours when we become covetous. Like a sullen little boy who was not given a piece of bread though he had seven loaves in his arms, Ahab plunged himself into his divan and cried unashamedly over his fruitless trip. But there is always a way for the exercise of evil. There is always a Lady Macbeth who would tell the thane how to become a king. There is always a door for an impure thought to come out, and though at the moment it looks half-closed, yet at the whisper of Satan it would fling wide open. "Don't you worry," comforted Jezebel, "I will take care of it. Come on and be merry, for in a short time you will have the vineyard." And, using her husband's seal, she sent letters to plot the judicial murder of an innocent man.

What a woman, we might say. She had the nerve to please her husband even in a way that displeases God. And the subservient people who were either afraid of Jezebel's cruelty or envious of Naboth's piety followed her order to the letter and therefore became participants in the murder of an honest citizen. Great influence is great mischief if the spirit that controls it is not of God.

Look at the procedure employed by Jezebel in grabbing Naboth's vineyard. She used a religious ceremony. "Make a fast," she instructed. "Be ceremoniously religious. Accuse Naboth of the crime of blasphemy against God and the king ." She was an expert in using religious means in grabbing a poor man's land.

Of course, we recall that her husband was also like that. He was to be visited by a religious man, King Jehoshaphat of Judah, and Ahab alerted 400 prophets who might be summoned any moment during the state dinner in honor of the royal visitor. And sure enough, when Ahab told his guest about his plan to conquer Ramoth-gilead, Jehoshaphat suggested that they seek the mind of God on the matter by consulting with the prophets. And with almost lightning speed, 400 religious leaders were assembled in the palace. And when the question was put before them as to whether or not Ahab should conquer Ramoth-gilead, with one voice they answered, "Yes." Religion is perverted whenever it is used to serve the will of man rather than the will of God.

Ahab and Jezebel are proof of the fact that people can be religious and land grabbers at the same time; that people tend to prefer to give a semblance of legality in what they do, when in truth they are the real masterminds in the death of innocent people. In short, Ahab and Jezebel are examples of a common human weakness of resorting to religious activities to cover up the moral and spiritual ugliness in our life.

Going back to the story, when Ahab heard about Naboth's death, he rose up early the next morning to see the vineyard for himself. He could have sent his soldiers to inspect the place. He could have the detailed description of the land through the services of surveyors and technicians. But because it was a great delight to see for himself the object of his unholy obsession, he went there himself. But, as the Scripture says, when Elijah appeared before him, the king exclaimed in horrified tone, "Have you found me, O my enemy?" Let us reflect on that for a while. Who was the enemy?

We will remember who Elijah was. Elijah was one of the greatest prophets in the Old Testament. He was a man of God, whose commitment to truth and justice and honesty was beyond suspicion. He was a guardian of morality, with a sincere concern for the plight of his fellow men. He would not allow any evil in society to go unchecked.

No wonder when Ahab met him, the king could not help but exclaim, "Have you found me, O my enemy?" We see, to a guilty conscience God's ambassador appears like an enemy. A guilty conscience cannot stand face to face with righteousness and honor. He trembles at the mere suspicion that he is found out. He hates the shadow of the true prophet because his works are not acceptable to God.

We would do well to resolve once again to seek first the Kingdom of God and His righteousness, and never mind whether or not the other things that we desire will be added unto us. God who knows our real needs will rightly apportion what He deems should be given unto us. If we dedicate our time to the glory of His name, the blessings of eternity shall crown the days of our life.

68

The Pharisee and the Publican

Scripture Reading: Luke 18:9-14

Here is the parable of the Pharisee and the publican, or tax collector. The Pharisee was a highly respected person in society. The word **pharisee** means "separated" and the implication is that the Pharisees were a group of people with a certain degree of moral and spiritual superiority for they were the spiritual guardians of the nation. They knew the law, the Torah, by heart; it was their duty to teach the people about good manners and right conduct. The people looked up to them for the interpretation of difficult religious and theological questions. Of course, they were laymen but they were very influential; their secular connections, so to speak, made their presence in the community very conspicuous. They represented the most religious segment of the Jewish world and were among the most highly educated temple authorities.

The publican, on the other hand, was a tax collector — an employee of the BIR or the Bureau of Customs. And his image in the community was not exactly glamorous. The tax collectors in the days of Jesus were known for their industry in collecting not only legitimate taxes but also illegitimate "grease" money. A New Testament scholar, Joachim Jeremias, writes: "While the taxes, such as poll tax and land tax, were collected by state officials, the customs of a district were farmed out, probably to the highest bidder; so the collector of the customs saw himself as a businessman and tried to keep his profit as high as possible. Tariffs were, no doubt, fixed by the state, but the collectors did not lack devices for defrauding the public. In public opinion they were on a level with robbers."[1]

I just wonder whether the author of this statement has ever visited the Philippines.

And yet in the parable the publican was justified and, inferentially, the Pharisee's prayer was not heard. Here is a solemn reminder that those who frequent the holy precincts of the church are not automatically assured

---

[1] Joachim Jeremias, *Rediscovering the Parables*, p. 112.

of a place in heaven, and those being despised by their fellow men are not necessarily beyond redemption.

But while those two men were miles apart in their social standing, they had some striking similarities in their religious upbringing. For instance, both of them prayed. They sought fellowship with God. Both of them approached God through prayer. Helmut Thielicke, a German theologian and pastor, writes: "The publican, even though his prayer is expressed in the form of a petition, gives thanks that there is such a thing as the mercy of God, that even someone like himself can approach God, that even an unworthy man can enter the sanctuary and need not go shuffling about outside, sick for home and crying for paradise lost."[1] In a sense, therefore, both the Pharisee and the publican offered prayers of thanksgiving.

For another thing, both men prayed in the temple. William Barclay, commenting on this parable, says: "Prayer was held to be specially efficacious if it was offered in the Temple." They could have prayed at home, in the privacy of their rooms, or somewhere in the garden, under the mango tree. But they exerted efforts to go up to the Temple, and there offered their prayers.

If we may paraphrase his prayer, it will sound something like this: "Look, partner, I am not like other men you see around here: they are extortioners, crooked, unjust. Unlike this tax collector beside me, I have not stolen anything; I have nothing to do with the disappearance of those gold bars; I have not misspent the people's taxes. On the contrary, I fast twice a week, I receive communion everyday and I give the tithes of all I earn. I see no reason why I should not have a special place in the kingdom of heaven."

Now let us consider the differences of these two men. Note, for instance, how they differed in their concept of God. In the words of Dr. George A. Buttrick, "The Pharisee regarded God as a corporation in which he (the Pharisee) had earned a considerable block of stock, so that at any moment he might be invited to become a director. His 'prayer' told God that he was waiting for well-deserved honors."[2]

A prayer like that betrays a certain intimacy which reduces God into a mere equal who is expected to be impressed by our achievements and

---
[1] Helmut Thielicke, *The Waiting Father*, p. 130.
[2] *Interpreter's Bible*, Vol. 7, p.309f.

our righteousness. God is regarded as a kind of being whose thoughts are like our thoughts and whose ways are like our ways. People who think of God that way will hastily question Him when sorrow or tribulation or misfortune come their way, believing that they have reasons to be exempted from the tumults of this life. The Pharisee in our parable typifies all those who believe that since they have done some virtuous things they should be entitled to some special divine favors.

The publican, on the other hand, saw God as "burning holiness," as the Supreme Being whose nature is love and whose mercy can save him from the quagmire of his sin. Before that God he forgot whatever little goodness he might have done to his fellow men; all he saw was the blackness of his soul in the presence of a consuming holiness.

Because of this basic difference in their concept of God, the Pharisee and the publican were far apart in their attitude towards their fellow men. The Pharisee despised his neighbors and thanked God he was not like them. He saw not only the worst that was in them — their moral impurities, their wanton injustices, their insatiable greed. He also saw the best that was in him — his matchless religiosity, his untarnished faithfulness to the Temple, his unquestionable devotion to the Law. That's why he despised his neighbors; they were not as good as he was.

The tax collector, on the other hand, "stood afar off from other men such as the Pharisee, because he felt himself unworthy of their friendship." He dared not freely associate with them, lest he hurt their sensibilities.

Furthermore, the Pharisee and the publican differed in their estimates of their own selves. The Pharisee was cocksure of his righteousness; the publican was so ashamed of his wickedness. Naturally, the Pharisee looked at life with himself at the center: even his prayer was replete with I's. "I thank thee I am not like other men... I fast twice a week, I give tithes of all I get." It was not a prayer anymore; it was putrid autobiography.

The publican, on the other hand, was so convicted of his sin that he looked up to God for the salvation of his soul. His mind was centered on the Lord who alone could give him peace.

And so those two men, who differed in their concept of God, also differed in their outlook of life and in their attitude towards their fellow beings. And this is what we need to remember always: that our belief in God and our relationship with Him, indeed, affect the way we deal with our fellow men and the way we think of ourselves. The Christian teachings on God we offer in the Sunday Schools are not merely for our intellectual stimulation; they are intended to be the very foundation of a lasting faith and a source of guidance for our daily life. We proclaim the Word of God not to observe a decent custom but in obedience to His will, and with the conviction that the cleansing power of His Spirit can remake us and the world. Calling men to right relationship with God can bring about renewal in society. The radical change we need these days is to bring God back into the center of human existence.

At this point, let us see why the Pharisee was a colossal failure. Why did he pray as he did? Why was he so sure of himself yet, in the end, was a tragic loser? Very clearly, it was because he looked at his fellow men, the publican more particularly, as his standard. He appeared so high and exalted because his standard was so low and despicable. He appeared so good because the publican was so bad. He compared himself with a sinner.

Is that not a common human weakness? How often have we felt exceptionally good because we see someone who is exceptionally bad, and we are glad we are not like him? If we want instant happiness, just think of someone who is quite below our stature. Make him as our standard and we will see ourselves passing the mark with flying colors. But that is an illusion which the children of God must try to overcome.

But the publican in our parable looked up to God, and in the presence of the Divine he saw himself as a wretched being. Yet, he could not be completely bereft of some goodness. He must have contributed something to the Community Chest. He must have put something into the offering plate. He must have said a word of comfort to a sorrowing friend. Yet, in the presence of the Almighty he saw the woeful depravity of his spirit and the alarming emptiness of his life.

And this is also the case when we look to Jesus as the Captain of our soul, as our Model, as our Lord. This is not to say that we literally forget the deeds of goodness He enables us to do, the words of kindness we say to lonely hearts, the gifts of love we give to those in need. Jesus himself encourages us to let our light so shine before men that they may see our good works. Certainly, there is a place for some personal testimony on what God has done for us and for the changes He has wrought in us when we are gripped by the power of His forgiving love. But when self usurps the place of God and our good works blur the grace of Christ, the danger signal is on and we better watch out. For if we don't, we will soon be like the Pharisee whose overconfidence prevented him from detecting the malignant cancer in his soul.

In summary, we may say that the parable is a warning on the inherent destructiveness of pride. Though not clearly hinted in the parable, the Pharisee could be a victim of intellectual pride since he was either a doctor of laws or a doctor of theology. And if he was like most of the Pharisees in Jesus' days, he must have felt he had nothing to learn from a poor Carpenter of Nazareth who did not have much formal education and whose followers were a bunch of ordinary fishermen. Intellectual pride can make the mind closed. It can lead us to believe that only our opinions matter and that only we are right.

Pride of power, whether it be economic or political power, can bring havoc to men and nations. The Pharisee belonged to a religious-political party and, therefore, had both religious and political influence. We are not surprised if, because of his pride of power, he therefore thought he needed no mediator to secure a passport to heaven.

We need to remind those who have been entrusted with power that they are stewards of such power. If they allow themselves to be corrupted by it, they and the rest of us will suffer.

But it is spiritual pride which can cause the worst damage to our life. And this was the lot not only of the Pharisee in our parable but of all who seriously believe they are holier than their neighbors. Spiritual pride cuts us off from vital links with God, even if every Sunday we find ourselves in church. It converts our prayers into pious declarations of our virtues; it makes us gloat over the failings of our fellow men.

There is another kind of pride which can impoverish us beyond all measure. It is what Helmut Thielicke calls the publican's pride. It is not exactly like the Pharisee's pride but can be equally destructive. The publican's pride may prompt us to pray, "I thank thee God that I am not so proud as this Pharisee: I am an extortioner, unjust, and an adulterer. That's the way human beings are and that's what I am, but at least I admit it, and therefore I am a little bit better than the rest of the breed. I commit fornication twice a week, and at most ten percent of what I own comes from honest work. I am an honest man, O God, honest enough to admit I am no good."

Is this not what we sometimes say to God, to our friends, and to ourselves? While honesty is indeed a virtue, this kind of honesty is but a form of pride. And it is from pride that we need to be delivered. It is from this hell that we need to be rescued. And who can save us from this sin which causes us so much miseries and griefs?

The merciful God can. The grace of our Lord can. But first we need to surrender our pride, and give God a chance to make us whole again. Then we will truly know what it means to be free.

69

The Beginning of Wisdom

Scripture Reading: Proverbs 1:1-19

In the Old Testament, there are three recognized religious and cultural leaders in society: the priests, the prophets, and the sages (or wise men). Of these three, the priests and the prophets are the more popular, and often, the more outspoken. But the sages exert tremendous moral influence because they are mainly concerned with the practical aspects of religion. At times they appear to be a little different from the prophets in that, for one thing, theirs is the voice of moderation while the prophets often find it necessary to be extremists. The sages tend to place emphasis on what man can do for himself, but the prophets are intent on calling the people's attention to what God can do. The sages, furthermore, tend to be prudential and even utilitarian in their teachings, but the prophets often suspect worldly success and therefore they pursue difficult causes without regard for their own safety and popularity.

But actually the sages seek to be true to the prophetic spirits: what the prophets say to the nation, the sages teach the individuals; and the standard of morality they try to cultivate is simply a response to the prophetic demands for a godly life.

One of the greatest sages the world has ever known is Solomon. In the book of I Kings, we read the following: "Solomon's wisdom surpassed the wisdom of all the people of the east, and all the wisdom of Egypt. . . His fame was in all the nations round about. He also uttered three thousand proverbs. . ." (1 Kings 4:30, 31, 32). This is why the proverbs which we have in the Old Testament are often linked with Solomon, just as the psalms are often associated with King David.

Modern biblical scholarship, however, informs us that the proverbs are not entirely of Solomonic authorship; the book of Proverbs is actually the work of many people and the product of many centuries.

The study of this book can be made more interesting by the fact that we in the Philippines have our own saying which we take as gospel truths.

Examples:

"Ang hindi marunong lumingon sa pinanggalingan, di makararating sa paruruonan."

"Ano mang haba ng prosisyon, sa simbahan din ang tungo."

"Ang lumalakad nang matulin, kung matinik ay malalim."

"Walang matimtimang birhen sa matiyaga na manalangin."

These and other native sayings have universal values because they deal with the universal truths of life. The perversion of these sayings which we sometimes make is only a reflection of our own perversity. Take the following example: *"Walang matimtimang dalaga sa patas ng dilata."* This obviously is an attempt to canonize the seemingly successful method of winning a woman's heart by flooding her with gifts.

No doubt Jesus and His disciples have learned much from the Proverbs. Jesus' discourse on the fool who built his house on the sand and the wise man who built his upon the rock; His admonition to trust God for the right things to say; His teaching on recompense, humility and the uncertainty of the future which we find in various parts of Matthew and Luke are all taken from the book of Proverbs. The Apostle Paul is quoting from Proverbs when in Romans 12 he says, "Be not wise in your own conceits." The writer to the Hebrews is merely repeating the teaching of the Proverbs when he, in chapter 12, admonishes, "My son, regard not lightly the chastening of the Lord, nor faint when thou art reproved of him; for whom the Lord loveth he chasteneth, and scourgeth every son whom he receiveth." Peter is quoting from the Proverbs when, in Chapter 5 of his epistle, he says, "God resisteth the proud, but giveth grace to the humble."

Now let us point out that while the Proverbs are meant to instruct people, they were originally directed to people of means, particularly the young people of well-to-do families. The reason is that while the sages taught publicly for free, they depended for their livelihood on the honorarium or salary they received as private tutors. And only the well-to-do and the rich could afford to hire private tutors. Thus we will note that most of the follies which the book of Proverbs deprecates are the follies which only the sons of the gentry could afford. Prof. S. H. Blank is correct in suggesting that "The social background and philosophy of the book are decidedly upper-class."[1]

This book, therefore, has something to say about the sins of the privileged and the upper-class in our society. The late Teodoro Valencia used to say that the vandals at the Rizal Park he was trying to beautify were not the poor and the lowly, but the rich and the influential who knew they could break the law and get away with it. They do as they please at the Rizal Park because they believe they cannot be touched by the police. To them and to the members of their company, whose power is the sign of their patent weakness and whose security only betrays their insecurity, the message of Proverbs can be a redemptive experience and a call to sobriety. And if the book can be helpful to them, it can be helpful to all of us, whatever our lot in life may be, because the book speaks of eternal verities and offers practical guides on charity, chastity, truthfulness, and chivalry which all of us ardently need.

In the book of Proverbs, God is the source of both knowledge and wisdom. We may acquire knowledge through formal education, through reading, or by traveling around the world, but Proverbs maintains that God is the fontal source of knowledge. And when this book speaks of wisdom, it means not primarily the intellectual system or the deposit of philosophical truths; rather, it means the practical manifestations of the highest virtues of life and the highest truths of religion. In this sense the uneducated can be wise, and his wisdom is not that he can understand complicated theological postulates but that in the simplicity of his daily life he can experience the deepest mysteries of God. Thus, the proverb says, "the fear of the Lord is the beginning of wisdom."

In other words, if our life is to be deeply satisfying, we must have a right relationship with God. Whether we like it or not, there is a vacuum at the center of life and of the universe which only God can fill. We only deceive ourselves when we try to fill up that vacuum with something else in order that we can do away with God. But we know from experience that even our good works cannot overcome the terrifying emptiness in a godless life, and no amount of activism will satisfy the purest longings of the human spirit.

In the American Translation, the wording is: "Reverence for the Lord is the beginning of knowledge." This gives us a clue to the meaning of fear. Prof. Charles T. Fritsch tells us that "the idea of fear goes back to the terror which was felt in the presence of the Deity," but later on it came

---
[1] *Interpreter's Dictionary of the Bible,* K-Q, p. 939.

to mean reverence or awe.[1] Therefore, the fear of the Lord is actually reverence for God.

The fear of the Lord is the fear that cuts into all other fears. The man who fears God will not be afraid of life's vicissitudes. Though he walks through the valley of the shadow of death, he will fear no evil.

But how do we fear the Lord? And how does God impart His wisdom? The answers are difficult to find. But we find pertinent hints in our Scripture reading. After verse 7 which reads: "The fear of the Lord is the beginning of wisdom," the next verse reads: "Hear, my son, your father's instruction, and reject not your mother's teaching." What does this suggest? It suggests that the children's first teachers are their parents, and that the home is also a school. It also suggests that the children should respect the teaching of their parents; they must learn to honor the instructions of their elders.

Let us elaborate on this. The parents' responsibility in the spiritual upbringing of the children cannot be delegated to the maids; it cannot be passed on to their preschool teachers, not even to their Sunday School teachers. If parents today can teach their young ones how to manipulate the television set and the airconditioner, there is no reason why we cannot teach them to say a word of prayer before eating and before sleeping. The formative years of a child's life are the best years for the cultivation of good manners and right conduct, and failure to take advantage of that opportunity can be unforgivable. The Proverbs says, "Train up a child in the way that he should go, and when he is old he will not depart from it" (22:6). The best place to teach and to learn the Christian religion is not the church but in the home.

Verse 8, let us also note, is a direct injunction to a young man: "Hear, my son, your father's instruction, and reject not your mother's teaching." The tutor here is almost pleading, praying that the son may give up his rebelliousness and give some consideration to the loving concern of his parents. How many of our young people today need this kind of an admonition?

Someone has observed that not long ago the word of the father was the law in the family; today, the word of the children is the law. Of course this is not always the case, but the fact remains that many homes are made desolate by the moral bankruptcy of those young people whose selfishness and perversity are divesting them of all sense of respect for parents and parental authority. Such people should be solemnly warned that only cowards try to prove their manhood by crucifying their parents.

---
[1] *Interpreter's Bible*, Vol. 4, p. 784.

There is no denying that parents can be wrong and that the delinquency of some young people is simply an outgrowth of the delinquency of their parents. The indignation of our youth can be righteous; at times there are valid reasons for their negative reaction to parental intervention. All that we are saying here is that the loss of reverence for parents and the spread of moral laxity among the youth cannot be tolerated; we have certain principles that cannot be altered by whims and caprices, and the young men or women who indulge in capriciousness will have to be reproved. They must be made to know that reverence for God should lead them to face squarely whatever problems they may have with their elders, in the hope that their common love of God may somehow enable them to transcend even the most bitter family squabbles.

Finally, let us consider verse 10. It says: "My son, if sinners entice you, do not consent." Whatever we may say about negative religion, it has a place in the practice of the Christian faith. Even the ten commandments say, Do not do this; do not do that. Norman Vincent Peale's "positive thinking" has a good amount of don'ts without which positive thinking is not possible. So is the fear of the Lord. It means we should not consent when sinners entice us. It means nonconformity with the workers of iniquity. It means rejection of fraud and dishonesty. It means refusal of any system that is not conducive to the growth of freedom and righteousness.

Thus, determined to resist evil, the man who fears God will fight for truth and justice. He will have compassion for the poor and the oppressed. He will work for social betterment. He will endeavor to live with dignity because he knows that a good name is better than great riches. He will handle excited people with the knowledge that "a soft answer turns away wrath, but a harsh word stirs up anger." And having learned that "pride goes before destruction," he will seek to walk humbly with his God.

And so to all young people in this land, I say: Fear God, reverence the Lord, seek His kingdom and His righteousness — that is the beginning of wisdom. And to all of us who are searching for that faith which can make us strong, I say: "Trust in the Lord with all your heart, and lean not unto your own understanding. In all your ways acknowledge Him, and He will direct your paths." (3:5,6).

70

"A Big Man in a Little Church"

Scripture Reading: III John

The sermon topic is borrowed from Prof. Dwight Stevenson. It is the title of a chapter in his book on preaching — the chapter which deals with the preaching value of III John. This epistle has only 15 verses and, like II John, is one of the shortest writings we have in the New Testament.

The author of this epistle is simply called the Elder, or John the Elder. Apparently he enjoyed some apostolic leadership in the early church and was very much concerned with the welfare of the local congregations within his district. His third epistle, while addressed to a man named Gaius, is intended for the whole fellowship because the author discusses a vital problem that affects the very life and witness of the congregation.

And what is the problem? The problem is Diotrephes, a church leader who is making a lot of trouble. Here is how the Elder puts it: "I have written something to the church: but Diotrephes, who likes to put himself first, does not acknowledge my authority. So if I come, I will bring up what he is doing, speaking out against me with evil words. And not content with that, he refuses to welcome the brethren, and also stops those who want to welcome them and puts them out of the church."

In other words, John the Elder is burdened with Diotrephes' insubordination. The man simply refused to acknowledge John's authority, probably because he resented being under the supervision of a bishop, or maybe because he was against church polity. Whatever the problem, he probably had his reasons for being so independent. For all we know, he could even be right in his differences with the Elder. We should at least give him credit for being so courageous as to defy a strong and powerful church leader like John. We may have something to learn from him. We should not always say "Yes" to our bishop. The bishop may be wrong, and to please him may only do more harm. We cannot think highly of those who have no guts to fight for their conviction for fear that they might displease a powerful bishop — or general, or cabinet member, or president. When a leader is bent on having his way without regard for the feelings of his people, it would be healthy to challenge him. For his own good and for the good of the church — or country — such leader should be disciplined.

But in the case of John, we can hardly say he is abusing his power. From what we know about him, we are sure that he is a man of faith. That his dealing with his fellow men has been fair and just can hardly be doubted, and his epistles reflect the warmth and the glow of Christian love that must have dwelt richly in his heart. We wish all bishops and leaders were like him. He is that rare combination of intellectual alertness and humility of spirit. He never tolerates any deviation from the truth. He opposes with firmness the various forms of heresy and immorality; yet great is his compassion for the heretics and constant are his prayers for the profligates. Surely his authority deserves our deepest respect. It is the authority of love and truth — the authority that comes from Christ himself. Diotrephes, therefore, is guilty of insubordination of the highest degree. His refusal to acknowledge the authority of John is not only a violation of the accepted polity in the church; it is also a willful disregard for the wisdom and guidance that can come only from a chosen man of God.

Furthermore, Diotrephes has been notoriously loose in his speech. He prates against the Elder with evil words. And evil words can be worse than libel or slander. People who cannot argue without being sarcastic must have descended from Diotrephes and we seem to have a good number of them in our churches. The Christian fellowship is not the exclusive fraternity of the well-behaved and the godly; it also includes the sharp-tongued and the hardheaded who have no control of either temper or words.

Again, Diotrephes refuses to welcome the brethren. The word brethren in John's epistle refers to the wandering missionaries who are commissioned to preach the gospel. In the early days of the Christian era the apostles and prophets and other missionaries were itinerant teachers of the new religion, and because they did not yet have the organization that would support their mission, Christians in the different localities were enjoined to give them hospitality. Church members must open their homes to these Christian workers. And they should give them *baon* when they depart, and give them enough to last until they reach the next destination. The Apostle Paul in his letter to Timothy tells us that a bishop, or a Christian for that matter, must be given to hospitality.

Of course, the picture is quite different during this generation. A missionary to our country, for instance, is not likely to cause us any trouble by insinuating himself and his family into our homes. Very likely, even before they arrive here, they already know that a well-furnished house or apartment is already waiting for them, and, with the twist of good fortune, they may even have two or three housemaids.

But not in the days of John the Elder. Their missionaries did not have mission houses. They did not have a stable salary; they only depended on the generosity and hospitality of their hosts. Christians, therefore, were admonished to open their homes to such messengers of peace. Diotrephes, being a church leader and most probably a man of means, is logically expected to be sympathetic with the brethren who happen to be in his community. But John tells us Diotrephes does not welcome them.

At first glance, it appears that Diotrephes is a very selfish man. He does not seem ready to suffer the inconvenience that temporary house guests may create. But John's epistle reveals that something other than selfishness is involved. For if Diotrephes is only selfish, then he would not mind other people saving the situation. But he does, and in fact threatens those church members who would welcome the missionaries to their homes with excommunication. In other words, aside from insubordination, he is also guilty of trying to divide the church — to exclude from the fellowship those who do not see things his way. He wants to rule the church with an iron hand and will get rid of those who stand in his way.

This type of high-handedness is a common phenomenon in our social life, especially in business and in politics. Men, by nature, are arrogant and self-centered and, whenever there is an opportunity, we want to control our fellow men. But when we see this happen in the church, we find it hard to dismiss as a simple human weakness. For if the church claims to be the agent of God's redeeming grace, it must bravely wrestle with every taint of human sin that weakens its message and its witness. It must exhibit convincing proofs that as a part of the Body of Christ, its purest desire is to obey the will of God.

Our study of Diotrephes' character leads us to see that the main cause of his viciousness is his excessive self-love. In the words of John, Diotrephes likes to put himself first or, as we have it in the King James Version, he loveth to have the pre-eminence. For him to live is to make himself important — the reversal of Paul's guiding motto, "For me to live is Christ." He wants to be the big man and, unconsciously, in so doing he actually makes his church small.

We can be sure that like Diotrephes, the devil will always tempt us to aspire to become big people. And when such temptation comes, we should not forget that it is essentially the temptation to put ourselves first and have pre-eminence. The consequence of such ambition is insubordination to the leading of God's Spirit and, ultimately, the falling to pieces of the fellowship itself. As Prof. Stevenson observes, "Men who are all the time striving to make themselves big create 'little' churches, churches little in vision, little in love, little in power." And we may add that such little men and little churches can never be our answer to the gigantic problems of our world.

Indeed, they cannot be our answer to the little problems we have in our personal and family life. For when we trace the roots of our problems, we discover that many of them start from inordinate self-love, from the very fact that we often want to put ourselves first. This feeling that stems from pride can easily be the cause of relationships going bust, of bitterness and resentment that make life seem like hell. This petty littleness which issues from spiritual poverty can ultimately lead to failure and despair.

But the simple teaching of the gospel and the Apostle is that life, to be rich and meaningful, must be centered on Christ. Christianity is the brave attempt to put Christ first, rather than ourselves. Self-denial in the Christian sense is merely putting self under the control of Christ in the sure knowledge that only in so doing can one achieve genuine personal fulfillment. This means that some measure of self-giving and sacrifice is needed to overcome the trifling littleness of men, that some degree of magnanimity or big heartedness is required to redeem those who are lost in self-conceit. The man or the woman who is ready to be last and to be the servant of all can be, in the providence of God, the bearer of our hopes for the salvation of our world. It is the big heart that makes men big and can make the church great.

The third epistle of John which exposes the littleness of Diotrephes is, as we have noted, addressed to a man named Gaius. But Gaius, we are told, is a very common name in the New Testament world. There was a Gaius who was with Paul in a riot in Ephesus. There was a Gaius chosen by his church to convey the collection for the poor in Jerusalem. Paul's gracious host in Corinth was Gaius by name, and one of the few whom Paul personally baptized. In the letter of John, Gaius simply stands before us "as a man with an open house and an open heart" (Barclay).

The Elder does not tell us much about him and the following verses are all we have about the man. "For I," writes John, "greatly rejoiced when some of the brethren arrived and testified to the truth of your life, as indeed you do follow the truth. No greater joy can I have than this, to hear that my children follow the truth." And then, commending Gaius for his hospitality, John continues, "Beloved, it is a loyal thing you do when you render any service to the brethren, especially to strangers, who have testified to your love before the church."

These few words about the man, however, are enough to give us the impression that Gaius is curiously the exact opposite of Diotrephes. He seems to be a quiet man but he is a doer of the truth. He may not be as outspoken as Diotrephes, but he welcomes the missionaries to his home. He may not be among the top leaders of the early church, but he has faithfully given his share in the missionary endeavors of the early Christians. We can be grateful that while Diotrephes is bent on disturbing the church, Gaius is equally determined to remain faithful within the fold.

All through the centuries, it is the Gaiuses who have preserved the splendor and the majesty of the Christian Church. A lot of schisms and corruption have crept into the institutional church, but the Gaiuses have remained true and strong. Precisely because the faith of the Gaiuses is built on the Rock, they cannot be shaken by the storms of whims and caprices. They have continued the work of calling men and women to repentance.

To raise more Gaiuses in our midst is our best strategy in strengthening the church. This means enlisting church people to become missionary Christians. For us these days, this does not necessarily mean we should have a guest room for wandering missionaries. Many of us do not even have enough room for ourselves. And missionaries would rather stay by themselves. It may be that once in a while we will have the honor of having in our homes some religious dignitaries, but even our best Filipino hospitality should not be confused with mission-mindedness.

To be mission-minded is to be church-minded, for the church is mission. Mission is the very expression of the church's being — it is not just the commissioning of some exceptionally pious people to heal the sick or preach the gospel in some remote villages or distant lands. The mission of the church is to spread the love of God unto the ends of the earth — that divine love which has a claim upon the whole man, body and spirit. And to take part in that mission is to take part in the very life of the church itself.

Let our involvement in our respective congregations become deeper and more enduring, that it may bring honor to Him who is the supreme Shepherd of our souls.

71

The Wheat and the Tares

Scripture Reading: Matthew 13:24-30,36-43

Among the parables of our Lord Jesus Christ, the parable of the wheat and the tares is one of the most difficult to expound. To understand it, we need to know the context of the story, the peculiar style of the author of the first gospel, and the situation at the time the story was written, especially the disturbing problems of the church to which Matthew belonged.

Some scholars believe that the parable of the wheat and the tares is simply a rewriting of a parable in the book of Mark, the parable of the self-growing seed, in chapter 4, verses 26-29. It reads: "The kingdom of God is as if a man should scatter seed upon the ground, and should sleep and rise night and day, and the seed should sprout and grow, he knows not how. The earth produces of itself, first the blade, then the ear, then the full grain in the ear. But when the grain is ripe, at once he puts in the sickle, because the harvest has come."

In this parable, the intention is to teach that man can only sow the seed; it is God who gives the increase. But this is not the central thought in the parable of the wheat and the tares. Other scholars, therefore, prefer to take the Matthean account at its face value; that is, take it as an original utterance of Jesus.

In the latter part of Matthew 13, we have an explanation of the parable. Jesus, speaking to his disciples, says that the sower of the good seed is the Son of man (meaning, Jesus himself); the field is the world, and the good seed means the sons of the kingdom of God. The enemy who sows the weeds is the devil, the weeds are the sons of the devil, the harvest is the close of the age, and reapers are the angels. Such an explanation, however, may not have come directly from Jesus himself, according to reputable New Testament scholars; it may be the work of Matthew, the author, or of someone who edited the gospel. The reason for this conclusion is that the so-called explanation hardly explains the central thought of the parable, which is allowing both the wheat and the tares to grow together until harvest time.

We will not settle this problem here, but some important points should be emphasized. For instance, the parable is intended to teach us about the kingdom of God. In the gospel of Matthew, the phrase "kingdom of heaven" is synonymous with the kingdom of God. But whether it be the kingdom of heaven or the kingdom of God, the word kingdom has a political connotation. The kingdom of heaven is the kingdom where God is King — and here the word **king** also has a political connotation. Of course, Jesus also teaches about the Fatherhood of God — the imagery is taken from the family. He talks about the justice of God, using legal concepts. But the phrase kingdom of heaven is not just a figure of speech; it has some political connotation.

Time and again we have been told not to mix religion and politics. The fact, however, is that in many cases they are mixed. To talk about the kingdom is to talk about politics; and to talk about God is to talk about religion. To talk about the kingdom of God is to talk about politics and religion.

This is not to say that a church should engage in partisan politics by supporting a particular candidate (although some churches do that). It is a mistake for a church to support a candidate even though such candidate is a Sunday School teacher. The church should be bigger than partisan politics. It should not be reduced into another political party.

But when public issues (whether they be economic, cultural or political) have moral dimensions, and such moral dimensions are at stake, it is the duty of the church to speak out with prophetic courage in defense of the Christian morality. When human rights are being violated, when our sense of decency and honesty is being offended, when the dignity of people is being taken for granted, the church must raise a voice of protest — even at the risk of being suspected of meddling in politics.

After all, that was the lot of Christ himself. He who came as an itinerant preacher, a teacher of religion, the Friend of the friendless and Savior of mankind, was accused as a subversive, and was crucified as an enemy of the government. Because He talked about the kingdom, Pilate thought He was talking about an earthly kingdom. Because He talked about being a king, Pilate thought He was a political rival. The sign placed on the cross above His head which read, "Jesus of Nazareth, King of the Jews," was a political label marking Him as a subversive.

Of course, we believe in the separation of the church and the state. In fact, Jesus taught us to give unto Caesar the things that are Caesar's and unto God the things that are God's. But the gospel we proclaim is for the spiritual edification of human life in its totality. Even politics needs the cleansing power of the Word of God. The state is an order of God's creation, and the civil servants are accountable to God and to the people. The politicians are not exempted from the stringent demands of the Christian gospel.

At the height of martial rule, the National Council of Churches in the Philippines issued a "Statement on the Use of the Pulpit." The last paragraph says: "The sermon is normally the form in which the Word of God is interpreted from the pulpit in the midst of a worshipping congregation... It aims to preach the Word of God in any of its dimensions... To interpret the Word of God in a sermon means making the Word of God bear upon a specific problem, a particular situation, a concrete issue, a definite life-situation... If therefore the Word of God is properly interpreted in a sermon, a preacher may have to draw out specific implications and conclusions that indicate the significance of God's Word, for now, or today, in our contemporary life-situation. And the implication or conclusion could be critical of current trends." In other words, when a sermon sounds a bit critical of current trends or of prevailing situations, the preacher does not have to be accused as an amateur in political science. He is just trying to be faithful to the Word of God. We should continue preaching about the kingdom of God that has a message for earthly kings, and about the kingdom of heaven that begins here on earth.

The second point we get from the parable of the wheat and the tares is that evil is a reality in our world, including the church. Bible scholars tell us that Matthew's purpose in writing this story is to describe the nature of the church in the early days of the Christian era. The church of Matthew and the churches of today include both the wheat and the tares. There are enemies that sow weeds among the wheat, and the weeds grow together with the wheat. This is a way of saying that the worst enemies of the church are those who are within its fellowship.

Throughout history, the church has withstood the persecutions and vilifications of its outside enemies: the cruelties of governments, the barbarity of the pagans, the slander of the agnostics. But their oppressiveness only serves to strengthen the faith of the Christians. Believers hold on to the promise of Christ that the gates of hell will not prevail against the church.

But the Judases within the fellowship prove to be much more insidious and destructive. They undermine the unity and mission of the church. They are capable of betraying the gospel and the Master himself. They are a thorn in the Body of Christ.

What to do with them is the haunting question. The way this question is handled in the parable is the central thrust of the story, and also the most difficult to explain. Here is how it goes: A man sowed good seeds in his field. While his men were sleeping, an enemy came and sowed weeds among the wheat. Naturally, when the wheat came up and bore grains, the tares also appeared. So the servants asked the Master, "Sir, we planted only the good seeds. How come there are tares with the wheat?" The Master simply answered, "An enemy has done this." So the servants asked again, "Do you want us to go and gather the tares?" The Master said very reflectively, "No, lest in gathering the weeds you root up the wheat along with them. Let both grow together until the harvest; and at harvest time I will tell the reapers to gather the weeds first and bind them in bundles to be burned, but the wheat shall be gathered in my barn."

Let us confess that we, too, are sometimes tempted to do what the servants wanted to do: gather the tares so the wheat can grow alone. Sometimes we feel the church should be exclusively for the saints — the sinners and the heretics and the Pharisees should be excluded and excommunicated. But Jesus says: No, don't do that. Does that mean that Jesus treats the saints and the sinners as if there is no difference between them? No. Does it mean that Christian discipleship is not appreciated since the Pharisees are not excluded from the temple? No. In fact, Jesus calls the scribes and the Pharisees hypocrites who could not escape the damnation of hell. Then why not allow the tares to be uprooted?

The answer is that by uprooting the tares, we may also uproot the wheat. So what's the use of uprooting the tares when you also uproot the wheat? What's the use of curing a mosquito bite when you kill the whole person? What's the use of exterminating your enemies when you also exterminate your friends? What's the use of saving the republic when you end up without a republic? Put in the language of our time, Jesus is saying that we should not throw the baby with the bath water.

Let us make that clear: Jesus is not trying to preserve the tares; it is the wheat He wants to preserve. He knows that the tares have been planted by His enemy; He knows the power of the evil one. And Jesus will not have any compromises with evil. Whenever the time is right, He wages war against the forces of evil. He turns the tables of the temple money changers upside down; He drives the corrupt businessmen out. He calls Herod a fox; He condemns the scribes and the Pharisees as hypocrites. And He summons us to follow in His steps — to proclaim the gospel to all and sundry, to liberate the victims of hunger and oppression, to bring healing to the sick, sight to the blind, comfort to the lonely. He calls us to spread the gospel of love and righteousness and justice and truth — precisely in order that the forces of evil may collapse.

But now, in this parable, we are reminded that there are times when uprooting the tares may also uproot the wheat; and in cases like that, we better let the tares and wheat grow together. In other words, a good objective is not enough; the method of achieving the objective is equally important. One does not have to be cruel in order to be kind. What can be more heroic than to uproot the tares? But that may also uproot the wheat. What can be more patriotic than to eliminate the enemies of democracy? But the method may kill democracy itself. What can be more blessed than to preserve the purity of our creeds? But that may lead to the disappearance of the creed.

And so we ask: If we allow the wheat and the tares to grow together, what will happen? To that question, Jesus answers: During the harvest time, the tares will be gathered and burned; the wheat likewise will be gathered for the benefit of mankind. Jesus in effect is saying the tares will not escape divine judgement. Ours is a moral universe and God is a righteous God. Truth will ultimately reign supreme and falsehood will be unmasked.

Finally, when the wheat and the tares are allowed to grow together, what we need is patience. Patience in seeing to it that the wheat get enough protection and care, so that it may bring forth grains and blessings to the world. Patience in hoping that God will not forget His promises, that in the fullness of time He will allow us to harvest the grains. Patience in doing the work of love and brotherhood, in planting the seeds of understanding among the members of the family, among the members of the church, among the people of the land and the inhabitants of this world, so that suspicion and mistrust may be supplanted by goodwill and the desire to help each other in every way possible. We need patience to overcome evil with good.

Such patience can be ours if we but put our trust in the power and wisdom of our Lord, who alone can give us the grace to be patient and the courage to be faithful.

72

The Appearances of the Risen Lord

> *I passed on to you what I received, which is of the greatest importance: that Christ died for our sins, as written in the Scriptures; that he was buried and that he was raised to life three days later, as written in the Scriptures; that he appeared to Peter and then to all twelve apostles. Then he appeared to more than five hundred of his followers at once, most of whom are still alive, although some have died. Then he appeared to James, and afterward to all the apostles.*
>
> — I Corinthians 15:3-7

Here Paul does not elaborate on Jesus' appearance to Peter. He also says that Jesus appeared to the twelve, and we wonder whether he means eleven because Judas was already out of the picture. Or could he be referring to the group after the election of Matthias (Acts 1:26) who took the place of Judas? If this is so, then we have no details of the appearance to that group. Furthermore, Paul says that Jesus appeared to more than five hundred of his followers, but he does not give further elaboration.

Fortunately, in the gospels the appearances are recorded with some details. In Mark 16:9 we read: "Now when he rose early on the first day of the week, he appeared first to Mary Magdalene, from whom he had cast out seven demons." Have you ever wondered why Jesus first appeared to a woman from whom he had cast out seven demons? It seems that the Easter story has a large place for women. We will recall that it was the women who first discovered that Jesus' tomb was empty. In Luke 24:1 we read: "But on the first day of the week, at early dawn, they went to the tomb, taking the spices which they had prepared." Who are **they** in this verse? The answer is in verse 10 — "Now it was Mary Magdalene and Joanna and Mary the mother of James and the other women with them who told this to the apostles." In other words, not only three women but many more. In the Philippines, we rejoice that for the first time in our history we have a woman president. Should we not rejoice even more that the risen Lord first appeared to women?

Before we get carried away by this woman-first business, let us note that the important thing is not that Jesus first appeared to a woman but that He appeared to someone who may well be the symbol of gripping sadness. Mary Magdalene was weeping because she thought the body of her Lord was stolen. Of course she was wrong because Jesus' body was not stolen. But her grief was real because her love for the Savior was real. However, her untold sadness suddenly became a blessed experience upon discovery that the man she was talking with turned out to be the risen Lord Himself. The lesson here is that, like Mary Magdalene, those of us who are buffeted by sorrows and despair can find sustaining strength in the company of the living Lord. The awareness of His presence can buoy us up beyond the grip of loneliness; it can drive away the atmosphere of gloom and make us see again the beauty in this world.

In spite of the dawning of a new day in our land, the traces of sadness can still be seen on many faces. For we have had some very painful losses and the pain is still with us. The promise of a better government may help. The lowering of prices of certain commodities may help. The implementation of some needed social reforms may help. But we also need the assurances of the resurrection faith because we know we do not live by bread alone. We need the presence of the risen Lord because we are also citizens of heaven and children of the spirit.

This is why we are grateful that the risen Christ comes to the rescue of the sorrowing. No longer shall we feel forsaken and forlorn, for Jesus comes to give us joy.

In the second place, the risen Christ appears to the disappointed. The Emmaus travelers were a couple of disappointed people, as the gospel of Luke tells us. When Jesus asked them what they were talking about, they answered, "Concerning Jesus of Nazareth, who was a prophet mighty in deed and word before God and all the people, and how our chief priests and rulers delivered him up to be condemned to death, and crucified him. But [listen to these words] we had hoped that he was the one to redeem Israel" (Luke 24:19-21).

Obviously these people had a deep concern for the plight of their country and they had hoped that Jesus would be the mighty deliverer. But now their hope was gone because Jesus, so they thought, ended up hanging on the cross. Happily they insisted that Jesus stay with them overnight, and when they saw the wounds on His hands as He was breaking the bread, they knew that their guest was no other than the risen Lord.

We, too, are seriously concerned about the plight of our country, and such concern gives us some real disappointment — disappointment with the imperfection of the present system, disappointment with some newly appointed officials, disappointment with the emerging group of new cronies. Added to this is the nagging disappointment of the personal kind: disappointment with husband or wife, disappointment with some friends, and who knows, even disappointment with God, especially when we think that God has not listened to our prayers. But the Easter message is that whatever disappointment we may have, it need not bug us perennially. The risen Christ can set us free from the suffocating cell of our blighted hopes. If things cannot be changed, He will give us grace to accept them; and if they are not hopeless, He will give us strength to make the necessary changes. That is our resurrection faith.

In the third place, the risen Christ appears to the doubting. And here we have in mind not only Thomas but also the other unnamed disciples. Matthew informs us that the eleven disciples "went to Galilee, to the mountain to which Jesus had directed them. And when they saw Him they worshipped Him; but some doubted" (Matthew 28:16,17). Thomas was not alone in his search for more evidences. There were others who doubted whether Jesus had really resurrected, even though they had already seen and worshipped Him.

We should be careful in condemning Thomas too hastily. His doubt need not be equated with lack of faith. There is a valid distinction between faith and mere credulity. As Prof. G. D. Harnold aptly observes, "To doubt is by no means sinful, when all evidence is lacking. In these circumstances, to doubt may be the proper response of a keen mind — and keen minds are the gift of God. The faith of a man who has known doubts is often stronger in the end than a simple uncritical faith."[1]

Today, as a church leader said, it is necessary not only to believe but also to understand. And the good Lord, we can be sure, is always patient with our honest doubts.

We may be convinced about the fact of the resurrection, but that is not the end of our doubts. Deep within our hearts we may be wondering whether God really cares. We may be troubled by the appalling increase of evil in the world, and even wonder whether the forces of goodness have not become impotent. When our home is made desolate by the death of a

---

[1] Harnold, *Risen Indeed*, p. 61.

loved one in spite of our goodness to our neighbors and our faithfulness to the church, are we not sometimes inclined to raise some questions about the goodness of our God? But moments like that can be moments of spiritual transformation, and our doubts can turn into a confident faith.

In the fourth place, the risen Christ appears to those who are at work. This is the testimony of Peter and his companions who went out fishing one night. The gospel of John (21:1-14) tells us that they labored the whole night, but caught nothing. And they were supposed to be experienced fishermen. At the break of dawn, they decided to go home and they saw a man standing on the shore. The man, whom they could not yet recognize, asked, "Have you caught any fish?" And they said, "No, we haven't caught anything." Then the Stranger said, "Cast your net on the right side of the ship, and ye shall find." Readily they obeyed, and lo and behold, it was a big catch; they could hardly pull the net back into their boat. The beloved disciple, often identified as John the son of Zebedee, whispered to his companions saying, "That's Jesus on the shore."

I do not know if there are fishermen in this congregation. I know some of you are teachers, lawyers, businessmen, government employees, doctors, engineers (I hope there are no smugglers here). But I want to say that if we know the gloriousness of the Resurrection, Christ is real in our work. When we are tired or worn out, and especially when we are low spirited because of some problems that make us unproductive, Christ speaks to us in some special way and our obedience to His command may bring us blessings beyond all expectation. The joy of Easter can be a daily experience in our places of work.

In the fifth place, the risen Christ appears to those who gather to worship. In the evening of the first Easter, so John tells us (20:19-23), the disciples (minus Thomas) gathered in the Upper Room. For what purpose we do not know, but students of the Bible surmise that they assembled for prayer. The gospel of John tells us that the following week they gathered in the Upper Room once again, and this time Thomas was with them (20:26). And Jesus appeared to them. That was the beginning of the custom of gathering together for worship on the first day of week, instead of the last day. Easter is the Lord's day and every Sunday worship should be a celebration of the resurrection.

It inspires us to know that Jesus appears to us in our act of worship, when our common loyalty to Him binds us together in Christian fellowship. He appears to those who truly seek Him through prayer. He appears when two or three are gathered together in His name. He appears to honor our praises and thanksgiving and to make us more equipped for the tasks we have to do. He reveals His presence through the reading and preaching of the Word, through the singing of hymns and anthems, through the sacraments, through every act of communion with God. In spite of all our unworthiness, God is in His holy temple.

Finally, the risen Christ appears to those who persecute the church of God. This is the witness of the Apostle Paul. In his letter to the Corinthians he says, "last of all, as to one untimely born, he (Jesus) appeared also to me. For I am the least of the apostles, unfit to be called an apostle, because I persecuted the church of God"(I Corinthians 15:8,9). You will recall that Paul was on his way to Damascus precisely to crush the courageous Christians who were secretly meeting there. But the risen Lord appeared to him, and he who was the chief of all sinners became the greatest of all saints.

Who are the persecutors of the church today? Perhaps, we would say they are the atheists who make mockery of our faith. They are the communists who defy the state. They are those who are aggressively working for the downfall of the Christian enterprise.

But can we find them also within the fellowship of the church? What about those whose Christianity is more of a label than life? Those whose worship of God is more of a ceremony than experience? Those who simply do not care, whose ways are creating scandals inside and outside the church? I submit they are also persecutors of the church of God.

I would hope we are not in that category, but in case we are, the good news is that Christ appears to those who are apathetic, if not totally antagonistic, to the Christian fellowship. And when we respond to His divine manifestation, we begin to look at life from a higher perspective and we cannot help but be on fire for God.

Let us, therefore, make this day a day of rededication and reconsecration. It is the most fitting act to celebrate God's boundless mercy and goodness unto us.

He wipes away our tears when grief visits our homes. He gives us solid hopes when we are sorely disappointed. He grants us the certainty of His abiding love even when we are being assailed by honest doubts. He gives us the courage and the strength we need for our daily work. He responds to our needs when we come to him through prayer and worship.

He calms our nerves when in our anger or impulsiveness we behave as persecutors of the Christian fellowship.

That God is the God who appears to us through the risen Christ. He deserves the fullest measure of our devotion.

73

One Foot in Heaven

Scripture Reading: 1 Thessalonians 1:1-10

To appreciate Paul's letters to the Thessalonians, we need to take a quick look at the city of Thessalonica. This great city was named after the wife of Cassander, daughter of Philip of Macedon and half sister of Alexander the Great. It was a link between the East and the West and was said to be "in the lap of the Roman Empire." The preaching of the gospel there paved the way for the making of Christianity into a world religion.

The story of Paul's stay in Thessalonica is recorded in the 17th chapter of the book of Acts. It seems that Paul preached in the synagogue there for three Sabbaths, which means that his stay there could not have been more than three weeks. Yet his brief visit was a tremendous success, in the sense that within that short time he and his associates were able to organize a church. At the same time, however, he provoked some enemies there. And since his life was in peril, he had to escape to Athens, leaving Timothy and Silvanus behind.

So concerned was Paul about the Thessalonians that when Timothy joined him in Athens, he sent him back to Thessalonica to gather more accurate information about the latest developments in the life of the church there. Fortunately, the information gathered by Timothy was very encouraging; it made Paul more determined to preach the gospel unto the ends of the earth.

But Timothy also brought some rather disturbing news. For instance, the so-called second coming of Christ, a theme which characterized much of the preaching in Thessalonica, seems to have produced an unhealthy situation. Believing that Jesus would come back very soon, some Christians abandoned their jobs; they gave up their ordinary pursuits to await the second coming with hysterical expectancy. In his first letter to the Thessalonians, Paul makes a brief reference to this problem and appeals to them to live quietly, and to do their work with their hands (4:11).

Another disturbing news brought by Timothy to Paul was that the

Thessalonians were quite worried about their loved ones who died before the second coming of our Lord. Paul tackles this problem in chapter 4 of his first letter to them (4:13-18). His advice on this subject is admittedly difficult to interpret, but the point is that Paul does not ignore this problem and that in fact he discusses it more lengthily in his second letter to the Thessalonians.

Thirdly, Timothy brought the news that some people in Thessalonica had some very serious charges against Paul. They charged Paul of preaching the gospel there because of what he could get out of it materially, that he was some kind of a dictator, and that he was after the praise of men rather than the approbation of God. Paul defends himself against these accusations in chapter 2. Part of his defense reads as follows: "We never used either words of flattery, as you know, or a cloak for greed, as God is witness; nor did we seek glory from men, whether from you or from others, though we might have made demands as apostles of Christ. But we were gentle among you, like a nurse taking care of her children. So, being affectionately desirous of you, we were ready to share with you not only the gospel of God but also our own selves, because you had become very dear to us" (2:5ff). In the latter part of chapter 2, Paul makes it clear that he and his companions worked very hard day and night that they might not be a burden to any of the Thessalonians; that indeed he never asked for financial support in exchange for his ministerial services. You will recall that in his letter to Timothy, Paul maintains that the preachers of the gospel are entitled to support from the congregation ("The labourers are worthy of their hire" — Luke 10:7; 1 Tim.5:18), but because he does not want people to misunderstand his motive, he supported himself by working as a tent maker during his spare time.

Another disturbing news brought by Timothy was that some of the church members in Thessalonica had the tendency to relapse into immorality. It was hard for them with pagan background to unlearn their paganism and to adhere faithfully to the new ethics of a new religion. Hence Paul finds it necessary to remind them that their sanctification is the will of God and that they should abstain from immorality.

In establishing the relevance of these epistles to our contemporary life, we should note that the good news brought by Timothy to Paul rekindled the fire of hope in the heart of Paul and revived his enthusiasm for mission. We would recall that Paul had met with so much opposition and discouragement at Philippi, in Thessalonica itself, in Berea, and in

Athens, so that when he set foot in Corinth his morale was exceedingly low. Deep within his heart the light of hope was beginning to flicker. But now comes Timothy with the news that on the whole the Thessalonian Christians were trying to remain steadfast in their faith. To Paul, that means the rebirth of a new hope, the revival of a daring spirit which propels him to declare the wonderful deeds of God from Asia Minor to the leading centers of Europe.

In others words, if Paul finally braved the hazard of long trips in sea and land, if he gallantly endured the extreme difficulties in his missionary journeys, if he ultimately succeeded in paving the way for making Christianity into a world religion, it was because a group of humble Christians, who remained loyal to God, gave him a real shot in the arm, so to speak, which resulted in the rebuilding of a faith that turned the world upside down and won many souls to Christ.

Has this not been the repeated experience of the Christian church? Behind the crusading spirit of a John Calvin and a Martin Luther, behind the missionary zeal of a William Carey and a James Rodgers, behind the evangelistic fervor of a D. L. Moody and a Billy Graham, behind the scholarly preaching of a Robert McCracken and a Peter Marshal, behind the many spiritual ventures that assailed the decaying moral sensibility of civilized men and redeemed them from total failure is the abiding faithfulness of some Christians who never tired of gathering together for prayer, for worship, for fellowship, and for their mutual edification in the faith.

Could it be that one reason many ministers and missionaries who could have become spiritual giants in the Kingdom of God but instead became forgotten and useless is the lethargy and indifference of church people who did not bother to come to the rescue of their spiritual leaders when, in their human weakness, they got lost and discouraged and confused? How many bishops and shepherds of souls became total failures when they were low-spirited and brokenhearted, and no one came to give them the much-needed encouragement?

Perhaps, we need to remind ourselves that in a truly Christian fellowship, it is not enough that the church leaders minister to the needs of the congregation. The members of the church must also be concerned about the spiritual health of their leaders. Our Elders and Deacons and Trustees and ministers are not spiritual Atlases who can carry the whole world upon their shoulders. They, too, can be assailed by discouragement and bitterness, and in such trying moments they also need the sympathetic understanding of their fellow Christians. They also need the guidance and encouragement of the congregation.

In his first letter to the Thessalonians, Paul takes cognizance of the problem raised by the people's misunderstanding of the second coming of Christ. With frantic expectation of the Lord's coming, the people left their offices and farms and devoted themselves to an eager waiting for the second coming of the Lord. This is the problem which the Apostle Paul discusses in his second letter. He reminds the Thessalonians that no one knows exactly when the Lord will come again. He echoes the words of Jesus recorded in Matthew's gospel, "But of that day and hour no one knows, not even the angels of heaven, nor the Son, but the Father only" (Matt. 24:36)

Prof. Dwight E. Stevenson tells us that in the United States, in the middle of the nineteenth century, the so-called Millerite movement exhibited the same symptoms the Thessalonians had when hundreds of people "abandoned their callings, sold their possessions, robed themselves in white and waited on hilltops for the coming of Lord." Stevenson recalls that again in 1954, "a small group of disciples attached to a Chicago prophetess set a date for the arrival of a spaceship which would inaugurate the Last Days." We had some similar stories here in the Philippines. We will never lack people who are queer enough to predict the end of the world. Not long ago, we witnessed a group of people who gathered on a hill somewhere in Cavite to wait for the end of the world. But the end did not come and we are still here. I hope they are back to some productive activities now, but in the case of the Thessalonians, their exaggerated millenialism led them to idleness.

Actually, the serious defect of the Thessalonians which alarmed the Apostle Paul was not their falsely understood doctrine of the Second Coming. Rather, it was their attempt to minimize earth and exaggerate heaven. Because the end was drawing nigh, they severed their connections with the world; they stopped working for a living, and devoted their time to a prayerful waiting for Christ's coming. In other words, they tried to plant both their feet in heaven and forgot the demands of their earthly life.

That was the problem of the Thessalonians. They tried to live as if they were no longer here on earth. In an effort to have an experience of the full consummation of the Lord's coming, they abandoned even the necessary duties of everyday life. They did not like to go back to their farms, they did not like to work anymore. All they wanted was to sit down and pray, eat and pray, sleep and pray.

But Paul advises them to go back to work. He reminds them that they are citizens of two worlds; that one foot should be on earth and one foot in heaven, and that, in fact, they are not safe citizens of either world "when that world is cut off from the other." Paul tells them that while it is their bounden duty to wait and to be ready for the end, nevertheless, the multiform relationships and responsibilities of life continue to be binding, for after all we are also children of nature and we need food, clothing, and shelter.

How is it with you and me these days? Is our problem that of minimizing earth and exaggerating heaven? Perhaps, to some Christians that is so. I am afraid, however, that to the great majority of our church people the problem is the other way around: we try to plant both our feet on earth. We are often too busy to pray, too busy to worship, too busy to think of God. Here is a poem which describes this dilemma of our generation.

Too Busy
By Walt Huntley

We sing "Take time to be holy,
And speak oft with thy Lord,"
When really what we ought to sing
Is time we can't afford.

We're all so busy doing things
And going here and there,
That if we really told the truth
We've hardly time for prayer.

There was a day we spent more time
To meditate and pray,
And how we'd wait upon the Lord,
Sometimes 'till break of day.

But somehow that has all been changed,
Like cars that once had cranks,

> For now we live as if we all
> Have tigers in our tanks.
>
> We're living in a world gone mad,
> Where time has lost its place,
> And speed is making busy wrecks
> Out of the human race.
>
> Yet, those who want to serve their God
> And all His will obey,
> Don't let "too busy" get between
> The Lord and us each day.

Planting both our feet on earth, being too busy for God and His church, is a serious malady of our age. And this, according to Jesus, is one of the real signs of the coming end of our world.

We should remind ourselves that while we are in the world, we are not of the world; that we do not live by bread alone, but also by the words which proceed from the mouth of God.

74

The Feeding of the Multitude

Scripture Reading: Luke 9:10-17

The miracle of feeding the multitude with five loaves and two fishes is the only miracle of our Lord recorded in all four gospels. The Evangelists must have seen something deeply significant in that miracle that they included it in their individual accounts of Jesus' life and teachings. Indeed, in Matthew and in Mark the feeding narrative occurs in two places. Matthew 14 (vss.13-21) is a parallel passage to the Lucan account and tells us about the feeding of five thousand men, besides women and children, and in which 12 baskets full of broken pieces were left over. But in Matthew 15, which is parallel to Mark 8, four thousand men, besides women and children, were fed, and in which seven baskets full of broken pieces were left over.

Students of the Bible differ in their theories of these narratives. Some contend that these two incidents are actually two versions of the same story. The differences in the number of people fed and in the amount of leftovers are considered very minor, and that no one can really be very accurate with statistics. But other scholars insist that Matthew and Mark had two incidents in mind. One took place in Decapolis and the other in Bethsaida. One was done during the spring time, and the other during the summer. At one time, twelve basketfuls of the fragments were gathered. At another time, seven hampers of leftovers were collected.

The gospel of John speaks only of the feeding of the five thousand and adds some other interesting features. For instance, when Jesus saw the multitude, he asked Philip where they could buy some bread so the people could eat. Why ask Philip who was among the least known of the disciples? The answer is that Philip was from that place and he should know where the nearest bakery was. But Philip answered, "Two hundred denarii would not buy enough bread for each of them to get a little." (In the Good News Bible, two hundred denarii is translated "two hundred silver coins," and a "silver coin was the daily wage of a rural worker." Other scholars suggest that two hundred denarii was approximately 40 American dollars.) At any rate, at that late afternoon it was not likely that the nearest bakery would have enough bread for five thousand people. But Andrew, who was good at introducing people to Christ, said, "There is a lad here who has five barley loaves and two fishes."

Whether these are accounts of different incidents or just versions of the same story should not bother us too much. Our bigger problem is: How are we to interpret this miracle? How are we to understand the feeding of the multitude, knowing that there were only five loaves and two sardines?

There are at least three possibilities open before us: One is to take the record as it is. This is the literal interpretation: Jesus, after saying a prayer of thanks, multiplied the meager food before him, so that all the people were able to eat not only bread and fish but perhaps also corned beef and butter and fried eggs and Nescafe. After all, did not Jesus miraculously produce wine at a wedding feast in Cana? Did He not cause the lame to walk and the blind to see and the dead to come to life again? Why should He not multiply the lad's *baon* to enable five thousand men plus women and children to have supper to their hearts' content? This is the argument of those who take the literal approach to this miracle.

The second possibility is for us to look at this miracle as a symbol of the messianic banquet in the Kingdom of God. In other words, it was a symbolic supper rather than an actual meal. The people were given a morsel of fish and bread which they ate in celebration and in anticipation of the great Messianic banquet in the Kingdom of God. And they were satisfied not in the physical sense but in the spiritual sense because Jesus Himself was in their midst as the Host. In short, it was a foretaste of the Lord's Supper which Jesus instituted just before His crucifixion. Some Bible scholars believe that this was the purpose of John in whose gospel account Jesus is pictured as the Bread of Life.

This theory cannot be easily dismissed especially when we remember that in both the Old and the New Testaments, life in the Kingdom of God is very much associated with deliverance from hunger and poverty. In the book of Isaiah, for instance, God says, "They shall not hunger or thirst, neither scorching wind nor sun shall smite them" (49:10) and in Revelation 7 (vs. 16) the same words were said by the Elders in describing the lot of the Christian martyrs. A very interesting interpretation. My only problem here is that it does not have any explanation for the leftovers.

And so we consider the third possibility, namely that the people brought their own *baon*; at the beginning they would not open it for fear that the others did not bring any provision and therefore might ask for food from them and if they gave anything, there might not be enough left for them. However, when the disciples (or the little lad, according to the Fourth Gospel) brought what they had to Jesus to be shared with the people after saying grace, the people themselves were challenged to bring out their own food and shared it with one another. In other words, the true miracle here was not the multiplication of food, but the change of hearts from morbid selfishness to loving generosity.

Bible scholars tell us that it was customary among the Jews to bring food with them wherever they went. The people who followed Jesus were not stupid to embark on a nine-mile journey without any provision. For all we know, many of them brought more than what they needed because they were not sure to have an audience with Jesus right away. They might have to wait for some time. And when they saw the disciples bringing out their *baon*, they, too, brought out their own and even shared what they had with one another; and to their great amazement, twelve baskets of broken pieces were gathered after supper.

Ernest Fremont Tittle, in his book on the gospel of Luke, cites an example of this miracle from recent history: "After World War II," he writes, "there was very real danger of mass starvation in Europe and Asia, but the situation was relieved by prompt and vigorous action on the part of governments and individuals. There was no multiplication of food, but there was on a vast scale a sharing of food. And whence did it come, this impulse to share which saved millions from a slow and torturing death? The answer of religion is, it was the will of God that hungry multitudes should be fed, and the Spirit of God at work in human hearts brought it to pass that they were fed."

Jeremias Montemayor, analyzing the plight of the poor Filipino farmer, writes, "There is no question that the farmer has grave economic problems which demand immediate action. But actually, there is enough wealth to go around. And modern technology has created wonders of production. But the trouble is these wonders are too often used to serve the greed of a few. And the more goods are produced, the more greedy these few become. Thus, in the midst of plenty for a few, the masses are left destitute, hungry and demoralized. The main problem, then, is not so much economic as moral, not so much a matter of technology as that of justice, not so much how to produce more goods as how to control greed and luxury and to share the goods of the world with one's neighbor." [1]

---

[1] J. Montemayor, *Barangay*, May 1996, p. 4.

We therefore submit that the cultivation of the spirit of sharing is what we ardently need today, and we would do well to pray hard for it. It is the *bayanihan* spirit, as the late Dr. Salvador Araneta calls it in his booklet, *Bayanicracy*. It is the spirit which we as a people have lost temporarily, says Dr. Araneta, "due to urbanization and affluence and influences coming from other lands." Yet it is something "inborn" and "congenital" in the Filipino people; something that is naturally revived in a great emergency. It is something that can be rekindled in the hearts of men in the power of the Spirit, by the touch of the Master's hand. It is something that can cause great rejoicing not only among men on earth but also among angels in heaven.

This, then, is the first lesson we can trace in this miracle of feeding the multitude: that the problem of hunger in our country and in the world is not just a simple economic problem; it is also spiritual and that, therefore, the answer must also touch the spirit of man. It is not enough that we take advantage of modern technology which enables us to produce as much as we can; we must also subject ourselves to a kind of spiritual surgery so that our greedy and stony hearts may somehow know the joy and the virtue of sharing.

In the second place, the miracle of feeding the multitude underscores Christ's abiding concern for the physical needs of men. This, of course, is explicit all throughout the story, but must be stressed separately to avoid the impression that Christianity's main concern is for the spiritual and is only superficially concerned about the material aspects of life. The Bible does not make absolute demarcation between the material and the spiritual; it holds that man is a unity of body and soul, and that salvation is not only for the soul but also for the body. When Jesus said, "Man does not live by bread alone, but by the words which proceed from the mouth of God," he did not mean to ignore the importance of bread. On the contrary, he was concerned that everyone should have enough bread to eat. What Jesus was guarding against was the absolutizing of bread as man's all-embracing need and the consequent deification of material wealth as an answer to that need. Christianity has a social gospel, and all the mundane problems of men, including the comprehensive agrarian reform program, are not beyond the sphere of the Christian's concern.

But now let us remember that our concern for the physical needs of men, which we cannot help if we are lovers of God, could mean the invasion of our privacy at times. Jesus and his disciples were tired and weary, and they went to Bethsaida precisely to have some rest. But the people followed them because of their own pressing need.

And what was the disciples' reaction? They told Jesus, "Send them away; let them go to the villages and country round about, to lodge and get provisions. Send them away." And what was Jesus' reaction? He told His disciples, "You give them something to eat." He who knew the importance of privacy and who took time to be alone with God, also knew how to convert an emergency into a rare missionary opportunity.

I submit we have something to learn here. While certainly we must take time to rest and be alone with ourselves and with our families, there are times when such privacy has to be sacrificed for the sake of a greater need. Our failure to sense such need can spell disaster in human relationships. This is what Premanand, an Indian writer, says in his account of the Evangelical movement in Bengal. He writes that the "Metropolitan Bishop of India failed to meet the late Pandit Iswar Chandar Vidyasagar of Bengal through official formality. The Pandit had been sent as spokesman of the Hindu community in Calcutta to establish friendly relations with the Bishop and with the Church. Vidyasagar, who was the founder of a Hindu College in Calcutta and a social reformer, author and educationalist of repute, returned disappointed without an interview, and formed a strong party of educated and wealthy citizens of Calcutta to oppose the Church and the Bishop, and to guard against the spread of Christianity... The formality observed by one known to be an official of the Christian Church turned a friend into a foe."

How many opportunities for Christ have we lost because our privacy cannot be invaded? One mark of Christian maturity is to be able to know when we can be disturbed, and to welcome such disturbance as an opportunity to be of help.

Finally, if we are to be God's agents in feeding the nameless multitudes around us, if we are to be a part of God's answer to the crying need of men, we must learn to bring what we have to Christ for His blessing and consecration. This is what the disciples did. The five loaves and two fishes bespeak of penury, but when blessed by Christ became the source of great abundance.

Let us be grateful for the divine assurance that in order to achieve self-fulfillment and to help meet the needs of our fellow men, it is not necessary that we first amass great wealth. What is necessary is that we consecrate our possessions and our life to Christ, and He will make us the channels of His grace. That is the miracle that we must covet for ourselves, for the members of our families and for our world.

75

The Man with One Talent

Scripture Reading: Matthew 25:14-30

In Palestine, the talent was not a coin; it was a weight. And the value of the talent depended on the kind of metal which was being used as a measure of weight. The commonest metal used was silver, and the value of a talent of silver was about 240 British pounds. Some American Bible scholars suggest that a talent was about one thousand US dollars, which is more than twice 240 British pounds under the current rate of exchange. In our currency that would be roughly 9,360 pesos. Whichever figure we use, a talent was certainly not too small an amount to be ignored.

We are told that he who was given five talents made five talents more, and he who had two made two more. But he who had only one hid his money in the ground and therefore did not earn anything.

Let us try to look at the one-talent man with understanding. Perhaps he thought that a small capital could not go too far, anyway. Do not businessmen of our time tell us that the more capital we have, the better? He who has a million pesos will know. He may double his money within a period of time. But if he has only 100 pesos to begin with, he does not have enough to build a small chicken house. And if he manages to build a chicken house for 100 pesos, then he has no more money for the chicken. And if he is lucky to have 2 or 3 chickens, he has no more money for the feeds. In short, he does not have enough to start with. Why should we therefore blame the one-talent man? Probably his performance would be different if he were given two or five talents, instead of only one.

But now let us remember that there is a parallel story in the gospel of Luke. In Luke 19, we have the parable of the ten pounds. Of course, in Luke, 10 people were involved, but each one of them was given a pound. Let me read the pertinent verses: "When he (the nobleman) returned... he commanded these servants, to whom he had given the money, to be called to him, that he might know what they had gained by trading. The first came before him saying, 'Lord, your pound has made ten pounds more.'

And he said to him, 'Well done, good servant: Because you have been faithful in very little, you shall have authority over ten cities.' And the second came saying, 'Lord your pound has made five pounds...' and he was given the same commendation. Then another came saying, 'Lord, here is your pound, which I kept laid away in a napkin...' " In the Lucan version, the servants were given a pound each. They had exactly the same amount to begin with — one earned 10 times, another 5 times, but the third man just hid his pound. In other words, the argument that the one-talent man in Matthew should not be blamed because he was not given two or five talents does not hold water because in the parallel story in Luke they were given the same amount.

Now in Matthew, the parable clearly hints that men differ in their abilities. Of course, all men are created equal in the sense that God gives us equal opportunities to develop ourselves, but in an equally real sense we are not created equal. Some are large, some are small; some are tall, some are short; some can sing at the Cultural Center of the Philippines or at the Phil-Am Life Auditorium but there are those who have no ear for music at all. Certainly some of us have 5 talents; others have 4; still others have 3; but, perhaps, most of us have only 1 or 2.

At this point, we should note that the parable was intended for the scribes and the Pharisees. The central point in the parable is that the man with one talent wanted to preserve what he had got, and one cannot help but remember that it was the scribes and the Pharisees who wanted to preserve their laws and their traditions. But the riches of God are not meant to be hoarded. They are to be used and multiplied. If we do not use them, we will surely lose them.

Let us look more closely into the character of the man with one talent. First, let us observe that when required by his master to give account of his talent, he said, "Sir, I knew that you are a harsh man, reaping where you did not sow and gathering where you did not winnow." That was his concept of God; God was a harsh Master gathering where He did not winnow, reaping where He did not sow. He was not a just God. God was rather unreasonable. The servant, therefore, acted the way he did for his God, after all, was not capable of treating him with fairness.

So we have here a case where belief determines action, where a distorted concept of God led to a disappointingly irresponsible act. If one's ideology is atheistic, one cannot be expected to be religious. In like manner, if we believe in a loving Father, the world has the right to expect us to be loving.

When an ideology is patently nihilistic, when a philosophy of life is grossly fatalistic and full of morbidity, we need not be suprised if it breeds despair and pessimism, and immaturity. When one cannot see anything beyond the confusion of his age and the hopelessness of his situation, one may conceivably resign himself to hopelessness and meaninglessness. If we believe that God is a harsh Master we may just as well bury the talents He has entrusted to our care.

But man is not always an honest animal. His heart can be deceitful. He does not always say what he means, and sometimes does not mean what he says. If the parable was really intended for the scribes and Pharisees, then the man's distorted image of God does not jibe with reality. The scribes and the Pharisees may have hundreds of shortcomings, but a distorted concept of God was certainly not one of them. Their theology may not be perfect, but they would not say that God was harsh. Those teachers of strict monotheism would be insulted by any suggestion that they held God to be unreasonable. They would rather just admit that irresponsibility could issue from doctrinal sophistication; or to put it in another way, the best of religious creeds do not necessarily prevent the commission of moral sins. While we believe in doctrinal purity, while we uphold the importance of correct interpretation of the faith, doctrines are no guarantee that believers will always do what is right and what is good.

Perhaps there was a deeper reason why the man with one talent buried the gift that was given him. So we proceed and examine his argument. And this was what he said, "I was afraid, and I went and hid your talent in the ground." "I was afraid..."; that sounds very revealing, and it may well be the reason for the way he acted. He was afraid.

There is no denying that fear is a common human experience. This is what Basil King is trying to say in his book *The Conquest of Fear*. He writes, "When I say that during most of my life I have been the prey of fear, I take it I am expressing the case of most people. I cannot remember a time when dread of one kind or another was not in the air... In some form or other fear dogs every one of us. The mother is afraid for her children; the father is afraid for his business; most of us are afraid for our job. There is not a home or an office, a school or a church in which some hangdog apprehension is not eating at the hearts of the people who go in and out. I am ready to guess that all the miseries wrought by sin and sickness combined would not equal those we bring on ourselves through fear. We are not sick all the time. We are not sinning all the time. But most of us are always afraid — afraid of something or somebody."

This kind of fear is a normal part of our existence. And it has some positive functions. It prevents us from being lackadaisical; it challenges us to resist the feeling of overconfidence; it hinders us from being too sure and too careless. It is fear that we can control; it can be made into an asset. But when fear controls us, when it paralyzes us into uselessness and reduces us into mere puppets, then it becomes woefully dehumanizing, and that was why the man in the parable buried his talent. He was afraid. He was frozen with fear. He was petrified and did not venture at all.

When people cannot do anything because of fear, even their ability to think for themselves is greatly weakened. In that condition, decisions that affect their lives may have to be made for them. But something within us makes us realize that human development requires that we be enabled to overcome our fear and thus create an atmosphere where people can act, out of their honest convictions. Does not the Apostle Paul assure us that "God has not given us the spirit of fear; but of power, and of love, and of a sound mind?" (2 Tim 1:7). Love, says John, casts out fear (1 John 4:18), and if we are to overcome fear, we have to grow in love. When there is a climate of fear in any society, the church must do its share in removing it.

Now, being at the mercy of fear, the man with one talent was therefore afraid to fail. He must have said to himself that if he engaged in trading, he might lose; and so he decided to play safe. He buried the talent so that when the Master came, he could return the money intact. He was so afraid to fail he did not try at all. And that was his tragic mistake: he did not try at all. We find no hint on the parable that failure would be condemned; the Master knew that in business there are risks involved. Precisely, that was the test: the Master wanted to know if the man was willing to face the risks.

And that is one test we will always have in life. And the Christian should have the courage to face the test. We may not always succeed; sometimes we may fail, but failure need not be dishonorable. It is the failure of courage that is dishonorable. He who has no courage is a failure even in victory.

When the Master commended the men entrusted with five and two talents, he did not say, "Good and successful servants;" he said, "Good and faithful servants." Whatever importance we may attach to success, success is not the most important thing in the eyes of God. It is faithfulness.

Our calling is to be faithful. Faithfulness may lead us to success; it may also lead us to failure, but it is faithfulness that counts.

Again, the man with one talent allowed his feeling of littleness to dominate his life. Comparing himself with those who had five and two talents, he must have said to himself, "I have only one, and I cannot do as much as those people can." Of course he could not do as much as those people could, but that was no reason for him not to do anything at all. And we are in the same condemnation when we shirk from using our talent because it is only one and a small one; when we refuse to do anything because we cannot do a great deal; when we refuse to give because we cannot match the other givers. That miserable fear of being insignificant prevents or cripples many good works. But we may not do any great thing unless we learn to do little things. No one becomes a strong and full-grown man without first becoming a child.

Let us therefore stop pitying ourselves for having only one talent. As the old saying puts it, it is better for us to light our little candles than curse the darkness. If God has given us any talent, let us use it to His glory, and never allow fear to paralyze us into uselessness.

Finally, just a quick look at the men with five and two talents. One thing we should notice is that both of them received the same commendation. To him who was given five talents and made another five, the Master said, "Well done, good and faithful servant; you have been faithful over a little I will set you over much; enter into the joy of your master." And those were the same words spoken to the man who was given two talents and made two more. They received the same commendation, even though one had more talents than the other. In other words, it was not the number of talents but their faithfulness that mattered.

Secondly, for work well done, the reward given them was more work to do. "You have been faithful over a little, I will set you over much." In the kingdom of men, when we have done a good job, we will be given a month's vacation and perhaps some extra money to spend. But in the Kingdom of God, for every good work we do, we will be given more work to do. For being faithful over a little, we may be promoted to do something bigger. That is the nature of the Christian life: it continues to grow in stewardship and in service. And that is the promise which Jesus gives: if we use our talents, He will give us more.

But if we do not use our talents, even the little that we have will be taken away. Not by force, to be sure, but by the natural course of life. Most of us have learned a little Spanish in college but since we have not used it after college, we have forgotten even the little that we learned. The parable tells us that if we are to preserve our talent, we better use it with a sense of stewardship.

Let us thank God for the talents He has given us. Let us resolve to use His gifts faithfully not only that we may glorify Him but also that we may be the channels of His grace to our fellow men.

76

"Do You Want to Get Well?"

Scripture Reading: John 5:1-16

A sick man was healed on a Sabbath. The rabbis thought that he who had waited for 38 years could have waited till the following day. The religious leaders would have been happy for his healing had it not happened on a Sabbath.

Let us analyze the story. In general, what is portrayed here is a great human suffering. Verse 2 makes reference to a pool, which in Hebrew is called Bethzatha (or Bethesda). It is a place with five porticoes. Verse 3 is a description of what we find in that place. "In these lay a multitude of invalids, blind, lame, paralyzed." Something like that can be seen at the Philippine General Hospital, where the porches and corridors of some wards are at times flooded with the sick and the dying — a similar situation in Bethzatha. If we are stricken with pity to see a loved one agonizing in great pain, we will know the consuming sadness in the homes of those people suffering from dismal diseases. Bethzatha represents the homes made desolate by death or quarreling. It also is a symbol of the anguish of a struggling person who is left alone to wrestle with his sickness. Indeed, it represents the whole wide world of sick people — people who suffer from physical, emotional, spiritual ailments.

Let us come closer to the scene and look more particularly at the man beside the pool. He is a picture of gripping loneliness and helplessness. He had been lying there for 38 years with no one to lend a helping hand. That is what he told Jesus, "I have no man to put me into the pool." He was a man without a friend, forsaken and helpless.

Furthermore, he was a frustrated man. For 38 years beside the pool, whenever the water was troubled, someone would step down ahead of him. Thirty-eight years — what a long period of disappointment. His life was a long rosary of frustrations and defeats.

This is why in this passage we have a picture of untold suffering, helplessness, loneliness and disappointment. And the picture becomes even uglier when we see the distinct element of selfishness or unconcern on the part of those who had gone ahead of him. Obviously, they never bothered to help him. They never had enough compassion to care for that needy one. Surely his suffering was made more bitter by the fact that those around him never thought to give him a chance.

But now, in the midst of his sullen obscurity, in the abyss of his morbid loneliness, Jesus came. And, the Scripture reading says, the sick man was made whole. The light of life dispelled the darkness in his heart. His spirit was revived and his tears were wiped away.

That is the message of the gospel in a capsule: Jesus cares; He can rescue us from perishing; He can sustain us in times of our greatest needs; He can give strength to the weak, hope to those in despair, comfort to those who have been blighted by tragedy and sorrow. Is it not a tiding of great joy to be assured that our God can, in Christ, go far beyond the reach of our human resources? The God we worship is the God who can enter into our deepest thoughts and feel the throbs of our hearts. He is the God who knows our every need and weakness and who graciously invites us to be made whole again.

And this is the message that we proclaim: that Christ is the Great Physician and the Great Shepherd of our souls. He can cure the sick mind which entertains sinister thoughts and evil plans. He can cure the wagging tongue that is infected by the germ of gossip. He can cure the sick heart which is suffocated by envy and bitterness. To all of us who are sick souls Jesus comes to snatch us from our home-made hell and to give us life abundant. If we will but look unto Him as author and finisher of our faith, we may yet run the race of our life with quietness and courage; we may yet behold the beauty of this world in spite of the aberrations of our time. For those who put their trust in Jesus, the supreme reality is not the excruciating suffering of men, but the sufficiency of His grace that enables us to rise above the tumults of our age. The real wonder of this life is the redeeming presence of our Lord who alone can save us from the nagging indifference and the cruel greediness of our fellow men.

Now, when Jesus saw the sick man by the pool, He asked him, "Wilt thou be made whole?" Or, in the language of our day, "Do you want to get healed?" Let us for a while examine the significance of that question. Why should Jesus ask a man who had been sick for 38 years if he wanted to get well? Does not the question sound annoying, if not insulting? If you have tuberculosis or are suffering from some kind of cancer, and a physician asks you if you want to get well, how would you feel? Probably, if you are a bit ill-tempered you might shout at the doctor and say, "Are you kidding?" But that is what Jesus did: He asked the man, "Wilt thou be made whole?" And His question was absolutely necessary. Why? Because there are those who do not like to get well. There are those who love the peculiarity of being sick, or of being always disappointed or of being in the state of hopelessness and friendlessness. And it is worth noting that some Bible scholars believe that the sick man had been there beside the pool for 38 years because he had lost his desire to get well.

Does that not sound familiar? Are there not people around us who have become accustomed to the darkness of resentment and isolation? They may not be in speaking terms with relatives or friends because of some petty misunderstanding which can easily be overcome with a simple greeting or a sincere smile. They still see each other at birthday parties or wedding receptions and when they are about to greet each other, one may suddenly feel the urge to go to the comfort room or get another drink in the kitchen or make a telephone call. And the wall that separates them remains unbroken, until they get used to it and even enjoy the isolation that it provides.

This is why Jesus has to ask you and me, "Wilt thou be made whole?" It is not enough that we behold Him coming to the ruins of our hopes as the Savior of the helpless. It is not enough that we see Him passing by the pool to give us a helping hand. He also examines us right on the pallet where we are and challenges us to know what we really want. Do we really want to get well?

And if we do, Jesus will say, "Arise," meaning "Arise now." Do not wait until tomorrow or next week or next year. Do not wait for 38 years. Do not wait until we reach the twilight years of our life. The response should be now. If we are to be delivered from the pang of bitterness and resentment and cowardice; if we are to be freed from the mighty tentacles of vice and fear and greed, the time to act is NOW. Many worship services have become void and meaningless because they are mere performances of traditional ceremonies, and because the Spirit of God finds no place in the hearts of men. But today, we must remind ourselves that "Now is the time of salvation." Jesus wants us to rise up from the ashes of failure now so that He can show us the wonder of living in the power of His forgiving love.

Then there is His command which says, "Take up thy pallet," pick up your mat. Allow no provision for relapse. Cast out all thoughts of sliding back. Look unto Jesus as the faithful Author of your destiny. Remember when He says, "No man, having put his hand to the plough, and looking back, is fit for the kingdom of God" (Luke 9:62). Take up thy pallet. . . don't leave it there lest it tempt you to lie on it again, and be the sorriest victim of stupidity for a long, long time.

"Arise, take up thy pallet, and walk." Walk unto the highways and byways of life. Participate actively in the affairs of the family of God. Let the life given by an Immortal Love be a part of the life of all, giving its best and its noblest to the happiness of all. Walk humbly with your God for He has made you whole again.

Healing or salvation in the Bible is not adequately portrayed by a person sitting on a swivel chair. It is better represented by one who is walking in response to the mandate of the Lord. To be made whole is to be where the action is, or to be involved in the liberation of life from anything that oppresses it.

Verse 14 of our Scripture lesson describes the man in the temple. He was there to worship God for the great deliverance that had come upon him. A strong sense of gratitude had led him to the house of prayer. For the healing of his infirmity, he offered his thanksgiving to God.

How I wish we would have the same experience in our life. Gratitude should characterize our dealings with God, just as graciousness characterizes His dealings with us. We need to know from our own experience that gratitude is the essence of Christian worship. To thank the Lord for the blessings we cannot count, for health and strength and mind, to thank Him even for the pain and misfortunes that serve to purge the souls is, indeed, to worship Him in spirit and in truth.

This story of a man who was sick for 38 years is a treasure of great value. It is a testimony on the goodness of our God and the faithfulness of our Saviour. It reminds us that a personal infirmity — be it physical, moral or spiritual — can be due to our own complacency or the appalling avarice of our fellow men. But Jesus is our Friend who can strengthen our resolve to turn a new leaf. He gives us grace to rise up from where we have fallen, and to walk again with dignity and honor.

Today, before the throne of His divine mercy, let us confess our desire to be made whole, to be healed, to get well — physically, of course, but spiritually in particular — so that the clangor of self-pity and hate may be obscured by the sweet melody of His pardoning spirit. Then we can tread the path of life with music in our hearts, able to see the true and good and beautiful, and willing to be God's instrument of peace. Then our worship will be an offering of our gratitude and praise for the wonderful goodness of the Lord.

77

The Promise of Paradise

Scripture Reading: Luke 23:39-43

The gospels tell us that Jesus was crucified between two thieves. That is the word in the gospel of Mark, in the King James Version. In the gospel of Luke, they are called malefactors. In the Revised Standard Version, Luke calls them criminals and Mark calls them robbers. Other translators use the words bandits and evildoers. But whichever word we use — malefactors, criminals, robbers, bandits, evildoers, thieves — the meaning is not complimentary at all. Of course one legend depicts them as the Robin Hoods of ancient times. They molested the rich and shared the spoils with the poor. But they must be more than Robin Hoods. They must be more than thieves and robbers. Otherwise their sentence should be lighter than capital punishment.

Bible scholars believe that these men were members of the so-called zealot movement which was a political organization for the liberation of the Jews through violent means. They armed themselves to fight the oppressors, especially the Romans who were the colonizers at that time. But because they were few in number, they resorted to guerilla tactics. Theirs was a secret organization: the members could roam around Jerusalem and other places. But those who became known to the authorities had to keep themselves in hiding, and in order to stay alive they were forced to steal. Hence they were called thieves and robbers.

But actually their crime was political in nature. They had wanted to overthrow the government, and that was punishable with death. If they were caught because of smuggling gold bullions from one country to another, perhaps they need not be crucified. But they were guerrillas determined to sacrifice themselves for their cause; they were, therefore, a real threat to the security and peace of the constituted authority.

But now these two guerrillas, whose love for freedom and independence led them to the cross, suddenly found themselves in the presence of the Saviour. And in that divine presence their political aspirations had to be reassessed. Both of them spoke, and their words revealed the quality of their spirits. One reviled Jesus, saying, "If you are the Christ, save yourself and us." The other was penitent and humbly asked Jesus to remember him in paradise. He who reviled wanted Jesus to use His messianic power not only to free themselves but also to achieve their political goals. But the other calmly accepted the fairness of their plight on the historical level, but craved for Jesus' companionship in His eternal Kingdom.

Like those two radicals, we, too, have our own aspirations — aspirations for the peace and prosperity of our country, for the good and welfare of our people. And in our eagerness to realize our fondest dreams, we, too, are sometimes tempted to use God to achieve what we want. This is not to suggest that we need not pray for what we desire. After all, Jesus taught us to ask and it shall be given. But when our dreams and ambitions become the controlling forces in our life, even our prayers may become no less than a command for God to do as we wish. A stronger faith will save us from such myopic religiosity and will enable us to subject our best intentions to the higher will of our heavenly Father.

It should be noted that the conversation between Jesus and the two thieves did not touch on the question of violent revolution. One wanted Jesus to prove His messiahship by breaking loose from the cross into freedom. The other rebuked his comrade for being so cowardly and for his failure to acknowledge that their lot was their just reward. Neither one of them asked Jesus about the wisdom of their social and political involvement. In fact, one of them simply presumed that joining the zealot movement was the right thing to do, and that Jesus must set them free if they were to continue their struggles for liberation. The other, however, simply prayed to be remembered in the kingdom, betraying his belief that even the radicals like him could have a place in the Kingdom of God.

In other words, if one of the thieves went to hell, it was not because he was radical but because he was a slave of his political aspirations. The other went to heaven, not because he was a radical but because he acknowledged that Jesus was greater than his dreams for his fellow men. He went to heaven not because of his radicalism but because in all sincerity he asked to be remembered in Jesus' Kingdom. He went to heaven not because of his ideology but because of his faith.

And that is what we need to remember all the time: that the person is more precious in the eyes of God than his belief; that it is more important to know about the communist than about communism; about the conservatives than about conservatism; about the pagans than about paganism; about Christ than about Christology. Our tendency to categorize people into party or movement or beliefs often overlooks the fact that they are persons who can be related to Jesus. It tempts us to forget that it is Jesus who saves, and not party or the church or the creed. Had Jesus judged the men beside him for their radicalism, He would not have promised paradise to one of them.

At this point we should clarify what is meant by paradise. This is an old Persian word which means garden or park. Later on, it was used to refer to the abode of the righteous who had died. But essentially, it means being with God or Christ. Sometimes it means an intermediary place for the righteous while waiting for their entrance into the Kingdom of Heaven. Sometimes it means heaven itself, or a place of exquisite beauty. But it is the presence of Christ that makes it a paradise.

Paradise, therefore, is not the absence of conflicts, but the overcoming of strifes; it is not the loss of fear but the triumph of faith; it is not the disappearance of hatred but the presence of love. Paradise is being with Christ — in sickness or in death, in poverty or in wealth. It is not the rule of the masses, nor is it the dictatorship of the leader; it is the rule of Christ in the hearts of men, the transcending harmony of life which overcomes petty jealousies and suspicions and rivalries so rampant in the world.

That paradise is for those who long for the Kingdom of God. It is for the faithful who will remain faithful unto the end; it is for the righteous who remain righteous in every strife. Paradise is for those who turn to God for help, who realize the bankruptcy of their human goodness and are prepared to obey the directives of the Holy Spirit.

But here we should note that Jesus' promise to the penitent thief was a response to the man's prayer. His petition was, "Jesus, remember me when you come into your kingdom." It was indeed a prayer of faith. He did not say, "Remember me if you come into your kingdom." Rather, he said, "Remember me when you come into your kingdom." He had no doubt about Jesus' coming into the kingdom. Deep within his heart, he knew that Jesus would be in the kingdom, and his prayer of faith was answered with the promise of paradise.

Let us confess that we, too, are dreaming of some paradise for ourselves, our families, our world; we long for a life of joy and happiness and peace, of health and prosperity and brotherhood. In fact, many of us work hard to enable our children to go to school, to provide a decent place for them to live in, and to secure the needed things that make life more pleasurable. Surely, we long to be in paradise. But the question is: How is our prayer life? Is it vigorous or shamefully anemic? Do we really feel the need for God's divine favor? It will be a pity if in all our labor for human betterment we find no time for communion with Him who alone is the fontal source of life and strength. Paradise cannot be achieved through human contrivance alone. It is a grace which only God can give, a gift that we can only receive. We can build churches, we may give pledges, we may send missionaries, and do all kinds of good works, but unless we pray and pray with faith, paradise cannot be promised.

We would do well to resolve once again to cultivate our prayer life and to nurture ourselves in the faith. For when faith is strong and prayer is a living experience, no Calvary will be too steep for us to climb and no cross will be too heavy for us to carry. Jesus will not only remember us in His kingdom; He will take us to Paradise.